CONSTRUCTIONS OF MASCULINITY IN THE MIDDLE EAST AND NORTH AFRICA

CONSTRUCTIONS OF MASCULINITY IN THE MIDDLE EAST AND NORTH AFRICA

LITERATURE, FILM, AND NATIONAL DISCOURSE

EDITED BY
MOHJA KAHF AND NADINE SINNO

The American University in Cairo Press
Cairo New York

First published in 2021 by
The American University in Cairo Press
113 Sharia Kasr el Aini, Cairo, Egypt
One Rockefeller Plaza, 10th Floor, New York, NY 10020
www.aucpress.com

Dar el Kutub No. 19393/19
ISBN 978 977 416 975 5

Dar el Kutub Cataloging-in-Publication Data

Kahf, Mohja
        Constructions of Masculinity in the Middle East and North Africa: Literature, Film, and National Discourse / Mohja Kahf and Nadine Sinno.—Cairo: The American University in Cairo Press, 2021
        p. cm.
        ISBN 978 977 416 975 5
        1. Masculinity in art—Middle East
        2. Masculinity in literature—Middle East
        I. Sinno, Nadine (jt. author)

        1 2 3 4 5   24 23 22 21

Designed by Adam el-Sehemy

CONTENTS

FIGURES

Chapter 1

Chapter 12

ACKNOWLEDGMENTS

Special thanks to contributor Nicole Fares for initiating the conversation on constructing masculinities by organizing a Middle East Studies Association (MESA) panel in 2016, as well as for sending out the initial call for papers, reviewing early abstracts, and identifying existing works on masculinities—and for believing in this book project from the start.

NOTES ON CONTRIBUTORS

Amal Amireh is an associate professor of English at George Mason University. She received her BA from Birzeit University and her PhD in English and American Literature from Boston University. She is the author of *The Factory Girl and the Seamstress: Imagining Gender and Class in Nineteenth-Century American Fiction*, and is co-editor of *Going Global: The Transnational Reception of Third World Women Writers* and *Etel Adnan: Critical Essays on the Arab-American Writer and Artist*. Her essays have appeared in many publications and some have been translated into Arabic and Farsi. Her current research focuses on Palestinian literature, gender, sexuality, and nationalism.

Jedidiah Anderson attended the University of Pittsburgh where he received a BA in Japanese and Linguistics. Upon graduation, Anderson joined the U.S. Army, serving as an Arabic linguist in Mosul, Rawah, and Baghdad, Iraq. After achieving the rank of sergeant and being honorably discharged, he attended the American University of Beirut in Lebanon, where he earned a master's degree in Middle Eastern Studies, focusing on gender and sexuality in the Middle East. For his PhD, Anderson attended Indiana University Bloomington. His research focused on LGBTQI activism in Lebanon, Iraq, and Israel/Palestine, and on the cultural history of the Arab world and minorities in the region from 1850 to the present day. After spending a year doing fieldwork in those countries, Anderson returned to the United States and did a postdoc at Wofford College. He joined the faculty at Furman University in 2017. His book based on his dissertation—tentatively titled *Sexual Intifada Now!*—has been accepted for publication with Indiana University Press.

Oyman Basaran is an assistant professor of sociology at Bowdoin College. His research specialties are in Sociology of Medicine and Health, Economic Sociology, and Political Sociology. Currently, he is working on a book project that examines the discursive, organizational, and institutional transformations of the market for male circumcision from the 1920s until the present in Turkey.

Kaveh Bassiri is a writer, translator, and PhD candidate in Comparative Literature at the University of Arkansas, where he has taught a range of Iranian literature and film courses. His essays have been published in *Iranian Studies*, the *Journal of Middle East Women's Studies*, the *Michigan Quarterly Review*, *Film International*, and *Senses of Cinema*.

Alessandro Columbu completed his PhD in Modern Arabic Literature at the University of Edinburgh in 2017, and is currently Lecturer in Arabic at The University of Westminster, London. Originally from Sardinia, he obtained his BA and MA from the University of Bologna. He learned Arabic in Damascus and Tunis, and has studied at the University of Barcelona, SOAS University of London, and the French Institute of the Near East in Beirut and Amman. His translation of Zakariya Tamir's *Taksir rukab*, published in October 2015 by Condaghes, was the first book to have ever been translated from Arabic into Sardinian.

Nicole Fares is a translator, writer, and educator. Her works have been published in journals and magazines across the United States. She has obtained a PhD in Comparative Literature and Cultural Studies from the University of Arkansas (Spring 2018), and her recent research centers on the LGBTQI communities in the Middle East and North Africa (MENA), Europe, and North America following the Syrian Civil War and the subsequent refugee crises. She is currently translating her third novel from Arabic into English.

Robert James Farley works at the interstices of Arabic, queer, and translation studies as a PhD candidate in Comparative Literature at the University of California, Los Angeles (UCLA), where he is writing a dissertation on grassroots productions of a language and archive of gender and sexuality in Arabic-language digital periodicals across the Mashriq and Maghrib. He teaches courses at UCLA on postcolonial literatures, and works as a research and instructional technology consultant in the digital humanities. Farley has presented his work at annual meetings of the National Women's Studies Association and the American Comparative Literature Association, and some of his translations can be found in *Banipal* magazine.

Andrea Fischer-Tahir (PhD) specializes in Kurdish Studies. She has conducted extensive field research on issues such as political history, gender, media, and urban–rural dynamics. She worked at Koye University Kurdistan; the Zentrum Moderner Orient, Berlin; and Philipps University of Marburg. Her dissertation discussed martyrdom, mobilization, and memory in Kurdistan. She is the author of *Brave Men, Pretty Women? Gender and Symbolic Violence in Iraqi Kurdish Urban Society* (2009), and co-editor of *Peripheralization: Spatial Differentiation and Social Injustice* (2013) and *Disciplinary Spaces: Spatial Control, Forced Assimilation, and Narratives of Progress since the 19th Century* (2017).

Nouri Gana is professor of Comparative Literature, and Near Eastern Languages and Cultures at UCLA. He has published numerous articles and chapters on the literatures and cultures of the Arab world and its diasporas in such scholarly venues as *Cultural Politics*, *PMLA*, *Public Culture*, and *Social Text*. He is the author of *Signifying Loss: Toward a Poetics of Narrative Mourning*, and the editor of *The Making of the Tunisian Revolution: Contexts, Architects, Prospects* and *The Edinburgh Companion to the Arab Novel in English*. He is currently completing a book manuscript on the politics of melancholia in the Arab world and another on the history of cultural dissent in post-colonial Tunisia.

Kifah Hanna is an associate professor of Language and Culture Studies at Trinity College in Connecticut. She earned her MSc and PhD in Comparative and General Literature, and Middle East Studies at the University of Edinburgh. She is the author of *Feminism and Avant-Garde Aesthetics in the Levantine Novel* (2016). Her work has appeared in peer-reviewed journals and edited volumes. Her research interests broadly include twentieth- and twenty-first-century Arabic literature, feminist and queer theory, (trans-) nationalism, (trans-)cultural studies, cinema studies, postcolonial theory, war literature, comparative literature, and world literature.

Sarah Hudson is an instructor for the Communications and Fine Arts division at Connors State College. Her research areas include Palestinian Film and Literature, Middle Eastern Literature and Culture, and Gender and Sexuality Studies. She is currently working on a project that examines the ways in which social- and environmental-justice concerns intersect in the Palestinian context and how those intersections can be seen in the fictional films from the area.

Mohja Kahf is a professor of Comparative Literature and Middle Eastern Studies at the University of Arkansas. Her research interests include Arab and Arab-American feminism, Arab women writers, classical and modern Arabic literature, postcolonial and decolonial feminisms, gender and sexuality, the literary traditions of Spain from 711 to 1615 CE, nonviolence, and the Syrian Revolution. Her work has appeared in journals including *Feminist Studies*, the *Journal of Middle East Women's Studies*, *Arab Studies Quarterly*, *World Literature Today*, *Banipal*, and *New Geographies*. Academic articles by Kahf appear in volumes including *Gender, Violence, and Belonging: Arab and Arab American Feminisms* (2011), *Muslims in American Popular Culture* (2013), and *Going Global: The Transnational Reception of Third World Women Writers* (2000). She has published four books: *Hagar Poems* (2016); *The Girl in the Tangerine Scarf* (2006); *E-mails from Scheherazad* (2003); and a scholarly monograph, *Western Representations of the Muslim Woman: From Termagant to Odalisque* (1999), which has been translated into Turkish.

Kathryn Kalemkerian is a post-doctoral research fellow at McGill University in Montreal. She earned her MSc in Middle Eastern Studies at the University of Edinburgh, and her PhD in history at the Institute of Islamic Studies, McGill University. Her research interests include the history of late-Ottoman Beirut and Greater Syria, gender and masculinity history of the Middle East, and the history of Ottoman material culture.

John Tofik Karam is an associate professor in the Department of Spanish and Portuguese and associate director of the Lemann Institute for Brazilian Studies—both at the University of Illinois, Urbana-Champaign. His first book on Arab cultural politics in neoliberal Brazil (2007) won awards from the Arab American National Museum and the Brazilian Studies Association. It was translated into Arabic and Portuguese by the Centre for Arab Unity Studies and the Editora Martins Fontes, respectively. Supported by the National Endowment for the Humanities (NEH) and Fulbright programs, his current book project is titled, *Manifold Destiny: Arabs at an American Crossroads of Exceptional Rule*.

Ebtihal Mahadeen is lecturer in gender and media with a focus on the Arab world. She is based at the department of Islamic and Middle Eastern Studies at the University of Edinburgh. Her research focuses on the intersection of gender, sexuality, and media within an Arab context, and has addressed questions of female virginity, militarist masculinities and femininities, and LGBTQI media activism. She has a professional background in reporting and online media, and offers consultancies on gender, media, and higher education in the Arab region.

Matthew Parnell is a post-doctoral fellow and assistant professor in the Department of History at the American University in Cairo. He is a specialist in the history of modern Egypt and the Middle East. His research and writing focuses on changing concepts and experiences of children and youth in history.

Nadine Sinno is an associate professor of Arabic in the Department of Modern and Classical Languages and Literatures at Virginia Tech. Her research interests include modern Arabic literature and cultural studies, particularly focusing on gender and sexuality, ecocriticism, and Lebanese visual culture. Her work has appeared in journals including the *Journal of Arabic Literature*, the *Journal of Middle East Women's Studies*, *Interdisciplinary Studies in Literature and Environment*, *Critique*, *Middle Eastern Literatures*, *MELUS: Multi-Ethnic Literature of the United States*, *College Literature*, and *ASAP/Journal*. Her publications also include a translation of Nazik Saba Yared's novel *Canceled Memories* (2009) and a co-translation of Rashid al-Daif's novel *Who's Afraid of Meryl Streep?* (2014) from Arabic to English.

INTRODUCTION: COLONIAL TO POSTCOLONIAL MASCULINITIES IN THE MIDDLE EAST AND NORTH AFRICA

Mohja Kahf

A crisis in masculinity may have catalyzed the grassroots uprising of 2011 in Tunisia—which, in turn, inspired grassroots uprisings in Egypt, Syria, Yemen, and Bahrain. Muhammad Bouazizi had been harassed numerous times by corrupt municipal police while pursuing his livelihood as a street vendor in an impoverished southern region of Tunisia, but the last straw was when a policewoman slapped the twenty-six-year-old man. Bouazizi set himself on fire on December 17, 2010. The photograph that onlookers took of his burning body circulated via mobile phones and social media and became a rallying image as Tunisian protestors organized around human rights and an end to police brutality in the long-standing dictatorship. Bouazizi's street vending helped him to provide, however meagerly, for his mother and siblings after the death of his father, in a country with high unemployment. The Middle East and North Africa (MENA), a region that is better termed 'Southwest Asia and North Africa,'[1] contains many authoritarian states with high levels of government corruption, police impunity, double-digit unemployment, underemployment, and high poverty rates. At the same time, most cultures in this region[2] construct 'breadwinner' as an important role for males, despite much flux in that concept, and even though women have been 'breadwinning' in increasing numbers for decades now in nearly all of these countries. The combination of these factors—authoritarian states, high unemployment, and men's sense of self that is invested in breadwinning—makes for high levels of stress in many men around the issue of their masculinity. At the other end of the Arab Spring's trajectory, the counter-revolutionary Islamist group, often mockingly known among Syrians and Iraqis as 'Da'esh' (an Arabic acronym derived from the Arabic name of the Islamic State in Iraq and the Levant/ISIL), gains recruits in part by banking on the frustrated concepts of masculinity of alienated men who cannot find adequate livelihoods and therefore cannot marry and can scarcely help out their natal families (this in no way means that all or even most men facing such conditions end up in extremist groups). The group provides these marginalized and jobless men with income and an outlet for efficacious action, as well as with an ideology for dominating women (Packer). In a sense, then, various anxieties around masculinity may well be at the hub of several crises in North Africa.

Grassroots uprisings during 2011 in many Arabic-speaking countries, as well as the 2009 Green Movement in Iran and the 2013 Gezi Park protests in Turkey, showed that a new wave of questioning is simmering in the millennial generation in the MENA region, questioning that touches nearly everything about the *status quo ante*—masculinity included. In Iran, "rebellious young people . . . view their bodies and the articulation of their sexuality as a site of resistance against the government" (Yaghoobi, 53). Frequently absented from Orientalist-inflected global-media accounts and from masculinist local accounts of these events, women played crucial roles in the 2011 uprisings at the grassroots level, where they started. In Egypt, Asma Mahfouz's vlog—especially her call to assemble in Tahrir Square on January 25—helped to spark the revolution (Fahmy, 373). Women laborers were a key part of the April 6 Youth Movement, which from 2008 laid the ground for Egypt's uprising (Naber, Fall 2011, 11). In Syria, Suheir Atassi repeatedly calling men and women together in street protests during January, February, and March 2011 laid the ground for later protest organizing in Damascus (Human Rights Watch, 2011). Syrian human rights lawyer Razan Zaitouneh, with her Violations Documentation Center (VDC), became a focal point in the uprising, for both men and women—well before Zaitouneh's iconic status for anti-regime Syrians rose even further because of her abduction from the VDC office in Douma on December 9, 2013, reportedly by Islamist militia Jaysh al-Islam (Human Rights Watch, 2016).[3] Before the Syrian uprising militarized in autumn 2011, women were leading two of the first four coalitions composed of local protest committees. Bahraini activist Maryam al-Khawaja continues to be a prominent voice for the Bahraini protest movement from abroad, her father and her sister imprisoned by the regime (Nallu). At the same time, the urgent need for continued gender struggle in the revolution arena was highlighted when eighteen women in Cairo's Tahrir Square, protesting the still-authoritarian conditions in Egypt after the 2011 Revolution succeeded in deposing president-for-life Hosni Mubarak, were arrested and subjected to virginity tests by the interim authority. The interim authority administered the 'test,' or gender-based torture method targeting women, in collusion with the accusation that the women were prostitutes, a charge aimed at undermining their protest actions (Amnesty International). This form of sexualized torture was declared illegal by a Cairo administrative court later that year (Butt and Hussein). However, the violence against women protesters continued; when the square filled on July 3, 2013, as Muhammad Morsi, Mubarak's civilian successor as president, was ousted, multiple women were subjected to mass sexual assault by men in the square (Kingsley). The testimony of a female member of Operation Anti-Sexual Harassment/Assault, a grassroots activist organization formed by Egyptian women and men in 2012, describes going into the pressing crowd with her Op-Anti-SH teammate to try to rescue a woman they had spotted being mob-assaulted, then becoming separated from her teammate and alternating between being pushed to the ground and facing suffocation or raising herself up and facing sexual assault as men tried to grope under the many layers of clothing she had worn in preparation (Operation Anti-Sexual Harassment/Assault, Testimony from an Assaulted Op-Anti-SH Member). She describes the look of horror (at the assault) of one man whose face met hers as he attempts to stop the other men. Women, whose actions and voices were initially *heard* and effectual in that rupture moment at the dawn of the uprisings, were then subjected to violent, sexualized attempts to shove them aside from its center and silence them, and the overall trajectories of many of the uprisings toward militarization ultimately marginalized the very women whose work had built the uprising.[4] These charged moments show that in MENA as elsewhere, gender role change is (again, and continually) shifting, with some men right in step with it and others vehemently pushing back. They also underline the need to bring research on men up to speed with research on women of MENA. With its primary focus on masculinities in semiotic discourses and cultural production, this volume contributes to an aspect of that research.

Syrian queer folk and their allies were also a vital part of the early nonviolent uprising in the Syrian streets. In 2010, the Assad regime had arrested groups of gay men in sweeps in Damascus ("Gays Join the Syrian Uprising"). According to Mahmoud Hassino, who is Syrian, gay, and out, "the regime started a homophobic campaign to say that the revolution is immoral because people who own the news channels, which are supporting it, are homosexuals. They went further by saying that everyone who is active in the revolution is gay" (Luongo). Homophobia, though perhaps as present there as anywhere, was not a prominent characteristic of the nonviolent phase of the Syrian uprising. By 2012, after the uprising had begun to militarize, homophobia was evident in Syrian-grown armed rebel brigades and when, in 2013, Islamist extremists from Da'esh (ISIL) joined the armed rebellion, public executions for alleged homosexuality became their all-too-frequent practice; one website keeps a tally (Outright Action International). In October 2017, well after the initial grassroots uprising in Egypt had been commandeered by Islamists and the military in quick succession, Egyptian authorities conducted an arrest sweep against gay men in the wake of the Cairo concert by the Lebanese band Mashrou' Leila, which has an openly gay member, Hamed Sinno. On one hand, the fact that the band, which "had been outspoken about LGBTQI issues in their music and public statements" (Holsiln), managed to snag a Cairo gig attended by 35,000 concertgoers is a significant indicator of ongoing change in social attitudes. On the other hand, after a photo of a concertgoer waving a rainbow flag went viral, the regime of Abd al-Fattah al-Sisi proceeded to arrest dozens on charges of 'debauchery' in an anti-LGBTQI sweep, an appeasement of conservative social attitudes. Change, powerful pushback—but a residual increment of change, nonetheless: these developments around heteronormative, as well as queer, male gender roles place an array of issues about masculinity at the center of current debates about the future of state and society in Southwest Asia and North Africa. This volume is about masculinity, inclusive of queerness, not centered around queerness—but MENA queer and trans issues can no longer be relegated to afterthought status in any book about masculinity anywhere.

While these recent events suggest that constructions of masculinity are in flux, what this volume suggests, in all its variety, is that masculinities are always in a process of being constructed. There is no 'before' that was a stable gendered environment. The early twentieth century in the Middle East and North Africa saw a swirl of older Ottoman-era and Qajari-era concepts of normative masculinity along with a plethora of new ideas reconfiguring masculinity, moving from Nahda[5] models to masculinities under the Mandate and decolonization struggles of the mid-century, then toward the coups and dictatorships of the third quarter of the century in much of the Arabic-speaking world. Dominant norms in masculinity, and resistances to them, shifted in Turkey with the rise of the Young Turks and the inception of the modern Turkish state in 1923, and in Iran from the Qajari state's demise and the Constitutional Revolution to the Pahlavi dynasty and then to post-Islamic Revolution changes. In the Arab world, Nahda models of masculinity themselves formed under the European colonial influence at which they chafed, and were not timeless and unchanging prior to modernity. For example, Nahda-era masculinity rigidified against more flexible (but not necessarily better) earlier attitudes toward male same-sex desires and practices, which colonizing and Orientalist discourses typically highlighted as part of the inferior nature of 'Oriental' males. At the other end of the century, as Frédéric Lagrange has noted, "[t]he limited treatment of same-sex relationships in modern Arabic literature in contrast to classical literature is somewhat puzzling" (Lagrange, 174). Afsaneh Najmabadi explores a parallel shift in nineteenth-century Qajari culture, when "homoeroticism and same-sex practices came to mark Iran as backward; heteronormalization of eros and sex became a condition of "achieving modernity" (Najmabadi, 3).[6] Besides heteronormalization, other configurations linking male identity to modernizing nationalisms began emerging over a hundred years ago. *Zeynab* (1913) by Muhammad Husayn Haykal is among the first Arabic novels, and with it Arabic national narrative right away has the trope metaphorizing a fertile woman into the land of the nation, whose honor men must protect. Our contributor Amal Amireh, in earlier work, has shown that the cost of this metaphor is paid by women, because "the national story becomes the story of possession of the land/woman by a man" (Amireh, 751) and female subjectivity is not centered in such a narrative. In Iran, nation, or *vatan*, is not a young woman but a mother figure whom the sons must protect (Najmabadi, 125). Different in their specifics, both tropes equally imagine the modern national citizen in a protective male role, leaving the presence of female citizens an enigma to be puzzled over. Perhaps even this is reactive to the ways in which colonial discourses themselves metaphorized the colonized territory of MENA as a (veiled) woman to be possessed; perhaps the nationalist is metaphorized as a man because of anti-colonial nationalist discourse's will to power over a position of being victimized (emasculated) by colonialism, as theorized in numerous works by Frantz Fanon. The dichotomy of 'tradition verses modernity,' in any case, is outdated, or at least needs more precision, because usually what is signified by 'tradition' is itself a product of older shifts in masculinity.[7] This volume hopes to problematize antecedents of masculine formations in a specific geographic region.

A word about conceptualizing and naming this geographic region is in order before proceding further. The 'Middle East' is geographically meaningless as well as being unhelpfully Eurocentric. Our region is not east of, say, India, China, Russia, or Indonesia. It is a naming created by European colonialism and owes its widespread hold to the global power of colonial terminology. 'West Asia' or 'Southwest Asia' is a more geographically accurate term to pair with 'North Africa.' It also disorients the Orientalizing gaze, asking the reader to question the cohesion and content of what these terms name. The editors of this volume would have liked this book to be part of the interrogation of colonial and postcolonial formations that inheres in the circulation of these newer terms. We attempted to transition to using 'Southwest Asia and North Africa' ('SWANA') in mid-course during manuscript preparation. However, 'Middle East and North Africa' is firmly wedged into existing publishing and marketing realities in ways that proved difficult for our publisher to circumvent or ignore, so the final manuscript reverted to 'MENA.'

Masculinity in MENA at the start of the era covered by this volume was already reactive to European imperialism and changes in world economies, and even before that always-already in flux. In fiction, a model frequently evoked by Arab writers as the granddaddy patriarch of their past appears in the characters of al-Sayid Ahmad Abd al-Jawad in Naguib Mahfouz's *Cairo Trilogy* and Miteb al-Hadhal in Abdulrahman Munif's *Cities of Salt*. Shaikh Khaled in Ibrahim Nasrallah's *Time of White Horses* is another example. Mahfouz's patriarch acquires, in film adaptation, the epithet Si al-Sayid, meaning "master the Master:" doubled masterliness. A religious variation on this patriarch is the Sufi ideal of tender-hearted spiritual knighthood, a man who behaves gently with women and can be moved to tears by pondering the Divine presence but, like Algeria's famed Emir Abd al-Qadir (1808–1883) or Sudan's Mahdi (1844–1885), also can jump on his actual horse, weapon in hand, ably to protect home and community in a crisis. Secular or religious, the old-school patriarchs of modern Southwest Asian and North African literary depiction have Antar[8]-like virility, bravery, and generosity; are obeyed by loyal wives and children; and are expected to defend the honor of women kin, demonstrate both forcefulness and forbearance, and model anti-colonial nationalist stances. Feminist writers tended to be less sanguine, depicting darker variations that equally, however, create old-school patriarchs as the 'before' figures—as evident in most of Nawal Elsaadawi's novels (*Woman at Point Zero, God Dies by the Nile, The Fall of the Imam*). In the iconic first novel of Turkish feminist Duygu Asena, *Kadının Adı Yok* (The Woman Has No Name, 1987), the protagonist Cici's father is the epitome of violent and abusive patriarchal authoritarianism.

These patriarchs, depicted as left over from the nineteenth century in ways this volume seeks to problematize, were represented as dwindling once the twentieth century moves forward, and the ways in which they seemed to embody masculinity were replaced with a number of other models. We see the venerable Haji Mahmoud, the patriarch at the Qajari-era beginning of Shahrnush Parsipur's novel *Touba and the Meaning of Night* (1989), worrying over how British and Russian machinations will affect his shop, and how to consummate his wedding with the intimidating young title character, Touba (Parsipur, 18). Mid-century decades in Iran saw the emergence of new classes of urban professional men, and the reconfiguration of gendered spaces in the home, state, street, and prisons, as the work of Joanna De Groot shows. In the above-mentioned Arabic novels by Mahfouz and Munif, the evaporation of the old-school patriarchs happens with a great deal of narrative nostalgia and ambivalence. The narratives of these male authors keep a sheen on these patriarchs, for all the insistence on their outdatedness. Miteb rides off on a white horse into the desert in *Cities of Salt* to attain mythic stature in the eyes of the entire village, and in the *Cairo Trilogy* al-Sayid is constantly described as larger than life. "What am I, compared to my father?" thinks Yasin, al-Sayid Ahmad's son at forty during the 1930s, in *Sugar Street*, third book of the *Cairo Trilogy* (Mahfouz, *Sugar Street*, 1038), even as his aging father finds himself confined by ill health to his house, then his bed. Yet Yasin also muses about his children that "he had never wished to play the cruel role with them that his own father had with him" (Mahfouz, *Sugar Street*, 1042). Si al-Sayid has become a stereotype, and stereotypes "are resilient, get reproduced and carry social power," as Emma Sinclair-Webb points out (Sinclair-Webb, 12). The patriarchs of old still resurface, even if they are superseded by 'new men' of the mid-century. Communist activist Ahmad Shawkat, grandson of the patriarch in Mahfouz's *Cairo Trilogy*, works for a magazine called outright *The New Human* in the 1940s; he marries his editor-boss, and they wish neither for children nor a conventional life. The liberal father who, to an extent, encourages his daughter's education is one of the urban upper- and middle-class 'new man' models of the mid-century Arabic-speaking world, as in Assia Djebar's *Fantasia* (1985; trans. 1993). It opens with a scene set in the 1940s: "A little Arab girl going to school for the first time, one autumn morning, walking hand in hand with her father. A tall erect figure in a fez and a European suit . . . a teacher at the French primary school" (Djebar, *Fantasiat*, 3). This mid-century 'new man' is marked sartorially in much of the former Ottoman Empire as secular by wearing a fez without a turban, and a suit rather than a robe; Reza Shah of Iran actually instituted clothing laws, which accompanied the emergent new forms of masculinity. The affable henpecked husband as portrayed by Dorayd Lahham in his recurring 'Ghawar al-Tosheh' character on Syrian state television of the 1970s, often fez-topped and placed in settings from earlier decades, expresses a comical variation on this 'new man.' The narrative that produces Ghawar is conservatively sympathetic to 'new man' bewilderment at what is seen as the growing assertiveness of women, figured by Ghawar's shrewish wife, Fattum Hisbis. In the 1957 Egyptian musical, *al-Kumsariyat al-fatinat* (The Pretty Ticket-takers), one of many Egyptian films of that era orienting audiences to the changing realities of middle-class women's work,[9] male bus laborers feel in danger of losing their jobs to 'new women.' Women in smart bus-conductor uniforms sing a rousing nationalist number calling all 'daughters of Egypt' to take on new jobs for the nation. They stride exultantly to work (this, in the 1950s, when the U.S. nationalist narrative was pushing Rosie the Riveter back into conventional domesticity). By film's end, the men neutralize the threat by marrying the 'daughters of Egypt' who then readily quit their jobs—but dozens of women apply for bus jobs the next day. Change, pushback, regrouping of patriarchy in a new form in reaction to the change, and some small net change, is the tally of the film.

The straightforwardly controlling patriarch is, however, not the only aspect of masculinity seen (often reductively) as belonging to the earlier, so-called 'traditional' period before national decolonization struggles. Legal scholar Lama Abu-Odeh describes the male "virgin by default" in her typology, a vestige of "traditional, pre-nationalist" masculinity (Abu-Odeh, 943) whose "aspects include a sense of estrangement from the other sex, shyness and embarrassment in their presence"—paradoxically combined in some men with behaviors such as harassing women on the street, watching belly dancers, and visiting prostitutes. Perhaps this virgin-by-default is just the young form of a male who morphs into the authoritarian patriarch after crossing the threshold of marriage; perhaps deflowering the virgin wife to whom he feels entitled will usher in his acquisition of grand patriarch status. Meanwhile, however, the male virgin must contend with his heritage of the passionate, chivalric lover of classical Arabic literature and in his real world must "negotiate his sexuality" within "the often violent structure of honor" (Abu-Odeh, 943). Postcolonial nation-building partially limited the violence of honor killings (often upheld in MENA during the colonial period by sexist British or French laws that bear striking overlap with the system permitting honor killing)[10] through the introduction of new laws against it—whose enforcement by the postcolonial states was lackluster. Nationalist projects, Abu-Odeh says, also partially dismantle the separation of gender in the social spheres (though not in the Gulf states, which were not directly colonized), causing a transition to new normative masculinities and femininities. The predatory type 'decouples' from its virginal-twin to become a masculine type on its own, as with the protagonist in Sudanese author Tayeb Salih's novel, *Season of Migration to the North* (1966), an icon of postcolonial literature. In contrast to the predator, Abu-Odeh notes the emergence of "the new 'feminized' Arab man" of the postcolonial era; he "tends to be gentle, soft-spoken . . . vulnerable to the agonies, anguish, and yearnings of love" (Abu-Odeh, 945).

In this last part, he has ample precedent in classical Arabic culture. That chivalric Arab lover of lore who elevates his love-longing to near-worship is a trope that Arabic culture gifted to Europeans, who had no such romance in literature before multiple contacts with Arabic and Persian culture through Spain, Sicily, and the Crusades. Persian literature and art is rich with the figure of Biblical/Qur'anic Joseph, a paragon of male beauty, and with the bewildered figure of the Sufi 'Shaykh San'an' of Faridudin Attar's creation, who falls in love with a Christian maiden and learns that this most dangerous love outside his faith is the love he needed to experience to break through to the next level of spirituality—a trope often reworked in Iranian modernity.

Arabic love literature is abundant and variegated, from raunchy to spiritual, but it can also be a troublesome heritage. Ahdaf Souief's massive novel *In the Eye of the Sun* (1992) has a female protagonist whose husband is too chivalrously invested in his wife's feminine-princess persona to have bed-rocking sex with her, so she seeks it elsewhere. On the other hand, the princess-bride femininity ideal (one among several normative femininities) can inculcate a rape-culture masculinity when a man is taught that a good woman will resist sex out of modesty, and so must be taken—and that then the experience will rouse her sexual response.[11] The sexual double standard survived all these postcolonial projects, in any case, even if it was modified somewhat in its stridency. Syrian poet Nizar Kabbani (1923–1998) famously attacked the double standard in iconoclastic poems from the 1950s onward advocating women's sexual freedom.[12] Islamists also attack the extra-licit parts of the sexual double standard, by having no tolerance for the whoring characterizing Mahfouz's patriarch al-Sayid Ahmad as well as his sons, and by expecting virginity of a man before marriage as much as a woman and so ostensibly leveling the playing field. However, Islamists bring the sexual double standard in through the back door, by offering men quantitatively more licit types of sexual outlets (in the form of polygyny, which is generally opposed by the postcolonial nationalist projects) than women have. Polyandry is not on the table (except in niche Muslim subcultures such as that of the Tuareg), so the best deal for multiple sexual outlets that women can get in the Islamist blueprint is serial monogamous marriages, with maybe an extra dash of *mut'a* (temporary marriage) on the Shi'a side of things.[13] (In the range of divorce and remarriage routes, Muslim women in the Middle East had wider options than most women in the first three-quarters of the twentieth century in countries termed 'Western.') Meanwhile, the modern Iranian feminist project has gone hand in hand with "modernist embarrassment over what to do with the homoeroticism of Sufi love" says Najmabadi. She asks, "How could we reenvisage a feminism that brings out homosocial and homoerotic possibilities that earlier feminists (women and men) felt compelled to cover over . . . without denigrating the integrity and gains of early Iranian feminism?" and her question is no less pertinent to Arab feminism (Najmabadi, 237–39).

Older (but still not timeless) notions about masculinity competed with newer ideas after the social changes of the mid-to-late century and the emergence of left-wing regimes in Iraq (1958), Syria (1963), Libya (1969), and other states, heralded by the Free Officers' Movement in Egypt taking over the state in 1952 and its key officer, Gamal Abd al-Nasser, nationalizing the Suez Canal in 1956 to widespread adulation in the Arabic-speaking world. Politicized young men with Ba'thist allegiances in Turki al-Hamad's Saudi male-entitlement coming-of-age novel *Adama* (2003) (themselves virgins by default, in a still firmly gender-segregated and sexually strict Saudi society, having only furtive glances, a stolen kiss or two, prostitutes, and the sexual double standard working for them) excitedly discuss the 1969 overthrow of Libya's King Idris as news of the Libyan Free Officers coup emerges. It's "better to have Libya governed by Nasserites than for it to remain under the control of imperialists and their reactionary traitor henchmen," one of the young men enthuses (al-Hamad, 186). Out of this second wave of anti-colonial struggle, the modern secular figure of the *fida'i* (literally self-ransomer) fighting against imperialism or Israeli occupation comes to center stage in Arab masculinity, idealized as a hero volunteering to stand bravely and selflessly against impossible odds, who is quick-tempered when it comes to nationalist pride and who can also sweet-talk a young woman into sleeping with him the night before his self-sacrificing mission for the greater good. The fiction of Ghassan Kanafani (1936–1972) often features men who fall through the cracks of that idealization, and the male protagonist of Palestinian feminist Sahar Khalifah's novel about the West Bank under Israeli occupation since 1967, *Wild Thorns* (1976), tries and fails at this ideal while the working-class pragmatist who never aims for the heroic ideal seems to provide a more enduring model of resistance to the Israeli occupation. These mid-century young ideologues typically see themselves in some part as allies of women's liberation, and see their nationalist, modernist, anti-imperialist ideologies as requiring men and women to work hand-in-hand against older gender barriers that hold the nation back. In a key transition moment of MENA neopatriarchy, however, those anti-imperialist *fida'i* types morph into male identities that provide a masculinist ideological excuse for the hypermasculine militia men of Lebanese and Algerian civil wars, or the predatory paramilitary thugs called *shabiha* cultivated by the 'anti-imperialist' regime in Syria from 1982, just as those clean-chinned, handsome officers who had led anti-colonial coups became brutal dictators-for-life of enormously corrupt police states—setting the stage for the Arab Spring, where we began.

Indeed, perhaps we end where we began because many of the liberatory, anti-colonialist, even progressive discourses in MENA countries in the twentieth century have replicated patriarchy and have hegemonized a violent model of masculinity in their methods even when eschewing them in their embraced ideologies, and even when this neopatriarchy is more nuanced than, and different in many ways from, the older classic patriarchy. If we keep on analyzing the old-form straightforward patriarchy, we waste energy on a straw man and fail to recognize the clever twists in MENA neopatriarchy. Lisa Wedeen examines the ways in which rhetoric of state in the 'anti-imperialist' Assad regime of Syria "not only emphasized Asad [sic] as national patriarch, but also stressed his masculinity or manliness" (Wedeen, 54). The same state apparatuses that built up the 'manliness' of the modern state leader—be he Habib Bourguiba of Tunisia, Jaafar Nimeiry of Sudan, or any number of others—on the one hand humiliates all citizens through police-state authoritarianism, creating pressure that distorts identity for everyone, and on the other hand does so in specifically gendered ways. Many of the surrealistic short stories of Syrian writer Zakariya Tamir bring out the way in which this pressure operates in specific ways to create a sense of emasculation in some men who then turn around and dominate women in their private lives, replicating on a domestic level the politics of modern but still authoritarian neopatriarchal 'manliness' (although not all non-elite men compensate by doing so).[14] Authoritarian states perpetuate, on the national stage, the authoritarian patriarch but in tricky modern guises, even while they may be sending the opposite message in state propaganda about modernity requiring the equality of women. Whenever new dissident or liberatory movements espouse masculinist methods, they too bode for the reproduction of the master's tools. The study of masculinities is thus profoundly involved in the relationship of gender roles to macro-politics, and to region-wide struggles to move out from under authoritarianism.

Arab, Turkish, Kurdish, Coptic, Amazigh, Iranian, Azeri, Nubian, Assyrian, Somali, and Mizrahi men, Shirazi men of the Comoros islands, men of the Druze ethnoreligious group, and other men of MENA, may share some cultural practices—such as ritualized hospitality and generosity—although the specific rituals differ even within each group according to class and other factors. They may share a higher likelihood of kissing men on the cheek in greeting, or of wearing scent (and that goes whether straight or gay, secular or religious, young or old) in richer fragrances than is common for men in, say, Western Europe—but constructions of masculinity are contingent, multilayered, and always in a state of reconfiguring, in the MENA region no less than elsewhere. One hegemonic male type does not exist; the formation of male identities depends on many different factors including but not limited to class, ethnicity, and access to social as well as economic capital—and some kinds of male identities marginalize other types of men as much as marginalizing women. Still, in our world at large including MENA, it "is hard to ignore the fact that most of the means of organized violence and brute force—weapons and the complex knowledge associated with them—are in the hands of men . . . most positions of power in the public sphere are held by men" (Whitehead and Barrett, 16). Those men in Tahrir Square assaulting women were not aliens from another planet whose presence is not explicable by human knowledge but ordinary men; the men trying to stop the assault were also men of MENA; it is crucial that we study how male identities are produced that led each of them to that place.

The above survey of MENA masculinities, by no means comprehensive, is obviously longer and more complex than the short, simple list of stereotypes about 'Middle Eastern' masculinity held by many outsiders to the region and by dominant global discourses: terrorist; fanatic; misogynist. Orientalism, as Edward Said lays it out (Said), that is, as a system of knowledge in the aid of violent imperialist power may not have caused the sexual torture of Iraqi men by U.S. soldiers at Abu Ghraib Prison in 2004, but it contributed in specific ways to the 'cultural awareness' training that the soldiers received and selectively deployed in conceiving how to sexually humiliate Arab prisoners, as well as buoying in innumerable ways the policies of the 2003 U.S. invasion and occupation of Iraq. Orientalism undergirds Israeli 'pinkwashing,' in which the state of Israel deploys propaganda depicting its supposedly progressive stand on gay rights in a manner that veils its daily racist violence against Palestinian human rights. In the regime of Orientalism, MENA masculinities seem always to be on the wrong side of civilization; when imperialist Orientalism was anti-gay, MENA men were condemned as shockingly gay and sexually permissive, but after the sexual revolutions of the twentieth century in the U.S. and Europe, MENA men were reduced to being shockingly macho and sexually repressive. This reveals how Orientalist stereotypes are as much about projections of the 'Other' inside the internal identities of their producers as about realities on the ground. Of course, realities on the ground were also changing; as Lagrange remarks regarding gayness in modern Arabic literature, "if censorship has become so wary of the mention of homosexuality it is because public morality has changed" (Lagrange, 190). The problem with Orientalist stereotypes is not that they are simply untrue, but that the way they frame and construct their subjects in alliance with hegemonic power clouds conscientious searching for truths. Orientalist stereotypes of MENA masculinity[15] chop up their subject unrecognizably and put him back together in grotesque Frankensteinish parodies; this leg may be true and that hand partially true, but they and everything else are affixed ass-backwardly. As Nadine Naber points out, "Orientalist approaches . . . obscure the ways in which cultural values are shaped within historical contexts and material realities such as the pressing struggle for jobs, food, health care, dignity, and an end to the interconnected problems of harassment, violence, and state repression" (Naber 2011b). What Orientalist supremacism offers is not understanding of the subject, but the will to hate and to dominate it.

"Masculinity is neither natural nor given. Like femininity, it is a social construct" (Peteet 107). How then, specifically, in this instance and that, is masculinity constructed in our region—especially in literary, cinematic, and other semiotic texts? The chapters in this multidisciplinary volume speak to each other intelligently on that question across disciplines, geographies, and historical periods. Together they examine constructions of both hegemonic and marginalized masculinities in the MENA region, through literary criticism, film studies, discourse analysis, anthropological accounts, and studies of military culture. Because this volume is multidisciplinary, each contributor contextualizes and theorizes their argument in their own field of research.

Within a queer-studies framework, Jedidiah C. Anderson's typology—in his opening chapter, "Exotic and Benighted, or Modern yet Victimized? The Modern Predicament of the Arab Queer"—theorizes three Orientalist narratives currently colonizing the space of Arab queerness. The first, a pinkwashing narrative, renders queer Arabs uniquely and exceedingly oppressed by a homophobia that can only be remedied by being more 'Western,' ignoring their oppression under systems of dictatorship and occupation in which Western powers are also implicated. The second Orientalist narrative is older, dating from the era of high imperialism by European powers, and Anderson shows that it is still alive and thrashing; this is the narrative which denounces Arab homosexuality as a sign of the sordidness of Arab societies generally, and sees queerness as an inherent, and perverted, part of 'their' nature. The third hegemonic narrative in circulation flips this, seeing Arab queerness in equally essentialist terms, but making a positive out of it, declaring its prurient attraction to a queer Arab male body that it hypersexualizes. It bears remembering here (and elsewhere in this volume) that 'hegemonic' does not simply mean 'dominant,' it also means dominant to the extent that it is willingly reproduced even by those whose interest it does not serve. One might suggest also that while the pinkwashing narrative and the third narrative appeal, though not exclusively, to those left of center in dominant global discourses, the second narrative appeals to those right of center, with its implication that the Arab world is in need of moral discipline. There is something for everyone to exploit, in the racist smorgasbord that Anderson describes. Queer Arabs are positioned as intensely visible for all the wrong reasons, he argues, and made hypervisible at the intersection of various "matrices of Western hegemonic power."

It bears remembering that Britain had an 'anti-buggery law' from 1533, and it took a struggle from 1967 to 2013 for gay sex to be fully decriminalized in all parts of the United Kingdom (Tatchell), while same-sex sexual relationships were not criminalized in Ottoman law *(kanun)* and are not criminalized in modern Turkish law (noting that non-criminalization is not the same as social acceptance, in either period). However, being homosexual is enough to relieve a man of military service in modern Turkey. It is from an authoritative U.S. psychiatric handbook, albeit an outdated one (the American Psychiatric Association's *Diagnostic and Statistical Manual*—1968 edition), that this policy seems to base its medicalized rationale in the Turkish military. From Michel Foucault's work in *History of Sexuality*, we perceive that discourses in Western Europe and the United States transitioned in the nineteenth century (the age of high imperialism) to considering homosexuality a medical disorder, and from Joseph Massad's analysis in *Desiring Arabs* we know that when this medicalized rhetoric shows up in MENA, it is usually a residue of the ways in which MENA countries responded to the pressure of hegemonic European imperialist discourses to heteronormalize modernity in the early twentieth century.

After this detailed critique of imperialist grand narratives around same-sex-desiring Arabs comes Amal Amireh's chapter, offering exactly the antidote, aiming its internal critique at grand narratives of Palestinian masculinity without letting up on the anti-imperialist analysis. Amireh's chapter, "Of Heroes and Men: The Crisis of Masculinity in the Post-Oslo Palestinian Narrative," teaches us how to resist the longing that some critics express for the novel that will tell 'the great Palestinian story' in order to appreciate alternative stories. That hegemonic, masculinist Palestinian national narrative typically posits the *fida'i*, the freedom fighter, as the embodiment of both manliness and Palestinian-ness. It continues to be written in Palestinian literature after the watershed letdown of the 1993 Oslo Accords, and is also contested by other, less heroic, ways of telling. Amireh's chapter traces the masculinist national narrative through the vast historical novels of Ibrahim Nasrallah, written in Arabic. By examining the terse, diaristic Anglophone writing of Raja Shehadeh of the Occupied West Bank, she brings to light a different sort of Palestinian masculinity, which quietly asserts its right to be heard against the heroic thundering of those who, she devastatingly reminds us, brought forth the disappointing Oslo accords. Short-story writer Raji Bathish, who edits a queer-friendly online zine, is a Palestinian citizen of the state of Israel. Amireh outlines how his writing resists the domination of one Palestinian master-narrative of the Nakba, the moment of the loss of the bulk of the Palestinian homeland to the state of Israel in 1948. Like many of the young men and women in his cohort who took to the streets in the uprisings of 2011 in many MENA countries, Bathish opens space for questioning the masculinist master-narratives of Arab nationalism that have brought us to this pass.

The protagonist in Lebanese novelist Rashid Al-Daif's *Tistifil Meryl Streep* (2001; *Who's Afraid of Meryl Streep?*, 2014) subscribes to a narrative of domineering manhood, but the novel itself does not, Nadine Sinno argues in her contribution to this volume, "'I get to deflower at least one. It's my right!': the Precariousness of Hegemonic Masculinity in Rashid Al-Daif's *Who's Afraid of Meryl Streep?*" Sinno's chapter explores the repercussions of performing a hegemonic type of masculinity, the type that Amireh's chapter has just displaced for the reader of Palestinian literature. Despite the fact that Rashoud, the protagonist of the novel that Sinno analyzes, views himself as a liberal man supporting women's emancipated status, his liberalness goes out the window when he thinks his masculinity is at stake in his marriage. Lebanon's multilingual code-switching, and the global incursions of U.S. culture, factor into Rashoud's concept of male selfhood. He finds himself both awed and threatened by actors such as Meryl Streep, whom he loves dearly but blames, at least in part, for modeling transgressive behavior that Lebanese women, including his wife, have begun to emulate—thereby sabotaging their honor and the nation itself. Rashoud's obsession with his wife's alleged promiscuity and the status of her hymen prior to marrying him ultimately leads to the disintegration of his marriage as his wife tires of being demonized and humiliated for her 'questionable' past. Along with his marriage, Rashoud loses his pride and confidence as he is cast away by a woman that he does not even respect. Unable to see his wife as anything but an extension of himself, Rashoud cannot help but think that whoever penetrates (or may have penetrated) her body has essentially violated him, sexually. He shudders at his own construction of his body as effeminate and penetratable. The novel's plot and story chip away not only at Rashoud's concept of masculinity, Sinno demonstrates, but also at his heterosexuality, revealing the fragility of his masculine construction of self. As the novel progresses, not only is Rashoud disabused of his rigid beliefs with respect to gender, sexuality, and the body but he also pays the price of enacting hegemonic masculinity. His toxic masculinity backfires, as he becomes subject to anxiety, sexual humiliation, stigmatization, and abuse—all of which he had inflicted on numerous women. Al-Daif's novel, which some readers might understandably find cringe-worthy and unsettling, echoes important, and sometimes uncomfortable, conversations that are taking place in the Arab world and elsewhere with regard to gender performance, chastity, intimacy, sexual assault, and marriage.

It is important to note here that, in the Lebanon of the novels treated in Sinno's chapter and the following one by Kifah Hanna, accelerated change in gender roles brought on by political and economic modernity has already been going on for at least three or four generations. Al-Daif's protagonist Rashoud, for example, lives in a moment when Lebanese women divorcing, or working (in the modern and middle class sense),[16] is not news; where men who do not identify as 'liberal' in the way that Rashid does are not therefore necessarily 'traditional' but may be illiberal in other, modern ways. In fact, Rashid is all about processing the anxieties residual in those several cycles of already-moving-on changes in gender roles. In "Crises of Masculinity in Huda Barakat's War Literature," Kifah Hanna argues that the Lebanese Civil War exerts pressure toward specific new variants of heteronormativity on male characters in three novels by Huda Barakat: *Hajar al-dahik* (The Stone of Laughter, 1990), *Ahl al-hawa* (Disciples of Passion, 1993), and *Sayidi wa habibi* (My Master, My Lover, 2004). Barakat's first novel, *The Stone of Laughter*, "is probably the first . . . Arabic novel with a male homosexual as main character" (Lagrange, 184). The protagonist, Khalil, is alienated not from some frozen-in-time 'traditional' Arab manhood but from "two very attractive versions of masculinity," the narrator says, that are very specific to Lebanon on the cusp of its civil war, when the novel is set. The first type of men, in the novel's words, "busy themselves shaping the destiny of an area of patent importance on the world map, concerned with people's public and private lives, even with water, with bread, with dreams, with emigration," while those in the second type "have laid down plans to fasten their hold on the upper echelons . . . in politics, in leadership, in the press" (Barakat, 12). Both types are concerned with power, with controlling large forces and wide swathes of discourses, but 'traditional' is not an accurate description of them and neither is 'conservative' quite precise enough. These new Lebanese masculinities, with their powerful hegemonic pull in different ways on the protagonists of all three novels, are post-civil-war iterations of masculinity that Barakat is peeling back for us and dissecting layer by layer. Hanna argues that Barakat's writing goes far beyond parsing available gender identities, to posit that sexual identity is ultimately fluid and indeterminate, "dispersed across 'male' and 'female' alike . . . androgynous." Hanna's reading of these novels opens up for us the possibility of imagining a "post-heteronormative future Lebanese society."

Naguib Mahfouz's *Cairo Trilogy* is 'the great Egyptian novel,' canonical and grand as its master protagonist, Al-Sayid Ahmad, even as it sows seeds of doubt in grand masculinity. It is not al-Sayid but his slender, elegant grandson Radwan who is the focus of Robert James Farley's chapter, "Mahfouz, al-Mutanabbi, and the Canon: Poetics of Deviance from the Masculine Nationalist Discourse of *al-Sukkariya*." Farley notes that critics have argued over whether Radwan's same-sex desire comes from pre-colonial Arab models or from Western models, and from what is called 'tradition' or from what is called 'modernity.' Anderson's chapter comes to mind, as this debate as a whole fits nicely within one of his three modes describing how same-sex-desiring Arabs are viewed. What critics have not done, Farley points out, is analyze Radwan's role in the nationalist narrative that is so central to the novel and the trilogy as a whole. On one hand, Farley argues, "we witness Radwan outside of a national discourse that appears divided on many philosophical, social, and political questions, but can unite on a masculine, heteronormative platform," feeling himself an outcast for not liking women. While his cousin's straight sexual thoughts are interwoven with nationalist themes in the interior monologues that are such a regular part of the novel's narrative pattern, Radwan's sexual interior thoughts are entirely absent, present only in the negative. On the other hand, by becoming a protégé of the aristocratic Abd al-Rahim Pasha Isa, a political bigwig, Radwan becomes the most politically influential member of his family, even finagling his father's long-delayed promotion in the civil service. The novel indirectly makes it obvious that Radwan's relationship with the Pasha has what Radwan himself calls its "nonpolitical" side, the side that he is terrified people will discover. Thus, Farley argues, "Radwan is at once an insider and outsider, political but not national." Further, Farley demonstrates that Radwan's homosexuality, rather than being rooted solely in a medicalized Western concept of 'deviance,' is intertwined with his affinity for the pre-modern corpus of Arabic–Islamic culture, placing him outside the Nahda-era narrative of heteronormative nationalism and its rationalist break with the classical past—or at least, belonging to both.

How does queer Arab masculinity construct itself in the diaspora? In "Diasporic Queer Arabs in Europe and North America: Sexual Citizenship and Narratives of Inclusion and Exclusion," Nicole Fares examines the social capital available to gay Arab men as they try to maintain membership in multiple social groups (Puar), in Ahmad Danny Ramadan's novel *The Clothesline Swing* (2017) and the novella *God in Pink* by Hasa Namir (2015). Rather than use the older paradigms of 'assimilation' and 'integration' with regard to immigrants in their new country, Fares reaches for 'inclusion' and 'social cohesion.' The narrative of acceptance of LGBTQI rights as part of human rights has come at the cost of casting certain countries and religions as 'traditional and backward,' Fares points out, building on Jasbir

Puar's work in *Terrorist Assemblages*. Both the narrator of *The Clothesline Swing* and his dying lover to whom the text is addressed in the second person are Muslim Syrian men who have settled in Canada as refugees. The narrator calls himself a "*hakawati*," which means "storyteller," and refers to men who plied the craft of performing orally the folkloric epics of premodern Arabic culture, typically to a group of men in a public café and usually after training with another *hakawati* (the craft is dying out). *The Clothesline Swing*'s narrator creates, through the narrated text, an archive of the life that he and his partner have experienced together, a sort of family photo album in words. Point of view in *God in Pink* alternates between a young man in Iraq and the local imam to whom he reaches out for help in dealing with his gender non-binary self-identification and his attraction to men. This triggers a process of self-recognition in the imam, a husband and father, who realizes that he, too, is gender non-binary, although this term is never used in the text. Fares mines these literary texts for the possibility of retaining localized discourses of homosexuality that do not adhere to 'homonormative' global discourses, with their single story and uniform goals of outness and independence from family for all LGBTQI people.

Alessandro Columbu's contribution, "Of Knives, Mustaches and Headgears: The Fall of the *Qabaday* in Zakariya Tamir's Latest Works," argues that new configurations of masculinity appear in stories published by Tamir in three collections: *Sanadhak* (We Shall Laugh, 1998), *al-Hisrim* (Sour Grapes, 2000) and *Taksir rukab* (Breaking Knees, 2002). While Sinno's and Hanna's chapters look at literature that reveals how the Lebanese Civil War changed male identities, Columbu examines how Tamir's stories reveal the gendered dimension of the unrelenting authoritarianism in Syria throughout the 1980s, 1990s, and the 2000s, signifying a subtle shift from how gender roles are portrayed in Tamir's earlier work. The failures of nationalist and liberatory ideologies in this period, combined with persistent authoritarianism, have a castrating effect on masculinity in Tamir's stories, Columbu argues. Tamir offers crushed men who have internalized the obedience and submission demanded by the modern authoritarian state, and shows that this makes them all the more vicious and unethical in relation to women, indeed twisting masculinity into another new contortion that is no less patriarchal. Columbu points out that all the characters in Tamir's brutally surreal stories become complicit "in self-enforcing strategies of domination, deconstructing a state-versus-citizens binary opposition, but attributing an equal amount of responsibility to the state's practices of coercion and the citizens' continued, albeit hypocritical acceptance." Culpability is everywhere, Tamir's *oeuvre* seems to suggest, and Columbu's analysis shows how gendered that culpability is.

Together, the cluster of chapters focused on literature demonstrates the increasingly complex literary representations of both straight and queer masculinities—and their dynamic interactions—in modern Arabic literature, produced at home and in the diaspora. From the iconic work of Naguib Mahfouz to post-Arab Spring queer novels, nuanced and complex ideas about masculinity in the Arab world are available to those who wish to explore alternatives to Orientalist narratives. These essays map intricate faultlines in MENA masculinities that are explored in Arabic novels. Many texts in which outsiders view MENA masculinity, however, continue with their stereotyped portrayals of MENA masculinities. The next chapter, by John Tofik Karam, analyzes Orientalist images of heterosexual Middle Eastern masculinity in two mid-century cultural texts produced in North and South America. Karam draws attention to the racialization of the immigrant body, even when the protagonist is male and straight—and seeks to assimilate in his adopted country.

Karam's chapter, "Romancing Middle Eastern Men in North and South America," shows the truth of Sara Ahmed's assertion that "We cannot isolate the production of racial bodies from the gendering and sexualizing of bodies" (Ahmed, 47). In the U.S., Rodger's and Hammerstein's Broadway musical *Oklahoma!* (1955) features the comical Persian peddler Ali Hakim, a minor character. In Jorge Amado's novel, *Gabriela, Cravo e Canela* (Brazilian; 1958); a major male character is 'seu' Nacib, a member of Brazil's '*turcos*,' as those of Syrio-Lebanese ancestry were historically called—at first pejoratively. Both characters are depicted as having "shrewd," which is to say slightly shady, business practices. Both texts enact national narratives involving ethnic, gender, and class hierarchies—but in different ways. Karam argues that while "the Middle Eastern man is contained by marriage with a rural white woman in the U.S. narrative, his sexuality must be exercised with a mulatta mistress in order to belong in the Brazilian narrative." Peddler Ali in *Oklahoma!* is comically forced into a shotgun wedding. Nacib has to transform by accepting that Gabriela, the sensual mestiza lover, is not meant for the bonds of marriage, and to let go of controlling her. Note that the 'seu' prefix affixed to Nacib's name is merely a Portugese-inflected version of 'Sayid,' the same as in 'si al-Sayid,' (Mahfouz's old patriarch), meaning 'master.' Nacib's title may evoke that imagined all-powerful patriarch for readers who recognize the roots of the term, but Nacib is not that patriarch—even if the society around him thinks he may be. "Orientalism in the southern hemisphere, like its counterparts in northern climes," Karam argues, posits Arab masculinity as alpha-macho (my term, not his), in contrast to masculinity of the civilized world which harbors a secret worry that it may have civilized manhood a little too much. Yet the novel offers a more nuanced view of Nacib, Karam shows. Further, Nacib becomes a recognizable icon across Brazilian culture living on in multiple adaptations of the novel, while Ali Hakim of *Oklahoma!* stays in a tiny cultural niche of mainstream U.S. culture.[17]

Our next cluster of chapters addresses masculinity in national cinematic corpuses—the first dealing with Iran's narrative cinema before and after its Islamic Revolution, the second with Tunisian films before and after the Bourguiba dictatorship, and the third with masculinity in Palestinian cinema. Read together, these chapters show us how war, resistance, and regime change impact the constructions and performance of masculinity, thereby highlighting the historic specificity and malleability of gender and sexuality. Kaveh Bassiri's scope in "Tough Guys, Martyrs, Dandies, and Marginalized Men: Changing Masculine Roles in Iranian Cinema" encompasses normative and transgressive models of masculinity in the Pahlavi era (1925–1978) as well as the 1979-onward era of the Islamic Republic of Iran, surveying a rich array of films. In the military monarchy of the authoritarian Pahlavi shahs, the state encouraged pro-Western models. Films of that era portraying historical or legendary Iranian heroes such as Rostam weight them with the normative values of the state, Bassiri argues, while in action-hero films that subtly transgress the hegemonic norms of that era, the virile, lower-class 'loveable rogue,' or *luti*, represents "the struggles and anxieties of the lower classes" alienated from Westernizing state discourse. Elite masculinity was Westernized in dress and ideology in Pahlavi Iran, and another critique of Pahlavi discourse appears in the portrayal of the Westernized urban upper-class man as an effeminate dandy, or *fokoli*, his manliness weakened by his lame attempts to be Western. The *fokoli* had not not always been seen as effeminate; it is modernity in Iran which marks him thus, recalling that, in the Qajari era, nineteenth-century Iranian culture "had other ways of naming, such as *amrad* (young adolescent male) and *mukhannas* (an adult man desiring to be an object of desire for adult men), that were not equated with effeminacy" (Najmabadi, 238). With the Islamic Revolution of 1978, Islamizing discourses replaced Westernizing discourse as the agenda of a new kind of authoritarian state; soon Iran faced war with Iraq, and hegemonic masculinity in films that adhered to the state narrative came to be represented by the unassuming citizen of modest means who sacrifices for the defense of his nation, embodying the spiritual journey toward becoming a martyr, or *shahid*. Some films attempt to capitalize on the older commercial popularity of the action-hero *luti*, converting him into an Islamic version of himself and, through his conversion journey on the screen, proselytizing cinemagoers. Typically, through love of a woman the rogue learns the spiritual value of shedding a material life for the sweet and melancholic self-sacrifice in defense of nation, along the way "earning the higher love of God." Not all post-revolution cinema endorses the 'idealized Muslim male subject' promoted by the regime, Kaveh shows; many filmmakers bring to the screen other, "subordinate and dissident masculinities, from the rebellious youth to the forgotten veteran."

Tunisia's Personal Status Code (PSC), passed on August 13, 1956, was a strident leap into modernity-from-above in gender equality, much like the Turkish Civil Code of 1924. The PSC was imposed by Habib Bourguiba, who would serve four terms as president and then finally give up the pretense and declare himself president for life in 1975, initiating a cult of personality in which worship of Bourguiba became embedded in the concept of modern Tunisian nationalism—in much the same way that public profession of adoration of Hafez al-Assad became a mandatory practice in Syrian nationalism, as analyzed in Wedeen). With a single swipe, in a manner that Nouri Gana says many saw as charged with neocolonial paternalism, the PSC illegalized many practices of gender iniquity—but did it eradicate them, coming as it did from the top down in an authoritarian regime? Or did it create a regime of neopatriarchy, and ensure a retrenchment of conservative reaction that could find ample fodder for implicating the PSC in Bourguiba's neocolonialism? Gana's chapter in this volume, "Men and Modernity in Postcolonial Tunisian Cinema," argues that Tunisian men have never quite recovered from Bourguiba's authoritarian paternalism, from being 'Bourguiba's sons.' "Not a homogenous group," he says, "they have been able neither to come to terms with the challenges of modernity, of which gender equality is part and parcel, nor to relinquish fully the shelter of traditional patriarchy." Examining over a dozen Tunisian films produced from 1978 to 2009, Gana argues that "Tunisian cinema is invested in unraveling the ways in which Tunisian men are stranded in the pull of neopatriarchy even while attempting, timidly or defiantly, to break from its confines. Like Bourguiba, while they can be enlightened about the workings of patriarchy they nonetheless perpetuate it." This confusion, straddling two contradictory regimes, "the logic of gender equality and the logic of male privilege," creates a melancholic narrative of manhood. It is a melancholia perhaps somewhat akin to the mournful spirituality ascribed by Bassiri to the marginalized male in Iranian cinema, who seems to stand in silent reproval of dominant masculinity. Gana points out that the masculine melancholia of 'Bourghiba's sons' in Tunisian film could be an incubator of more equitable futures.

Palestinian land is still under colonial-settler occupation, with Palestinians fractured into several groups inside it and in the diaspora. The term 'postcolonial' in its chronological sense is not yet applicable to Palestinians, as the regime of settler colonialism still exists. Palestinian film at one time, which seems very long ago (2002), denied entry into the Oscars competition by the U.S. Academy of Motion Picture Arts and Sciences because Palestinians had no nation-state, is the subject of Sarah Hudson's chapter in this volume, "Constructions of Masculinity in Palestinian Film." Without a nation-state but with a nationalist discourse that is 'postcolonial' in the sense of resistant to colonialism, ideas of Palestinian masculinity still have undergone many of the shifts in relation to national narratives that happened in other Arabic-speaking countries during the time from the Nahda to postcolonial modernity. While Gana's study analyzes the neopatriarchal nuances of the mid-century 'new men' who are 'Bourghiba's sons' in Tunisian film, Hudson's study follows the twists and turns of Palestinian filmic narratives that cast doubt on hegemonic patriarchy in a nation without a dictator-Bourghiba parallel. Drawing on Julie Peteet's work, which emphasizes the significant impact of Israel's occupation, oppression, and daily acts of violence—including beatings, raids, and imprisonment—on the construction and performance of Palestinian masculinities, Hudson analyzes three Palestinian feature films, focusing on father–son relationships. She argues that Palestinian directors Michel Khleifi, Hany Abu Assad, and Elia Suleiman manage to critique hegemonic Palestinian masculinity while maintaining the moral-ethical superiority of the Palestinian struggle for human rights and national self-determination. Extended colonial occupation by Israel, and Palestinian resistance to it, complicates Palestinian masculinities in numerous ways, deteriorating or inverting the father–son hierarchy, for example. Israeli national discourse promotes a militaristic model of Jewish-Israeli male hypermasculinity, particularly in the illegal settlements. If, as Hudson argues, "masculinity is inextricably entwined with the state of the nation and the state of the nation is kept perpetually in limbo by Israel, then nationalist masculinities cannot bear fruit" for Palestinian men. In practical terms, on the ground, Israel 'wins' the macho context, for Palestinians are contained and constrained whether they are citizens of Israel, in diaspora, or living under brutal and intense occupation in the West Bank or, especially, Gaza. Still, Hudson argues, the films offer narratives in which Palestinians can win the moral higher ground, and do so in ways that operationalize new turns in Palestinian masculinities. Thus, Hudson's chapter links up with Amireh's in this volume, to show us another set of alternatives to the grand, hegemonically masculine, Palestinian narrative.

Two chapters that follow deepen this book's historical richness at the beginning of the century-plus span that it covers. The first researches the gendered depiction of colonizers and colonized in political caricatures in

Egypt and Britain; the second examines masculinity in Ottoman Beirut and early Egyptian nationalist discourse, looking at cultural practices, dress, work, and military roles. These texts highlight the role of the visual in fashioning 'Self' and 'Other,' particularly with regards to projecting (or denying) a specific masculine image.

In his chapter, "Gendered Politics in Late Nineteenth-Century Egyptian Nationalist Discourse," Matthew B. Parnell analyzes cartoons and caricatures that appeared in popular British and Egyptian journals in the late nineteenth century, highlighting the gendered representations that depicted the struggle for power in Egypt. The satirical images possess potent symbolism, he demonstrates, particularly as they serve as vehicles for promoting imperial and nationalist agendas. Conceptualizing cartoons as "a visual equation to the struggle," Parnell argues that in both the imperial and nationalist cases, the emphasis on gendered difference serves to expose, mock, and undermine the 'Other,' including the Other's alleged masculinity or lack thereof. As an example, following political developments between June and August 1882, British satirical journals such as *Fun* and *Punch* depicted the khedive as an 'emasculated' or 'child-like' figure in need of pacification and guardianship—by the British. By the same token, Egyptian journals, most notably Yaqub Sannu's *Abu naddara zarqa'* (The Man with the Blue Glasses), mobilized an array of images that sought to undermine the khedival regime and protest European intervention in Egypt in addition to promoting support for the Egyptian nationalist movement. Parnell demonstrates that the Egyptian press adopted tropes of masculine crisis to belittle Isma'il and Tawfiq in ways that were similar to the images circulated in British satirical journals. These representations highlighted the impotence and ignorance of Egypt's rulers in the face of dominant European encroachment and nationalist resistance. In contrast to the depictions mocking khedival effeminacy or childishness, Sannu' produced images of nationalist leaders, inlcuding 'Abd al-Halim Pasha and 'Urabi, in social scenes that feature their subscription to and performance of an 'idealized Arab masculinity,' wherein traits such as loyalty to the nation, courage, honor, and benevolence are central. In that sense, the cartoons that appeared in Egyptian journals both converge with and diverge from those presented by the British journals. Parnell's text reminds us of the ways in which gendered images can serve as weapons for branding the 'Other,' advancing imperialist and nationalist agendas, critiquing ruling elites, and mobilizing public support. Parnell's chapter read in conjunction with Farley's offers a colonial backdrop for the debate that Farley outlines over how to interpret the same-sex-desiring figure of Radwan in Naguib Mahfouz's *Sugar Street*.

Usefully contesting the phrase "crisis of masculinity" for the way it implies a prior stability in masculinity, Kathryn Kalemkerian, in her chapter, "Men at Work: The Politics of Professional Pride in Ottoman Beirut," parses the rise of a male professional class in Beirut during the last decades of the Ottoman Empire, contextualized by the *Tanzimat*, the Ottoman governmental reforms of the nineteenth century. She highlights a shift from an older form of mostly hereditary bureaucratic service in which members were seen as lifelong servants of the sultan rather than modern men rising on merit. This new white-collar class, cutting across ethnic and religious lines, was marked sartorially by the fez and by physical 'orders' in the form of medals and sashes that were worn with a tailcoat and tailored trousers. 'Devotion,' 'Effort,' and 'Loyalty' are examples of specific merits rewarded by orders; the acts that entitled a man to these epithets varied over time (the nineteenth century had already seen a shift from military to civilian values rewarded by these orders), yet all serve to construct ideals of manly virtue. One Ottoman order, introduced in 1878, was given to women, for 'Compassion,' usually signifying charitable work, but because it was given only to women already related to the palace or to elite men, it did not mark an emerging class. Imperial orders were bestowed on Armenian, Jewish, Greek, Christian, and Muslim men, "weaving together segments of Beiruti society" whose histories are so often treated as separate, Kalmerkian argues, around the specific combination of ideas of masculinity that was becoming common to this class of men. The system of bestowing orders was a global imperial one promoted in the British, French, Ottoman, and other empires, and thus it linked these men to a system of honors recognized internationally. The era of orders peaked around 1900, until their use petered out as empires themselves faded. Bureaucratic officials were ridiculed in the press as state ideology shifted to militarism, and the erstwhile 'new men' became the 'old' men of declining forms of masculinity.

Taking with us the long historical perspective offered by Kalemkerian's essay, we can question how long the military narratives treated in the neighboring group of chapters will last. These final three chapters analyze narratives of masculinity in the military. While the volume's first essay focuses on the 'external' Western gaze to which the queer body of the MENA region is constantly subjected, the chapter by Oyman Basaran focuses on the 'internal' gaze that gay men must reckon with, particularly when navigating masculinist institutions. In "You Are Like a Virus: Dangerous Bodies and Military Medical Authority in Turkey," Basaran argues that while affectionate homosocial bonding is an encouraged part of Turkish military service, military authorities see homosexual bodies as 'dangerous/feminine,' endangering the Armed Forces' homosocial, but straight, masculinity. Compulsory military service for men has been part of the modern Turkish state since 1927, embedding such service firmly into the story of modern Turkish masculinity. However, the long-standing Turkish war against the Kurdish armed struggle has diminished subscription to this ideal of Turkish masculinity, and gay men who wish to avoid the draft for various reasons have grounds to do so in their homo-sexuality. The catch is that the draftee's gayness must be certified by a panel of psychologists as 'gay enough' (in their eyes) to seduce other men and disrupt the military order. Bosaran's analysis reveals that a masculine gay man would not be likely to be exempted, nor would a man whose practice of same-sex desire is expressed in any but narrow stereotyped ways. Draftees seeking the exemption must exhibit the kind of behavior and appearance that military medical authorities see as homosexual, in a remarkably invasive inspection process that can include days of observa-tion in a psychiatric ward, and anal examinations. Medical, military, and national discourses thus intersect in Turkey to fix in place a stereotype of gay men as 'feminine.'

In conversation with each other, two final chapters analyze the dis-course of militarized conflict between the state and non-state actors, in Iraqi Kurdistan and Jordan respectively. "Gendered Memories and Masculinities: Kurdish Peshmerga on the Anfal Campaign in Iraq," by Andrea Fischer-Tahir looks at masculinity in the personal narratives of Kurdish militia members in Iraq. Armed struggle as a part of the Kurdish movement for self-determination came to the fore in 1961 in Iraq, but the term *peshmerga* (literally, those who face death) was in use from the 1940s as a Kurdish-lan-guage parallel to the Arabic-language term *fida'i*, describing those who take up arms in the national struggle of a stateless people. From 1986 to 1989, the Iraqi state systemically attacked peshmerga and their Kurdish civilian sup-porters through ground and air bombardment as well as mass displacement and chemical warfare against civilian populations. The Iraqi regime used a Qur'anically derived term, the "Anfal campaign," to name these atrocities, due to Iraqi dictator Saddam Hussein's newfound interest in religion after he lost the Kuwait War. Anthropologist Fischer-Tahir compares construc-tions of masculinity in two narrative accounts of the Anfal campaign: Awat Qaramani's *Narrow Ways. The Novel Biography of Awat Qaramani. The Events of 1963–1999* (2009), and an oral account by a younger, lower-ranking pesh-merga who uses the pseudonym Soris, born in 1961. Fischer-Tahir carefully explains her positionality and relationship to the Kurdish movement, and accounts for how it may play a role in her interview with Soris in terms of audience, as she examines "the situatedness of memory production" in both accounts. Arguing that Qaramani and Soris emphasize resistance and victimhood in different ways, and paying close attention to language practices, Fischer-Tahir shows how each of their historiographies of Anfal construct hegemonic masculinity by a weave of specific relationships to concepts of honor, bravery, and decisiveness, as well as by their responses to "dealing with the experiences of defeat and harmed masculinity."

What are the implications for masculinity of Jordanian discursive responses to the Islamic State of Iraq and the Levant? In "Militarist Masculinity, Militarist Femininity: A Gendered Analysis of Jordan's War on the Islamic State," Ebtihal Mahadeen examines the response of the Jordanian government and media to the heavily broadcast immolation of newfound, a Jordanian Air Force pilot who was captured by ISIL after his F-16 fighter crashed in hostile territory in Syria. The twenty-two minute video of Muadh al-Kasasbeh's gruesome murder was played repeatedly on Arab television stations as well as on social media, causing outrage in Jordan and shock all over the world. In response to the Islamic State's performances of violent masculinity, the discourses circulating in the Jordanian media reinforced a militarist Jordanian masculinity that was "capable of rising to the occasion" in the face of the enemy. This militaristic masculinity, often embodied by the Jordanian king and Armed Forces, was endowed with the promise to exterminate the enemy and avenge al-Kasasbeh's murder, Mahadeen argues. Women, too played a key role in advancing this militarist masculinity through performing militarist femininities—as exemplified by the female soldiers aiding the campaign (but not directly participating in it), as well as the figure of 'the martyr's mother,' who was constructed as 'the mother of all Jordanians' and the mother of the devastated but strong Jordanian nation. Drawing on Cynthia Enloe's work, Mahadeen argues that "[i]f on the surface the experiences of the soldier and the mother seem different, they perform similar functions within a militarist society that uphold the ideology of militarism itself." Mahadeen further contends that such militaristic masuclinities and femininites are not new; on the contrary, she demonstrates that the social acceptance of militarism in Jordan has long existed, and that this ideology has long manifested itself in public discourse and cultural productions. However, she points out, it is at times of national crisis that militarist masculinity "truly comes to the fore," often as a strategic means of unifying the fractured nation.

What is the purpose of this volume? José Martí (1853–1895), a founding figure of Cuba, said, "A knowledge of different literatures is the best way to free one's self from the tyranny of any of them." A knowledge of different masculinities may not necessarily free anyone from the actual tyranny of any of them, but may well free us from imagining masculinity immutable in the Middle East and North Africa. This volume sets before the reader a strong set of work on masculinity in specific literatures, cinemas, and other semiotic practices in the Middle East and North Africa. Such work offers conceptual apertures for thinking our way through to more ethical configurations of masculinity and femininity. Academic scholarship takes account of knowledges and exposes gaps and provisionality within them, against the logic of any tyrannical power—secular or religious—that imagines itself grounded on foundations of absolute knowledge. Cultural Studies investigates, through multiple disciplines, the workings of power in culture, to make it all the more naked. This, so that we can be clear-sighted about power's multi-valenced workings in everyday human practices—so that we equip ourselves and our societies with knowledges, however modest and piecemeal, that can begin to redress inequity. Investigating masculinities is "organically linked" to feminist projects whose aim is social justice (Sinclair-Webb, 8). By excavating masculinities, we also unearth the ongoing resistances of marginalized identities to hegemonic masculinity—in the military, in civilian society, in sartorial symbolism. Current movements for gender justice, such as the #MeToo movement against rape culture and sexual harassment, reaffirm the value of excavating the scaffolding of hegemonic masculinity and witnessing the resistances of marginalized masculinities and femininities. When we expose, in small and specific ways, the scaffolding of hegemonic masculinist discourses, we create the potential to give power back to those who are assumed to be powerless. Patriarchy is alive and thrashing in our world in new–old ways, as the hearings for U.S. Supreme Court nominee Brett Kavanaugh highlighted. Orientalism is alive and thrashing in new–old ways, and this volume aims to trouble imperialist representations of MENA masculinities. To study the multiple and contingent formations of masculinity in culture, literature, film is to wrest away claims made about the timelessness and authoritativeness of any particular mode of masculinity, whether such claims are made by outsiders or from within the region. This study, gathering critical mass with others of its ilk on other regions as well as MENA, can help to shore up the daring needed for imagining genders and human collectives arranged in ways that are more compassionate than the arrangements of today.

Notes

1   We problematize the term 'Middle East' in the text that follows.
2   In much of the world, as well as in MENA, 'breadwinning' is, to varying degrees, historically associated with masculinity.
3   As of late 2019, Zaitouneh is still missing.
4   The international '#MeToo' movement against sexual harassment is another such highly charged moment, accompanied or followed by great

pushback, which features women's voices being heard efficaciously in a context where they have not usually been given equal weight.

5 The Nahda: a term referring to a period of cultural renaissance beginning roughly in the last quarter of the nineteenth century in Egypt and other parts of the Arabic-speaking world, encompassing philological research, literary and journalistic activity, religious reform, and Arab-nationalist political awakening. When the Nahda period ended is open to interpretation and differs depending on the country; it can be said to go on until roughly World War II, or to the era of decolonization struggles.

6 For a parallel discussion on this issue in the Arabic-speaking world, see Khaled Rouayheb, *Before Homosexuality in the Arabic Islamic World 1500–1800* (Chicago: University of Chicago Press, 2009).

7 Every educator reading this is hereby enjoined to tell their students to think harder if they are about to use the notion of 'tradition versus modernity' to frame their course papers.

8 Antar ibn Shaddad was a pre-Islamic knight and poet born in the sixth century to an aristocratic Arab father and an enslaved Ethiopian mother; his adventures, described in his own poetry and in the voluminous heroic epic that later formed around his figure *(The Epic of Antarah)*, have made his name a byword for manliness in Arabic culture.

9 Such as *Lawyer Madiha* (1950), *Stronger than Love* (1954), *My Wife the General Manager* (1966). See Rania Mahmoud's forthcoming analysis of the gender ideologies in these films.

10 In Jordan, for example, one (Article 98) of the two laws (the other is Article 340) whose reform is needed to close the loopholes for honor killing is based on the Napoleonic Code.

11 The international #MeToo movement of 2006/2017 has pointed out that this male fantasy informs the modern Hollywood film genre of romantic comedy; versions of it exist in many cultures.

12 Such as Kabbani's book-length poem, *Yawmiyat imra'a la mubaliya*, 1968. His use of a female first-person voice in this and other poems is, however, a charged topic.

13 In the Gulf, divorced women do not face the same social stigma that they do in the Levant and North Africa, and female serial marriage is not infrequent.

14 This is a major theme in those of his stories collected in the English translation titled *Breaking Knees*, Garnet, 2008. The 2017 dissertation of Alessandro Columbu, "Modernity and Gender Representations in the Short Stories of Zakariyya Tamir: Collapse of the Totalising Discourse of Modernity and the Evolution of Gender Roles," offers a full-length study of this dynamic in Tamir's writing.

15 Such as can be found in Raphael Patai's *The Arab Mind*, first published in 1973 but revived by Hatherleigh Press in the post-9/11 year of 2002.

16 Lower-class women have always worked outside the home—in the fields and in domestic service, for example. When people offhandedly say 'women working' they are often unconsciously focused on middle- and upper-class women.

17 *Oklahoma!* also erases the indigenous population, male and female, although the happy musical is set in a state that was designated as 'Indian territory' and used as a target of forced displacement of native peoples by the US government.

Works Cited

Abu-Odeh, Lama. "Honor Killings and the Construction of Gender in Arab Societies." Paper for Georgetown University Law Center, 2010. Washington, DC.

Aghacy, Samira. *Masculine Identity and the Fiction of the Arab East since 1967*. New York: Syracuse University Press, 2009.

Ahmed, Sara. "Racialized Bodies." In *Real Bodies: A Sociological Introduction*, edited by Mary Evans and Ellie Lee, 46–63. New York: Palgrave, 2002.

Al-Kumsariyat al-fatinat (The Pretty Ticket-takers). Cairo: al-Hasan Aflam Hasan al-Sayfi, 1957. -

Amireh, Amal. "Between Complicity and Subversion: Body Politics in Palestinian National Narrative." *South Atlantic Quarterly* 102, no. 4 (2003): 747–72.

Amnesty International. "Egyptian Women Protesters Forced to Take 'Virginity Tests,'" March 23, 2011.

Barakat, Huda. 1990. *Al-Hajar al-dahik*. Lebanon: Dar al-Adab.

Butt, Riazat, and Abdel-Rahman Hussein. "'Virginity tests' on Egyptian protesters are illegal, says judge." *The Guardian*, December 27, 2011.

De Groot, Joanna. "The Bureacrat, the Mulla, and the Maverick Intellectual 'at Home': Domestic Narratives of Patriarchy, Masculinity, and Modernity in Iran, 1880–1980." *Gender & History* 27, no. 3 (2015): 791–811.

Djebar, Assia. 1993. *Fantasia: An Algerian Cavalcade*, translated by Dorothy S. Blair. Portsmouth, NH: Heineman.

Duetsche Welle. "Gays join the Syrian uprising," September 7, 2012.

Encyclopedia Britannica. "Mohamed Bouazizi: Tunisian Street Vendor and Protester."

Fahmy, Hazem. "An Initial Perspective on 'The Winter of Discontent:' The Root Causes of the Egyptian Revolution." *Social Research* 79, no. 2 (2012): 349–76.

Ghazzawi, Razan. "Decolonising Syria's so-called 'queer liberation': On Rojava's new international LGBTQI brigade, the 'war on terror' and the Western left's erasure of local struggles," *Al Jazeera Opinion/LGBT*, August 5, 2017.

Hamad, Turki al-. *Al-Adama*. London: Dar al-Saqi, 1997.

Holslin, Peter. "Inside Egypt's LGBT Crackdown: One Band's Story," *Rolling Stone*, October 25, 2017.

Human Rights Watch. "Today Is Razan Zaitouneh's Birthday," April 29, 2016.

———. "Syria: Gang Attacks Peaceful Demonstrators; Police Look On," February 3, 2011.

Kingsley, Patrick. "80 Sexual Assaults in One Day," *The Guardian*, July 5, 2013.

Lagrange, Frédéric. "Male Homosexuality in Modern Arabic Literature." In *Imagined Masculinities: Male Identity and Culture in the Modern Middle East*, edited by Mai Ghoussoub and Emma Sinclair-Webb, 169-198. London: Saqi Books, 2000.

Luongo, Michael. "Gays and the Syrian Revolution," September 28, 2012.

Mahfouz, Naguib. *Palace Walk* (1956; trans. 1990 by William Maynard Hutchins and Olive E. Kenny), *The Palace of Desire* (1957; trans. William Maynard Hutchins, Lorne M. Kenney and Olive E. Kenny), *Sugar Street* (1957; trans. William Maynard Hutchins and Angela Botros Samaan), In *The Cairo Trilogy*, New York: Alfred A. Knopf (Everyman's Library), 1991.

Naber, Nadine. "Women and the Arab Spring: Human Rights from the Ground Up," *International Institute Journal*, University of Michigan: 11–13, 2011a.

———. "The Meaning of the Arab Revolution," *Against the Current*: 9–10, 2011b.

Najmabadi, Afsaneh. *Women with Mustaches and Men without Beards: Gender and Sexual Anxieties of Iranian Modernity*. Berkeley, CA: UCB Press, 2005.

Nallu, Preethi. "Q&A: Bahrain rights defender Maryam al-Khawaja," *Al Jazeera*, September 13, 2014.

Operation Anti-Sexual Harassment/Assault. "Testimony from an Assaulted OpAntiSH Member, January 25th 2013," posted on OpAntiSH's Facebook page, January 26, 2013.

Outright Action International. "Timeline of Public Executions for Alleged Sodomy by the Islamic State Militias," 30 June, 2016.

Packer, George. "Exporting Jihad: The Arab Spring Has Given Tunisians the Freedom to Act on Their Unhappiness," *New Yorker*, March 28, 2016.

Parsipur, Shahrnush. *Touba and the Meaning of Night* (Farsi ed., 1987), translated by Havva Housmand and Kamran Talattof. New York: The Feminist Press, 2006.

Peteet, Julie. "Male Gender and Rituals of Resistance in the Palestinian Intifada: A Cultural Politics of Violence." In *Imagined Masculinities: Male*

Identity and Culture in the Modern Middle East, edited by Mai Ghoussoub and Emma Sinclair-Webb, 103–26. London: Saqi Books, 2000.

Pinault, David. "Zeynab bint Ali and the Place of the Women of the Household of the First Imams in Shi'ite Devotional Literature." In *Women in the Medieval Islamic World*, by Gavin R.G. Hambly. New York: St. Martin's, 1998.

Puar, Jasbir K. *Terrorist Assemblages: Homonationalism in Queer Times*. Durham, NC: Duke University Press, 2007.

Said, Edward. *Orientalism*. New York: Vintage, 1978.

Sinclair-Webb, Emma. "Preface." In *Imagined Masculinities: Male Identity and Culture in the Modern Middle East*, edited by Mai Ghoussoub and Emma Sinclair-Webb, 7–16. London: Saqi Books, 2000.

Tatchell, Peter. "Don't fall for the myth that it's been 50 years since we decriminalized homosexuality," *The Guardian*, May 23, 2017.

Wedeen, Lisa. *Ambiguities of Domination: Politics, Rhetoric, and Symbols in Contemporary Syria*. Chicago: University of Chicago Press, 1999.

Whitehead, Stdphen M. and Frank J. Barrett. The Masculinities Reader. Cambridge, U.K.: Polity, 2002.

Yaghoobi, Claudia. "Iranian Women and Shifting Sexual Ideologies." In *Sexuality in Muslim Contexts: Restrictions and Resistance*, edited by Anissa Hélie and Homa Hoodfar, 52–57. London and New York: Zed Books, 2012.

1

EXOTIC AND BENIGHTED, OR MODERN YET VICTIMIZED? THE MODERN PREDICAMENT OF THE ARAB QUEER

Jedidiah Anderson

Introduction

"The gay man or lesbian in the Arab World is oppressed. She or he is not only oppressed by the government that he or she lives under, she or he is also oppressed by Islam. It is the moral duty of us white and enlightened ones to liberate him or her—if only she or he could move to the West (or to Israel) and get away from those backward people! At least we have freedom."

"The gay man or lesbian in the Arab world is perverse. Don't they fuck little boys and camels there, and no one cares? It's because they are segregated by gender; it's because they make their women cover up from head to toe—of course the guys only want to fuck other guys, and the girls only want to fuck other girls. It is the moral duty of us white and enlightened ones to bomb him or her—if only they could be like the West and not be these backward perverts! At least we have decency."

"The gay man in the Arab World is FUCKING HOT!! Aren't the guys over there all tops, all muscular, tough, ready to pounce on the first bottom that they find? It's because they aren't like us, they have to be tough, it's their culture, and even the straight ones will fuck a guy because they are so horny. It is the moral duty of us white and enlightened ones to let them occupy the territory of our asses—if only we had cocks as big as theirs! At least we can buy a plane ticket there."

"Wait—there are Arab lesbians?"

33

The above statements are examples of the ways in which the Arab queer[1] is Othered and Orientalized. Colonialism, neoliberal paternalism, economic exploitation, military aggression, and white guilt have all contributed to (and stemmed from) an Orientalist discourse that constitutes the Middle East as an *a priori* 'Other' that is to be excavated, penetrated, and controlled as it is a subject that cannot rule itself. By extension, the Arab queer has become the subject of this discourse. Due to a number of discursive forces, the Arab queer has become a flashpoint for this Orientalizing discourse, a point at which multiple fields of Orientalizing discourse intersect. I further claim and will show in this chapter that this Orientalizing discourse regarding the Arab queer centers around three poles that contradict each other and at the same time are all simultaneously in play in Orientalist discourses surrounding the Arab queer. Those poles are the Arab queer as uniquely and exceedingly oppressed subject (exemplified by Israeli pinkwashing efforts); the Arab queer as polymorphously perverse monsterterroristfag[2] (exemplified by the Abu Ghraib prison abuse pictures, in which they were forced, ironically, to enact this trope); and the Arab queer as hypersexual, inchoate savage (as exemplified in the writings of André Gide, Jean Genet, and William S. Burroughs, and also in the queer tourist literature about the Arab world [particularly Lebanon] that exists in the present day). While all three poles of discourse surrounding the Arab queer have been discussed in depth, it is my intent to call attention to the inherently contradictory nature of three poles in relation to each other and at the same time draw the reader's attention to the fact that they all exist in Orientalist discourse, and all serve to facilitate the 'Othering' of the Arab queer—and, by extension, Arabs in general.

Theoretical Framework(s)

These three constructions of the 'Arab queer' are frequently discussed separately in academic works, with only one being examined in any particular work as if the other two tropes did not exist.[3] Joseph Massad, in his book *Desiring Arabs*, does perhaps the best job of acknowledging at least two of these Orientalist tropes (the Arab queer as "oppressed victim," which dominates the book, and the Arab as "monsterterroristfag," which he merely points toward in his introduction). This chapter will analyze the trope of the Arab queer as hypersexual, inchoately desiring savage through the theoretical framework of Frantz Fanon's writings, the trope of the Arab queer as "monsterterroristfag" through the theoretical framework put forth by Jasbir Puar (particularly in her book *Terrorist Assemblages*), and the trope of the Arab queer as (my words) "uniquely and exceedingly oppressed," through the lens of the concepts put forth in Chandra Talpade Mohanty's essay "Under Western Eyes: Feminist Scholarship and Colonial Discourses."

All three of these theoretical frameworks are already grouped under the greater theoretical umbrella of postcolonialism—Fanon is often mentioned in the same breath as Mohanty, who is often paired with Puar. The claim that one theoretical framework excludes use of the other(s) is incorrect. Additionally, I acknowledge the importance of Gilles Deleuze's and Felix Guattari's concept of the assemblage and the rhizome in shaping how I have approached this topic. In Deleuze and Guattari's words, "the rhizome is an acentered, nonhierarchical, nonsignifiying system without a General and without an organizing memory or central automaton . . . [w]hat is at question in the rhizome is a relation to sexuality" (Deleuze and Guattari, 21). It is within the framework of the rhizome and the assemblages that it creates that I hope to locate and analyze these discourses.

The topic of sexuality, particularly queer sexuality, is something that cannot be looked at as possessing only one genealogy, only one discursive path of development. In this chapter, I attempt to acknowledge the fragmented nature of (queer, Arab) sexuality by also openly acknowledging the fragmented, multifaceted, hybridized nature of my analysis, in which I hope to illustrate that Arab sexuality (and the manifold ways in which it is constructed) is not only 'X' but is also always already at the same time 'Y' and 'Z' and 'A' and every other letter and more as well.

But first, I will begin with what is perhaps the most polite (but still covertly deeply oppressive) of the Orientalist tropes—that of the Arab queer as uniquely and exceedingly oppressed subject.

The Arab Queer: Uniquely and Exceedingly Oppressed

I have chosen to indicate this particular Orientalist trope of the oppressed Arab queer with the term "The Uniquely and Exceedingly Oppressed Arab Queer" to indicate that while it is not problematic to describe Arab queers as an oppressed category, when the Arab queer is constructed as a subject that is oppressed by homophobia in a manner that is found nowhere else in the world—and also oppressed by that homophobia to a greater extent than anywhere else in the world *in a manner that is worse than any other form of oppression that for any other reason the Arab subject can bear*—one is creating discourse indulging this particular Orientalist trope.

That Arab queers endure much greater oppression in their home countries than their queer Western counterparts is a truism that, on the most basic level, I will not even attempt to deny or downplay. That being said, one must ask: is this oppression the most odious of the oppressions that the Arab queer faces? Is Arab queer subjectivity characterized by a perception of oppression that is *not* shared by non-queer Arabs—and if so, is this oppression unique in its odiousness?

The answer to these questions must be no. Perhaps the clearest, most concrete example that shows that this is not the case took place on November 9, 2009, when Helem (the LGBTQI-rights advocacy group in Lebanon) protested in front of the Ugandan Consulate in Beirut (an action in which I participated) and presented the officials that worked there with an open statement condemning what has since become known in the mainstream media as the "Kill the Gays" bill. Activists at Helem claimed that they felt that their protest was morally necessary because of the greater privilege that they enjoyed as Lebanese as opposed to Ugandans, even though they did not have a strong relationship with the Ugandan group SMUG (Sexual Minorities in Uganda) that called on them to protest. Helem's activists' understanding of their relative privilege when compared to the situation in Uganda, paired with their awareness of the necessity of acting in solidarity with the Ugandans when asked to do so *and* in the manner that they asked for the international gay community to help them, illustrates how genuine, non-exploitative global activism toward their common goal of freedom for LGBTQI individuals throughout the world can work. At the same time, it also stands in stark opposition to public-relations efforts by the Israeli government to call attention to LGBTQI oppression elsewhere in the world by highlighting (what it likes to portray as) its LBGTIQ rights agenda vis-à-vis other countries for the purpose of obscuring its human-rights abuses in the context of the occupation.

This exploitation of gay people and the discourses surrounding them has been given the shorthand term 'pinkwashing.' Even Israeli Prime Minister Benjamin Netanyahu, when speaking before the United States Congress, has engaged in it, claiming that "Israel has always embraced this path [of Western human rights] in a Middle East that has long rejected it. In a region where women are stoned, gays are hanged, Christians are persecuted, Israel stands out" (Netanyahu, 2011).

The discourse of pinkwashing does not restrict itself to making comparisons between Israel and its neighbors with regard to gay rights, but also attempts to highlight the (allegedly) more liberal gay-rights policy of Israel in relation to other Western nations, including the United States. In it, two Israeli male soldiers are shown holding hands, with a caption that announces, "It's Pride Month. Did you know that the IDF treats all of its soldiers equally?"[4] This is coupled with the creation of websites like gay-middleeast.com, although this website has been greatly downscaled since its inception. While gaymiddleeast.com (according to human-rights activist Scott Long) was ostensibly created to serve as a clearing house for information about LGBTQI individuals in the Middle East, it was run by Israeli citizens in order to create a platform from which the LGBTQI-rights situation in Israel was glorified, and contrasted with homophobia and oppression of LGBTQI individuals elsewhere in the Middle East for the purposes of both rendering Israel legible as a modern state that protected human rights and framing the Palestinians and Israel's Muslim and Arab neighbors generally as backward and in need of enlightenment through external intervention (be it military or otherwise) (Long 2012).

Pinkwashing is perhaps one of the most malicious examples of the covert imperialism in human-rights discourse that Chandra Talpade Mohanty speaks of in her essay "Under Western Eyes: Feminist Scholarship and Colonial Discourses." Mohanty talks about Western feminists whose writings create the monolithic idea of 'the Third World woman,' a unified group of women who are 'powerless' *a priori* because of their gender. Such Western feminist approaches, Mohanty suggests, are incapable of creating a genuine analysis of the actual situation. The Western feminists end up failing to see how women in the developing world are oppressed for reasons other than their gender, reasons that they may share with men, but instead constructing knowledge that is flawed by starting with the assumption of the category of 'woman' as oppressed group. Instead of seeing the real reasons why specific groups of women are oppressed or disempowered, these feminists see women as oppressed or disempowered *because* they are women, and because they are 'Third World' (Mohanty, 261–62).

If one substitutes 'LGBTQI individuals' for 'women' and 'LGBTQI rights activists' for 'feminists' in the argument proposed by Mohanty, a more benign version of pinkwashing emerges. However, it is the seemingly willful creation, by pinkwashing, of 'the oppressed Arab queer' that is indeed disturbing, as it is done without genuine concern for what it constitutes as oppressed subject; rather, it is done *in the name* of helping the oppressed while actually intended to benefit only the oppressor.

In more concrete terms, the concept of the "uniquely and exceedingly oppressed Arab queer" actively obfuscates other forms of oppression faced by Arab queers that have nothing to do with being queer. It would be absurd and racist to say that American queers of color should join mainstream LGBTQI activisms (particularly when those mainstream activisms ignore or are willfully antagonistic toward the realities of queers of color, working-class queers, rural queers, and so on) to the exclusion of anti-racist struggles simply due to the homophobia of some straight people of color—and yet this is what Arab queers are always insistently asked to do, and neoliberal hegemony is bewildered by their unwillingness to comply.

The trope of the 'exceedingly and uniquely oppressed Arab queer' also ignores the very real issues surrounding the ways in which Arab queer identity is constructed. In his book *Before Homosexuality in the Arab Islamic World*,

1500–1800, Khaled El-Rouayheb argues that people in the pre-modern Arab world viewed homosexual acts as something that anyone could potentially do, and not as something that one needed to have a particular nature in order to do (6).

Accepting El-Rouayheb's basic premise and expanding on it, Joseph Massad, in *Desiring Arabs*,[5] discusses how Western colonialism and cultural imperialism brought the sexual category of 'the homosexual' through epistemic violence to the Arab world, and how this epistemic violence, by creating 'gay people,' has thus also created 'straight people' that could then in turn oppress the 'gay people' (Massad, 18889). Massad also claims that 'the homosexual' as a category of identification has been further reified through what Michel Foucault called "incitement to discourse" in his book *The History of Sexuality*.[6] This "incitement to discourse," according to Massad, has been spearheaded by what he calls "The Gay International," a collection of Western human-rights groups and activists who have sought to bring Western gay rights to the Arab world. Massad problematizes these efforts of "The Gay International" as imposing Western concepts of gayness on the Arab world, and erasing other knowledges of sexuality, thus creating a scenario in which those that object to this understanding are constructed as opposing 'gay rights' (Massad, 174).

Not only does the trope of the "uniquely and exceedingly oppressed Arab queer" facilitate the proliferation of hegemonic and colonialist discourses by creating an 'oppressed' subject that suffers by not being located in the realm of 'the modern' (and thus directly benefitting from 'liberation'), it also oversimplifies the extremely important issue of how Arab queer identity has been constructed, and puts those who would interrogate the process by which the discursive 'homosexual' came about in the Arab world in the category of 'homophobe' without looking at the epistemic violence that was deployed by colonialism in creating 'the homosexual' in the Arab world.

While this particular Orientalist trope is, on the surface, the most well-meaning, another trope that will be discussed in this chapter does not even pretend to be concerned with the well-being of the Arab queer. This is the one that I, borrowing from both Sigmund Freud and Jasbir Puar (by way of Edward Said and Joseph Massad), will call "the polymorphously perverse monsterterroristfag."

The Polymorphously Perverse Monsterterroristfag is Coming for You!

In her book *Terrorist Assemblages*, Jasbir Puar contends that in order to harness queer Americans for the bio-power that is needed to sustain U.S.

hegemony, American queers are no longer always already construed as engaging in perversions that are inimical to the state. In place of this, the Western queer has been situated in relation to two constructions of 'the queer' that have been formed: the 'homonational'—that is, the Western or Westernized queer who has been integrated into the nation and the forces of the market, and what Puar has termed the Orientalized "monsterterroristfag," who may not be a monster, terrorist, or a fag (and almost always is none of the above), but who is constructed and perceived as all three of these things. Through the incorporation of homonormative individuals into mainstream society under the banner of 'homonationalism,' those Western or Westernized queers that are constructed as modern are thus then able to serve as a foil against those that are called "terrorists" (Puar, 15–28, 45–47, passim). One of the most well-known (and most easily apparent) instances of the deployment of this trope is when American soldiers sexually and physically abused the Iraqi detainees who were held at the Abu Ghraib prison facility.

There are two major aspects of this sexual torture that took place at Abu Ghraib, and both play into the trope of Arab queer as 'monsterterroristfag.' One is the torture of the detainees as Muslims and Arabs, and the (very intentional) cultural significance of this torture in that context. The other aspect is the implications of this sexual torture looked at vis-à-vis the United States' attempts to portray itself as a (sexually) tolerant and modern nation that *is liberating* Iraq.

Beginning with the first thread: it would be almost boilerplate in the field of Near Eastern Studies to mention at this point that the idea for this particular type of torture stemmed from Raphael Patai's *The Arab Mind*,[7] a book published originally in 1976 that has frequently been used to augment U.S. military 'cultural training,' and which according to Seymour Hersh in "The Gray Zone" (as cited by Puar) "[depicted] sex as a taboo [for Arabs] vested with shame and repression," suggesting that "Arabs only understand force and . . . that the biggest weakness of Arabs is shame and humiliation" (Puar, 83–84). Puar elaborates on this claim made by Hersh, discussing how in the case of this torture, the Muslim is marked as "sexually conservative, modest and fearful of nudity (and it is interesting how this conceptualization is rendered both sympathetically and as a problem), as well as queer, animalistic, barbarian, and unable to control his (or her) urges" (Puar, 86). This 'shame' attached to homosexuality has also been attached to Arabness as well, through discourse about the Arab world that has its roots in the initial colonial moment.

It is here that one can proceed on to the second thread. For Puar, one can see in this torture the state operating under the repressive hypothesis as described by Foucault: Muslims/Arabs are sexually conservative and because of this sexual torture is effective, homosexual torture especially so, and thus this homosexual torture is part and parcel of the mechanics of liberation (Puar, 94). At the same time this forcing of the prisoners to engage in homosexual acts makes the Muslim/Arab body the site of perversion and queerness. Clear examples of this can be seen among the infamous Abu-Ghraib pictures. The Western queer is neatly sliced out of this by what Deleuze and Guattari call the "apparatus of capture" (Deleuze and Guattari, 424–27), in which Western capitalism finds that the Western queer is more useful as compliant and cheerful consumer than as a perverse Other, against which the state can construct itself as a civilizing enterprise, thus transforming the Western queer from perverted monster-terrorist(communist?)-fag to the example *par excellence* of the repressive hypothesis according to the overarching power structure. That is, liberated from sexual repression thanks to the beneficence of the state in sanctioning his or her sex and relationships, she or he cannot be like the perverse Arab; he or she is liberated, enlightened, without pent-up libido, and thus can serve as an agent of 'freedom.' It is not the queerness that is the issue anymore; it is the repression that makes the pervert, the other.

Freud, Polymorphous Perversion and the Arab Queer

While Said and Massad both use the term "polymorphously perverse" to describe Orientalist constructions of Arab sexuality, it is important and useful to go back to the writings of Sigmund Freud, who originally coined the term. In his essay "Infantile Sexuality" Freud explains polymorphous perversion as the sexual irregularities that sometimes manifest themselves in children: "the mental dams against sexual excesses—shame, disgust, and morality—have not yet either been constructed at all or are in the course of construction, according to the age of the child." A "clever seducer," according to Freud, can arouse this same "polymorphously perverse" inclination in women (Freud, 57).

It can be argued that the term "polymorphous perversion," when looked at through the lens of Freud, figures in Orientalist discourse (such as in *The Arab Mind*) as a concept that infantilizes the Arab, makes her or him uninstructed in "shame, disgust, and morality" and too easily led astray by a "clever seducer." This has been the position of the colonizer toward the Arab colonized (and his or her sexuality) as can be seen in European travel literature regarding the Arab world decrying the "sin of Sodomy" that the writers observed in the region (El-Rouayheb, 1–2), and has led to greater policing of homosexuality in these colonized countries even after the colonizers have left. M. Jacqui Alexander, in her essay "Erotic Autonomy as a

Politics of Decolonization: An Anatomy of Feminist and State Practice in the Bahamas Tourist Economy," discusses how concern on the part of the British colonizer with the sex engaged in by colonial subjects led to the criminalizing of homosexuality in the Bahamas, in order to construct the inhabitants of the islands as 'civilized' through the process of colonization (Alexander, 82, 83).

Through these discourses of colonization, the colonized are cast in the role of needing protection from Freud's "clever seducer"[8] and the colonizers reify their *mission civilisatrice* (and its efficacy) in both the land and the psyche of the colonized. 'Whiteness' is not only produced in Europe *a priori* of the identity, culture and social mores of the colonized but also becomes a product of the act of colonization: to be 'truly European (white)' is to *not* be like the colonized—indeed, to cultivate modes of behavior and mores that are expressly unlike those of the colonized subject. The colonized make the colonizer, and the colonizer in turn makes the colonized.

This process, by which the Arab queer is made legible as Puar's "monsterterroristfag," results in the Arab internalizing the norms and mores of the colonizer and holding them out as something to aspire to in order to avoid sinking into the 'polymorphous perversion' that she or he has been made to believe they have been saved from and that is yet, according to the colonizer, inherently a part of him or her. Influenced by Jean-Paul Sartre's writings about anti-Semitism, Fanon writes about how the Jew is inculcated with self-loathing by the anti-Semitism surrounding her or him, and how this anti-Semitism in turn makes the Jew into an anti-Semite:

> The Jew, authentic or inauthentic, is struck down by the fist of the "*salaud*." His situation is such that everything he does is bound to turn against him. For naturally the Jew prefers himself, and it happens that he forgets his Jewishness, or hides it, hides himself from it. That is because he has then admitted the validity of the Aryan system. There are Good and Evil. Evil is Jewish. Everything Jewish is ugly. Let us no longer be Jews. I am no longer a Jew. Down with the Jews (Fanon, 140).

Describing the psychological processes that the Jew goes through in encountering anti-Semitism, Fanon claims that this same process happens with black people, and that this leads to "Fault, Guilt, refusal of guilt, paranoia—one is back in homosexual territory. In sum, what others have described in the case of the Jew applies perfectly in that of the Negro" (Fanon, 141). It is possible to see how this same self-loathing is instilled in the Arab colonial subject as well vis-à-vis sexuality.

Let us pause and unpack Fanon's statement that with these feelings "one is back in homosexual territory." It might seem that Fanon is implying that "Fault, Guilt, refusal of guilt, paranoia" inhere in the homosexual more than anywhere else. While this statement seems on the surface a little more than slightly homophobic, it is interesting and important to note that in the case of the Arab queer,[9] and representations of him or her, this "fault, guilt, etc." does, often inhere around representations of the (homo)sexual Arab. No less an authority than Joseph Massad has made this claim, saying that the incitement to discourse regarding Arab sexuality has not only Othered the Arab world with respect to the West but has also Othered the Arab world with regard to its own sexuality, for the purpose of creating shame and anxiety in the Arab world about this sexuality in order to make it easier for it to be exploited by the West. Examples of this include the censorship and marginalization of Arabic homoerotic poetry from the 1850s on, as well as the Islamist preoccupation with sex—both of which, Massad claims, had their beginnings in the colonial moment (Massad, 73, 175).

One can see here how the two tropes that I have discussed, that of the oppressed Arab queer and that of the monsterterroristfag, feed off the same discourses. The Arab queer is portrayed as a monsterterroristfag, and colonial hegemony sees him as "polymorphously perverse" due to the seductions of her or his 'backwardness' and 'lack of civilization,' and thus she or he is disciplined through horrific and brutal torture, and bombed ostensibly for his or her 'liberation' from perversion. Equally, though, this same 'backwardness' and 'lack of civilization' is cited as the primary reason for her or his oppression and, contradictorily, hegemony calls for their 'liberation' as queer, oppressed subject while blithely ignoring the fact that colonialism's construction of the Arab queer as polymorphously perverse, and then calling for him or her to be rendered legible in the LGBTQI framework, is *precisely* what has led to her or his local oppression.

The Arab queer, as has been shown, not only serves as a source of colonialist fear but also is a major site for the deployment of discourses of paternalistic concern for his or her oppression. Both of these contribute to forming the Orientalist discourses that surround her or him, but at the same time this hegemony cannot turn a blind eye to the opportunities for pleasures that he or she also presents as an Other. Because of this, there is yet another Orientalist trope through which the Arab (virtually always male) queer is Othered by Western colonial discourse—the trope of the Arab queer as oversexualized, hypermasculinized subject.

Sexy Times with the Sheikh of Araby

> Well I'm the Sheik of Araby / Your love belongs to me / Well at nights
> when you're asleep / Into your tent I creep.
> —Harry B. Smith and Francis Wheeler, "The Sheikh of Araby"[10]

The trope of the sexualized, savage, male Arab queer (and the male
Arab heterosexual) is one that is not unique to him alone. The stereotypes
of the black man with the large penis, the passionate Latin lover, and the
sexually neurotic Jew or 'Jewess' also provide examples of this trope. That
being said, the way in which colonialism took root in the Arab world and
its unique discourses have informed the manner in which this trope has
formed in regard to the Arab queer. This trope is particularly present in
discourses surrounding gay tourism in the Arab world (particularly in Lebanon) and in gay male pornography (again, particularly in Lebanon). The
additional dimension of pinkwashing and Lebanon's position as the most
liberal of the Arabic-speaking countries—and as a country that also neighbors, and is still technically at war with, Israel—presents an additional and
very different aspect to this discourse, which will be discussed in further
depth later in this chapter. In this discourse, queerness is conflated with
modernity and the way in which the two countries try to outdo each other
in practically everything—creating the largest dish of hummus, having
the best gay-tourism packages, even in having the best pornography made
about and in their respective countries

The aforementioned polymorphous perversion of the Arab queer
also provides, within Orientalist discourse, an opportunity for the white
colonizer to 'free himself' (or herself) from the rules and restrictions
of his civilized society through the primitivism of the Orient. Fanon
has noted this as well in white, racist constructions of the black man,
observing that "[t]he civilized white man retains an irrational longing for
unusual eras of sexual license. . . . In one way these fantasies respond to
Freud's life instinct. Projecting his own desires onto the Negro, the white
man behaves as if the Negro really had them" (Fanon, 127). Having projected his own 'polymorphous perversity' onto the Arab queer (or other
colonized 'Other'), the white colonizer must then, of course, leave 'civilization' (not because it is actually necessary in order to fulfill his or her
desires, but because it forms part of his or her fantasy of savage sex) and
go to the place that he or she sees as the repository of the polymorphous
perversion that they seek. Because of these colonialist and Orientalist
desires, gay tourism in the Arab world has existed almost since the beginning of colonialist projects there.

One sees here the incorporation of Arab bodies into the global capitalist system—as things to be consumed, exploited, and desired for the pleasures that they potentially offer. Because of the economic benefits to be derived from this consumption, gay clubs are allowed to operate in Lebanon, sometimes with prostitution deals being conducted practically in the open air. The difficulties and oppressions that these bodies experience are never addressed by the Lebanese government, which turns a blind eye to them every summer during the tourist season, and at the end of summer these same queer Arab men who are exploited by organized crime and global capital then risk raids and arrests by the police. M. Jacqui Alexander also writes about a similar situation in the Bahamas, where "[b]lack women are also sexualized and exoticized in this tourist drama; in fact, white imperial tourism would not be complete without eroticized blackness. . . . European fantasies of colonial conquest, the exotic, the erotic, the dark, the primitive, of danger, dread, and desire all converge here" (Alexander, 96). An example of the commodification of gay male Arab bodies can be seen in pictures posted on gay tourism websites, where the two primary attractions of Beirut are depicted as its stunning coastline and hot, hirsute Arab men.

At the same time that these bodies are construed as oversexualized sites of polymorphous perversity, they are also, in gay Lebanese circles (and tacitly by the Lebanese government), constructed as yardsticks of civilization and modernity. For example, *World of Men: Lebanon* was produced in Lebanon in 2006 by Collin O'Neal, as part of a series of films with a global perspective, with most of the sex scenes taking place in buildings that had been bombed out in the civil war.

1.1. Cover of Collin O'Neal's Men of Lebanon Video, featuring three shirtless men standing in front of an abandoned building in Beirut.

This usage of Lebanese bodies (as well as some non-Lebanese porn stars who acted as Lebanese) for the purpose of portraying the country as an Orientalist gay paradise was then countered by Israeli pornographic-film producer Michael Lucas (whose blog mixes pinkwashing, far-right Israeli politics, and stills of gay Israeli sex from his movies for the explicit purpose of showing freedom in Israel), who in 2009 produced a film entitled *Men of Israel*, whose actors have sex in destroyed Palestinian villages (Schulman, 117). This one-upmanship continues in the gay tourist industry. While the gay Lebanese tourist industry promotes the fact that one can go to a gay club in an Arab country (apparently the ultimate marker of gay freedom), the Israeli government misses no opportunity to proclaim that Israel is the one country in the Middle East that has gay rights.

Conclusions

In this paper, I have mapped out the three primary Orientalist tropes that have been deployed for the purposes of both Othering the Arab queer and also justifying the imposition of Western hegemony and homonationalism on Arab bodies. Arabs are portrayed as oppressed in order to justify military actions for their ostensible liberation; they are subject to the projections of the colonizers' desires onto their bodies; and they are cast as 'polymorphously perverse' and thus in need of discipline, of the instilling of guilt, shame, fear, morality, and anxiety, which both reifies Western gay identity (something not necessarily wished for) in the Arab queer and constructs the Arab queer body, again, as the site of punishment by their heterosexual compatriots. They are then further constructed as oversexualized, as the site of indulgence of this same polymorphous perversity by the white colonizer, made into commodities for global capital, and in the end have their sexuality recast not as perverse but as the very yardstick by which modernity is determined.

It is important for the reader to understand that the Arab queer is, in fact, one of the most visible of the intersections of matrices of Western hegemonic power, for it is not only the Arab queer that is marked as oppressed, as polymorphously perverse, or as uncivilized, sexual savage it is the Arab world *as a whole*, through the discursive processes of Orientalism, that is reified as all of these things. Furthermore, it is essential particularly in the field of Middle Eastern Studies to expand the application of the rubrics of queer theory to spaces outside of queerness. Natalie Oswin also calls for this in the field of geography, writing that

> [r]ather than clinging to the fiction that we can locate queer spaces that exist in coherent opposition to heterosexual spaces, we need to

intensify examinations of what comes together in processes of sexualization. By abandoning belief in the existence of facile geometries of heroes and hegemons, analysis is opened up to the myriad uses of sexuality. While a critique of the concept of queer space has been the vehicle through which I have come to make this argument for a broader use of queer theory in geography, it should by now be clear that I am simultaneously arguing against the division of space into queer and 'straight' space (Oswin, 97).

The theoretical interventions provided by queer theory will prove to be useful in discussing issues of marginality, modernity, and postcolonialism in the Arab world. Furthermore, in a region where Western LGBTQI categories do not necessarily apply, it is particularly important for the Middle East scholar to not look at discursive space as always already divided into queer and 'straight' space but to look more closely at the role of sexuality in the construction of colonialism, Orientalism, and Western hegemony.

Notes

1   I use the term 'queer' throughout this paper as a convenient shorthand to describe people in the Arab world whose desires do not necessarily fall along unproblematic heterosexual lines, and do not intend to imply by its usage that the term queer would be one that would be chosen by the people I am discussing to describe themselves.

2   To use the term coined by Sigmund Freud (57) (which Joseph Massad and Edward Said later used in describing this trope) and Jasbir Puar's term for it in rapid succession.

3   While Edward Said in *Orientalism* definitely touches on aspects of all of these tropes, he does not fully unpack their implications—instead, grouping all of them under the nebulous umbrella of Orientalism.

4   It is worth mentioning that the *Times of Israel* later established that this photo was, in fact, staged, and that the two men in the photo "are not a couple, only one is gay, and they both serve in [the IDF] spokesman's unit" (Ginsburg 2012).

5   *Desiring Arabs*, despite its often problematic arguments, is probably the best work that has been published that discusses the dilemma of modern Arab same-sex desire and the construction of (homo)sexual identity in the context of Arab culture. However, it is my deepest desire for scholarship regarding this topic to move beyond discussion of only Massad's theories, and to examine queer (non)identity in the Arab world not only through the lens of Orientalism, but also through the lenses of Gender Studies, queer theory, and critical race theory. Thus, I will

break from standard form in academia when discussing this topic, and will discuss Massad's arguments in depth in this chapter (something that I have done in many other texts) only if they relate specifically to the arguments that I am making.

6   I must point out a problem with Massad's attempt to look at the construction of modern-day Arab sexuality from a Foucauldian perspective. This is the problem of agency. For Foucault, power is diffused along multiple matrices that stem from multiple centers (Foucault, 49; passim), which makes Massad's idea of a single, coherent "inciter of discourse" (that is, the West) deeply problematic.

7   *The Arab Mind* is a deeply racist book that, in my opinion, ought to be banished from Near Eastern Studies until it is understood solely as the racist object that it is; thus, I will only cite it through Puar and Hersh in order to avoid mentioning it in the bibliography.

8   Whoever that might be!

9   And perhaps in the case of Arab sexual subjectivity as a whole.

10   Spike Jones and His City Slickers give (in brownface) a rather ghastly performance of a heterosexualized version of this trope in a rendition of this song, which can be seen on YouTube.

Works Cited

Alexander, M. Jacqui. "Erotic Autonomy as a Politics of Decolonization: An Anatomy of Feminist and State Practice in the Bahamas Tourist Economy." In *Feminist Genealogies, Colonial Legacies, Democratic Futures*, by M. Jacqui Alexander and Chandra Talpade Mohanty, 63–100. New York: Routledge, 1997.

Boone, Joseph A. "Vacation Cruises; Or, the Homoerotics of Orientalism," *PMLA* 110, no. 1 (1995): 89–107.

Deleuze, Gilles, and Felix Guattari. *A Thousand Plateaus: Capitalism and Schizophrenia*, translated by Brian Massumi. Minneapolis, MN: University of Minnesota Press, 1987.Fanon, Frantz. *Black Skin, White Masks*, translated by Charles Lam Markmann. London: Pluto Press, 2008.

Foucault, Michel. *The History of Sexuality, Volume 1: An Introduction*. New York: Pantheon Books, 1978.

Freud, Sigmund. *Three Essays on Sexuality*. New York: Basic Books, 1962.

Ginsburg, Mitch. "Army's 'gay soldiers' photo was staged, is misleading," *Times of Israel*, June 12, 2012.

Ibish, Hussein. "Joseph Massad, homophobia, gay rights and the structure of modernity," *Ibishblog*, February 4, 2010.

Long, Scott. "Why Gay Middle Easterners Can't Stand gaymiddleeast.com," *Pinkwatching Israel*, January 28, 2012.

Massad, Joseph A. *Desiring Arabs*. Chicago: University of Chicago Press, 2007.

Meronek, Toshio. "De-Pinkwashing Israel," *Truthout*, November 17, 2012.

Mohanty, Chandra Talpade. "Under Western Eyes: Feminist Scholarship and Colonial Discourses." In *The Post-Colonial Studies Reader*, edited by Bill Ashcroft, Gareth Griffiths, and Helen Tiffin, 259–63. New York: Routledge, 1995.

Netanyahu, Benjamin. "Transcript of Prime Minister Netanyahu's address to U.S. Congress," *Globe and Mail*, May 24, 2011.

Oh Yes I Am Blog. "Israeli Defense Forces Posts Photo of Gay Soldiers Holding Hands to Official Facebook Page," *Oh Yes I Am: Mantra of the Fabulous*, June 13, 2012.

Oswin, Natalie. "Critical geographies and the uses of sexuality: deconstructing queer space," *Progress in Human Geography* (2008): 89–103.

Puar, Jasbir K. *Terrorist Assemblages: Homonationalism in Queer Times*. Durham, NC: Duke University Press, 2007.

El-Rouayheb, Khaled. *Before Homosexuality in the Arab Islamic World, 1500–1800*. Chicago: University of Chicago Press, 2005.

Said, Edward. *Orientalism*. London: Penguin Books, 2003.

Schulman, Sarah. *Israel/Palestine and the Queer International*. Durham, NC: Duke University Press, 2012.

Spivak, Gayatri Chakravorty. "Can the Subaltern Speak?" In *The Post-Colonial Studies Reader*, by Bill Ashcroft, Gareth Griffiths and Helen Tiffin, 24–29. New York: Routledge, 1995.

Stoler, Ann Laura. *Race and the Education of Desire*. Durham, NC and London: Duke University Press, 1995.

2

OF HEROES AND MEN: THE CRISIS OF MASCULINITY IN THE POST-OSLO PALESTINIAN NARRATIVE

Amal Amireh

In a widely circulated essay, prominent Palestinian literary critic Faisal Darraj laments that Palestinian literature produced in recent years is inferior to that produced by the Palestinian literary founding fathers such as Jabra Ibrahim Jabra, Ghassan Kanafani, and Emile Habibi. According to him, these authors penned what he calls the "great Palestinian narrative," something that recent writers have failed to do (Darraj). Critic Ismail Nashif defends the younger generation of Palestinian writers against Darraj's dismissive judgment by declaring that the time for "the grand Palestinian narrative is over" (Nashif). This chapter discusses what I see as two contending trends in recent Palestinian literature written in the post-Oslo Accords period.[1] The first trend may give Darraj some hope for the future of Palestinian literature because it insists on writing the Palestinian grand narrative. The second trend goes in the opposite direction and seems to vindicate Nashif's assessment, for it rejects grand narratives in favor of micro narratives. In what follows, I show how both types of narratives, which define the post-Oslo literary scene, coexist but do not overlap. More importantly, I argue that in both grand and micro narratives contrasting concepts of masculinity play a central role in the authors' aesthetic choices, something not acknowledged by either Darraj or Nashif.

Nationalism, Narrative, and Masculinity: An Intimate Triangle

Nationalism offers a *narrative* of the nation that symbolically constructs a community. Correspondingly, and as Benedict Anderson showed in his influential *Imagined Communities*, the novel played an important role in forging modern national identities. Timothy Brennan builds on Anderson's claim and argues that "[n]ations . . . are imaginary constructs that depend for their existence on an apparatus of cultural fictions in which imaginative literature plays a central role" and that the novel especially, as a composite but clearly bordered work of art, was crucial in defining the nation as an "imagined community" (Brennan, 173). While Anderson's and Brennan's observations were made in discussions of European identities, their views have been extended to other national identities. Frederic Jameson's declaration that third-world narratives are national allegories does just that, as do Arab critics who have noted the important role the Arabic novel plays in forging national identities. According to two such critics, by "critically reading modern Arabic history, [the Arabic novel] sought to answer the questions: who are we? And how did we get here? And where are we going?" (Obaid and al Bayati, 34). Perhaps the most iconic expression of the intimate connection between nation and narrative is the one made by Edward Said in a 1984 article when he declared that the essence of the Palestine question—that is, Palestinian nationalism—is the "permission to narrate"—a permission denied despite the "coherent narrative direction pointed toward self-determination" that the "history, actuality, and aspirations" of the Palestinian people possess (Said, 246).

Alongside being intimately connected with narrative, nationalism has a similar intimacy with masculinity. As Joane Nagel puts it, "[t]he culture of nationalism is constructed to emphasize and resonate with masculine cultural themes. Terms like honor, patriotism, cowardice, bravery and duty are hard to distinguish as either nationalistic or masculinist, since they seem so thoroughly tied both to the nation and to manliness." She concludes that "the 'microculture' of masculinity in everyday life articulates very well with the demands of nationalism, particularly its militaristic side" (Nagel, 252).

In the Palestinian context, this articulation of nationalism and masculinity is hard to miss. Armed conflict, in particular, brings it to the fore unambiguously. During the Israeli attacks on Gaza in recent years, social media was usually ablaze with descriptions of Palestinian resistance as manly, protecting *women and children* and returning honor and dignity to the nation; Palestinian victories are usually described as victories "made by men." In contrast, Mahmoud Abbas, head of the Palestinian Authority in the West Bank, and Arab leaders in general, are described as "emasculated," and "neutered" figures who desperately "needed Viagra." There is nothing new here: this is a continuation of a hegemonic masculinist Palestinian national narrative that posits the *fida'i*, the freedom fighter, as the embodiment of both manliness and Palestinian-ness (Amireh, 747–72).

While hegemonic, this narrative is far from being static or uncontested. Literature is certainly one important site where this narrative is reproduced, but it is also a space where it is challenged. In what follows I will examine several literary texts by Palestinian authors to shed light on how this masculine narrative has been reproduced and reworked in post-Oslo literature. The three authors I discuss below articulate nationalism and masculinity in their works from three different geopolitical locations: Ibrahim Nasrallah as a Palestinian refugee living in Jordan; Raja Shehadeh as a Palestinian subject of Israeli military rule in the occupied West Bank; and Raji Bathish as a Palestinian in Israel, a member of an Arab minority in a self-identified Jewish state. Writing from these disparate locations, and making different aesthetic choices, these Palestinian authors have one crucial thing in common: they engage questions of national identity via narratives of masculinity. While Nasrallah does that by embracing grand narratives, Shehadeh and Bathish question and ultimately reject such narratives and the subject positions they entail.

Heroic Masculinity and the "Palestinian Iliad"

Born in 1954 to a Palestinian family that was displaced during the Nakba of 1948, Nasrallah grew up and was educated in a refugee camp in Amman, Jordan. He saw Palestine for the first time in 1987 when he returned as a visitor. He searched for his village near Jerusalem, which his father had often talked about, but he found no trace of it. It has been erased and a weapons factory was built on its lands (Obaid and al-Bayati, 11). Nasrallah's experience of exile and dispossession is at the root of his creative project, which began with poetry but has shifted to the novel and culminated in his monumental *al-Malhat al-falastiniya* (The Palestinian Tragicomedy). This multi-volume work was started in 1985, when the writer began working on one "big novel," as he explains:

> At the beginning I was thinking of writing a big novel. But as work progressed [it] showed me that a story so rich and big like the Palestinian story cannot be told in one single novel. . . . This is where I got the idea of several novels that tell the Palestinian story from different angles. . . . Palestinian exile created Palestinian communities that live under different conditions . . . There is one people joined by the big Palestinian dream but in its living conditions it looks like many Palestinian peoples (Quoted in the orginal Arabic by Obaid and al-Bayati, 21; author's own translation).

That first big novel was eventually completed twenty-two years later and was published as *Zaman al-khuyul al bayda'* (released in English as *Time of White Horses*). The novel relies on thousands of pages of oral testimonies of diaspora Palestinians who were displaced following the Nakba of 1948. Nasrallah weaves their stories and the written historical resources he relies on with myth and poetry to create what critic Salma Khadra Jayyousi has hailed as the long-awaited "Palestinian Iliad."[2]

Five other volumes appeared in between and more since, spanning 250 years of Palestinian history, from the seventeenth century until the second *intifada*.[3] While the multi-volume project allows Nasrallah to narrate the diversity of the Palestinian experience without giving up the "big novel," his grand narrative, which has loss and dispossession at its core, risks being a tragedy, a *"ma'sat."* To counter the narrative's tragic bend, Nasrallah calls it a *"malhat"*—a tragic-comedy, thus negating the defeated ending that comes with tragedy.

Nasrallah's 'epic' appears at a particularly low moment in Palestinian history. The defining feature of the post-Oslo period for Palestinians is the fragmentation of their body politic. While geographic fragmentation of Palestinians as a people came about as a consequence of the Nakba and later military occupation, there was a moment when Palestinians seemed to rise from the ashes of catastrophe and form a unifying leadership, represented by the Palestine Liberation Organization, which developed a consensual political agenda that brought them together despite their geographic and ideological fragmentation. This golden age of Palestinian nationalism, which shaped the political consciousness of Nasrallah's generation, allowed the Palestinians to ignore the factionalism of various Palestinian political groups; the exclusions of the PLO; the autocratic way in which it was run; and, finally, the disjunction between a unifying political rhetoric and divisive actions on the ground. The Oslo Accords, in both their content and the way they came about, were a consequence of all these factors. They also became the catalyst that exposed and worsened the state of fragmentation. It is not overly dramatic to say that the current state of division and fragmentation of Palestinians is unprecedented, or at least reminiscent of the immediate aftermath of the Nakba: Palestinians in the West Bank are still under occupation, though partly ruled by the Palestinian Authority; those in Gaza are ruled by Hamas, and are under Israeli siege; Palestinians in the diaspora feel forgotten and leaderless; while those inside Israel continue to occupy the liminal position of citizens in a state that officially tells them it is not theirs.

Nasrallah's grand, if fragmented, narrative is an intervention in this malaise.[4] In what follows, I focus my discussion on his novel *Time of White Horses*, which I argue is neither an epic nor a tragedy but rather historical fiction. As such it seeks to do what the historical novel has traditionally done: to understand, shape, or recreate a present by inventing a usable past. The purpose of this usable past is "to build the imagined community of nations" (De Groot). Nasrallah's return to history, then, should not be seen as retreat from the present but rather as a way to reorient it. Like other historical fictions, his grand narrative is about 'nation creation'—or what one critic of the historical novel calls "the substantiation of a sense of national identity [which] has been part of the historical writer's purpose and mode of working" (De Groot, 140). Thus at a time when the facts on the ground are negating Palestinian identity and national aspirations, and a national homeland seems more remote than ever, when the refugee issue seems to be forgotten, Nasrallah's fiction urgently tells the story from the beginning—to mourn a lost past and to insist on its relevance to a stale and dead-ended present.

Key to the novel's historical narrative is the recollection of a past geography.[5] While it tells the story of how one village, Hadeya, lost its land to Zionist settlements, it is crowded with names of other villages, the majority of which were erased from existence. The author not only maps lost villages but also writes a cartography of Palestinian cities, marking their landmarks and institutions which testify to the rich history of these cities and to their cosmopolitanism. The novel also recalls and records many details of practices of daily life specific to particular regions and groups—from etiquettes of coffee drinking; to wedding customs; to songs that celebrate different occasions such as marriage, harvest, pilgrimage, and rain. All the songs recall a Palestinian dialect and bring to life the oral culture of the villagers. Nasrallah's historical fiction contains a large dose of fictionalized history. He uses footnotes to remind his readers of actual historical events and historical figures.

While the story Nasrallah tells is a collective one, at its center, larger than life, stands the individual hero of the romance: in *Time of White Horses*, it is the legendary Sheikh Khalid, who tirelessly battles the Ottomans, the British, and the villain who works for them, al-Habbab. The novel retells his adventures: his life as a vagabond chased by the Turks, his leading a rebellion against British forces, and his escape from British prison. He is also celebrated for his generosity, hospitality, and chivalry. When he is offered a bride in humiliation, as a 'secondary wife,' to expiate for the father's transgression against him, he refuses her and returns her to her father's house more dignified than when she came to him. He refuses to kill prisoners of war, declaring, "We're rebels, not murderers!" and "I'm not fighting to win. I'm fighting to preserve what's rightfully mine" (Nasrallah, *Time of White Horses*, 397, 458). Because of his physical prowess and honor code, Khalid becomes a legend: "a story told by young and old alike, to the point that some thought he actually was nothing more than a legend" (Nasrallah, *Time of White Horses*, 182). Even his British enemy, Peterson, at the moment of his death testifies to his honor and courage, lamenting, "This was a courageous man, and it's shameful to congratulate each other on his death. . . . He was an honorable man. Where will I ever find another opponent like him?" (Nasrallah, *Time of White Horses*, 461). Like the hero of *Qanadil malik al-jalil*, Sheikh Thaher al-Omar, who challenged the Ottoman Empire in the seventeenth century, Sheikh Khalid is an idealized military leader, who embodies idealized masculine qualities: physical prowess, courage, honor, and dignity. He administers justice, punishes villains, and saves women from their rapists.

Sheikh Khalid is a 'true man' who stands tall in contrast to effeminate men. These men are intellectuals like Sheikh Khalid's son, Mahmud, who studies at the American Friends' School in Ramallah, becomes a journalist, and refuses to ride the horse on his wedding day. At a climactic point in the narrative, he is compared to a "lady of the night in front of some nightclub," standing naked and impotent (Nasrallah, *Time of White Horses*, 567). Along with intellectuals like Mahmud, the upper-class Palestinian leadership is embodied by Salim Bek al-Hashemi, an entrepreneur who studied in England and is described as "a calm, sedate man, soft to the touch, with a simile on his lips, reticent and secretive" (Nasrallah, *Time of White Horses*, 370). In lamenting the weakness of the leadership of the Palestinian national movement that succumbed to the British policy of bringing Jews and Arabs together in parties and feasts, Nasrallah relies on sexual language, as in the following passage:

> Hence, as a result of Palestine's double affliction with, on one hand, the British and the Jews and, on the other hand, the weakness of its nationalist movement, there emerged what might be termed a dual, or 'hermaphrodit,' nationalism. No one could fail to note the weakness and apathy that came over the independent nationalist movement, or the disunity and chaos into which it fell (Nasrallah, *Time of White Horses*, 470).

In the Arabic original, Nasrallah uses the word *khunthawiya*, which, in the above passage, is translated as "Hermaphrodit" (Nasrallah, *Zaman*, 380). A translation closer to the meaning of the Arabic original is 'unmasculine' or 'effeminate.' This gendered description of the weakened national movement appears a couple of pages after the assassination of Sheikh Khalid by a British soldier, in a chapter that describes Salim Bek al-Hashemi and other Palestinian upper-class people at a British dinner party, humiliating themselves playing games and getting drunk. At some point, al-Hashemi is rewarded with a British woman but he is too drunk to be able to have sex with her. The woman describes his abject impotence: "He chased me from room to room, and in every room he would take off a piece of his clothing. By the time we finally made it to the bed, he'd forgotten why he was chasing me, and fell asleep" (Nasrallah, *Time of White Horses*, 476). Eventually, al-Hashemi sells his businesses and farms just before the Nakba and escapes to Lebanon. With heroes like Sheikh Khalid and Thaher al-Omar taking center stage in these narratives, Nasrallah's national and aesthetic project becomes a narrative nostalgic for heroic masculinity, a masculinity embodied by the men of yore but lost in the present.

The Writer as Anti-Hero

The other trend I want to engage rejects grand narratives altogether and turns away from macro politics. It is also a result of Post-Oslo disappointment. The best representative of this trend is Raja Shehadeh. Trained as a lawyer, Shehadeh was founder of al-Haq, an organization that documents Israeli human-rights violations under occupation. Like Nasrallah, he comes from a family of refugees but he lives in Ramallah under Israeli occupation. Shehadeh started identifying as a writer when he stopped being a political activist. Writing in English for a foreign audience about life under occupation became, paradoxically, his refuge from politics. In *Palestinian Walks* (2007), which won the George Orwell Prize in 2008, he explains how he felt before and after Oslo:

> I had perceived my life as an ongoing narrative organically linked to the forward march of the Palestinian people toward liberation and freedom from the yoke of occupation. But now I knew this was nothing but a grand delusion. There was no connection outside my own mind between my knowledge and reality. It was only my way of feeling I was part of the rest of the struggling society, a way of enduring hardships by claiming and holding on to the belief that that there was a higher meaning to the suffering—that it wasn't in vain; it wasn't without purpose. As long as I was gaining a better understanding of the grand plan within which all this misery was taking place, my efforts had a point. I was not just a sufferer. I was an interpreter and a challenger, acting in solidarity with others.
>
> But the Oslo Agreements buried my truth. The only resistance that was recognized was the PLO's armed struggle. The generally accepted claim was that it was the military struggle that was responsible for bringing us to this "peace." The legal battles waged for years against Israel were never recognized by the leadership, which, as I discovered, had the power to deny them at will. When the Oslo Peace Accords were signed I distinctly remember feeling the final rupture, the termination of what for years I had called my narrative. My bubble, my illusion, was burst (Shehadeh, *Palestinian Walks*, 123).

It is instructive that Shehadeh expresses his national disappointment as a grand-narrative failure. Therefore, in all his writing he avoids grand narratives, choosing to write instead as a diarist. His style is terse, dispassionate, and elegiac. In contrast to Nasrallah, he is not interested in stories of beginnings but in the here and now, taken one day at a time.

As a diarist, Shehadeh is unheroic: he is a man who withdraws from public life to tend his private garden—a witness to a decidedly ruptured world. He suffers from the "persistent pain of failure . . . to save the land." He wants to "face the fact of our defeat." He writes, "This is not the first time we have arrived at defeat that was trumpeted by the leadership as a victory . . . Our history is rich with similar instances. The price of living a lie is too high for me. I'd rather face facts and take stock. Israel has won this round" (Shehadeh, 169).

Even when he allows for moments of resistance or confrontation with the Israeli Army, they are moments happening to others—like, for example, the neighborhood barber who during the invasion of Ramallah in 2002 lectures an Israeli soldier by insisting on his own humanity then asks him to leave. But these moments are few and far between. Shehadeh does not allow himself even these confrontational daily moments of resistance. When he is getting ready to face the soldiers who barged into his house, he worries in a Kafkaesque manner about what to wear—whether to be formal or informal—thus highlighting the absurdity of the situation and his own helplessness.

Shehadeh no longer believes in heroes—particularly the ones idealized in Nasrallah's fiction. In fact, he reserves his harshest cynicism and critique for a leadership that pays lip service to idealized militaristic heroes but leaves young men to die at the hands of the Israeli Army's superior military machine. In his book *When the Birds Stopped Singing* (2003), he refuses to celebrate the military masculinity of the second intifada. In *Palestinian Walks*, he and his wife during one of their hikes are shot at by Palestinians, and during another walk with a foreign friend he is absurdly mistaken for a kidnapper and is surrounded by Palestinian soldiers eager to save his friend from him. Such incidents prompt him to declare that soldiers do not belong to this landscape. Neither do Israeli settlements, he often laments, which are responsible for changing the hills he loves so much.

Some may say that Shehadeh is an exception: he after all is writing in English to a foreign audience and is hardly thought of as a 'writer' in the Palestinian context.[6] But I would argue that he is no exception; post-Oslo Palestinian literature is teaming with unheroic masculinities. Often these are included purely in order to be shot down because they are blamed for defeat; sometimes they are foils for something held up as a true masculinity. Shehadeh is different in that, unlike them, he is not writing about the others' defeat: he is that man and he will have a voice as that man even if his voice is not deemed worthy of inclusion according to those who engineered Oslo.

Narrative from the Margin

I want to conclude this chapter by discussing another writer who rejects grand narratives and questions heroic masculinities in a radical way. Raji Bathish is a Palestinian poet and short-story writer who is a citizen of Israel. He is founder and editor of an online zine called *Qadita*, which is a queer-friendly site. Bathish identifies as queer himself. In talking about his literary project, he says he wants to shock readers, especially Arab readers and Palestinians in the diaspora, out of the national clichés and taboos by which they live. He believes there is a huge gap between reality and what Palestinians believe. Those who romanticize Palestine fail to see what he calls the complex reality of the Palestinians living in Israel. He wants to demolish the ready-made Palestinian image that dominates the imagination. According to him, there is no one Palestinian. There are Palestinians—there are Palestinians who die a normal death, not only martyrs as everyone wants to believe (Bathish, Interview).

This attempt to rewrite the romanticized Palestinian imaginatively is evident in Bathish's short story "Nakba Lite." It is about five friends who have a blog to commemorate the Nakba and want to tell the Nakba stories they get from their parents, who were witnesses to the event. Bathish uses the mode of the mock epic to criticize particular narratives of the Nakba. What he calls the "revolutionary endeavor" of the Nakba consists of searching for "a shocking three-line summary; one that would make the walls quake with awe, and the cracked and crumbling surfaces weep blood mixed with salty waters" (Bathish, Nakba, 145). The friends each return with a story to include in the blog. One account is of a family who were kicked out of their house by the Jewish paramilitary organization, the Haganah, but kept returning to it and are living in it now. It is rejected as not interesting enough; it lacked the 'proper,' predetermined ending (Bathish, Nakba, 145). Thus, a story about a family that was, in the end, not displaced and whose members stayed in their home does not fit the Nakba narrative these young men are trying to tell.

The other narrative is also cut short: it is about a family who try to escape through the port but arrive too late to find a ship that will evacuate them as the rest of the Arab population was evacuated. So they change route and settle down in Nazareth, where they stay. The story is rejected again as having no ending, as being "'reconciled with history'—It forces one to ask in exasperation: where is the Nakba. Where did it disappear all of a sudden?" (Bathish, Nakba, 146).

The most zealous of the Nakba bloggers is described this way: "he seemed to be living his life partly in some epic film, like *Shindler's List* or *Gate of the Sun*" (the novel by Elias Khoury that has been hailed at the first real big Nakba narrative). His story is that all his family was annihilated by the Haganah's gangs, all burned and their features effaced. This, we are told by the narrator, is "wishful thinking" (Bathish, Nakba, 147). Seeing the Nakba as a tragedy means embracing annihilation.

Then there is the story of the aunt who is dying from cancer, which she blames on the trauma of sixty years of suffering. She dreams she was gang raped by soldiers. Although this is exactly the kind of story the bloggers want, they cannot use it because the moment they start to talk about rape as a real thing, a fight breaks out. The storyteller is offended: "You lowlife, have some shame! They should have raped your mother or grandmother. How dare you insult the honor of our family" (Bathish, Nakba, 147). Thus, rape of women cannot be included in this narrative because it violates men's sense of honor.

The bloggers try to tell the story of the house keys that many refugees kept. "The key is the key to the Nakba. It is overdone but viable because after all we are not doing an ad campaign." But the story turns out to be about a lost key, not a kept key. The man concerned puts it in his *sirwal* (traditional trousers) and puts the *sirwal* at the bottom of the closet in his house in Ramallah, but the pants are lost or stolen when his wife dies. Five years later he dies of grief over his lost key. The story is judged excellent but the question asked undermines it: "how do you know he died of grief over the lost key?" The answer: "Is there anything more tragic to die for?" (Bathish, Nakba, 148).

Then, however, the narrator tells the friends that he received a stupid message in his inbox by mistake. It turns out to be a narrative of the Nakba, or rather a fragment of one, about April 1948:

> In the city . . . and behind that window (now smashed) the two comrades—who were believed to be more than just friends—were planning to write, act and produce the first, second or possibly third ever Palestinian feature film. And here, in some single frozen moment, the final rehearsal of the theatre group came to an end, never to be resumed, except in the mirror of drizzle produced by departing seas. And behind the window of the city, Claudette was cheating on her simpleton husband with a youthful Moroccan sailor. . . . At this window, and behind that one, and the other, this is where the frustrated writer did not complete the novel he began two years ago. Yet the coordinates of the place slipped from his fingers, and the novel turned into a story . . . a short story, and an oblivion (Bathish, Nakba, 149).

This is a story of loss, but not heroic loss. It is about frozen moments of culture, interrupted. The Palestinians appearing in it are possibly gay lovers; a cheating wife (an Emma Bovary type); a cuckolded, simpleton husband; and a frustrated writer. These characters are usually outside the national imaginary. They may not be suitable for a grand narrative, but for Bathish they should be at the heart of any Nakba story. They are ordinary, multidimensional characters who would complicate the national narrative if they were included in it. The 'ordinary' Palestinians that appear in the other rejected fragments—those who did not leave, those who were internally displaced but continued to exist, those who died ordinary deaths, and those who lost their key to their lost house—all of them experienced the Nakba but are not included in its narrative. Bathish would like to change that by giving those unheroic men and women a place and a voice, even if it means rewriting the Nakba as a mock-epic.

Raji Bathish's characters in his mock epic, like Raja Shehadeh's persona in his diaries, seem to belong to a different place and time than Nasrallah's epic heroes. Yet all three writers share the same historical moment of post-Oslo defeat; they just make different aesthetic choices in response to this defeat. Nasrallah insists on reviving the masculine hero of yore, as if willing him into existence by writing a historical novel that seeks to go back to the beginnings. Shehadeh embraces his non-heroic self and gives it a voice that is critical of the militarized masculinity of the hegemonic Palestinian narrative. Similarly, Bathish seeks to include those who were excluded because they did not fit: ordinary, unheroic, Palestinians, some with non-normative sexualities, who have been invisible in the big picture of Palestinian dispossession and survival.

Notes

1   The Oslo Accords were signed in 1993 in Oslo, Norway between the Palestine Liberation Organization and the Israeli government. The accords provided for the withdrawal of the Israeli Army from part of the West Bank and Gaza and the creation of the Palestinian National Authority (PNA), a limited self-government to administer those areas. This was meant as an interim agreement to be followed by a final agreement that settled the Palestine–Israel conflict. This has not happened.

2   Quoted on the back cover of the Arabic edition.

3   The books are, in order of publication: *Tuyur al-hathar* (1996), *Tifl al-mimhat* (2000), *Zaytun al-shawari'* (2002), *A'ras Amina* (2004), *Tahta shams al-duha* (2004), *Zaman al-khuyul al-bayda'* (2007), *Qanadil malik al-jaleel* (2012), *Arwah Kiliminjaro* (2015) and *Thulathiyat al-ajras* (2019). All published by Arab Scientic Publishers in Beirut.

4   This interest in writing historical fiction post-Oslo is not limited to
    Nasrallah. Other writers have revisited the Nakba recently; among them
    is Sahar Khalifeh, in her two recent novels *al-Hub al-awal* (First Love)
    and *Asl wa fasl* (translated as *On Noble Origins* by Aida Bamia. Cairo: The
    American University in Cairo Press, 2012). Also, see Mahmoud Shuqair's
    latest novel, *Faras al-'aila* (The Family's Horse).
5   In *Qanadeel* he includes a map crowded with the names of fifty particular
    villages and cities, which form the setting for the narrative.
6   Some of Shehadeh's works have been translated into Arabic but an Arabic
    Google search of him yields almost nothing.

Works Cited

Amireh, Amal. "Between Complicity and Subversion: Body Politics in Pal-
    estinian National Narrative," *South Atlantic Quarterly* 102, no. 4 (2003):
    747–72.

Anderson, Benedict. *Imagined Communities: Reflections on the Origins and the
    Spread of Nationalism*. London: Verso, 1983.

Bathish, Raji. "Nakba Lite," translated by Suneela Mubayi. *Banipal: Magazine
    of Modern Arab Literature* 25 (2012): 145–49.

———. Interview: "Raji Bathish: I Write Against the Stereotype of the Pales-
    tinian in the Arab Imagination," *Safahat suriya*, June 28, 2009.

Brennan, Timothy. "The National Longing for Form." In *The Post-Colonial
    Studies Reader*, edited by Bill Ashcroft, Gareth Griffiths, and Helen Tiffin,
    170–75. London: Routledge, 1995.

Darraj, Faisal. "Why Has Palestinian Literature Changed?" *Al Jazeera*, August
    6, 2011.

De Groot, Gerome. *The Historical Novel*. London: Routledge, 2009.

Jameson, Frederic. "Third-World Literature in the Era of Multinational
    Capitalism," *Social Text* 15 (1986): 65–88.

Nagel, Joane. "Masculinity and Nationalism: Gender and Sexuality in the
    Making of Nations." *Ethnic and Racial Studies* 21, no. 2 (1998): 242–69.

Nashif, Ismail. "In Search of Raji Bathish." *Qadita.net*.

Nasrallah, Ibrahim. 2012. *Time of White Horses*, translated by Nancy Roberts.
    Cairo: The American University in Cairo Press, 2001.

———. *Zaman al-khuyul al-bayda'*. Beirut: al-Dar al-'Arabiya li-l-Ulum,
    2007.

Obaid, Mohammad Saber and Sawsan al Bayati. *al-Kawn al-riwa'i: qira'at
    fi-l-malhama al-riwa'iya al-malhat al-falastiniya li Ibrahim Nasrallah* (The
    Novelistic Universe: A Reading of the Narrative Epic the Palestinian
    Tragic Comedy, by Ibrahim Nasrallah). Beirut: al-Mu'asasa al-Arabiya
    li-l-Dirasat wa-l Nashr, 2007.

Said, Edward. "Permission to Narrate." In *The Edward Said Reader*, edited by Moustafa Bayoumi and Andrew Rubin, 243–66. New York: Vintage Books, 2000.

Shehadeh, Raja. *Palestinian Walks: Forays into a Vanishing Landscape*. New York: Scribner, 2008.

———. *When the Birds Stopped Singing: Life in Ramallah Under Siege*. South Royalton, VT: Steerforth, 2003.

3

"I GET TO DEFLOWER AT LEAST ONE. IT'S MY RIGHT!": THE PRECARIOUSNESS OF HEGEMONIC MASCULINITY IN RASHID AL-DAIF'S *WHO'S AFRAID OF MERYL STREEP?*

Nadine Sinno

> But Superman, again, is a lie. And the only thing that needs to be saved today is the sinking ship called manhood.
>
> —Joumana Haddad (22)

Introduction

In Rashid Al-Daif's *Tistifil Meryl Streep?* (2001; *Who's Afraid of Meryl Streep?*, 2014), the newly-wed Rashoud strongly agrees with his friend that it is every man's right to deflower "at least one [woman]" (Al-Daif, *Who's Afraid of Meryl Streep?*, 57). When he suspects that his wife may have engaged in premarital sex, he subjects her to a humiliating medical examination and personally inspects her body to determine if (and how) she had engaged in vaginal intercourse prior to their wedding night. The possibility that his wife may have had a hymen reconstruction surgery terrifies him, since he sees her action as a reflection of not only her dishonor but also of his own violated masculinity. While more empathetic than Rashoud could ever be, Habib, the scorned narrator in *OK, ma' al-salama* (2008; OK, Goodbye) considers suing his lover Hama for ending their relationship abruptly and causing him irreparable physical and emotional damage. He accuses Hama of using him as a "cane that she leaned on" until finding "the right man" (Al-Daif, *OK, ma' 'al-salama*, 56). And in *'Awdat al-almani ila rushdih*, (2006; *How the German Came to His Senses*, 2015), a novelized account of Al-Daif's intercultural exchange with the gay writer Joachim Helfer, the narrator Rashid struggles with accepting homosexual desire and identity; he candidly explains that in his society homosexuals are considered "perverts and their practices are considered sex acts against nature" (Al-Daif, *How the German Came to His Senses*, 3).

Clearly, Rashid Al-Daif's male narrators can hardly be considered exemplary, let alone sympathetic characters. They often articulate their flawed, sometimes disturbing visions of the world—particularly with respect to gender and sexuality—without tact or reservation. Despite their narrators' often revolting proclamations and actions, however, Al-Daif's texts have much to teach us about the tenuousness of constructing masculinity in contemporary Lebanon. In the face of shifting material realities—such as women's increased participation in the public space, late capitalism, evolving gender roles, and personal circumstances—Al-Daif's male protagonists must confront what Homi Bhabha refers to as the "prosthetic reality" (Bhabha, 57) of their masculine identities. They learn, often the hard way, that their conceptualizations and enactments of gender and sexuality are far from being natural, innocuous, or irreversible. Rather than casting these men as inherently or inexplicably oppressive, however, Al-Daif's texts explore the ways in which the narrators' perceptions and enactments of gender and sexuality are shaped by interlocking factors, including religious ideology, local and global conditions, and the narrators' unique life histories.

Dismissing Al-Daif's narrators as male chauvinists unworthy of critical attention precludes us from engaging in fruitful conversations about the still-existing cultural norms that engender these men's hegemonic performances of masculinity. Furthermore, as many scholars have argued, critiques of dominant masculinity must strive to illuminate their detrimental impact on men, not just women. As Stanley Arnowitz reminds us, "unless—and until—men are shown how they will benefit from ending their own cultural privileges, no real change will take place" (Arnowitz, 1995). In Al-Daif's narratives, the male narrator must reassess the high cost, and depreciating value, of his male privilege.

Despite dominating the narrative, Al-Daif's male narrator is rarely depicted as a positive role model who should be respected or emulated. Rather, Al-Daif ensures that his unreliable narrator (or anti-hero) is sufficiently humbled, and that his tragicomic life serves as a cautionary tale for his male counterparts in the real world. Employing irony and self-deprecating humor, Al-Daif creates a literary space where social issues may be addressed in a culturally resonant manner. For example, in *How the German Came to His Senses*, the narrator, Rashid, overstates his fears of being mistaken for a homosexual by the gay writer Joachim Helfer. Because he believes that homosexuals tend to be lecherous, effeminate, and disrespectful of personal boundaries, he worries that Helfer might make sexual advances toward him—particularly as Rashid happens to be hairy, and believes himself therefore sexually appealing to gay men (Al-Daif, *How the German Came to His Senses*, 4). As Ken Seigneurie persuasively argues, however, Rashid's statements should not be accepted at face value, or without careful attention to the author's strategic use of irony and counter-irony. In other words, Al-Daif ensures that the narrator "assumes a position close to popular opinion" in his discussion of homosexuality, "instead of pretending that this reality does not exist by emphasizing the small haven of alternative lifestyle that exists in Beirut" (Seigneurie, 182). This allows the homophobic narrator to initially establish solidarity with his imagined Arab reader, before taking him/her on a personal journey whereby simplistic cultural myths about homosexuality are tested against a more complicated reality.

In this chapter, I offer a close reading of *Who's Afraid of Meryl Streep?*,[1] highlighting the anxieties and contradictions of performing masculinity, as experienced by al-Daif's male narrator. Engaging with studies of masculinity by R.W. Connell, among others, the chapter elucidates the challenges and repercussions of performing a hegemonic type of masculinity, one that legitimates and enacts male dominance, while undermining female and other gendered identities in "both direct interactions and a kind of ideological warfare" (Connell, *Gender and Power*, 186).[2] It demonstrates that the narrator's seemingly domineering narrative is always already undermined by opposing counter-narratives that draw attention to the precariousness of his proclaimed masculine identity. In other words, while al-Daif's narrator may articulate dominant notions of Arab masculinity, or *rujula*, the text exposes the narrator's vulnerabilities and the unfortunate predicaments of his internalized masculinist ideals. By demonstrating the perpetual crisis of its tormented-but-complicit narrator and revealing "the cracks and fissures that belie the complications and contradictions embedded in the masculine project" (Whitehead and Barret, 19), the text warns against the pitfalls of clinging to essentialist notions of both masculine and feminine identities.

Bearing the Brunt of Failed Femininity

From the outset of the novel, the male narrator Rashoud emphasizes that he is a progressive man who values principles such as religious coexistence and women's liberation. When he and his friends convene for lunch, in the aftermath of the Lebanese Civil War, they toast their beloved country, "the land of public and personal liberties; the land of free press . . . [the country] where women enjoy more freedom than anywhere else in the entire region and participate fully in the media revolution, in television and in radio, etcetera, etcetera" (Al-Daif, *Who's Afraid of Meryl Streep*, 18). However, despite his proud championing of women's increased emancipation and visibility in the public space, Al-Daif's unreliable narrator holds dear his traditional notions of "real femininity"—particularly as they relate to the performance of gender and sexuality. Rashoud admits that "deep inside [he] really like[s] for a woman to be shy and sweet and bashful," (Al-Daif, *Who's Afraid of Meryl Streep?*, 61) and that while he is not a "fundamentalist," he is still a "big believer in modesty and discretion" (Al-Daif, *Who's Afraid of Meryl Streep?*, 63).[3] Despite Rashoud's aspirations for a liberated but bashful wife, the text denies him the ideal partner he thinks he deserves. Rather, Al-Daif playfully pairs up the self-righteous narrator with a female partner who defies rigid gender dichotomies and subverts dominant cultural norms unapologetically, thereby causing the self-righteous narrator continual anxiety. By clinging to essentialized ideals of "real femininity," Al-Daif's narrator experiences resentment (of self and partner), powerlessness, and emasculation at the hands of a defiant wife whose gender-variant behavior threatens his entrenched beliefs about gender polarity.

Rashoud's partner, whom he likens to "assertive and confident young men in Lucky Strike commercials" (Al-Daif, *Who's Afraid of Meryl Streep?*, 66), unsettles his notions of gender differentiation by "interrogating the supposed self-evidence of femininity" and demonstrating that "the possession of a conventionally defined penis has nothing to do with securing manhood" (Noble, xvii, xxvviii). For example, on their first date, Rashoud's future wife orders a beer, which shocks him, since women are generally expected to order non-alcoholic beverages or, at the very least, seek a man's permission before ordering an alcoholic drink. While she sips her unauthorized beer nonchalantly in public, Rashoud wrestles with feelings of insecurity and self-doubt after repeatedly failing to get her to recognize and fix her mistake (Al-Daif, *Who's Afraid of Meryl Streep?*, 66). He is incapable of detaching his wife's 'failure' to comply with dominant cultural norms from his own masculine identity and self-worth. Rather, his wife's aberrant gender performance becomes the criterion against which his *rujula* is measured, since he considers it part of his manly duty to "uphold and protect cultural definitions of gender-specific propriety" (Peteet, 107). Since he firmly believes that "men [are] the guardians of women and that this was just the way God had designed the world and intended it to be" (Al-Daif, *Who's Afraid of Meryl Streep?*, 66), he feels inadequate every time he fails at deterring his wife from exhibiting seemingly deviant behavior.

The incident at the café foreshadows the couple's contentious marriage, as it signifies Rashoud's future wife's disregard for cultural norms and his futile attempts at setting her on the 'right path.' On another date, she shares a joke she had heard about the sun looking like a "man's erection" as it sinks into the sea. While she erupts in boisterous laughter, Rashoud seethes at her for ruining the romantic mood. He feels disturbed by her vulgar choice of words, wondering "where she had heard that kind of talk" and "the kind of people she had been associating with" (Al-Daif, *Who's Afraid of Meryl Streep?*, 31–32). The traditional gender roles are reversed, as Rashoud acts bashfully while his future wife behaves in a manner that he finds boorish and unfit for a lady. And when she compares porn to "chemical fertilizers" that "make the fruits and vegetables grow faster and bigger, but make them lose their flavor," he is bewildered by her astounding analogy (Al-Daif, *Who's Afraid of Meryl Streep?*, 33). Rashoud's concerns about his future wife are two-fold: On the most obvious level, he disapproves of her seemingly unfeminine mannerisms, including her audacity at using vulgar language and making sexual innuendos. On a deeper level, he is terrified by what his wife's treacherous words reveal about her practical knowledge of sex. This explains why he obsessively analyzes her jokes and casual comments in order to determine if she is simply repeating things that she has heard or if any of her verbal utterances betray secrets of unforgivable, firsthand sexual experiences.

For Rashoud, exhibiting coyness and decorum is a cherished trait in a female partner. More critically, he firmly believes that it is ultimately a woman's (perceived) sexual purity, or what Christa Salamandra refers to as her "chastity capital," that determines her value. As Salamandra argues, the absence of a woman's chastity capital often leads to disastrous consequences not only for the woman herself but her entire family, as it may be used as a form of ammunition by other families (Salamandra, 156). Similarly, Roseanne Khalaf's study of young people's perceptions of sex in contemporary Lebanon highlights the "disjunction between normative expectations which condone, indeed cajole, young women to be *sexually attractive* but condemns them if they become *sexually active*" (Khalaf, 185). Like Khalaf's respondants, Rashoud has internalized his society's dissonant dominant norms, which demand that a woman be sexy but not sexually experienced. However, the narrative deprives Rashoud of his peace of mind with regard to his partner's performance on the chastity scale. When he finds out that his wife had been fondled by her cousin as a child, Rashoud is flabbergasted and worries that she might have lost her virginity through sexual intercourse, or that she had engaged in *voluntary* sexual activities with other men after losing her virginity to her abusive cousin. He is less worried about the pain and trauma that she endured than he is about the state of her chastity on their first night of marriage. After all, Rashoud firmly believes that "[a] man should receive his wife's body in perfect condition. It should be complete. . . . This way, the woman will have her head up at all times, never needing to hide her face, whenever the talk about premarital chastity comes up" (Al-Daif, *Who's Afraid of Meryl Streep?*, 105).

Rashoud's stubborn preoccupation with his wife's "spoiled identity" (Goffman, 4) dictates his actions throughout the novel, driving him to embark on a futile journey in pursuit of the truth. We accompany him as he drags his wife to the gynecologist in order to determine whether she "had lost her virginity a long time ago, whether it had been by someone's finger, or if it had happened recently by something other than a finger" (Al-Daif, *Who's Afraid of Meryl Streep?*, 84). Rashoud is terrified by the prospect that he may not have been the one to take his wife's virginity, so he insists on investigating the matter while completely disregarding her right to dignity and privacy. However, not only does Rashoud's wife deny him the unabridged truth he seeks by verbally misleading him and by omitting crucial information, but her body itself resists readability, as demonstrated by the doctor's failure to reach any conclusions regarding her prior sexual activity. In fact, the doctor's final verdict is that Rashoud must decide whether or not he trusts his wife's account regarding her sexual history. Rashoud may objectify his wife's body, but the wife's indocile body consistently refuses to yield to his invasive inquisition. As Samira Aghacy notes, "if he insists on presenting his wife's body as readable, decipherable, and penetrable, the narrative reveals that his wife is illegible and undecipherable" (Aghacy, 163).

The narrator's failure to really 'know' his wife—by now, the mother of his unborn child—disabuses him of his illusion of power. If knowledge is power, then Rashoud's inability to collect any reliable information regarding his wife's body becomes a source of his powerlessness. He may be the first-person narrator, the one with the loudest voice and largest narrative platform,[4] but he has very little control over his household—let alone his own mental state. His imagined masculinity brushes up against a cold reality, one in which he is transformed from an authoritative patriarch to an emotional wreck with more questions than answers. Rashoud's preoccupation with his wife's questionable sexual history leaves him so tormented that he contemplates the possibility of being controlled by demonic forces:

> I did think that I had made a mistake in my marriage. In fact, I thought I was destined to suffer. I was a plaything in the hands of fate. . . . Perhaps demons were toying with me. They must have found a weakness and were using it to control me. . . . I never thought in a million years that I could become a victim of this sort of thing (Al-Daif, *Who's Afraid of Meryl Streep?*, 89).

Rashoud's introspection about his mistake, which he ultimately blames on his destiny, is revealing. His emotional, superstitious reaction contradicts his repeated proclamations about men's innate rationality and their God-ordained responsibility to guide women through life's challenges. Furthermore, his reference to himself as a 'victim' sounds unwarranted and insensitive upon first glance—after all, it is his wife who was sexually abused as a child. Yet, Rashoud is, indeed, a victim of a different order: a masculinist discourse that shackles him with the burdensome responsibility of monitoring his romantic partners' chastity capitals and diminishes his ability to feel empathy. Throughout the novel, Rashoud brags about abandoning women who made the mistake of sexually surrendering to him before marriage. By doing so, however, he constantly misses out on the opportunity of engaging in meaningful relationships and connecting intimately with women who view themselves as his equals. He is also incapable of showing any vulnerability, lest he be taken for a weakling. Rashoud's sexual vigilantism echoes Ghassan Hage's conclusions regarding the cost of embracing a 'penis-centered' masculinity. Hage persuasively argues that enacting misogynous masculinity minimizes one's chances of experiencing what Anthony Giddens refers to as "confluent love," which entails "opening oneself out to the other" and which "presumes equality in emotional give and take" (Giddens quoted in Hage 124). Rashoud's dream of finding an intelligent, chaste, and modern woman—who accepts his double standards of morality—proves to be unattainable in contemporary Lebanon. He ultimately relies on his aunt to find him a spouse, whom he marries without much thought, or love, because he is tired of waiting for his perfect match.

By the end of the novel, Rashoud is abandoned by his wife. To make matters worse, the unnamed wife undergoes an abortion without his permission. In fact, Rashoud only learns about the fate of the baby after "three long weeks," which felt like an "eternity" to him (Al-Daif, *Who's Afraid of Meryl Streep?*, 112). By divorcing Rashoud and aborting their baby, his defiant wife gains control of her life while he loses any semblance of agency. While Rashoud's former wife spends time on the beach and later travels to the Gulf, he remains trapped in his apartment longing for her return (to her senses and to their marital home). The novel thus ends with Rashoud's confinement in the domestic sphere, while his wife moves freely beyond her home and homeland.

Grappling with Globalization

As he interprets reality through his narrow masculinist lens, Rashoud cannot even enjoy the simple pleasures in life, including the escapism enabled by film. Even *Kramer vs. Kramer*, which features his beloved Meryl Streep, plunges him into a whirlwind of ambivalent emotions. The 1979 film—which revolves around a divorce and brutal child-custody battle between a couple played by Streep and Dustin Hoffman—disturbs Rashoud as he agonizes over Meryl Streep's decision to leave her marital home. He cannot reconcile her tenderness as a mother with what he sees as her unfathomable act of abandoning her husband and child. When Streep walks out the door,

Rashoud desperately yells at his television screen, "Please, Meryl Streep, no. Don't take my wife's side!"—thus projecting her actions onto his own wife (Al-Daif, *Who's Afraid of Meryl Streep?*, 40). Instead of bringing him comfort, Meryl Streep becomes the narrator's unwitting tormentor because of her perceived complicity in engendering "change in gender imagery, sexuality, and other forms of practice" (Connell, "Globalization, Imperialism, and Masculinities," 83). Rashoud's disappointment with Meryl Streep's 'un-motherly' behavior symbolizes his frustration with what he sees as a menacing side of globalization: the circulation of liberal worldviews and values, particularly with respect to gender roles and practices. He even wonders "who was more American" in her brutality, Meryl Streep or his wife (Al-Daif, *Who's Afraid of Meryl Streep?*, 62). He fears that Lebanese women, including his wife, have been influenced by global discourses of women's liberation, perhaps acting out in real life what American women dare act out only in film.

Not only is Rashoud disturbed by Hollywood films, he is also enraged by the safe-sex campaigns that have suddenly filled Lebanon's public billboards and television screens. He rages against the increasing frequency of advertisements that promote condoms, and he considers their stated goals of curbing sexually transmitted diseases as a mere pretext to "liberate sex from the strict confines of wedlock" (Al-Daif, *Who's Afraid of Meryl Streep?*, 63). Rashoud's objections to out-of-wedlock sex are, of course, hypocritical as they are self-serving because he does not have any qualms about engaging in pre- or extra-marital sex with women whom he brands as non-marriageable. Furthermore, while Rashoud is awed by the capabilities of new digital technology for transporting the viewer "from the Middle Ages to ages that have not even occurred yet and from places of worship to bars and night clubs," in a split second (Al-Daif, *Who's Afraid of Meryl Streep?*, 1), he is terrified by the fact that the global images that appear on his television screen—as entertaining as they may be to *him*—pose a serious threat to the innocent women and children of his traditional, conservative society. He explains:

> Personally, I do not see the difference between the bedroom and the television screen. Nor do I see the difference between the television screen and the living room where all the family gathers, in the company of well-intentioned and ill-intentioned guests. What kind of ideas would run through the ill-intentioned guest's mind whenever a commercial promoting the use of condoms appeared on the screen, while your own wife, young daughter, or older sister—whom you know has been dreaming of a man to brighten up her life—or even your mother, is sitting next to you? (Al-Daif, *Who's Afraid of Meryl Streep?*, 63)

Rashoud's emphasis on the importance of shielding one's female kin from the corrupting influence of cable television adds to his crisis and moral dilemma: he relishes consuming sexually explicit images, but he equally worries about the unregulated flow of such images that threaten to jeopardize not only the purity of his womenfolk but also the stability of the social order from which he obtains his privileges as a middle-class, straight man. As John Tomlinson notes, "[A]n acceptance of the technological culture of the West and of aspects of its consumerism may well co-exist with a vigorous rejection of its sexual permissiveness and its generally secular outlook" (Tomlinson, 23).[5] Rashoud's protest of the sexual permissiveness of the West complicates dominant Orientalist discourses that often construct Islamic religiosity and gender conservatism as an inherent combination, when in reality gender conservatism can also occur in a secular person (of either Muslim or Christian background), as in the case of Rashoud who insists that he is neither a "fundamentalist" (Al-Daif, *Who's Afraid of Meryl Streep*, 63) nor a "devout believer" (Al-Daif, *Who's Afraid of Meryl Streep?*, 109).

While Rashoud vehemently rejects the sexual permissiveness of the West (when it comes to women), his wife strongly objects to the dominant narrative that while women must remain virgins, men should have the liberty to sexually experiment outside the confines of marriage. She frowns upon and admonishes Rashoud for his sexual double standards and his mistreatment of former girlfriends whom he had judged as promiscuous or unfit for marriage. In her discussion of gender and globalization, Connell argues that "globalization also involves a powerful process of cultural change. Western cultural forms and ideologies circulate, local cultures change in response. . . . Some homogenization results as local cultures are destroyed or weakened. But new forms appear—hybrid and 'creole' identities and cultural expressions" (Connell, "Globalization, Imperialism, and Masculinities," 73). Connell's observations may be applied to Rashoud's wife, who has clearly benefited from a bilingual education and is cognizant of shifting ideas of gender and sexuality locally and globally. She is neither too traditional, nor completely 'westernized.' Her character typifies the hybrid identities facilitated by the crisscrossing of cultures: She speaks English fluently and often attributes her knowledge of sex, including contraception, to the English-language magazines she reads. By the same token, she code-switches between Arabic, English, and French depending on the topic about which she is speaking. When discussing birth control, for instance, she utilizes English medical terminology, whereas when she is yelling at Rashoud she resorts to Lebanese colloquialisms. And when she is in a romantic mood, she utilizes French idioms to refer to her preferred sexual acts. Unlike his wife, however, Rashoud does not know English very well since he had learned French as his second language—which is not uncommon among the Lebanese (due to the French mandate, 1923–1946). His struggle with deciphering the English language inevitably contributes to his feelings of inferiority and powerlessness, especially that his "satellite TV addict" (Al-Daif, *Who's Afraid of Meryl Streep?*, 81) wife can better comprehend the English-language media that eludes Rashoud and terrifies him in its dominance.

Rashoud's ambivalent relationship with English, which he sees as a marker of global imperialism, is comparable to Habib's predicament in Al-Daif's *OK, Goodbye*.[6] In this novel, the ageing Habib falls in love with the much younger—and very sophisticated—Hama. However, he often feels insecure about his age, (modest) income, and inadequate English. Similarly to Rashoud, Habib is frustrated with the prevalence of English, as well as his inability to master it. While Habib does make a sincere effort at learning English, he is bewildered by the sad reality that his English-language deficiency renders him a lesser citizen of the world. In fact, he painfully remembers a news story in which a self-taught, twelve-year-old Iraqi boy is quoted as saying, "If you can't read and speak English you're deaf and dumb" (Al-Daif, *OK, ma' 'al-salama*, 60). Habib finds that hypothesis quite "dangerous," and it becomes an incentive for him to increase his efforts at studying English so he may avoid such a disturbing destiny. Like Rashoud, Habib is also convinced that Hollywood films offer much insight regarding the dynamics of gender relations in the West; more importantly, Habib and Rashoud consider such films a window into the psyche of their respective female partners, including the women's aspirations for gender equality and mutual reciprocity in sexual intercourse. In Al-Daif's novels, the crisis of masculinity, which is ongoing, cannot be extracted from the material conditions in which it exists. If the civil war may have put young men in the difficult situation of either embracing aggressive masculinity by taking up arms (so they may defend their families) or risking being overpowered and dominated, then (relative) peace and stability may have posed a different dilemma regarding whether or not, or to what extent, they should embrace new technologies, worldviews, and practices made more accessible and attainable in the postwar era.

Rashoud's response to the "local instabilities in gender arrangements" facilitated by the proliferation of global media is "to reaffirm local gender hierarchies" (Connell, "Globalization, Imperialism, and Masculinities," 83) and to disavow any connections between Arab and Western women. Rashoud contradicts his own narrative about Lebanese women's extreme liberation by insisting that "*our* women" would never engage indiscreetly in premarital sex like "Meryl Streep and her kind" and that "every nation wears its own attire" (Al-Daif, *Who's Afraid of Meryl Streep*, 96). Rashoud's insistence on drawing rigid boundaries between 'us' and 'them,' on the basis of women's sexual conduct, reiterate Sheila Croucher's observation that "Women's actual bodies and behaviors also become signifiers of the nation and mechanisms for marking the boundaries between nations" (Croucher, 183) and that "just as globalization can enhance the capacity for world citizenship, it can also facilitate the maintenance and flourishing of particularistic identities and attachments" (Croucher, 190). In fact, Rashoud repeatedly rehashes the narrative that unlike the West, his culture prefers a "virgin, unsullied"—a narrative that his wife complicates by arguing that more women are engaging in premarital sex and "wouldn't marry a man who didn't accept them the way they were" (Al-Daif, *Who's Afraid of Meryl Streep?*, 51). The wife's counterargument not only complicates Rashoud's monolithic narrative about the value of virginity in contemporary Lebanon, but it also unsettles him because he considers her staunch defense of such 'reckless' women as further proof of her own fall from grace.

Disavowing Effeminate Homosexuality

Rashoud's wife's imagined fall from grace, due to her engagement in pre- or extra-marital sexual intercourse, devastates him as it threatens not only his gender identity as a manly man "who must deflower at least one woman," but also his perceptions of himself as a heteronormative, *straight* man, one who has sexual intercourse with women only (by being on top, no less). This is because Rashoud firmly believes that "[i]f someone were to lay a hand on my wife, he'd be violating me, too, in every sense of the word," and that "if another man has penetrated her, he's penetrated me too . . ." (Al-Daif, *Who's Afraid of Meryl Streep?*, 81). Rashoud's conflation of his wife's body with his own brings about his demise. It transforms him—according to his own paranoid logic—from a straight man, who penetrates female subjects, to a feminized "homosexual bottom," who is vicariously penetrated by another, more dominant, man.

Rashoud's reality offers a sharp contrast to his childhood dream of being "*al-malik*," that is, 'the king,' a persona that he had emulated because he believed that a king "possessed as many women as he wanted, and women dreamed of being possessed by him. They all dreamed of being loyal to their husband the king" (Al-Daif, *Who's Afraid of Meryl Streep?*, 89). Now, however, Rashoud must confront the painful reality that he had failed at securing the love and loyalty of even *one* woman—his own wife. His male ego is doubly bruised since he feels betrayed and discarded by a woman who is not even an "*'aya fi-l-jamal*" (Al-Daif, *Tistifil*, 15)—that is, a 'paragon of beauty'—and who should have felt lucky to be married to him. Rashoud's fear of having settled for "less" by marrying his average wife may be contrasted with Habib in *OK, Goodbye*, whose crisis of masculinity is exacerbated by his insecurity that his partner is perhaps too good for him. Habib worries that Hama may be "out of his league" because of her youth, financial independence, and worldliness (Al-Daif, *OK, ma' 'al-salama*, 101). If Rashoud feels emasculated by his wife's sexual transgressions, Habib's emasculation is partially prompted by Hama's avid consumerism and his inability to fund it. In both cases, securing (patriarchal) manhood remains an elusive endeavor.

Rashoud's dread of being perceived as an emasculated homosexual should also be explored in relation to his past experiences as a child who was chastised for choosing female roles in school plays and for engaging in same-sex amorous behavior. Rashoud recalls his mother's concerns about his masculinity and sexual orientation as a child, an adolescent, and even an adult male. Stumbling upon him and his friends in the midst of reenacting a romantic scene they had seen on television—where Rashoud had joyfully played the role of the female lover—Rashoud's mother is bewildered and enraged. Rashoud remembers his scandalized mother hitting him with "unforgettable brutality" for letting his "fiancé" (a man) kiss him on the mouth (Al-Daif, *Who's Afraid of Meryl Streep?*, 46). The flashback about Rashoud's gender nonconformity as a teenager is neither incidental nor insignificant. It invites the reader to consider the potential fluidity of his gender and sexual identity, thus deconstructing his heteronormative masculinity. In other words, it is not implausible that Rashoud's mother may have disrupted the flourishing of his same-sex desires by forcing him into compulsory heterosexuality instead of allowing him to fully explore his gender and sexual identity—even in play. As David Morgan argues, "If we see gender as a process rather than as a thing, then family relationships represent an important site where people do gender" (Morgan, 232). Since "[t]he fear of being seen as a sissy dominates the cultural definitions of manhood" (Kimmel, 131), Rashoud's mother may have aborted his attempts to "do gender" (and sexuality) differently by insisting that he *act* like a proper straight man. At the very least, she conflates homosexuality with femininity and instills in her son much fear and loathing for both. The "socially masculinized" Rashoud must, therefore, constantly prove his straight masculinity since he learned at an early age of the punitive consequences of acting like the "gay sissy man" his mother detests. His vicarious penetration by his wife's past or present lovers thus threatens to confirm the inescapable charge of effeminate homosexuality.

Rashoud's vivid memories about his mother's invasive search for evidence of his "deviant" sexuality are numerous. He recalls her irrational annoyance at his preference to play in goal during soccer matches, since it put him at the receiving end of the action:

> She assumed that I was not the male *doing* the deed but the female having it *done to* her. She got so carried away that she recalled the days I used to play soccer with my classmates, noting how I only liked to play the goalie position! [. . .] In my mother's mind, what connected a goalie and a female was the fact that they were both targets, about to be penetrated by something, and waiting for that something to happen while others initiated it. . . .What a sick imagination! (Al-Daif, *Who's Afraid of Meryl Streep?*, 47)

Rashoud's references to his mother's qualms about his proclivity for being penetrated as a child, and his emotional reactions to her accusations, help further explain his obsessive fear of being penetrated as an adult. His homophobia and sexism are heavily intertwined, for he has learned that his status as a real man cannot be established without disavowing both femininity and homosexuality, which are viewed as inextricable by the dominant culture that his mother enforces. As Michael Kimmel argues, "Women and gay men become the 'other' against which heterosexual men project their identities, against whom they stack the decks so as to compete in a situation in which they will always win, so that by suppressing them, men can stake a claim for their own manhood" (Kimmel, 280). Following Kimmel, Rashoud attempts to constantly reaffirm his hypermasculine persona as a means of distancing himself from the haunting stigma of the homosexual man, whom he sees as emasculated.[7] It is not surprising that he actively embraces a hegemonic, heterosexual masculinity, one that he must rigorously maintain through his social interactions, since "gender is always a doing, though not a doing by a subject who might be said to preexist the deed" (Butler, 25). Rashoud's fear of being labeled as gay is reminiscent of the anxiety experienced by the narrator Rashid in Al-Daif's novelized biography, *How the German Came to His Senses*. When Rashid's friend Nasr misinterprets Rashid's reference to Helfer as "*mithli*," (which could mean 'gay' or 'like me,' depending on the context), and assumes that Rashid is referring to Helfer as being gay "*like* [him]," Rashid is terrified by the miscommunication and swiftly disavows any connections to homosexuality. He professes, "Mine was the haste of a man soiled by impurity as I disavowed my connection and clarified the matter. I wanted not a trace of doubt to linger in his mind" (Al-Daif, *How the German Came to His Senses*, 7). Rashid's emotional response to his friend's misunderstanding and his use of the terms "soiled" and "impurity" highlight the association of homosexuality with "filth" and depravity in the dominant Lebanese imaginary.

Speaking of filth, in *Who's Afraid of Meryl Streep?*, Rashoud's mother continues to fret about the questionable stains of semen that she finds "on the backside" of his underwear, which make her "doubt [his] masculinity," well beyond his childhood and adolescent years (Al-Daif, *Who's Afraid of Meryl Streep?*, 46). She considers the stains as evidence of his (allegedly passive and dirty) homosexuality. Rashoud's monitoring of his wife's transgressive body mirrors his mother's surveillance of his suspect homosexual body. Like his mother, whom he accuses of having a pathological imagination, he is fixated on collecting any empirical evidence that would help confirm his verdicts regarding the sexual deviance of *other* bodies. After all, as Connell argues, "A specific masculinity is not constituted in isolation, but in relation to other masculinities and to femininities" (Connell, "A Very Straight Gay: Masculinity, Homosexual Experience, and the Dynamics of Gender," 737). Rashoud seeks to compensate for his alleged "lack of masculinity" by actively partaking in the dominant phallic order in his everyday practices. However, his private and public participation in the phallic order becomes increasingly difficult as the novel progresses.

Experiencing the Degradation of the Phallic Order

As Rashoud goes through life, abiding by and defending the heteronormative cultural norms he has inherited, he insists that he is merely a bystander in a patriarchal gender order that has been dictated by biology, religion, and tradition. In other words, he never admits, let alone reflects on, his complicity in the perpetuation of masculinist ideals that hurt both men and women. In fact, Rashoud even expresses dismay that some of the men in his life abuse their male power and privilege. He recounts with disgust how his friend shamelessly bragged about disciplining his wife by "grab[bing] her by the hair, flip[ping] her over, and ram[ming] it into her just like that!" For Rashoud, talking publicly about such inhumane behavior is "shameful" and "unacceptable" (Al-Daif, *Who's Afraid of Meryl Streep?*, 44). However, the novel exposes Rashoud's hypocrisy with regard to his complicity in embracing and legitimizing a phallocentric masculinity through his own interactions with women. When his wife refuses to give him fellatio, he is less concerned with her refusal to perform the act than by his conclusion that she denied *him* specifically. He vividly recounts the brutal scene in which he forced his wife into obeying him, thus unwittingly reproducing his friend's violent behavior:

Yes, I forced her, brutally, and without reservation, because one time at least, a man must prove to his woman that he is a man, especially if he can prove it without causing harm or pain . . . a man must thrust himself into his wife, into one of those spots she protects with such vigilance, so that she will feel her husband is a real man in every meaning of the word and that he is powerful and his might is justified and firmly established . . . God created man stronger than woman for a purpose, and that purpose manifests itself on precisely these occasions (Al-Daif, *Who's Afraid of Meryl Streep?*, 106).

Rashoud's behavior demonstrates his internalized belief that "real manhood" is directly linked to a man's ability to sexually overpower his female partner. In other words, he brags not merely about virility or sexual prowess as proofs of manhood, but rather about a man's willingness to enact "aggressive degradation" (Beneke, 567). He justifies marital rape by denying its potential damage and by appealing to religious ideology. For Rashoud, God designed men as physically superior so they can subdue women inside and outside the bedroom. As Connell notes, men who attack women "feel they are entirely justified [. . .] they are authorized by an ideology of supremacy" (Connell, *Masculinities*, 83).

However, the phallic order does not reign supreme in *Who's Afraid of Meryl Streep?* despite Rashoud's illusions of grandiosity, with their expectations of yielding female compliance in the "battlefield of the bedroom." Rather, Rashoud's wife subjects him to sexual humiliation by utilizing against him his own weapon: his penis. Feeling enraged for being forced into giving him fellatio, she bewilders him by forcefully spitting his semen, which he refers to as, "that fluid God created for her to receive, like a holy receptacle," into his own mouth (Al-Daif, *Who's Afraid of Meryl Streep?*, 107). By doing so, she desecrates his manhood and literally gives him a taste of his own medicine. Rashoud admits to feeling violated by his wife. He exclaims, "I did not feel dirty, but I felt something deeper than that, like having been despoiled, and I felt that I had been exposed to rape" (Al-Daif, *Who's Afraid of Meryl Streep?*, 108). Rashoud thus experiences, firsthand, a tiny taste of what it feels like to be sexually violated; he also confronts the limitations of his aggressive display of manhood in the face of subversive femininity. His wife's swift retaliation against sexual assault reiterates Connell's assertion that "some bodies are more than recalcitrant, they disrupt and subvert the social arrangements in to which they are invited" (Connell, *Masculinities*, 58). By using his penis as a punitive tool, Rashoud's wife forces him to experience his phallocentric masculinity as a double-edged sword that can be mobilized to sexually degrade him. By forcing him to experience a fraction of what it feels like to be "raped," she also destabilizes "rape" as something that is exclusively done to women by men, or the idea that it is only women's bodies that can become subject to being "despoiled."

Al-Daif explores (and explodes) the myths of penis-centered masculinity in *OK, Goodbye* in a way that both converges and diverges from its treatment in *Who's Afraid of Meryl Streep?*. From the outset of the novel, the sixty-year-old Habib learns that he must forgo everything he had learned about the (exaggerated) benefits of penetrative sexual intercourse with regard to pleasing women sexually and gaining their admiration. After he repeatedly fails to confirm his masculinity by ensuring that Hama reaches orgasm during sex, Hama informs him that she is incapable of having an orgasm through penetration—no matter how long he manages to stay erect and active (Al-Daif, *OK, ma' 'al-salama*, 68). When Hama finally experiences an orgasm, after Habib performs oral sex on her, he is so overjoyed that he "cries from happiness" (Al-Daif, *OK, ma' 'al-salama*, 74). Like Rashoud, Habib is initially misguided about pleasing women in the bedroom. Unlike Rashoud, however, Habib acknowledges the limitations of upholding a phallocentric masculinity, and he permits himself to be sexually attentive and vulnerable with his female partner—at least in the privacy of their bedroom.

It is important to note that Rashoud's misguided enactment of a penis-centered masculinity is not restricted to his wife or former lovers. Rather, he victimizes unwitting outsiders, such as the seamstress whom he lures into his home under the false pretext that the curtains need to be repaired—before proceeding to molest her. What makes Rashoud's behavior even more disturbing is the fact that he is convinced that the seamstress desperately longed to have sex with him. When he first meets the seamstress, a conservative single woman who wears the hijab, he concludes that she must be sexually repressed based on her appearance and their brief conversation. He confidently states that "[s]he was no doubt shaken by the fact that my wife and I were newlyweds, that we could enjoy each other as we pleased [. . .] whereas she was unmarried and dying of a desire that could not be consummated" (Al-Daif, *Who's Afraid of Meryl Streep?*, 20). More specifically, as he gazes at the seamstress, whom he accuses of ogling him and his wife, he concludes that "she blushed in a way that was concerning. It was not the kind of blushing associated with shyness" and that "Perhaps she was jealous of [his] wife and wanted to be in her place" (Al-Daif, *Who's Afraid of Meryl Streep?*, 20). Since he mis/interprets the seamstress's body as a lusting body, one that specifically longs to be sexually touched by him, it is no surprise that the narrator finds it not only legitimate but almost dutiful of him to sexually *liberate* her. In his discussion of rape, Tim Beneke writes,

I have suggested that men sometimes become obsessed with images of women, that become a substitute for sexual feeling, that sexual feeling becomes externalized and out of control and is given an undifferentiated identity in the appearance of women's bodies. It is a process of projection in which one blurs one's own desire with her imagined, projected desire (Beneke, 566).

Beneke's observations apply to Rashoud's interaction with the seamstress. Rashoud projects his own sexual feelings onto the image of the seamstress's allegedly desiring body, the body that is "asking for it," and he blurs his own sexual desires with her *imagined* desire. He even professes that her predicament made him "so sad [he] kept wondering how [he] could possibly help her!" (Al-Daif, *Who's Afraid of Meryl Streep?*, 21). It is no surprise, then, that he naturalizes the act of sexually assaulting her under the pretext of sexual emancipation and reciprocity—which exposes his moral double standards and his class bias. While he himself will not marry a "sullied" woman, he finds it legitimate to defile a woman of lower socioeconomic status and who comes from a conservative background no less. Even when the seamstress falls unconscious when he gropes her, he assumes that her inert body is an indication that she must be at "the stage of ecstasy at the peak of orgasm" (Al-Daif, *Who's Afraid of Meryl Streep?*, 22). Rashoud's misinterpretation of the seamstress's body parallels his failure to read his wife's body. In both cases, he inflicts harm rather than pleasure—and he does not find the validation he seeks with regards to asserting his sexual prowess. In both cases, he faces not only sexual rejection but also retaliatory violence.

When the seamstress's brothers find out about Rashoud's crime, they threaten to kill him after he refuses to financially compensate them for dishonoring their sister. In one tragicomic confrontation, her older brother whips Rashoud with his belt, slaps him, and disarms him of the knife he brandishes. As he leaves the wounded Rashoud, he tells him to "shove [the knife] up [his] ass!" (Al-Daif, *Who's Afraid of Meryl Streep?*, 74–75), as if symbolically sodomizing him and confirming his worst fear of embodying the effeminate man he reads as the homosexual. Rashoud is publically transformed—at the hands of "manlier men"—from a privileged predator to an emasculated prey.

Conclusion

Al-Daif's writings on gender and sexuality should be situated within a larger corpus of war and postwar novels that have drawn attention to Lebanese 'gender trouble' in its various permutations. Many novels set during the Lebanese Civil War have provided complex engagements with hegemonic masculinity and its toxic effects on men and women. Novels that explore the de/construction of dominant masculinities in war-torn Lebanon include, but are not limited to, Ghada Samman's *Bayrut '75* (1974; *Beirut '75*, 1975) and *Kawabis Bayrut* (1977; *Beirut Nightmares*, 1997), Hanan al-Shaykh's *Hikayat Zahra* (1980; *The Story of Zahra*, 1986), Hoda Barakat's *Hajar al-dahik* (1990; *Stone of Laughter*, 1995), and Elias Khoury's *al-Jabal al-saghir* (1977; *Little Mountain*, 1989) and *Yalu* (2002; *Yalo*, 2008).[8] In these novels, the reader often witnesses the transformation of men from ordinary civilians to militarized subjects who frequently enact hypermasculine identities bolstered by hostile acts such as looting, killing, and rape. By the same token, such novels also demonstrate the potential disempowerment of ageing patriarchs in the face of a new social order that erodes their authority as they become targets of violence, or as their womenfolk take on new responsibilities that are typically associated with men during peaceful times. In a related manner, al-Daif's *Who's Afraid of Meryl Streep?* invites us to consider the possibility that some men, like Rashoud himself, may be struggling to adjust in peacetime Beirut, where killing, looting, and rape are no longer 'viable' options (and may lead to incarceration). Perhaps, many are still dealing with residual violence that they are painfully and slowly 'working out of their system'[9]—sometimes at the expense of women. Furthermore, while they may no longer be bombarded by bombs, many find themselves bombarded by mixed messages—including those perpetuated by a ubiquitous global media—about what it means to assert one's masculinity in a country where women (and men) are increasingly embracing not only new technologies but also hybridized worldviews that defy simple categories such as 'traditional' versus 'modern.'

More recent novels, such as Alexandra Chreiteh's *Dayman Coca-Cola* (2009; *Always Coca-Cola*, 2014) and *'Ali wa-ummuhu al-rusiya* (2010; *Ali and his Russian Mother*, 2015), have focused less on the spectacular violence of war and more on the mundane violence of hegemonic normalcy. While Chreiteh's *Always Coca-Cola* acknowledges the lingering scars of war, the novel primarily explores the psychic anxieties of young women who must navigate a multiplicity of destructive discourses—propagated by family, local culture, and consumer capitalism—regarding what it means (and what it takes) to be a 'good' woman.[10] In a similar vein, even though *Ali and his Russian Mother* is set during the July 2006 war, the novel seems less concerned with the imminent destruction caused by the Israeli invasion than with the character Ali's construction of homosexual identity and masculinity.[11] As both Chreiteh's and the aforementioned novels demonstrate, gender upheaval is constantly taking place—literally and literarily—within and beyond the frame of war. Al-Daif's writings on gender and sexuality therefore contribute to and engage with an existing (and expanding) corpus of literary texts that have explored the destabilization of gender and sexuality in contemporary Lebanon, either directly or tangentially.

Like many of Al-Daif's first-person narrators, including those of *OK, Goodbye* and *How the German Came to His Senses*, in *Who's Afraid of Meryl Streep?* Rashoud finds himself in testing situations that force him to confront the consequences of performing a dominant masculinity in a postwar context, and to recognize that fostering more positive gender relations "may well require a de-structuring of the self, an experience of gender vertigo, as part of the process" (Connell, *Gender* 91). In the face of shifting gender identities and material realities, Rashoud recognizes that the construction of dominant masculinity is a progressively precarious undertaking. While he articulates a masculinist discourse that "naturalizes difference," "imputes male superiority," and "posits gender-determined mental propensities" (Arnowitz, 316–17), his first-person point of view is gradually undermined by the plot, which demonstrates "the material and spiritual costs of maleness" (Arnowitz, 320) and exposes the tenuousness of dominant masculinity as a lived reality.

Not only is Rashoud brutally stripped of his reified beliefs with respect to gender, sexuality, and the body but he also experiences the darker side of hegemonic masculinity as he becomes subject to perpetual anxiety, sexual humiliation, rejection, stigmatization, and even physical abuse—all of which are generally associated with female victimhood. By the time his wife has walked out the door, Rashoud resembles a *deflated* Superman whose claim to superiority has been debunked through physical, emotional, and mental defeat. He has experienced the crumbling of patriarchal ideals firsthand and has been sufficiently humbled by other men *and* women. Rashoud's identity crisis transcends the private realm of its narrator, however. The novel speaks to broader conversations that are taking place in Lebanon and elsewhere in the Arab world, including those about the significance of female chastity and the connection of female embodiment to (or its disarticulation from) the nation; the shifting notions of gender and sexuality and their impact on social interactions between men and women; and the 'price' of embracing, resisting, or simply adapting to our increasingly globalized and hybridized realities, with all the opportunities and vulnerabilities they engender. In typical Al-Daif fashion, however, *Who's Afraid of Meryl Streep?* sets up a platform for engaging with such complex discourses but it resists offering any simplified, definitive answers—particularly with regard to the ever-elusive question "what makes a man?"[12] Through its complex construction of plot and characterization, the novel does posit, however, that the "Arab Superman" has lost some of his power—and much of his popularity—in contemporary Lebanon.

Notes

1   This chapter refers to the 2014 English translation by Haydar and Sinno, unless noted otherwise.

2   It is important to emphasize that this chapter does not perceive 'hegemonic masculinity' as a fixed, homogenous or unchangeable trait. On the contrary, its analysis of Al-Daif's narrators reveals the myths and contradictions associated with the *process* of performing masculinity and the contestability and mutability of this process. For more information regarding R.W. Connell's clarification and reformulation of the concept of hegemonic masculinity, see Connell's article "Hegemonic Masculinity: Rethinking the Concept," which reiterates the dynamism of hegemonic masculinity and places emphasis on the importance of exploring the embodiment and contradictions within it.

3   Like many of his compatriots, Rashoud flaunts Lebanese society's 'openness' and its championing of women's rights while at the same time demanding that women act "*dumn al-hudud*" (within boundaries). As Joumana Haddad notes, propagators of this narrative of Lebanese exceptionalism often justify their exaltation of the country's progressiveness by comparing it with more conservative Arab countries such as Saudi Arabia, so they may bask in their "lame illusory satisfaction" (Haddad, 53–54). While Lebanon does generally grant women more rights than some of its Arab neighbors, it remains largely patriarchal in terms of official laws and dominant cultural mores. As an example, Lebanese civil law grants men, but not women, the right to transfer their nationality to their children. With regard to cultural norms, moral double standards still exist in ways that are comparable with the rest of the Arab world. For instance, it is considered acceptable, even commendable, for men to engage in out-of-wedlock sexual experiences, whereas their female counterparts are generally expected to remain (or appear to be) chaste until marriage. Haddad refers to this social phenomenon as "sexual hypocrisy syndrome" (Haddad, 66–67).

4   Ironically, Rashoud's wife is left unnamed in the narrative. While she is 'nameless,' in Rashoud's account, the plot and story indicate that she has a strong voice—one that her husband fails to silence.

5   Other scholars have also argued that globalization remains an incomplete, unfinished, and contested process in different parts of the world. Examples include but are not limited to Abu-Lughod 1991; Croucher 2004; Pieterse 1995; Robertson 1995; and Scholte 2000.

6   Al-Daif's novel *Lirning inglish* (1998; *Learning English*, 2007) also explores the trials and tribulations of its male character with learning the English language, as well as his struggles at navigating both traditional values and liberal ideals in contemporary Lebanon.

7   Expressing excessively 'effeminate' behavior is still considered by many Lebanese, including homosexuals, as unacceptable and shameful. As Sofian Merabet (2006, 216) notes in his study of queer spaces in Beirut, '[t]his eagerness to be different from—i.e. better than—the effeminate [*tante*] leads to a peculiar kind of homophobia that, I believe, is internal to the homosexual sphere in Lebanon as well as successively internalized by a great number of its protagonists.'

8   Rashid Al-Daif's novel *Fusha mustahdafa bayna al-nu'as wa-l-nawm* (1983; *A Passage to Dusk*, 2001) is also an example of such (post)war novels that demonstrate the destabilization of gender in the context of armed conflict.

9   The author wishes to acknowledge Mohja Kahf's contribution in helping her think more thoroughly about residual violence as it relates to Lebanese masculinities.

10   For a detailed study of the novel's depiction of the construction of gender in a globalized but socially conservative Lebanon, see Sinno (2015).

11   For a detailed study of Chreiteh's exploration of homosexuality in *Ali and his Russian Mother*, see Sinno (2017).

12   I borrow this expression from Ken Seigneurie's and Gary Schmidt's edited volume, *What Makes a Man?: Sex Talk in Beirut and Berlin*, which includes the English translations of Al-Daif's *How the German Came to His Senses* and Helfer's *The Queering of the World*, in addition to scholarly essays about these texts.

Works Cited

Abu-Lughod, Janet. "Going Beyond Global Babble." In *Culture, Globalization and the World-System*, edited by Anthony D. King, 131–44. Binghamton, NY: State University of New York, 1991.

Aghacy, Samira. *Masculine Identity and the Fiction of the Arab East since 1967*. Syracuse, NY: Syracuse University Press, 2009.

Arnowitz, Stanley. "My Masculinity." In *Constructing Masculinity*, edited by Maurice Berger, Brian Walls, and Simon Watson, 307–20. New York and London: Routledge, 1995.

Beneke, Tim. "Men on Rape." In *Men's Lives*, ninth edition, edited by Michael S. Kimmel and Michael A. Messner, 563–68. Boston, MA: Pearson, 2013.

Bhabha, Homi K. "Are you a man or a mouse?" In *Constructing Masculinities*, edited by Maurice Berger, Brian Walls, and Simon Watson, 57–65. New York and London: Routledge, 1995.

Butler, Judith. *Gender Trouble: Feminism and the Subversion of Identity*. New York: Routledge, 1990.

Chreiteh, Alexandra. *'Ali wa ummuhu al-rusiya*. Beirut: Arab Scientific Publishers. English translation by Michelle Hartman, *Ali and His Russian Mother*. Northampton: Interlink, 2015.

———. *Dayman Coca-Cola*. Beirut: Arab Scientific Publishers. English translation by Michelle Hartman, *Always Coca-Cola*. Northampton: Interlink, 2012.

Connell, R.W. "Globalization, Imperialism, and Masculinities." In *Handbook of Studies on Men & Masculinities*, edited by Michael Kimmel, Jeff Hearn, and R.W. Connell, 71–89. London: Sage Publications, 2005.

———. "Hegemonic Masculinity: Rethinking the Concept." *Gender and Society* 19, no. 6 (2005): 829–59.

———. *Masculinities*. Second edition. Berkeley, CA and Los Angeles: University of California Press, 2005.

———. *Gender*. Malden, MA: Blackwell Publishers, 2002.

———. "Masculinity Politics on a World Scale." In *The Masculinities Reader*, edited by Stephen Whitehead and Frank J. Barret, 369–74. Cambridge: Polity Press, 2001.

———. "A Very Straight Gay: Masculinity, Homosexual Experience, and the Dynamics of Gender." *American Sociological Review*, 57, no. 6 (1992): 735–51.

———. *Gender and Power*. Stanford, CA: Stanford University Press, 1987.

Croucher, Sheila. *Globalization and Belonging: The Politics of Identity in a Changing World*. New York: Rowman and Littlefield Publishers, 2004.

Al-Daif, Rashid. *OK, ma' 'al-salama*. Beirut: Dar al-Saqi, 2013.

———. *'Awdat al-almani ila rushdih*. Beirut: Dar al-Saqi, English translation by Ken Seigneurie, *How the German Came to His Senses*. In *What Makes a Man?: Sex Talk in Beirut and Berlin*, translated by Ken Seigneurie and Gary Schmidt, 1–54. Austin, TX: University of Texas at Austin, 2006.

———. *Tistifil Meryl Streep*. Beirut: Riad El-Rayyes Books. English translation by Paula Haydar and Nadine Sinno, *Who's Afraid of Meryl Streep?*. Austin, TX: University of Texas at Austin, 2014.

———. *Fusha mustahdafa bayna al-nu'as wa-l-nawm*. Beirut: Mukhtarat. English translation by Nirvana Tanoukhi, *A Passage to Dusk*. Austin, TX: University of Texas Press, 2001.

Featherstone, Mike, Scott Lash, and Roland Robertson, editors. *Global Modernities*. London: Sage Publications, 1995.

Goffman, Erving. *Stigma: Notes on the Management of Spoiled Identity*. New York: Prentice-Hall, 1974.

Haddad, Joumana. *Superman Is an Arab: On God, Marriage, and Other Disastrous Inventions*. London: Westbourne Press, 2012.

Hage, Ghassan. "Migration, Marginalized Masculinity and Dephallicization: A Lebanese Villager's Expereince." In *Sexuality in the Arab World*, edited by Samir Khalaf and Jon Gagnon. London and Beirut: Saqi, 107–30, 2006.

Khalaf, Roseanne Saad. "Breaking the Silence: What AUB Students Really Think about Sex." In *Sexuality in the Arab World*, edited by Samir Khalaf and Jon Gagnon, 175–98. London and Beirut: Saqi, 2006.

Kimmel, Michael S. "Masculinity as Homophobia: Fear, Shame, and Silence in the Construction of Gender Identity." In *Theorizing Masculinities*, edited by Harry Brod and Michael Kaufman, 119–41. London: Sage Publications, 1994.

Merabet, Sofian. "Creating Queer Space in Beirut: Zones of Encounter with the Lebanese male Homosexual Sphere." In *Sexuality in the Arab World*, edited by Samir Khalf and Jon Gagnon, 199–242. London and Beirut: Saqi, 2006.

Morgan, David H.J. "Family, Gender and Masculinities." In *The Masculinities Reader*, edited by Stephen Whitehead and Frank J. Barret, 223–32. Cambridge: Polity Press, 2001.

Noble, Jean Bobby. *Masculinities without Men?: Female Masculinity in Twentieth-Century Fictions*. Vancouver, BC: University of British Columbia, 2004.

Peteet, Julie. "Male Gender and Rituals of Resistance in the Palestinian Intifada: A Cultural Politics of Violence." In *Imagined Masculinities: Male Identity and Culture in the Modern Middle East*, edited by Mai Ghoussoub and Emma Sinclair-Webb, 103–26. London: Saqi Books, 2000.

Pieterse, Jan Nederveen. "Globalization as Hybridization." In *Global Modernities*, edited by Mike Featherstone, Scott Lash, and Roland Robertson, 45–68. London: Sage Publications, 1995.

Robertson, Roland. "Glocalization: Time-Space and Homogeneity-Heterogeneity." In *Global Modernities*, edited by Mike Featherstone, Scott Lash, and Roland Robertson, 25–44. London: Sage Publications, 1995.

Salamandra, Christa. "Chastity Capital: Hierarchy and Distinction in Damascus." In *Sexuality in the Arab World*, edited by Samir Khalaf and Jon Gagnon, 152–62. London and Beirut: Saqi, 2006.

Scholte, Jan Aart. *Globalization: A Critical Introduction*. New York: St. Martin's Press, 2000.

Seigneurie, Ken. "Irony and Counter-Irony In Rashid al-Daif's *How the German Came to His Senses*." In *What Makes a Man?: Sex Talk in Beirut and Berlin*, translated by Ken Seigneurie and Gary Schmidt, 171–97. Austin, TX: University of Texas at Austin, 2015.

Sinno, Nadine. "Crushing the Bones of the Other: Disability, Ethnicity, and Homosexuality in Rashid al-Daif's *Sikreeda's Cat* and Alexandra Chreiteh's *Ali and his Russian Mother*." *Critique: Studies in Contemporary Fiction* 58, no. 3 (2017): 258–75.

———. "Milk and Honey, Tabbouleh, and Coke: Orientalist, Local, and Global Discourses in Alexandra Chreiteh's *Always Coca-Cola*." *Middle Eastern Literatures* 18, no. 2 (2015): 122–43.

Tomlinson, John. "Globalized Culture: The Triumph of the West?" In *Culture and Global Change*, edited by Tracey Skeleton and Tim Allen, 22–29. London and New York: Routledge, 1999.

Whitehead, Stephen M., and Frank J. Barret. "The Sociology of Masculinity." In *The Masculinities Reader*, edited by Stephen Whitehead and Frank J. Barret, 1–26. Cambridge: Polity Press, 2001.

4

CRISES OF MASCULINITY IN HUDA BARAKAT'S WAR LITERATURE

Kifah Hanna

Introduction

In her debut novel, *Hajar al-dahik* (*The Stone of Laughter*, 1990), Huda Barakat minutely traces the traumatic impact of sexual self-discovery as her main character, Khalil, struggles with his newly awakened homo-erotic desires.[1] In *Ahl al-hawa* (*Disciples of Passion*, 1993), she shifts her attention to heterosexual violence through the narrative of her unnamed protagonist's traumatic, and eventually murderous, recognition of his lov-er's androgyny. Finally, in *Sayidi wa habibi* (My Master, My Lover, 2004) she explores the violence inherent in normative masculinity through her story of Wadi''s enforced adaptation to its strictures. The thread that ties these three novels together and exhibits the crisis of masculinity in Barakat's war literature is the narration of madness and violence in asso-ciation with rising forms of masculinities against unravelling social and national paradigms. This chapter examines Barakat's representation of masculinities during the Lebanese Civil War (1975–1990) through a close reading of *The Stone*, *Disciples*, and *Master*. I investigate Barakat's focus on representing marginalized male antiheroes as embodiments of the con-tradictions of gender and sexuality during the civil war. By positioning the male psyche as central to her exploration of the human in response to vio-lence, Barakat traces a (male) subject defined by traumatic sociopolitical experiences rather than by essential gender designations. The disman-tling of the social order that accompanied the war affords Barakat's male antiheroes the opportunity to release social, sexual, and political energies that had hitherto been repressed under Lebanon's peacetime patriarchal heteronormative economy. By narrating trauma and violence, the author unravels the emergence of intimate estrangement or alienation through her attention to masculinity and sexuality.

Barakat's employment of sexuality as the main framework to explore this pioneering subject matter demands a reconfiguration of this discourse in Arabic literary criticism. Revolving almost entirely around representations of women in contemporary Arabic literature, such discourse fails to account for—and, indeed, often explicitly represses or disavows questions of—male sexuality (whether heterosexual, homosexual, or androgynous) in the canon. The last few decades, however, have witnessed the rise of studies of masculinities in the Middle East that aim to remedy this neglect. One of the most prominent works in this field is Samira Aghacy's *Masculine Identity in the Fiction of the Arab East since 1967* (2009). In this groundbreaking book, Aghacy offers a detailed study of the construction of masculine gender and sexual identities in Arabic literary fiction in relation to the feminine and as reflective of recent social, political, and economic transformations in the region.[2] Crucially, she contests the dominant Arab gender discourse under which femininity and masculinity are seen as polar opposites, and which interprets sexuality in terms of innate biological differences (Aghacy, 1–2). Her readings revolve, rather, around a more flexible, socially mediated sense of masculine identity formation, which allows for precise analyses of types ranging from the "domineering" to the "precarious, unsure, and less typical, nearly feminine [. . .] struggling in a hyper-aggressive world of tyranny and wars" in her primary texts (Aghacy, 16). This critical framework models an engagement with questions of gender and sexuality attuned to non-normative identifications.

Building on Aghacy's work, I turn to Judith Butler, especially *Gender Trouble*, in my exploration of non-normative (heterosexual, homosexual, and androgynous) masculine gender and sexual identities as represented in Barakat's war literature. I draw inspiration from Butler's thesis that gendered identities are "constituted in time" through a "*stylized repetition of acts,*" and that, against the forms of normative heterosexuality produced and policed in patriarchal societies, new gender and sexual identities may emerge when such societies are disrupted or destabilized (Butler, 191). The Lebanese Civil War constituted immense *social* as well as political disruptions, and, with hegemonic masculinity under threat, new gender and sexual identities could and did emerge in this national milieu. Reflected vividly in contemporary Lebanese feminist literature, I aim to explore the question of masculinity within the context of war and sexuality. I maintain that Barakat develops a sophisticated politics of gender and sexuality as pertaining to traumatized Lebanese masculinity. Rather than sidelining questions of Lebanese femininity or feminism, this emphasis actually expands the remit of literary feminism by adducing subordinate or minority masculinities as a novel venue for its inquiries into gender and sexuality during war.

Masculinity, Madness, and Sexuality

In *How to Do the History of Homosexuality*, David Halperin argues the historicist case and reads the subjectivity of sexuality both within the "alterity of the past as well as the irreducible cultural and historical specificities of the present" (Halperin, *How*, 17). Paul Amar underscores Halperin's approach to the subjectivity of sexuality "in the experience of possession by demons that are generated by a community [. . .] the collective experience of [. . .] violence, and even immersive humiliation" (Amar, 55). Barakat's novels exhibit such elements of violence and humiliation, past and present, in her exploration of male sexuality in Lebanon. Her male characters are thrown into a world of repressive heteronormativity, and, as they experience forms of unconventional love and sexuality (whether heterosexual, homosexual, or androgynous), they at some point in the development of the plot succumb to states of madness and hysteria. These culminate in final violent acts as their only means of sexual, social, and political liberation. It is the particular social and political contexts of the Lebanese Civil War that mediate her characters' psychic breaks and exhibit a crisis of traditional forms of masculinity.

Driven by the imperative of working through the tensions of love and loss, belonging and estrangement, life and death, Barakat delves into the innermost recesses of her characters' psyches in search of that moment of madness—a sublime, revelatory moment when the pre-given binaries and hierarchies that structure social life dissolve.[3] She affirms this literary aptitude in her statement: "In moments of extreme tension, we experience madness" (Rakha, n.p.). Writing from "the place of madness" (quoted in Fer, 176), Barakat underscores marginalized masculinity, especially homosexuality, as a site where the male/female binary collapses. This gives her narratives a unique dream-like quality, renders them dreamworlds that trace what Jennifer Mundy describes as "path[s] beyond the potentially confining aspects of conventional desire and identity" (Mundy, 53). The paths of non-normative, marginalized Lebanese masculinity are strewn with the violent impositions of conventionality.

Such violence is evident in the critical reception of Barakat's novels as well. Although *The Stone* won the prestigious al-Naqid award for a first novel on its publication in 1990, and is now internationally recognized as one of the best novels about the Lebanese Civil War, it has received only sporadic attention among Arab critics due to its controversial placement of a young gay man, Khalil, at its very heart. Conscious of the provocative nature of her subject matter, Barakat claims that although "[t]here is a gay man [. . .] it's not shocking because he narrates a real sentiment of love" (quoted in Whitaker, 99). Whatever the resulting attitude of the critical establishment toward the novel, it seems to me that Barakat's aversion to shock for its own sake, or for publicity, is genuine, and her real intention is to portray the gradual unfurling of homosexual desire and love with a sensitivity and sophistication that have rarely been afforded in contemporary Arabic literature.

In *The Stone*, Barakat, teasing her (potentially antagonistic) reader into sympathetic identification, narrates Khalil's sexual self-discovery slowly but steadily—by increments, as it were. His desires first surface in a dream scenario where Ra'fat, a man he knows only by voice from his calls to a nightly radio program, seduces him: "Ra'fat came close to Khalil and pushed back a long strand of hair that was fluttering across his face. [. . . Khalil] was more sure that he was beautiful and ready for love" (Barakat, *Stone*, 68). Soon, Naji, Khalil's first love, appears in the dream in a sexual wish-fulfilment fantasy. The dream ends abruptly with a sudden shock when Khalil finds himself "standing next to his bed [. . .] drowning in his cold sweat," with "his pajama bottoms [. . .] clinging between his thighs," and, as he recollects the content of his dream, he succumbs to "a flood of tears" (Barakat, *Stone*, 69). While this outburst might be interpreted as Khalil's lamentation for what has become the impossibility of realizing his desires, its more fundamental cause is the realization of these desires itself—inevitably traumatic in a society which conditions its subjects into believing they are immoral, obscene, and unmanly. Thus begins Barakat's sensitive, sophisticated dialectic of homoerotic desire in confrontation with the strictures and inherited assumptions of a hostile culture.

In *Disciples*, the liminal experience that takes its protagonist to the edge of madness is that of violence rather than repressed desire. Indeed, the novel opens with its unnamed male protagonist recounting a murder with a hallucinatory intensity that befits an act that transgresses the established boundaries of reason, law, and being: "After killing her, I sat down on a high boulder. I closed my eyes for a long spell, keeping them shut until my breathing was calm and regular" (Barakat, *Disciples*, 1). While the "fresh, almost raw, and so near" sky evokes memories of his childhood, it is only through violence as signified by his murder that he can now, for the first time, "occupy [his] own being, the whole of it [. . .] as if [he is] giving birth" to himself (Barakat, *Disciples*, 1–2). Thus brought back to his prehuman existential immediacy, he becomes a "sacred being; a saint," and he is bestowed with a pure knowledge that—liberating him from "fancies," "suffering," and "the tensions of longing"—spurs his "search for wondrous salvation" (Barakat, *Disciples*, 2).

Barakat's nuanced investigation of the issues of madness, irrationality, and hysteria through the figure of the marginalized *male* protagonist in

Disciples comprises a significant novelty in the study of Lebanese masculinities in crisis. She shows that under the pressures of the civil war, the masculine, compelled to internalize the violence that surrounds it, can also become a compromised, fragmented subject-position. In what might be called her allegory of the psychology of war, Barakat suggests male madness, the collapse of the human through violence, as both cause and product of Lebanon's unfolding national crisis.

In *My Master*, Barakat draws on the main thematic strands that run through *The Stone* and *Disciples* to bring her exploration of masculinity and sexuality during the Lebanese Civil War to its culmination. Like her other two antiheroes, Wadi', the central character in this novel, inhabits the dreamworld of the unconscious. There, the desires and violent urges otherwise blotted out of waking life manifest themselves, leading to a radical estrangement from self. On board a ship carrying him and his wife, Samiyah, from Beirut—where his father had been murdered by members of a rival drug cartel—to Cyprus, Wadi', a marijuana trafficker, undergoes a hallucinatory and fearful fever. In direct contrast to the protagonist of *Disciples*, the moment of madness that ensues does not "transform [him] into a saint," but "change[s]" him nevertheless: "I do not know how I became another man. [. . .] I spent my entire life building up my might stone by stone, and now this one night on board the ship has abolished it as if in one blow" (Barakat, *Master*, 121).[4] What he discovers is the underside of the violence through which the *Disciples* protagonist had found a form of inhuman liberation: the vacuum of an identity that had been constructed through violence, and that had indirectly caused his father's death. Wadi' is now emptied "of all he had in the past," with nothing "inside him to replace what he had lost" (Barakat, *Master*, 128).

Stripped of the desires, attachments, and sense of self that constitute individual identity, including his heteronormative self-identification through marriage, Wadi' is now able to comprehend the true nature of his relationship with his current employer, Tariq. Wadi' realizes that "I loved him with an indescribable love," yet he promptly assures us that this love is indescribable not because of its profane or transgressive nature, but rather because it "remains mysterious": "I am yet," he concludes, "to hear someone speak of its like" (Barakat, *Master*, 7). By framing Wadi''s love outside of the conventional heterosexual and homosexual definitions through which such is either authorized or forbidden, Barakat inscribes her protagonist, or the place of madness from which he speaks, as essentially androgynous, as occupying a "mysterious" positionality that precedes conventional gender and sexual designations. Further, by linking what, prior to his exile, had been Wadi''s unwitting interpretation as a masculine, heterosexual subject with his violent past, she suggests the violence inherent in all modes of sociosexual differentiation, categorization, and hierarchization. It is, I would suggest, in search of androgyny as politics that Barakat writes her male antiheroes.

Narrating Love and Desire

At the heart of each of these novels lies an intricate love relationship. None of these, however, even the heterosexual relationships of Wadi', are conventional in the way they are experienced by Barakat's male protagonists. They are, rather, thoroughly mediated by the contexts of national crisis in Lebanon—a context which, involving as it does the crumbling of the social order and the destabilization of gender and sexual hierarchies, allows for the release of hitherto repressed (hetero-, homo-, and androgynous) sexual energies. Accordingly, Barakat's representation of desire and sexuality is reflective of the "pervasive anxiety about masculinity and about men who cannot live up to the grandiose standard of accomplishment and self-actualization" (Aghacy, 131). Such anxieties often cause a revival of traditional cultural and social values in order to reinstate hegemonic forms of masculinity through restabilizing notions of family, religion, and, ultimately, the nation. While this literary aptitude is illustrated in novels such as Rashid Al-Daif's *Who's Afraid of Meryl Streep?* (Aghacy, 157–68), Barakat opts for effecting a literary shift away from what might be called the "heteronormative assumption" dominant in contemporary Arabic literature, and toward a more complex engagement with the multiple forms of (male) sexuality rising in response to trauma and anxiety.

The reception of Khalil, the homosexual protagonist of Barakat's first novel, among Arab critics again stands as an outstanding example of the limitations of the current critical discourse, and the need for reinvigoration. Usually desexualized, and read either in terms of what Aghacy calls his "feminized positionality" or in those of what Mona Fayad calls his "strategic androgyny" rather than his homosexuality, critics have been keen to downplay or contain his significance as the first gay central character in the contemporary canon (Aghacy, 137; Fayad, 162).[5] Both illustrating and exemplifying my intervention in the discourse, my readings of Barakat's novels here seek to restore the hitherto disavowed (homo)sexual, and later androgynous, dimensions of her representations of Lebanese masculinity in crisis.

The Stone opens with Khalil chasing after Naji, "panting" as he tries to catch up with the man for whom his homoerotic desires will soon evolve (Barakat, *Stone*, 3). Thus infused from the outset with what David Halperin, describing "hot" hierarchies within male friendships, calls "an immediate and inescapable aura of eroticism" (Halperin, "How," 99), the novel unfolds as Khalil's dialectic of homosexual awakening in the social and political contexts particular to the Lebanese Civil War. Set at the outbreak of the conflict, the novel finds Khalil struggling to define his gender and sexual identity as the men around him, instinctively conforming to hegemonic models of masculinity, are conscripted into various militias and, by extension, into their own deaths. Alienated from hegemonic masculinity due to his feminine features, yet still insensible of his homosexual inclinations, he finds "the doors of both kinds of manhood [. . .] closed" to him, and thus becomes trapped in a "narrow passing place, in a stagnant, feminine state of submission to a purely vegetable life, just within reach of two very attractive versions of masculinity" (Barakat, *Stone*, 12). And so, he retreats to the private, interior space of his room—a richly metaphorical as well as a physical space—in order to work through the conflicts and contradictions of his identity.

Khalil's room bears multiple overlapping significations. Firstly, it offers him a refuge from the violence and brutality of the war that is starting to rage 'on the outside,' and, more importantly, from the exigency of gendered self-definition in relation to such. Secondly, it suggests, initially, that his retreat is one toward the sort of feminine subject-position associated with domesticity, safety, and exclusion from public life. Given his society's entrenched hierarchization of male over female, Khalil's retreat to the feminine frames his inability to adopt a coherent masculine subjectivity as an implicit adoption of a subordinate gender role. Thirdly, it comprises a site of homosocial interaction between himself and Naji.[6] It is where his highly charged, erotic 'friendship' with Naji is first initiated, but also where—due to the norms of homosociality inscribed in and as this innocent, desexualized space—Khalil is prohibited from expressing his underlying sexual desires. Finally, it is the metaphorical space of Khalil's interiority: a space where the memories, dreams, and desires locked away in his unconscious may be articulated and confronted.

Alongside Khalil, the character of Wadi' in *My Master* signifies transgressive, or at least ambiguous, male sexuality in Barakat's novels as examined here. He, like Khalil, is acutely self-conscious of his own physicality. Short, overweight, and suffering from a retractile testicle, he fails to live up to the internalized image of powerful, assertive, and sexually active Lebanese masculinity in circulation before and especially during the civil war, which saw the rise of what was almost a national cult of male vitality. Struggling to define his gender and sexual identity, Wadi' thus turns to a series of powerful male figures as a compensation mechanism for his own shortcomings—in childhood and adolescence, he forms an unhealthy attachment to Ayoub, which, unreciprocated, leads to despair ("How much I miss Ayoub. Oh lord. I don't want anything from this world but to see his face"), and in later life he unconsciously repeats this process with his employer, Tariq (Barakat, *Master*, 142). While similar circumstances cause Khalil to retreat into interiority in order to work through the challenges of what Halperin terms "personal individuation,"[7] Wadi' does the same upon his exile later in the narrative chronology. At first, he is compelled to rebel against his nature and adopt a strong masculine subject-position in response to the pressures of war. In distinction to *The Stone*, then, Barakat, in *My Master*, interpolates between the realization and acceptance of transgressive desire an account of normative masculinity as false consciousness, as a violent imposition upon the self necessitated by internalized social discourses of gender and sexuality. This adds an important new dimension to her representation of Lebanese masculinity in crisis.

Wadi's attempted adoption of a normative masculine identity pivots on masquerade as a practice of disguising his underlying gender and sexual ambiguity, his male vulnerability.[8] This first occurs in his encounter with Samiyah, his female other—responding to her body with "sheer terror," he is forced to "tame" himself into a relationship of conventional desire with it (Barakat, *Master*, 16). Heterosexuality here manifests as a conscious or willed assumption of heteronormativity, or, in Lacanian terms, as a symbolic relationship with the other that further distances the self from the freeform, thus transgressive, circulation of its real desires. Yet this private assertion of heteronormativity isn't sufficient to ensure Wadi's self-requisite conscription into the country of men—he must also assert and perform his masculinity in the public sphere. He thus joins a group of drug traffickers led by al-Rudiyo, a gangster subculture governed by exaggeratedly homosocial/homophobic discursive and relational norms, and rapidly exceeds even its paranoid performances of hyper-masculinity. His passport into this form of homosociality is sexually explicit language and imagery, and the anatomical preoccupations evident in his use of such language belie what the reader knows is one of the causes of his underlying vulnerability. "I do not sit on tires in order to preserve my testicles," he tells his peers, "I use them," continuing that "my woman asked me to pamper and treasure them as royal testicles should be treated" (Barakat, *Master*, 74). As Aghacy illustrates in her examination of male characters in Lebanese war literature, a man's "awareness of vulnerability intensifies his fear of being viewed as emasculated and plays a crucial role in intensifying his homophobia and his insistence on unequivocal gender dichotomization." Consequently, Aghacy continues, "he adopts a rigidly heterosexual, blatantly homophobic attitude to ward off the feeling that manhood has become a more complicated business, causing immense anxiety for men" (Aghacy, 166). This sense of *anxiety* transpires in Wadi''s employment of humorous remarks to assert his presumed power by evoking conventional perceptions of masculinity through active sexual roles.

Wadi''s narrative thus ends where Khalil's begins, in a retreat to silence and solitude. Like Khalil's, his exile from the physical and psychological violence of his society affords him the opportunity to reflect on himself and on his past relationships with men as a means of understanding his current, deeply traumatized predicament. In Khalil's case, this results in a recognition and eventual affirmation of his homosexuality. Meditating on Youseph one of his love objects, Khalil realizes the depth and permanence of his revulsion to female flesh—in comparison to Youseph, he sees Zahrah, his cousin, as "an old, rotten fish, its eyes covered with a thick film, which still swims around only to send out more rancid smells" (Barakat, *Stone*, 84).[9] Wadi''s case is more complex. Certainly, he at one point experiences a similar revulsion toward Samiyah—"I hate her," he contemplates, "I am filled with disgust when she nestles up to me at night [. . .] I am repulsed when I feel her body quivering in pleasure" (Barakat, *Master*, 143–44). Yet, when he embarks on his inward journey and fully comes to terms with his feelings for Tariq, the pre-definitional sense of 'mysterious' or 'androgynous' love that emerges mediates his renewed sexual desire for his wife. It is not that Barakat is suggesting here a more authentic heterosexuality than that imposed by a heteronormative social order through the overcoming or sublation of homosexual impulses. Rather, she suggests that all sexuality is essentially mysterious, undefinable, undirected—and that by channeling it in conformity to pre-given categories such as 'heterosexual' or 'homosexual,' we are engaged in a form of violence that corrupts its nature and gives rise to the revulsion experienced by Khalil and Wadi'. By liberating himself from the violence of socially imposed self-definitions in terms of these categories, Wadi' is able to reconnect with a sexuality that, indeterminate and freely dispersed across 'male' and 'female' alike, is in itself androgynous. In this way, he becomes the first subject of what might be considered a post-heteronormative future Lebanese society.

As if sensing the impossibility of subjectivities such as those of Khalil and Wadi' in the current sociopolitical order, Barakat closes both their narratives with the literal and figurative disappearance of her protagonists. At the end of *The Stone*, Khalil is left "rising upwards" into the ether while the narrator—now revealed to be, like Barakat, a woman—is consigned the responsibility of "writ[ing]" his disappearance (Barakat, *Stone*, 209). At the end of *My Master*, Wadi', his heart newly opened via the mediation of Tariq, collapses in upon himself when his employer is accused of embezzlement and it becomes evident that the world is as yet too venal to be capable of love. As significant as their presence, the absence of these protagonists marks out a space for the as-yet-unrealizable liberation of gender and sexuality in Lebanon, and in the wider region of the Levant.

Androgynous Subjectivities

At the heart of Barakat's depiction of androgyny is an objection to the normative gender and sexual identifications hegemonically imposed in Lebanese society. This objection is largely in response to forms of social and sexual *repression* which, as Michel Foucault asserts, "operated as a sentence to disappear, but also as an injunction to silence, an affirmation of nonexistence, and, by implication, an admission that there was nothing to say about such [sexual] things, nothing to see, and nothing to know" (Foucault, 4). Exacerbated by the war, it is the oppression of heteronormative masculinity that is of special concern to Barakat, and her 'moments of madness' are those of the destabilization of masculine and feminine subject-positions in response to such oppression. Thematically realized in Barakat's emphasis on non-normative or transgressive sexuality, androgyny is the existential site of liberation in her novels.

Ironically enough, given that the androgyny argument has been mainly mobilized to displace or dispel the impression of this character's homosexuality, Khalil has already been read in such terms by the Arabic critical establishment. For instance, Fayad, in a detailed article entitled "Strategic Androgyny: Passing as Masculine in Barakat's *Stone of Laughter*," has argued that by "refusing to become one [male] or the other [female], Khalil resists gender as a vector of power" (Fayad, 169). The text does indeed give rise to such an interpretation. Reflecting on his separation from his mother and the necessity of adopting a sexual identity at the onset of adolescence, Khalil realizes that "he was of a certain sex and he was of a certain age and that his sex and his age had begun the outward journey," and therefore that "the delight at being *outside* sex" was "lost for ever," having "abandoned" him "before he knew which string he would play to compensate for this loss" (Barakat, *Stone*, 142).[10] But my reading here goes beyond the androgyny argument. As I see it, the 'loss' culminates in Khalil's realization of his love and desire for Naji, and this can only be read as a step toward a non-essentializing, androgynous identity when contextualized with reference to the gradually unfolding dialectic of gender in Barakat's novels studied here. It is essential to foreground Khalil's homosexuality not only because of his significance as the first homosexual central character in contemporary Arabic literature but also in order to fully grasp that for Barakat, the flight from the violence of heteronormativity is a dialectical process with a variety of outcomes all stemming from, and leading back to, androgyny as their existential core.

My analysis here aims to highlight Barakat's overarching project by reading her three protagonists as points on a spectrum of non-normative masculinity. Such reading effects a progressively stronger understanding of gender politics manifest in each of her individual novels, which, in turn, reveals androgyny as the structuring mechanism of her oeuvre as a whole. Having already discussed Khalil and Wadi' in exactly these terms, I now turn to the unnamed protagonist of *Disciples* in order to complete my reading of Barakat's revolutionary cycle.

Disciples opens with its protagonist reacting hysterically to his murder of his female lover. While this symbolic act—a moment of madness— places him outside the boundaries of the human, a closer look at the precise nature of his response is important here. This is because in psychoanalytic theory, hysteria is a pivotal site of gender trouble. As Juliet Mitchell explains in her feminist reassessment of Sigmund Freud and Jacques Lacan, it is in "the body of the hysteric, male and female [that] the feminine protest against the law of the father" occurs (Mitchell, 404). The "law of the father" refers to the Lacanian theory that during early development the father's injunction against oedipal desires and attachments precipitates the child's adoption of a sexual identity defined by clear boundaries between legitimate and illegitimate objects of desire—this injunction prompts the child's entry into what Lacan calls "the symbolic order," a social structuring of desire in relation to familial, gender-based, ethnic, and various other identifications.[11] According to Mitchell, hysteria is a psychic manifestation of rebellion against this patriarchal law, and comprises a destabilization of the categories, such as 'male' and 'female,' by which desire and sexuality are channeled. When read in these terms, the murder committed by *Disciples'* protagonist—a radical rejection of an identity constructed around heteronormative desire—is almost by definition a hysterical act. Moreover, it leads him toward a recognition of androgyny as both the beginning and end of human sexual experience.

Perversely appropriate for an act that deprives the human body of time, the murder induces the protagonist to reflect on the effects of time on the body. "Our bodies," he meditates, "will no longer carry anything but a withered, dried-out sex. Thus do objects neutralize and hide their origins. Woman and man become a single form, one body, their organs and limbs fixed into a single sex" (Barakat, *Disciples*, 49). Like plants and animals that "self-reproduce," having "both male and female organs," he continues, the consummation of an androgynous body relieves the human of its self-division or makes for "a sex liberated from pain" (Barakat, *Disciples*, 63). From this vantage point, he then acquires a new appreciation for actual bodies that seem to suggest the overlapping or combination of gender-distinct attributes such as that of his former lover, whose facial hair; short, unpolished fingernails; and protruding veins had given her a masculine edge, or of the Egyptian diva Um Kulthum, whose lack of "prettiness appropriate to a woman's face" and voice "simultaneously" that "of a woman and a man" rendered her appealingly "asexual" (Barakat, *Disciples*, 63, 64). But this appreciation only comes to the protagonist retrospectively, as a working-through of the heteronormative fears and anxieties that had haunted him during his living relationship with his "manly woman," and that had led to the murder in the first place. *Disciples* thus consists of a cautionary tale of the losses suffered by both self and other as a result of the misrecognition of sexuality.

As he reflects on his relationship with his former lover, the protagonist realizes the full extent of his intimidation. Derived from his heteronormative conditioning, his fear is of being placed in a subordinate gender position by a "manly woman" of, essentially, being emasculated. The first stirrings of such fears occur when he notices that although she was "completely different," she was also "completely the same as she had been and *completely identical to me*," a woman who "is not a woman" but also "not a man" (Barakat, *Disciples*, 47, 125).[12] This incipient awareness of her "self-sufficien[cy]," her androgyny, provokes, at first, a misogynist response (Barakat, *Disciples*, 125). The protagonist attempts to neglect her and fails to do so given that he is no longer able to decipher her thoughts. He then decides to punish her by rejecting her sexual advances. Yet this resolution also fails, and he is unable to resist his desire for her when he hears "the sigh of her bare feet on the floor, padding over to where [he] stand[s]"; his "knees go limp and [he] fold[s]" (Barakat, *Disciples*, 62). With these forms of psychological violence having reproduced only his own weakness, the protagonist next turns to physical violence in order to contain the threat to himself posed by the androgynous other—"I pound at her," he recollects. "I rain blows on her, and she clings to me" (Barakat, *Disciples*, 126). Naturally, such violence can result only in death as its culmination. Embodying what Natalya Lusty glosses as Georges Bataille's thesis that there is "no possibility of a virile masculine subject without the possibility of its putative emasculation," this finale, also a beginning, demonstrates that the consequence of an act intended to guard the masculine from emasculation is nothing but emasculation itself—masculinity asserted, Barakat shows, is masculinity negated (Lusty, 116).

Alongside Khalil and Wadi', the protagonist of *Disciples* signifies a point in the spectrum of gender and sexuality as traced by Barakat throughout the novels examined here. This spectrum may now be mapped out in the following manner to illustrate Barakat's project on representing the crisis of masculinity during the Lebanese Civil War. Firstly, *The Stone* provides an articulation of homosexuality as a form of masculinity alternative to that imposed by a heteronormative social order. Secondly, *Disciples* demonstrates the violence inherent in heteronormative gender and sexual identifications, which are constructed around the misrecognition of an underlying androgyny. And finally, *My Master* represents androgyny as the existential core of all gender and sexual experience in its purest form.

In sum, the novels studied here comprise a dialectic wherein androgynous gender and sexuality is channeled into the socially acceptable forms of heteronormativity—a process which, exacerbated by the war, results in self-division, alienation, violence, and death. Consequently, Barakat's male protagonists adopt, often through heroic psychological and social efforts, a range of alternative masculinities, all of which both stem from and lead back toward androgyny as the site of liberated gender and sexuality. Barakat thus presents us with a unique, even radical, literary take on rising forms of masculinities illustrating the crises mediated by the Lebanese Civil War.

Notes

1   The following discussion draws from the broader analysis offered in the author's book on these novels, *Feminism and Avant-Garde Aesthetics in the Levantine Novel* (Palgrave Macmillan, 2016) as part of a 'Civil War series.' Reproduced by permission.

2   As Paul Amar contends, the interdisciplinary field of Masculinity Studies in general is relatively new. It revolves around the transposition of feminist and queer studies to studies of maleness and heterosexuality. See Amar (44–45).

3   For a brief biography of Barakat and the displacement, estrangement, and transgression she experiences in her own life, see Rakha.

4   Translations of the title and all quotations are the author's own—as are transliterations of characters' names.

5   Barakat, although she acknowledges the generosity of such critics, has herself explicitly contested their readings of Khalil in an article for *al-Akhbar*: "Literary critics were very generous with me, more than I expected. Perhaps because of the [al-Naqid] prize. But some of the criticism went almost in the opposite direction of the content of the novel. At first, I thought it was lack of professional experience on my part that made critics miss my point to the extent of praising a piece of writing that was meant to be condemned. Then I decided to consider myself 'not understood' because of the uniqueness and novelty of my 'pioneering' writing. To create an Arab

gay man, and take his side, making his pains and estrangement a shield to ward off social and religious criticism and a tool to grant him innocence of sexual deviance [. . .] all of this in addition to other literary 'considerations' was not easy to accept. Then with a little humility I started thinking that before this novel nobody had heard of my existence altogether, from the ocean to the gulf, and that I should be happy with it. So I became happy with it." (Barakat, *Hajar al-dahik*, n.p.). Translation the author's own.

6   'Homosocial' is employed here in the terms first articulated by Eve Kosof-sky Sedgwick as descriptive of "social bonds between persons of the same sex," but distinct from what might be considered the 'sexual bonds' implied by 'homosexual' (Sedgwick 1). The author also acknowledges, and seeks to move beyond, what Fedwa Malti-Douglas sees as the tendency among Western critics to read instances of homosociality in Arabic literature as "indexes of latent or overt homosexuality." In Arab–Islamic culture, she rightly asserts, 'homosociality' actually "takes precedence over heterosexu-ality" on the levels of both "social practice [and] mentalités," and thus must not be reduced to or confused with sexual motive (Malti-Douglas, 15, 110).

7   Halperin's concept of "personal individuation" is employed here as oc-curring in antagonism to pre-given gender and sexual designations. Such individuation defines the process by which the subject realizes, often through immense psychological and social struggle, a *unique* sexual 'ori-entation' and 'identity.' See Halperin ("How," 112).

8   The discussion of 'masculinity as masquerade' here draws strongly on Judith Butler's extension of Joan Riviere's thesis on "womanliness as mas-querade" to all gender identifications, and similarly sees such as produced and reproduced performatively. See Butler (63–72).

9   In his otherwise positive response to Barakat's representation of Khalil's homosexuality, Joseph Massad sees her as succumbing in this episode to "the Western stereotype of the misogynist homosexual." Massad (411–12, note 192).

10 Emphasis added.

11 See Lacan for his account of the law or name of the father.

12 Emphasis added.

Works Cited

Aghacy, Samira. *Masculine Identity in the Fiction of the Arab East since 1967.* Syracuse, NY: Syracuse University Press, 2009.

Amar, Paul. "Middle East Masculinity Studies: Discourses of 'Men in Crisis,' Industries of Gender in Revolution." *Journal of Middle East Women's Stud-ies* 7, no. 3 (2011): 36–71.

Barakat, Huda. "Hajar al-dahik." *al-Akhbar*, no. 2438, November 7, 2014.

———. *Disciples of Passion*, translated by Marilyn Booth. Syracuse, NY: Syracuse University Press, 2005.

———. *Sayyidi wa habibi (My Master, My Lover)*. Beirut: Dar al-Nahar, 2004.

———. *The Stone of Laughter*, translated by Sophie Bennett. New York: Interlink Books, 1995.

Butler, Judith. *Gender Trouble: Feminism and the Subversion of Identity*. London: Routledge, 2006.

Fayad, Mona. "Strategic Androgyny: Passing as Masculine in Barakāt's *Stone of Laughter*." In *Intersections: Gender, Nation, and Community in Arab Women's Novels*, edited by Lisa Suhair Majaj, Paula W. Sunderman, and Therese Saliba. New York: Syracuse University Press, 2002.

Fer, Briony. "Surrealism, Myth and Psychoanalysis." In *Realism, Rationalism, Surrealism: Art Between the Wars*, edited by Briony Fer, David Batchelor, and Paul Wood. New Haven, CT: Yale University Press, 1993.

Foucault, Michel. *The History of Sexuality*, vol. 1, translated by Robert Hurley. New York: Vintage Books, 1990.

Halperin, David. "How to Do the History of Male Homosexuality." *GLQ: A Journal of Lesbian and Gay Studies* 6, no.1 (2000): 87-123.

Hanna, Kifah. *Feminism and Avant-Garde Aesthetics in the Levantine Novel*. New York: Palgrave Macmillan, 2016.

Lacan, Jacques. *On the Names-of-the-Father*, translated by Bruce Fink. Cambridge: Polity Press, 2013.

Lusty, Natalya. "Surrealist Masculinities: Sexuality and the Economies of Experience." In *Modernism and Masculinity*, edited by Natalya Lusty and Julian Murphet. Cambridge: Cambridge University Press, 2014.

Malti-Douglas, Fedwa. *Woman's Body, Woman's Word: Gender and Discourse in Arabo-Islamic Writing*. Princeton, NJ: Princeton University Press, 1991.

Massad, Joseph. *Desiring Arabs*. Chicago: University of Chicago Press, 2008.

Mitchell, Juliet. *Psychoanalysis and Feminism: A Radical Reassessment of Freudian Psychoanalysis*. London: Allen Lane, 1974.

Mundy, Jennifer. "Letters of Desire." In *Surrealism: Desire Unbound*, edited by Jennifer Mundy. Princeton, NJ: University Press, 2001.

Rakha, Youssef. "Hoda Barakat: Starting Over." *Al-Ahram Weekly*, no. 457, November 25-December 1, 1999.

Sedgwick, Eve Kosofsky. *Between Men: English Literature and Male Homosocial Desire*. New York: Columbia University Press, 1985.

Whitaker, Brian. *Unspeakable Love: Gay and Lesbian Life in the Middle East*. Berkeley, CA: University of California Press, 2006.

5

MAHFOUZ, AL-MUTANABBI, AND THE CANON: POETICS OF DEVIANCE FROM THE MASCULINE NATIONALIST DISCOURSE OF AL-SUKKARIYA

Robert James Farley

In 2016, *al-Sukkariya* (1957; English translation: *Sugar Street*, 2019) made its way into the news as one of the works referenced by an Egyptian member of parliament to justify bringing Naguib Mahfouz to trial, were he still alive today. He would be charged with violating *al-adab al-'ama*, "public morality," and likely sentenced to two years in prison—as was Ahmed Naji in 2016 for a published excerpt of his novel *Istikhdam al-haya* (2014; English translation: *Using Life*, 2017), a text that according to the prosecutor, "spewed sexual lust and transient pleasures" (Farid). The parliamentarian had no actual issue with Mahfouz's book, for he stated later that he was referring to the film that had come out in 1973 ('Abd al-Hamid). Nonetheless, his comments situate Mahfouz's work in a discussion of literature, sexuality, and censorship in today's Egypt. That the notion of violating "public morality" has continually served to justify the incarceration of LGBTQI people in Egypt asks us to look further into Mahfouz's representation of sexual desire in his seminal *Cairo Trilogy*.

Before its publication in 1957, the first volume of the trilogy was serialized in *al-Risala al-jadida* from 1954 to 1956. Known to English readers as *Palace Walk*, *Bayna al-Qasrayn* (between two palaces) wove the stern authoritarian patriarch al-Sayyid Ahmad 'Abd al-Jawwad (popularly known as 'Si al-Sayid') into the fabric of Egyptian archetypes, which continues to this day—to such an extent that, nearly a half century later, Tamer Hosny released the single "Si 'L' Sayed" featuring Snoop Dogg, in which he boasts of his rule over his woman, chanting "*Ana Si al-Sayid*" ("I am Si al-Sayid") in the refrain. It may come as no surprise that Si al-Sayid emerged as a cultural icon that went far beyond the world of the trilogy, given his central role in all three volumes, the TV serial, and films that followed it. Neither is his influence ignored by Arabic literary studies in the American academy; Miriam

Cooke cites him as a prime example of Mahfouz's male characters who objectify women as a way to "weave fragile delusions of power and control" (Cooke, 104). But as much as spotlighting Si al-Sayid may let some indulge in the comfort of Orientalist tropes of the ruthless Arab man on the necks of secluded women, he is, in the end, merely one specific shade of masculinity in Mahfouz's trilogy—and one that signifies a hyperpatriarchal old order in the midst of Egypt's rapid modernization during the interwar period.

I am interested in a very different type of man in this chapter. Radwan comes of age in the second and third volumes of the trilogy. He is the eldest grandson of Si al-Sayid, but his world cannot be contained by a paradigm that categorizes him as 'modern' or 'traditional.' By the time of *Sugar Street*, he is a Wafdist, long after the nationalist political party had failed to oust the British in the 1919 Revolution. Well versed in classical poetry, he studies law at the university. He is not attracted to women. In fact, Radwan's sexuality complicates his relationship with the national project that remains a central theme of the book, and in doing so sheds light on the heteronormativity that underlies this national project. In what follows, I interrogate the novel's discourses of nation and masculinity and Radwan's alienation from them, which may tempt some readers to place him as a 'foreign' subject of Western modernity. However, I want to problematize this by looking at Mahfouz's deployment of the figures and language of premodern poets, signaling his connection to Arabic literary traditions. Understanding the contradictions in Radwan's presentation requires us to see beyond these exclusive philosophical categories and expose the inherent heteronormative violence that undergirds the national project.

Radwan is nominally included in studies that cross Arabic literature and Queer Studies. Two main mentions belong to Frédéric Lagrange and Joseph A. Massad. In his survey of homosexuality in Arabic literature, Lagrange notes Radwan as a "mere archetype" and sole character of the younger generation in the trilogy to choose the past, "almost as if to suggest that his sexual life were another remnant of *al-'ahd al-bā'id* (the ancien régime)" (Lagrange, 177). Indeed, relegating Radwan's sexual life to the past is not far-fetched, as I argue, but it is greatly problematized by the particularly modern terms in which he understands and expresses his sexuality. Specifically, the very idea of 'possessing' a sexual identity and further characterizing himself as *shadh* ('deviant') has been illustrated by a number of scholars, including Lagrange himself, to be a phenomenon of modern conceptions of sexuality. Therefore, "research on same-sex eroticism in Arabic literature has been very cautious with its vocabulary, preferring in place of 'homosexuality' terms such as 'homoeroticism' or 'same-sex sexuality,' or even *homosensualité*" (171).

Pushing this caution further, Massad contends that Radwan's "deviance" is intelligible by virtue of Arabs having internalized Western taxonomies of sexuality (Massad, 288). His reading of Radwan rests on two components of Mahfouz's representation of same-sex desire. First, Radwan's self-identification distinguishes him from the character of Kirshah from Mahfouz's *Midaq Alley*, published a decade earlier in 1947. Unlike bourgeois Radwan, Kirshah is of the lower classes, and while he is described as *shadh* by the narrator he never considers himself as such. Massad's second crucial point is the medicalized vocabulary with which the Pasha speaks to Radwan about his inability to desire women, as though it is a disease that plagues him. For Massad, the use or "infiltration" of Western categories and medicalized language is part of a shift in representing desire. He states,

> The difference between their desires and the desires of Kirshah is precisely what accounts for the transformation of same-sex attraction from one of many existing and tolerated deviances among the lower middle classes and the poor in society into a medicalized condition among the rich and upwardly mobile. Mahfouz's representation of Radwan as self-declared deviant is intelligible to readers precisely because of the transformation of Arab society since the late nineteenth century, where the epistemic shifts instantiated by the Arab Renaissance project and the simultaneous European colonial project began to seep through to the interstices of society at large, to be internalized by new modern subjects, no longer remaining within the purview of the literati and colonial officers (Massad, 288–89).

I do not intend to delve much into the critiques of Massad's paradigm, problematized in large part for a unidirectional Orientalism wherein knowledge flows from a monolithic and omnipotent 'West' into the passive, empty vessel of an 'Other.' In a *GLQ* issue on "Queer Politics and the Question of Palestine/Israel," both Sahar Amer and Gil Z. Hochberg separately take him to task for a number of issues, one being the very real violence that occurs today in Palestine that is predicated on this view of how same-sex desire operates in Arab cultures. This problem of conservative pundits associating homosexuality with the West remains an issue that the region's LGBTQI groups continue to challenge. Here, however, I am interested in complicating Massad's literary analysis of Mahfouz's representation of homosexuality in the trilogy, which firmly understands Radwan as a subject of Western sexual taxonomies.

What can we learn from opposing viewpoints of Lagrange's and Massad's work, which fundamentally place Radwan either in the realm of tradition or the modern, respectively? What these two views have in common is that they fail to take Radwan to be anything more than a kind of literary decoration. He is "a mere archetype in Mahfuz's panorama of Egyptian youth" (Lagrange, 177), or one of the "cases" of homosexuality in modern Arabic literature that are "used as sideshows or as enriching detail and not as social and national allegories" (Massad, 270). But how can we be expected to bracket the national allegory that engulfs Radwan in the trilogy? In the end, the contradiction we see between Lagrange and Massad indicates the way same-sex desire can be rendered illegible by the modernist paradigm. So other than determining whether or not Radwan is a modern subject, or what the 'true' source of his 'deviance' is, I am interested to know the ways in which Radwan is erased from the trilogy's nationalist discourse. I suggest we do take Radwan seriously and look deeper into those moments when he is constituted as a paradox. This entails first understanding him within what Hoda Elsadda calls a "canonical national allegory."

National Masculinity

To read the trilogy as a national allegory harkens back to the debate sparked in 1986 with Frederic Jameson's controversial claim, "All third-world texts are necessarily [. . .] allegorical, and in a very specific way: they are to be read as what I will call *national allegories*, even when, or perhaps I should say, particularly when their forms develop out of predominantly western machineries of representation, such as the novel" (Jameson, 69). Aijaz Ahmad offered up what has become one of the most oft-cited critiques of Jameson when he accused him of totalizing historical phenomena by propping up false binaries (East/West/Other/Self) with his "rhetoric of otherness" (Ahmad, 8). My objective is not to intervene in this argument over how Mahfouz *should* be read. Rather, I am interested in how the national allegory, as a private story that broadly tells the national story, takes the plurality of national stories for granted. What we are left with is one of many stories of the nation told from a particular vantage point that is not without its mediation, one that is gendered and classed.

Hoda Elsadda begins her study, *Gender, Nation, and the Arabic Novel*, with the notion that the novelistic canon in twentieth-century Egypt was formed to coincide with the way the male-dominated liberal Nahda-era elite imagined the nation, "in their own image, foregrounding their values, their ontological dilemmas, their fears and desires" (Elsadda, xiv). Part of this process included advocating for an image of Egyptian history in which a 'rupture' with tradition was a prerequisite for entering modernity. As a specifically *canonical* national allegory, Mahfouz's trilogy tells the story of Egypt through the story of the 'Abd al-Jawwad family from the perspective of a nationalist discourse espoused by the elite of the Nahda era. Elsadda makes it clear that a canonical national allegory

> is not the same as saying that the personal lives of the characters are linked to historical or sociopolitical developments. Rather, the events, characterization, and plot all reflect and constitute the dominant national discourse about the road to modernization, about the inevitable linear development from a traditional society to a modern one, about the radical opposition between traditional and modern values, and about the imperative of relinquishing the old ways in favor of new ones (Elsadda, 79).

In terms of the *Cairo Trilogy*'s constructions of masculinity, this means that the authoritarian patriarch Si al-Sayid, who Elsadda regards as "the icon of 'traditional' manhood," sits in stark opposition to the "*nahda*/national masculinity" of his son and main protagonist of the trilogy, Kamal. This kind of masculinity privileges a life of the mind, while maintaining an ambivalence toward women, either as modern objects of passionate desire (as shown in Kamal's infatuation with the Westernized socialite 'Ayda) or his 'embarrassing' traditional mother.

> The ambivalence of the nationalist discourse toward its constructed traditional motherhood is exemplified in Kamal's relationship with his mother. He loves her, was totally integrated in her world as a child, but ultimately rejects her and her world. His gentle dismissal of some of her more blatant blunders, about politics or other worldly matters, is symbolic of the *nahda* hero's attitude to tradition, to Egypt, to mothers: he loves her but is embarrassed by her shortcomings and wants to change her (Elsadda, 91).

The "traditional" and "*nahda*/national" masculinities of Elsadda's model are in large part constituted by their relationships with femininity, which seems to consistently represent the nation under European (Western), national, or Arabo–Islamic traditional influence. This binary gender dynamic of the masculine subject and the feminine nation lies at the heart of the trilogy as a canonical national allegory.

Arguably, the most important passage for Radwan in the trilogy in general is his moment of anxious self-reflection during an argument among his cousins and friends about halfway into the third volume. At the university, Radwan Yasin, his cousins Ahmad Shawkat and Abd al-Mun'im Shawkat, his friend Hilmi 'Izzat, and some other unnamed students discuss their upcoming exams and the recent marriage of 'Abd al-Mun'im and Na'ima. The topics quickly turn from exams and marriage to the Muslim Brotherhood, Islam's role in politics, and Egyptian independence. With the boys belonging to different political factions, the conversation develops into a heated argument but is diffused by a group of female students coming into their view. After a moment of silence while the boys gaze at them, the conversation picks up again on the topic of women's presence at the university and quickly turns back to the role of religion, but this time on a philosophical level. After an outburst by Hilmi, the scene goes quiet, affording Radwan a moment to reflect:[1]

> The reaction to this fierce quarrel was universal silence, which pleased Ridwan. His eyes roamed around, following some kites that circled overhead or gazing at the groups of palm trees. Everyone else felt free to express his opinion, even if it attacked his Creator. Yet he was compelled to conceal the controversies raging in his own soul, where they would remain a terrifying secret that threatened him. He might as well have been a scapegoat or an alien. Who had divided human behavior into normal and defiant? How could an adversary also serve as judge? Why were wretched people so often mocked? (Mahfouz, *Sugar Street*, 128-29)

He then asks the critical question, which I render here as, "Who divided people into natural [*al-tabi'i*] and deviant [*shadh*]?" (Mahfouz, *al-Sukkariya*, 164)

By now the argument has calmed, and the chapter closes with light-hearted Ahmad fantasizing about one of the female students showing up at his house. The passage has a number of tensions running through it that signal not only the depth of Radwan's alienation from the others in the scene but also his understanding of his own sexual life.

The role of history in the passage imbibes it with a sense of anxiety around the British presence in Egypt, expressed most directly in the students' argument over the implications of the recently abolished foreign capitulations in Egypt by the Anglo-Egyptian Treaty, negotiated and signed in August 1936. Led by Mustafa al-Nahas, the Egyptian leadership had signed a treaty with the British government to legally terminate the British occupation of Egyptian lands, with the exception of the areas around the Suez Canal—the exception being because the canal was deemed a "universal means of communication" between the various stretches of the British Empire. "The presence of these forces," the treaty states, "shall not constitute in any manner an occupation and will in no way prejudice the sovereign rights of Egypt" (Secretary of State for Foreign Affairs, Article

8). Abolishing the capitulations favoring foreigners was one of the key successes for the Egyptian leadership. Dating back to the sixteenth century under the Ottomans, these gave Europeans the permission to station consuls to bring their own nationals living in Egypt to trial, as well as the right to trade in the empire's territories. Europeans in Egypt eventually abused this ability to escape Ottoman jurisdiction, smuggling with impunity and evading taxes. Meanwhile, the Egyptian farmers bore the brunt of taxation and abusive moneylending interest rates (Marsot, 84–85). The *Times* hailed the August 26 treaty signing as a "contribution to the factors making for world peace" ("Anglo-Egyptian Treaty," 7). In Cairo, the occasion was commemorated by a twenty-one-gun salute, hoisting of the national flags, and a televised broadcast of the brief ceremony with speeches from al-Nahas and British foreign secretary, Anthony Eden ("Treaty Signed" 20). Yet, by that time, the British occupation had extended far beyond a physical military presence, and leading Egyptian intellectuals were concerned about foreign influence on their culture. Ahmad Hasan al-Zayat cursed the effects of *istbdad al-'ajnabi* ('tyranny of the foreigner') on Egyptian thought on the front page of *al-Risala* (Al-Zayat, 1941). *Al-Hilal*, too, published its November issue around questions of freedom, sovereignty, and democracy. It opens with editor Imil Zaydan's "Responsibilities of Independence: Our Need for New Types of Thought," and includes an article by Zaki Mubarak asking whether Arab culture would benefit from being independent of foreign ones (Zaydan, 2; Mubarak, 28). In a historical moment foregrounded by a shift in British military presence and questions of political sovereignty that had been lingering since the 1919 Revolution, intellectuals were concerned with British and other foreign influences in shaping Egyptian thought and culture.

It is this lingering presence and privilege of the foreigner that remains one of the concerns at the heart of the students' discussion. Mahfouz stages a number of viewpoints, and the spotlight is on Radwan's cousins, the Shawkat brothers. Abd al-Mun'im Shawkat of the Muslim Brotherhood asks, "Should we give up our religion in order to please the foreigners?" and the conversation turns to employment.

> "Not so fast. There aren't any positions waiting for us.
> What future is there for Law or Arts students? You can either loaf around or take some job as a clerk. Go ahead and wonder about your futures, if you want."
> "Now that the capitulations favoring foreigners have been abolished, doors will start to open."
> "Doors? There are more people than doors!"

> "Listen: Al-Nahhas broadened the system of admissions to the University after many had been arbitrarily excluded. Won't he also be able to find jobs for us?"
>
> Then tongues fell silent and faces looked off toward the far end of the park, where a flock of four young women approached from the University en route to Giza (Mahfouz, *Sugar Street*, 125-26).

The silence speaks volumes. Writing with a tinge of irony from the early- and mid-1950s, Mahfouz articulates the fear among students about their future at an unstable time of population growth and lack of trust in the political leadership. By 1937, the Egyptian-educated population was largely unemployed while graduates of foreign schools found work, which contributed to tensions with those educated in non-Egyptian institutions.[2] This concern over what it means to be Egyptian in 1936 undergirds the chapter and gives a national inflection to Radwan's internal monologue, particularly when he characterizes himself "*ka-l-gharib aw ka-l-mutarid*" ('as a stranger or a scapegoat').

The moment of silence comes about when the young men begin leering at their female peers, adding to Radwan's alienation from sharing the heterosexual object of desire. It is not until the women are out of sight that they resume their conversation, this time, on the number of female students in the Arts College. To explain this, Hilmi jokes, "That's true, but there's also something feminine about instruction in the arts. Rouge, manicures, kohl for eyes, poetry, and stories all fall into one category." (Mahfouz, *Sugar Street*, 127). At this, the boys laugh together and proceed on to the subject of gender equality. The cousins Ahmad and 'Abd al-Mun'im agree on the principle of equality between men and women, but soon begin their bickering again as the subject expands to human rights and religion. The silence, distraction, and jest all seemed to have momentarily united the arguing students, except Radwan, "Talking about the girls made him uneasy and sad" (Mahfouz, *Sugar Street*, 126). He is not interested in participating in the collective heterosexual gaze. On the other hand, he also does not participate in Hilmi's stilted attempt to define "feminine study." This momentary homosocial union among the arguing boys alienates Radwan, who despairs at having to keep his aversion to women a secret. Through the lens of national allegory, we witness Radwan outside of a national discourse that appears divided on many philosophical, social, and political questions, but that can unite on a masculine, heteronormative platform. In fact, he hardly contributes to the discussion at all.

But Radwan's absence from the national conversation does not constitute a lack of involvement in politics. He actually becomes the most politically influential of his family through his relationship with 'Abd al-Rahim Pasha 'Isa. In an especially telling passage in the following chapter, Radwan and Hilmi visit the Pasha's house during a lively meeting of Wafdists:

> As the two made their way inside, some of the young men shouted, "Long live solidarity!" Ridwan's face became flushed from excitement. He was as zealous a rebel as the others but wondered anxiously whether anyone suspected the nonpolitical side to his visits (Mahfouz, *Sugar Street*, 129).

In the midst of solidarity chanting, a blushing Radwan worries about anyone suspecting the "nonpolitical side" of his visit to the Pasha. This line drawn between sex and politics is clearly imaginary, as it shapes the entire relationship between him and the Pasha and thereby shapes the nature of Radwan's political involvement and affiliations. Through this apparent contradiction, Mahfouz presents Radwan's homosexuality as always undergirding the political.

In the context of an apparent anxiety among intellectuals around foreign influence, Mahfouz injects Radwan's pivotal reflection of feeling like a stranger for not being attracted to women. His exclusion from a specifically heterosexual definition of masculinity simultaneously constitutes his alienation from the national conversation. At the same time, his sexual relationship with the Pasha is the basis of his political influence, even if he understands it as a distinctly private affair. Radwan is at once an insider and outsider, political but not national.

Ars Erotica and a Premodern Poetic Lexicon

Back in the chapter of the student discussion, the structure heavily emphasizes dialogue with a few instances of interior monologue belonging to either Radwan or his cousin Ahmad. Radwan's thoughts are told in a style that Mahfouz deploys throughout the trilogy, whereby he remains mostly in the indirect form of interior monologue with strategic usage of the direct form. What makes the passage so poignant is that it is the only time Radwan identifies himself as *shadh*, and even so, he implies it through the question, "*Man alladhi qasama l-bashara 'ilā tabi'i wa shadhi?*" (Who divided people into natural and deviant?) (Mahfouz, *al-Sukkariya*, 163, translation author's own). Massad sees this question as a pivotal moment in modern Arabic literary expressions of same-sex desire, in which Arab readers' understanding of Radwan's self-identification as *shadh* indicates their internalization of concepts of sexuality that came from the West. I broaden Massad's reading of Radwan's moment of "self-declared" deviance by taking into consideration Mahfouz's intertextual references. In particular, I want to trouble the so-called 'Western' roots of Radwan's homosexual identification through Mahfouz's deployment of a literary figure that goes back to al-Mutanabbi—namely, the paradox of being simultaneously *khasm* (adversary) and *hakam* (judge).

As mentioned, Radwan's reflection stands out as one of the few moments of interiority throughout a chapter dominated by conversation. The narrator's presence is anomalously small with little description, to the point that there are a number of times we are not aware who is speaking—let alone what the speaker is thinking. In contrast, the passage itself narrows from a description of Radwan's thoughts in the indirect interior monologic form to the three questions at the end, told in the direct first-person form. His self-identification is not just implied in the question but thought as well. That is, Mahfouz juxtaposes Radwan's silent and indirect self-identification with his being in the midst of the spoken word, effectively magnifying his absence from the national conversation going on around him.

Moreover, he asks not how or why, but who? In a sense, this addresses the same concern for Massad, who would answer, "the West." In fact, Massad excavates the historical adoption of the term *shadh* from the Europeans. But Radwan's following question seems to imply something different: "*Kayfa takunu l-khasma wa-l-hakama fi 'ani?*" ("How can you be the adversary and the judge at the same time?"). The paradox of being both *khasm* and *hakam* appears in an ode by al-Mutanabbi, in which the poet writes to his patron, 'Ali ibn Abi al-Hayja' (known as Sayf al-Dawlah):

> Oh, you most just of people, except in your treatment of me, the feud is over you and you are both adversary and judge May God guard your faithful eyes from supposing fat in one whose fate is [mere] bloating For what use does a man have for his eyes if lights and darknesses are all the same to him?[3]

These couplets in particular accuse his patron of not using his sense of taste in assessing the poet. Sayf al-Dawlah's lack of discernment between al-Mutanabbi's rhetorical talents and those of the other poets in his court causes the *khisam* (dispute) (Larkin, 58). Looking back at Mahfouz's passage, Radwan's question is distinct in the monologue in that it is the only one that addresses a "you" who embodies the contradiction. Additionally, a *khisam* triggers the anguish as well, in this case from the intensity of a *khisam* between Radwan's nationalist cousins. The fact that he accesses a classical Arabic poetic lexicon to express his situations appears to problematize the idea that Radwan's understanding of his sexual life is simply lifted and transplanted from a Western system of sexual taxonomies. But the role of classical poetry is not limited to this instance. Arab–Islamic poetry and song constitute the main focus of Radwan's cultural interests, which he shares with his dear friend Hilmi. The arts play as much of a role in their gatherings with the Pasha as does politics. Poetry and music are in fact the only topics of conversation that rival politics in terms of time and energy. The Pasha even puts poets and politicians in the same position as victims of scandal in his first 'lesson' when meeting Radwan, saying that if he works hard in his public life he can act as he pleases in private. As explicitly in the realm of *al-haya al-khasa* (private life), desire can only be pursued if countered by *al-ijtihad* (hard work) and *al-nazaha* (righteousness). To which Hilmi responds with a quote from Abassid poet 'Ali ibn al-Jahm, "The noble man is the one whose faults can be counted" (Mahfouz, *Sugar Street*, 67). As I will show later, premodern Arabic poetry provides a lexicon for Radwan, Hilmi, and the Pasha to illustrate moral lessons.

The fact that poetry provides much of the content of conversations between Radwan and the Pasha gestures toward a Foucauldian model of sexual knowledge transmission. In *History of Sexuality, Volume 1*, Michel Foucault puts forth the paradigm of *ars erotica* (erotic art) and *scientia sexualis* (science of sexuality) when discussing the production of the truth of sex. He associates *ars erotica* with much of the world outside of the West, wherein sex is treated as an object of knowledge to be disseminated by a master, who "can transmit this art in an esoteric manner and as the culmination of an initiation in which he guides the disciple's progress with unfailing skill and severity" (Foucault, 57). He contrasts it with *scientia sexualis*, which he finds characteristic of modern Western civilization, that the West gradually came to practice over the *ars erotica*. It tells the truth of sex through the act of confession, by which an internal pre-existing truth is divulged. He aligns this transformation along that of the oral to the written, in which,

> we have passed from a pleasure to be recounted and heard, centering on the heroic or marvelous narration of "trials" of bravery or sainthood, to a literature ordered according to the infinite task of extracting from the depths of oneself, in between the words, a truth which the very form of the confession holds out like a shimmering mirage. (Foucault, 59)

Building on this idea, Gerald Doherty claims that since *ars erotica* transmits conditions of such intense pleasure that they transcend language it is therefore "profoundly resistant to articulation in narrative form," and its practice "elides the basic structures of narratability" (Doherty, 137). The Pasha and Radwan's relationship clearly dramatizes that of master and disciple in the *ars erotica* theory of pleasure, whereby the classical Arab–Islamic poetry spoken at their meetings is the oral mode that serves to express the truth of sex "in an esoteric manner." Toward the end of the novel, Radwan and Hilmi make one last visit to the Pasha as he bids farewell to go on pilgrimage. The three of them with the Pasha's deputy, 'Ali Mihran, playfully banter and flirt with each other, and the Pasha begins to reminisce:

> "The old days! Children, why do we grow old?
> May your wisdom be exalted and glorified, my Lord. A poet said:
> *My lance was not deflected by a foe's taunts.*
> *Auspicious times for it were dawn and dusk both.*"
>
> Wiggling his eyebrows, Mihran said, "'By a foe's taunts'?
> No, you should say, 'By Mihran.'"
> "You son of a bitch—don't spoil the mood with your nonsense. It's not
> right to joke around when we're reminiscing about those beautiful
> days.
> At times tears are more becoming than a smile, more humane, and
> more respectful. Listen to this too, by al-A'sha:
> *She rebuffed me, but the*
> *Events she rejected*
> *Were baldness and white hair.*
>
> What do you think of the poet's use of 'events'?"
> Imitating a newspaper vendor, Mihran called out, *"Events of the Day,*
> *the Egyptian, al-Ahram . . ."*
> Despairingly the pasha said, "It's not your fault but . . ."
> "Yours!"
> "Mine? I'm not to blame for your depravity. When we first met, you
> were so debauched that Satan would have envied you. But I won't
> allow you to spoil the ambiance created by these memories. Yes,
> hear this as well:
> *Just as a stalk is ravished of*
> *Its leaves, so I was stripped of youth."*
> Pretending to be shocked by the sexual allusion, Mihran asked, "A
> stalk, Pasha?"

> (Mahfouz, *Sugar Street*, 288-89)

The Pasha recites couplets from Jahiliya poets 'Amru ibn Qumay'a and al-'Asha, and then Abassid poet Abu al-'Atahiya. Mihran reacts to the first and third by making play of the phallic imagery, the poet's spear (*qana*) and rod (*qadib*). The second instance, however, is immediately drawn from its Jahiliya context into the current Egyptian political landscape vis-à-vis the newspaper titles. No matter how much the Pasha insists on reminiscing, the Jahiliya and Abbasid poetry takes on new meanings in the ever-changing years of modernity and is even considered anachronistic in this final gathering, when the Pasha deploys a pseudo-medical register:

> You can say you find women disgusting, but why don't other men feel that way? You fall prey to a feeling that's almost like a disease, an incurable one. It leads you to withdraw from the world and is the worst possible companion for your solitude. Then you may be embarrassed to despise women without having any choice about it" (Mahfouz, *Sugar Street*, 291).

Framing Radwan's lack of interest in women as "a sickness for which you do not know a cure," the Pasha's language signals a biological element to sexuality. As mentioned above, Massad takes this example in his reading of Radwan and the Pasha as indicating a shift in Arab societies toward Western understandings of same-sex desire as a "medicalized condition among the rich and the upwardly mobile" (Massad, 288). But the meaning of this biological definition of sexuality changes in the context of the *ars erotica*. At once inherent and learned, Radwan's sexuality is portrayed as a paradox, and as such illuminates the depth of contesting dimensions of sexuality in the novel. It is clear that the poetic language belongs to an Arab–Islamic trajectory. This sort of continuity with Arab–Islamic tradition vis-à-vis the arts runs diametrically opposed to the rupture required to enter modernity as it is figured in the liberal elite imagination. In this way, Radwan's situation outside of the nationalist discourse is twofold. His inability to perform heterosexual masculinity while also maintaining a cultural affinity to Arab–Islamic tradition places him outside the national project that his cousins embody. In the face of the spoken national conversation, he is a silent reflection which does not acknowledge a modern/tradition divide but understands himself in language that can be attributed to both.

Within the safety of silence, Radwan's sexual life still is not presented so much as life at all, but rather death or absence. Although we read the erotic fantasies in the minds of many of his male relatives, and especially his father Yasin, there is nothing of the sort for Radwan. Mahfouz structurally depicts the starkness of this difference by producing a kind of psychic foil that situates Radwan's interiority alongside that of Ahmad. But in contrast to Radwan's intense anxiety over his failed desire for women, Ahmad is taken by the mere thought of 'Alawiya Sabri's name:

The name galvanized him. She was a young woman with an Egyptian version of Turkish beauty. Slender and of medium height, she had a fair complexion and coal-black hair. Her wide black eyes had lofty eyelids, and her eyebrows met in the center. She was distinguished by her aristocratic demeanor and refined gestures. (Mahfouz, *Sugar Street*, 126).

As he details her appearance in his mind, we get the kind of visuality that does not exist in any of Radwan's thoughts. Ahmad's attraction for 'Alawiya on an atomic level accentuates a view of sexuality that is inherent to the individual's body, to be awoken by just the thought of the desired object. This biological view of sexuality further corroborates the treatment of same-sex desire as a disease by the Pasha mentioned above.

As a canonical national allegory, the trilogy is an example of how nationalist discourses render same-sex desire with silence and contradictory terms. Alienated from his nationalist cousins and fellow students, Radwan harbors a great deal of anxiety about not desiring women. Although a minor character in relation to those characters that develop across all three books and generations of Mahfouz's trilogy, centering Radwan exposes the heterosexist underpinnings of the homosocial national project. His best friend and near-double, Hilmi, tries to conform by leering at women, cracking gendered jokes, and proclaiming his support for the institution of marriage. Much more so than Radwan, Hilmi is disciplined by the nationalist discourse. But his nationalism like his performed heterosexuality is insincere, and he has an ultra-nationalist outburst that echoes a fascist call for eugenics, "to bring humanity to an ideal condition, pure and powerful!" (Mahfouz, *Sugar Street*, 128). Thus, Mahfouz draws a very clear and direct line between the nation, masculinity, and sexuality; to be deviant *(shadh)* in one means to deviate from the others. Yet, Radwan and Hilmi and the old Pasha who mentors them are far from 'Western': they have a mastery of classical Arabic poetry, unlike their peers. In this way, a queer reading of the trilogy illuminates the disciplinary modes of this modernity and its logics of exclusion along the lines of national heteronormative masculinity. For Radwan, such discipline bears on his psyche, while for Hilmi (a character of much less depth) it bears on his performance of nation and gender.

A Ghost in the Archive

Finally, the figure of the ghost seems to be fitting for understanding Radwan's role in Arabic literature. In his seminal work on Francophone literature of the Maghreb, Jarrod Hayes discusses the image of the specter as a metaphor for the presence of sexualities that do not fit the mould of nationalist discourses. He cites Terry Castle's image of ghosts to describe a "culturally constructed invisibility surrounding lesbianism," as well as Vito Russo's descriptions of homosexuality "ghosting" in Hollywood cinema. Placing this in the context of the Maghreb, Hayes looks to Jacques Derrida's construction of "hauntology" to revive queerness that has been rendered illegible by official national narratives: "Queering as a form of hauntology thus exposes the connection between sexual repression and political oppression, and the topos of this queering/hauntology [. . .] is the Nation" (Hayes, 19). Dina Al-Kassim likewise writes about the intersection of Queer Studies with Middle East scholarship:

> [B]ut this thought of the present disastrous fiction of East against West echoes throughout the chapters and recurs as an unanswerable question about the limits of knowing and naming the desire that we moderns hear in the archive. Hearing voices might be a figure for archival research of this kind, which is always incomplete and rarely a disinterested pursuit; haunting seems to me the best figure for the kind of history that can emerge from within queer studies (Al-Kassim, 298).

While problematic in many ways, Mahfouz's depiction of Radwan should not be ignored on the basis of flat characterization or as an archetypal decoration for his trilogy. Instead, we should look to him to see the limits of nationalist discourses in articulating subjects. Understanding him as a ghost reminds us that clarity for an illegible subject may never be accessible, but the contours of that subject may be found by interrogating those structures that discipline or work to erase it. Similarly, laws that have been mobilized to criminalize homosexuality often do not mention it, but claim to uphold a notion of "public morality" like Article 178 of the Egyptian penal code and criminalize "public outrageous actions" in Article 272 (Al-Farchichi and Saghiyeh, 13). To read silent desire when words are inadequate means looking to the limits of discourse to realize its representational violence in an attempt to see the ghosts beyond it.

Notes

1   Except where noted, all English citations from *Sugar Street* reference the published English edition, translated by William Maynard Hutchins and Angele Botros Samaan (The American University in Cairo Press, 2019).
2   "7,500 baccalaureate holders and 3,500 university graduates were jobless. Those who graduated from foreign schools and spoke foreign languages found jobs in foreign firms, but since members of minorities were the

ones who frequented foreign schools, that simply added to the bitterness of the native Egyptians" (Marsot, 113).

3   Margaret Larkin's translation, (Oxford: Oneworld Publications, 2008, 58).

Works Cited

'Abd al-Hamid, Ashraf. "Madha qalla barlamani masri athar jadalan hawla muhakimat Najib Mahfuz?" *al-Arabiya*, November 29, 2016.

Ahmad, Aijaz. "Jameson's Rhetoric of Otherness and the 'National Allegory.'" *Social Text*, no. 17 (1987): 3–25.

Amer, Sahar. "Joseph Massad and the Alleged Violence of Human Rights." *GLQ: A Journal of Lesbian and Gay Studies*, vol. 16, no. 4 (2010): 649–53.

Chicago Tribune. "Treaty Signed By Britain and Egypt as Allies: London Agrees to Move Troops from City," August 27, 1937.

Cooke, Miriam. "Naguib Mahfouz, Men, and the Egyptian Underworld." In *Fictions of Masculinity: Crossing Cultures, Crossing Sexualities*, edited by Peter F. Murphy, 94–120. New York: New York University Press, 1994.

Doherty, Gerald. "'Ars Erotica' or 'Scientia Sexualis'?: Narrative Vicissitudes in D.H. Lawrence's 'Women in Love.'" *Journal of Narrative Technique*, vol. 26, no. 2 (1996): 137–57.

Elsadda, Hoda. *Gender, Nation, and the Arabic Novel: Egypt, 1892–2008*. Syracuse, NY: Syracuse University Press, 2012.

Al-Farchichi, Wahid, and Nizar Saghiyeh. *Homosexual Relations in the Penal Codes: General Study Regarding the Laws in the Arab Countries with a Report on Lebanon and Tunisia*. Helem online, January 20, 2012.

Farid, Sonia. "Egyptian writer who 'violated public decency': An open-and-shut case?" *Al Arabiya English*, March 5, 2016.

Foucault, Michel. *The History of Sexuality, Volume 1: An Introduction*, translated by Robert Hurley. New York: Vintage Books, 1990.

Hayes, Jarrod. *Queer Nations: Marginal Sexualities in the Maghreb*. Chicago: University Of Chicago Press, 2000.

Hochberg, Gil Z. "Israelis, Palestinians, Queers: Points of Departure." *GLQ: A Journal of Lesbian and Gay Studies*, vol. 16, no. 4 (2010): 493–516.

Jameson, Fredric. "Third World Literature in the Era of Multinational Capitalism." *Social Text* 15 (1986): 65–88.

Al-Kassim, Dina. "Epilogue: Sexual Epistemologies, East in West." In *Islamicate Sexualities: Translations across Temporal Geographies of Desire*, edited by Kathryn Babayan and Afsaneh Najmabadi, 297–339. Cambridge, MA: Harvard University Press, 2008.

Lagrange, Frédéric. "Male Homosexuality in Modern Arabic Literature." In *Imagined Masculinities: Male Identity and Culture in the Modern Middle*

East*, edited by Mai Ghoussoub and Emma Sinclair-Webb, 169–98. London: Saqi Books, 2000.

Larkin, Margaret. *Al-Mutanabbi: Voice of the 'Abbasid Poetic Ideal*. Oxford: Oneworld Publications, 2008.

Mahfouz, Naguib. *al-Sukkariya*, fifth edition. Cairo: Dar al-Shuruq, 2014.

———. *Sugar Street: The Cairo Trilogy III*. Translated by William Maynard Hutchins and Angele Botros Samaan. American University in Cairo Press, 2019.

———. "Bayna al-Qasrayn: 1–4." *al-Risala al-jadida*, April 1954.

Marsot, Afaf Lutfi al-Sayyid. *A History of Egypt: From the Arab Conquest to the Present*. Second edition. New York: Cambridge University Press, 2007.

Massad, Joseph A. *Desiring Arabs*. Chicago: The University of Chicago Press, 2007.

Mubarak, Zaki. "Al-thaqafa al-'Arabiya: hal yanbaghi istiqlaluha 'an al-thaqafat al-ajnabiya." *Halal*, no. 1 (1936): 28–31.

Secretary of State for Foreign Affairs. "Treaty of Alliance between His Majesty, in respect of the United Kingdom, and His Majesty the King of Egypt." London, August 26, 1936. Treaty Series No. 6. H.M. Stationary Office, 1937.

The Times. "Anglo-Egyptian Treaty: Provisions of the Seventeen Articles." August 28, 1936.

Al-Wahidi. *Diwan Abi al-Tayib al-Mutanabbi wa fi athna matnih*. Berlin: Maktabat al-Muthanna, 1861.

Al-Zayat, Ahmad Hasan. "Ba'da al-mu'ahadah." *al-Risala*, no. 178: 194142, November 30, 1936.

Zaydan, Imil. "Tab'at al-istiqlal: hajatuna ila anwa' jadida min al-tafkir." *Halal*, no. 1 (1936): 2–5.

6

DIASPORIC QUEER ARABS IN EUROPE AND NORTH AMERICA: SEXUAL CITIZENSHIP AND NARRATIVES OF INCLUSION AND EXCLUSION

Nicole Fares

As human rights have become an indicator of the progress of nations, gay rights have become a mark of modernity, and the acceptance of gay rights a mark of embracing modernity, but this acceptance is framed discursively through casting other countries and religions—specifically Muslim and Arab immigrants to the West—as traditional and backward (Puar; Butler). This impacts the image of Arabs as either modern and liberal if they accept gay rights, and traditional and backward if they do not. The employment of gay and lesbian rights as a symbol of freedom and modernity has been addressed and analyzed by many scholars (Stychin; Puar; Butler). Western countries are using their status as sanctuaries for LGBTQI Arabs as a form of sexual exceptionalism, and the liberal gay politics of visibility employed by the West when discussing Middle Eastern LGBTQI communities—and, more recently, Arab queer refugees—is ultimately about the development of "a righteous critique of power from the perspective of the 'injured' (queer) victim, who demands the protection of the benevolent state from the 'social injury' of homophobia" (Ritchie, 562). The most visible queer Arabs in the media are men, because lesbians are seen as more tolerated in Arab culture—be it because their homoerotic behavior is assumed to be more tolerated in Arab societies (Habib) or because in both medieval Arabic literature and in the Qur'an, lesbians are not considered to be guilty of sin and the act of lesbianism is not considered a crime, and therefore not punishable (Amer, 221). Regardless of the reasons, the only acceptable visible queer Arab is the victim. This is why Judith Butler, among other academics and queer activists who interrogate the "Western male white-dominated organizations that advocate for the protection of victimized queer Arabs" (Georgis, 558), insists on the inseparability of the queer struggle and the

121

struggle against racism and occupation—in order to disrupt the effects of the globalized queer ideology that has labeled Arab LGBTQI individuals as victims and has rendered the queer Arab as acceptable and visible "only insofar as they mute or repudiate their Arabness" (Ritchie, 560). Employed in the discourse of Syrian LGBTQI refugees, and queer Arab refugees in general, liberal gay politics of visibility thus render the Arab "even on the metaphorical level of sexuality, the victim of the Western Phallus" (Lagrange, 189). An Arab masculinity in diaspora that is not a victim then, at the opposite end of the spectrum, is constructed as a dominant and active masculinity. This could also be attributed to the continued notion of homosexuality in the Middle East as the failure of the Arab man to resist the interference of the countries that once colonized his (Massad, 2007), which ultimately reproduces stereotypical and heteropatriarchal Arab and Muslim norms that define masculinity as heterosexual.

The U.S., Canada, and certain European countries—especially Germany—have become primary destinations for individuals applying for refugee status on the basis of their sexual orientation, in a sense offering a concept of 'sexual citizenship.' LGBTQI Arab refugees, however, and those who work with them, are involved in a system founded on highly malleable, historically and sociopolitically specific sexual terms and identities that benefit distinct gendered, classed, and raced interests—and, thus, place LGBTQI Arab refugees, or any refugees from non-North American societies for that matter, in a particularly vulnerable position.

At the same time, public policy discourses in the U.S., Canada, and Europe shifted focus regarding the concept of social cohesion in the 2000s. Until then, when cohesion had been defined, social scientists had emphasized the duration of a person's citizenship (Yorukoglu, 39). Dorwin Cartwright defines social cohesion as "the degree to which the members of a group desire to remain in the group" (Cartwright and Zander, 91). The emphasis, in this older view, is placed on the continuity of group membership. Value is located in the fact that members of a society stay together rather than in the elements that ultimately keep them together. Social cohesion thus becomes more of a resistance "to disruptive forces" (Gross and Martin, 554), which signifies a reliance on the relational bonds between individuals and social groups. This in turn implies an acceptance of inevitable conflict and incompatibility that may arise in a society and culture, but importance is placed on the ultimate result: the continuation of that social bond. More recently, however, the definition has shifted to an emphasis on "involving a sense of commitment, and desire or capacity to live together in some harmony" (Jenson, 15) and on the behaviors that ultimately lead to the end goal of social cohesion: "[Cohesion] is the property by which whole societies, and the individuals within them, are bound together through the action of specific attitudes, behaviors, rules and institutions which rely on consensus rather than pure coercion" (Green and Jamaat, 18).

The term "social cohesion" has gained ground in European, American, and Canadian social sciences and amid policy discourses since the early 2000s (Baun and Marek, 1).[1] The Organization for Security and Co-operation in Europe (OSCE), and the Council of Europe and the United Nations Scientific, Educational and Cultural Organization (UNESCO), for instance, have recently voiced their belief that social cohesion is essential for eliminating intolerance and discrimination, maintaining international peace and stability, and contributing to educational development and growth (Junuzović). In addition, "social cohesion" as a term and concept has been integrated within political discourse to achieve specific political agendas.[2] In the U.S., the Donald Trump administration has cut annual immigration intake in half, framing this as necessary to protect the nation's social cohesion: "high levels of immigration have damaged social cohesion in Europe," Stephen Miller, the president's policy advisor stated, "and threaten to do the same in the U.S." (Lauter and Bennett).

In economic research and politics, the term 'inclusion' has come to replace 'equality' and 'social cohesion' has come to replace 'integration' (Mayer, 112). These new terms focus on non-economic conditions for economic performance. Urban problems, for instance, stop being viewed as result of urban decline and become obstacles to social cohesion and healthy competition, which in turn leads to social and economic exclusion. When the older terminology is employed, it is introduced along with new terminology in such a way that "concepts such as security, integration and cohesion are all lumped together within a causal relationship" (Yorukoglu, 31). Presented as such, integration becomes integral to security, which in turn appears necessary for cohesion: "non-integration, in turn, is feared to have an unfavorable effect on societal cohesion" (Vasta, 3). It has become difficult to discuss cohesion without alluding to concepts of social order, stability, security, and integration (Holton), all of which are terms that are not easy to define. But it is through such terms as "generalized social trust, trust in institutions, political participation, the degree of involvement in associations and outsider-group hostility" that social cohesion is measured (Lægaard, 455). It is as result of these concepts and methods of evaluating cohesion that immigrants are adopting new ways to live with their adopted societies, or at least to demonstrate to officials and their adopted societies that they are able to live together in cohesion.

Ahmad Danny Ramadan's novel *The Clothesline Swing* (2017) is narrated by a queer Syrian refugee who left Syria roiled in conflict post-2011 to live in Vancouver with his partner. *God in Pink* (2015) by Hasan Namir blends narratives from Ramy, an Iraqi college student struggling to live as a gay man, and an imam of a Baghdad neighborhood mosque who, when he receives an anonymous plea for religious guidance from a young gay man, is drawn into the slow realization that he himself may be gay. Ramadan's novel shows the discursive development of sexual citizenship in the refugee-narrator's adopted country and helps us to look at the construction of a gay Arab masculinity in diaspora today, while Namir's novel offers several models of gay Arab masculinity struggling for modes of existence in the home country of the protagonist, Iraq. I argue that, viewed within the framework of recent shifts in policy discourses centered on the concepts of social cohesion and sexual citizenship, these works tell us something significant about the scope and limits of current global conversations on queer Arab masculinities.

The Clothesline Swing is the story of Rasa, a Muslim, Arab man who refers to himself as the *hakawati* (storyteller) because he spends his days recounting stories to his dying lover: "This is your life," Death tells the *hakawati*, "you will be sitting at the bedside of your loved one as he dies, and slowly, you will tell him stories, trying to keep him away from my final touch" (Ramadan, *Clothesline Swing*, 32). He often tells his lover memories of his past in Syria and Egypt, and stories of people, such as that of Evelyn McHale who committed suicide by jumping off her balcony, his lover is still capable of identifying the original characters in the stories, as he identified Evelyn MacHale as the *hakawati*'s mother (Ramadan, *Clothesline Swing*, 34). The *hakawati* is often accompanied by ghosts, most often of Death and of his own mother. He remembers his life with his abusive mother, whom he escaped, and his life with his father who almost beat him to death for "coming out" as gay (Ramadan, *Clothesline Swing*, 88). He speaks of his life in Egypt where his eight friends outed him then beat him to a pulp in a mall (Ramadan, *Clothesline Swing*, 30), then back to Syria where he reunited with his lover, and to Lebanon as a "displaced Syrian person" (Ramadan, *Clothesline Swing*, 189), and then finally to Vancouver as a refugee.

The *hakawati* and his lover are both Muslim and Syrian—and both met in Syria and emigrated to Lebanon, then to Canada together. He often describes their physical encounters: "That night in the tub, I made love to you as if I were reciting poetry about the beauty of Damascus. I woke your sense with opening lines and flirtatious gestures" (Ramadan, *Clothesline Swing*, 16), and speaks of the lengths to which they had to go in order to be close in Syria: "The sweetest kisses," the *hakawati* states, "are the ones we share in forbidden places" (Ramadan, *Clothesline Swing*, Prologue, 11). Mehammed Mack sees progress in any writing on Arab sexuality by an Arab author, since it distracts the reader from continuing trends in international LGBTQI publishing that grant an exclusive platform to the 'Western' narrator giving accounts of their sexual encounters in the "'lands of Islam,' from the spotty scholarship (or sex tourism literature) edited by Arno Schmitt and Jehoeda Sofer to the recent collection *Gay Travels in the Muslim World* by Michael Luongo" (Ramadan, *Clothesline Swing*, 326). European and now also Canadian gay magazines, like *Têtu* and *DailyXtra* single out authors like Abdellah Taïa and, more recently, Ramadan himself as courageous gay-rights pioneers for their homelands (Dryef; Ramadan, "Why I'm Proud"). *DailyXtra* went as far as to dub Ramadan "Trump's worst nightmare" (Ramadan, "Why I'm Proud"). Their coming-out interviews are conducted and shared by many magazines and newspapers, and their traumatic experiences in their homelands are often positioned alongside images of them at gay-pride parades (Browne). What these magazines and newspapers often omit, however, are the historical precedents that produced literatures celebrating non-identitarian homosexual practices. Khaled el-Rouayheb, for instance, is one author who has documented a wealthy pre-modern Arab and Muslim heritage of same-sex male and female sexualities. Rouayheb "details a homosexual praxis that places a greater emphasis on inter-generational dynamics, on aesthetic appreciation of the male form, and roles that may shift with age" (Mack, 324).

Geoffrey Nash, in *The Arab Writer in English: Arab Themes in a Metropolitan Language*, examines the writings of Gibran Khalil Gibran as an Arab author in the United States who preferred to frame his message in universal terms that would endear him to Western readers by its spiritual appeal (Nash, 62). In turn, Ramadan utilizes themes and terms that represent progress and modernity to the Western reader seeking to read the tale of a Syrian refugee. Ramadan uses "the evocative power of his Arab mystical heritage [. . .] to enhance his message" (Nash, 384)—for instance, by comparing himself throughout the novel to Scheherazade, a powerful character in *One Thousand and One Nights* that is highly contested among many Arab feminists. She regales the sultan with stories every night without revealing the ending, thereby keeping him from killing her as he wants her to continue the tale the next day—and keeping him from killing other virgins in the land as well. "Scheherazade did not love the sultan," Ramadan's narrator says. He goes on, "She didn't want to fix him. She murmured her stories to keep her neck away from the hands of the swordsman" (Ramadan, *The Clothesline Swing*, 33). The narrator speaks of his Christian lesbian friend in Syria, Maryam, and her attempt to escape marriage by having him pose as her husband (Ramadan, *The Clothesline Swing*, 140), and of his memory of his mother left weeping on the streets of Damascus after a man slaps her (Ramadan, *The Clothesline Swing*, 112), as well as of his many other memories of personal trauma and abuse in Syria. Women in *One Thousand and One Nights* are not solely portrayed as victims; Maryam, the mother, and even Scheherazade are nuanced and complex characters. However, the accumulation of victimized women suffering trauma in the homeland adds to the text's sense of appeal to the human rights narrative.

Ramadan is vague in his description of the political situation in Syria. The former Syrian president, Hafez al-Assad appears to the *hakawati* speaking of his father and his love for Syria and his people (Ramadan, *The Clothesline Swing*, 154). However, aside from brief narrations of historic periods in the Middle East, such as al-Assad's rise to power (Ramadan, *The Clothesline Swing*, 159) and the Palestinian refugee crisis in Lebanon (Ramadan, *The Clothesline Swing*, 189), the *hakawati* remains focused on his personal encounters—mostly in Egypt and Syria, and later in Beirut and Vancouver. Although the author does not necessarily portray himself as passionate about the Syrian cause of liberation from the Assad regime, he does paint himself as deeply committed to the Syrian gay cause of equal legal and social rights. He, in various ways, frames his appeal to the Western audience's ethical sense of rights: "the police running after another person to arrest. They would pull on the prisoner's shirt and drag him to the ground while the women in his family wailed in agony from their windows, tightening their white scarves upon their heads" (Ramadan, *The Clothesline Swing*, Prologue, 15). He yearns for help and intervention from the outside world in support of queer Syrians: "We queers were the loneliest people in Damascus" (Ramadan, *The Clothesline Swing*, 250). Ramadan thus positions the narrator as an avowedly invested mediator between lesbian and gay Arabs, in the Middle East and the West, pleading for Arab modernization and Canadian support. After leading the Vancouver Gay Pride Parade in 2016 (Takeuchi), Ramadan gave a speech in which he pleaded to the gay-rights organizations present. He spoke of the Arab gay and lesbian individuals forced to remain in the closet in the Middle East: "Like all of us they deserve to find what they're looking for" (Johnson).

In *Desiring Arabs*, Joseph Massad not only criticizes the "distorted" political and journalistic representations of Arab sexuality that focus on oppression, violence, intolerance, and phallocentrism, he also emphasizes the potential that Arabic literature and cinema possesses to change the current dominant view in Europe and the U.S. of Arab sexuality toward a less judgmental and alienating viewpoint (Massad, 319). In key ways, literature has been able to answer the demand for sexual knowledge; it could also complicate "sexual assumptions about the Arab/Muslim world and introduce another story in their place, perhaps less bleakly realist, more stylistically adventurous, and amenable to what cannot be easily explained or categorized" (Mack, 322). Literature has been able to represent a fuller scope of sexual diversity than other written works, but it remains lacking in that it continues to produce an abusive ethnography occupied with classification and truth claims of Arab and Muslim abuse of women and LGBTQI individuals in the Middle East. While European; US; and, more recently, Canadian publications have tended to present gay Arab immigration as an inexorable march toward greater visibility and freedom of sexual disclosure, one hopes that more people become aware of the globalization of homonormative discourses and the way in which they jeopardize the specificity of Arab and Muslim sexual practices and attitudes. The homonormative discourses dominant today, and which are being adopted by young generations worldwide, involve latent but unacknowledged class and racial privilege (Mack, 325)—positing, in particular, a universal drive toward "outness" and independence from family. Such homonormativity aspires to "move beyond a more undefined, working-class, non-globalized sexuality" (Mack, 325).

While attention and criticism have been directed toward the discrimination that LGBTQI individuals are facing in the Middle East, little has been written about the trials of Syrian LGBTQI refugees in Western countries. After facing persecution and violence in their home countries and enduring challenging transitions to neighboring states, many of the refugees given access to countries in Europe and North America face political, socioeconomic, and psycho-emotional stresses. In Ramadan's novel the *hakawati* recounts in detail the many sad events he has encountered in the Middle East, yet he seems to steer clear of recounting any unfortunate memories of his life as a refugee in Vancouver. He briefly mentions missing his apartment in Beirut and a fleeting feeling of not belonging to Canadian culture: "Neither of us could admit it, but I missed our home in Beirut, while you missed your family home back in Damascus [. . .] Whenever we met someone new, all they wanted to talk about was the weather and the traffic; it was part of this new strange culture we found ourselves in" (Ramadan, *The Clothesline Swing*, 121). But aside from that instance, his life in Vancouver is painted as his salvation from his life as a gay man in the Middle East: "'You'll be sponsored to come to Canada by a group of Canadians who will take care of all of your needs for a year' he said, glowing at the privilege his country had given its citizens, 'You'll be able to live here out of the closet, openly, and celebrate your love'" (Ramadan, *The Clothesline Swing*, 190). His salvation is described as lovers finding one another. He speaks of being afraid to lose his new city, afraid of it being taken away from him, which would ultimately result in his return to Syria: "Like a new lover, we embraced Vancouver; we didn't think of our futures or hopes, we just lived the moment. [. . .] We walked up the hill and refused to jaywalk the streets, even when there were no cars. We wanted to be model citizens and we feared that breaking any law might cause them to take away our new city from us" (Ramadan, *The Clothesline Swing*, 120–21).

On the other hand, data outside the novel contradicts the general impression in the novel that Muslim immigrants are given the opportunity and a welcoming fair chance to integrate within Canadian society and culture. Statistics Canada reports a 253 percent increase in hate crimes against Muslims in Canada since 2012 (Minsky). The Angus Reid Institute has also published a set of opinion polls taken between February 16 and 22, 2017, related to coherence between the Muslim Canadian population and the Canadian population of other faiths. The polls state that 46 percent of Canadians view Islam and clothing associated with the religion unfavorably compared with how they view other religions such as Christianity and Buddhism, and 32 percent of them completely oppose their sons or daughters marrying a Muslim. Another poll shows that 25 percent of Canadians believe that their country should have taken a similar stance to U.S. president Donald Trump's on refugee policy, while the majority believe that the 2017 refugee targets should have been decreased, as opposed to its increase to 55,000 refugees (Kurl). The numbers are not as bleak, however, as the polls conducted by Germany's *Stern* magazine, which assess coherence between Muslims and Christians in Germany. The polls were published in 2015 and show that one in eight Germans is willing to join anti-Muslim marches, and 29 percent of German people believe that Islam is having a negative influence on life in their country (Hudson). Two previous polls in 2006 by the *Frankfurter Allgemeine Zeitung* show that 82 percent of Germans are concerned about the rise of Islamic extremism, and 51 percent of Muslims in Germany believe that 'most' or 'many' Europeans are hostile to them ("Turks in Germany").

To be granted refugee status on the grounds of sexuality (referred to here as 'sexual citizenship') is to enter a highly charged discursive arena that has existed since the U.N. Convention of 1951 (McGhee, 145). The main controversy surrounding this topic is on account of its granting individuals asylum for persecution due to their belonging to a certain social group, making this provision the most contested in refugee law. To be granted refugee status, applicants must testify in person, which is an act charged with both the promise of 'freedom' and the threat of deportation. Adding to the complicated process and challenging experience are governmental measures that restrict the right to asylum (Murray, *Queering Borders*, 4). LGBTQI Arab refugees also face daunting challenges in negotiating a system that questions the authenticity of their sexual identity. These questions of legitimacy are constructed by consistently evaluating bodily appearances, conduct, and narratives to determine their suitability in Western homonationalist sexual categories (Puar). These modes of evaluation and investigation of the queer refugees' body across spaces and times create significant challenges for the refugees placed within the determination process (Murray, "Real Queer," 29). Queer Arab refugee claimants, then, become classified by legislators and Western governments as either unworthy claimants or as poor victims begging to be saved from the tyranny of their own cultures, communities, and nations. Sexual-orientation persecution, like gender persecution, as deployed in refugee discourse can function as a deeply racialized, culturally essentialist concept in that it requires Arab LGBTQI people to separate their experiences of sexual violence from their experiences as colonized people (Murray, "Real Queer," 24). Their application for asylum often entails generating a racialist and colonialist discourse that critiques their native state "while participating in an adjudication process that often depends on constructs of an immutable identity refracted through reified colonialist models of culture shorn of all material relations" (Luibheid, 179). Furthermore, as mainstream LGBTQI groups and human-rights organizations seek to support queer refugees, they may inadvertently utilize the refugees' statements and claims in ways that sustain homonationalist discourses that preserve "a narrow concept of diversity defined in terms of freedom and choice [. . .] that not incidentally chime with a neoliberal free market ideology whose inherent exclusions are harder to name" (quoted in Murray, *Queering Borders*, 29). Nevertheless, as refugees encounter homophobia and racism in their daily lives in Western countries, the homonationalist discourse will expose the selective dynamics of asylum procedures and interpretations, as well as the role they play in supporting the privileges of neoliberal states (Goldberg). But what is more important is the exclusion of the histories of imperialism, colonialism, and racism from queer refugees' narratives of sexual identity formation and migration such that "we are not able to see how these systems of domination produce and maintain violence against racialized sexual minorities both within and beyond national borders" (Goldberg, quoted in Murray, *Queering Borders*, 24).

Citizenship, regardless of its various definitions derived from typologies of states as legal and political concepts, distinguishes the individuals who belong to the culture and society in question from those who are not entitled to belong. The rules and criteria for granting an individual citizenship, 'naturalization,' are often challenged and altered—and as a result, more recent discussions have transformed these rules and criteria to become more "inclusive" and "human rights oriented" (Yorukoglu, 62). Citizenship remains, however, despite challenges and alterations, centered around the idea of rendering certain groups and individuals as included and others as outsiders. The latter is a dangerous result as it enables discourses "around migration, integration and citizenship to abuse the emotional aspect such as fear of 'the other'" (Yorukoglu, 64. See also Said; Labib; Puar; Ritchie).

Ramy, the protagonist in Hasan Namir's *God in Pink* (2016)—which, like *The Clothesline Swing*, was written in English—is a closeted Muslim university student in Iraq. He lives with his older brother, Mohammed, and his wife, Noor, who have raised him since their parents died. Ramy's unorthodox behavior, his refusal to marry, and the one incident when Noor saw him in the arms of a male colleague in a car all lead his strict brother and sister-in-law to exert further pressure on him to marry. As they began introducing him to available girls to make his final decision for marriage, Ramy makes a desperate attempt to seek counsel by contacting the sheikh at their local mosque, Ammar. The latter is then placed in a dilemma between helping young Ramy with his predicament to come out or leave the country in order to live freely as a gay man, or to follow the teachings of the Qur'an as the sheikh sees them. Ultimately, this struggle leads the sheikh to question his own belief system as well as his gender identity.

As'ad AbuKhalil posits that "the construction of modern masculinity in Western societies was not similar to that in Eastern societies. The rigid lines of separation and distinction between males and females, or between homosexuals and heterosexuals, were lines of qualitative moral designation. Males and heterosexuals represent the ideal social and natural roles, from the standpoint of established clerical opinion" (AbuKhalil, 101). In her article titled "Violence, Sexuality and Women's lives" (1995), Lori Heise makes the astute observation that in numerous cultures men seek to prove themselves as belonging to the more esteemed category of heteronormative male, because the alternatives are being reduced to the status of woman or queer. Pink, typically seen as a dominantly feminine color from the late 1940s (Maglaty), is prevalent in Namir's novel, as well as being in the book's title, *God in Pink*. The protagonist, Ramy, chooses 'pink' as a secret word between him and the sheikh: "I ask you now to talk about homosexuality next Friday—and condemn it. Please. Condemn it. But if you mention one word, then I'll know you want to help me. One word" (Namir, 21). 'Pink' is also the word that Ramy uses to identify himself when he first meets the sheikh in person: "I can't find the words; this is more difficult than I thought it would be. I finally blurt out, 'Pink.' Sheikh Ammar's eyes widen as he silently stares at me" (Namir, 100). Ammar struggles with pink as he struggles with accepting his sexuality: "Drowning in a sea of pink, I struggle, fighting to make it to shore" (Namir, 59). And toward the end of the novel—when the sheikh finally succumbs to his own homosexuality, which he had been suppressing for years—the color pink is coupled with the shaving of his beard—the latter being another symbol of masculinity, which the sheikh rejects: "I have a revelation. I go toward my night table and retrieve the trimmer that I sometimes use. I turn it on and begin to remove all my facial hair" (Namir, 143). In the last scene in the book, which is the final time Ramy sees the sheikh, he "notice[s] the smears of pink lipstick on his face" (Namir, 150). Heise addresses in her article the difference between being a male and being a man. She concludes that a distinction exists between 'man' and the inferior category of 'woman,' which is connected to the question of orientation of desire and eroticism as expressed by the heterosexual and homosexual binary (Heise, 121). Gibson Ncube and Heise both consider these questions to be vital in the construction of masculinity in the predominantly heteropatriarchal Arab-Muslim societies (Ncube, 50). As when the *hakawati* in *The Clothesline Swing* affiliates with the role of the male Scheherazade, a similar sense of pride in a male embrace of femininity is also found in Namir's novel as displayed by the sheikh, signaling a reclaiming of terms that were once derogatory.

Maxime Cervulle and Nick Rees-Roberts argue that masculinity survives by making itself unrecognizable and concealing its name (Cervulle and Roberts, 53). Arab-Muslim masculinity as a research field has remained unrecognizable in that it is difficult to comprehend what it is, how it is constructed, and how it is regulated. There is a need to deconstruct Islamic masculinity, however, in order to "render Muslim men visible as gendered subjects and show that masculinities have a history and are part of gender relations in Muslim counties" (Ouzgane, 1). The novels of Ahmad Danny Ramadan and Hasan Namir, through their open broaching of male homosexuality, question the roles and performance of masculinity in predominantly Arab-Muslim communities. Their works embody the "distinction made by modern Western 'sexuality' between sexual and gender identity, that is, between kinds of sexual predilections and degrees of masculinity and femininity, [which] has until recently had little resonance" in Arab-Muslim nations (Dunne, 8). They also provide vital alternative models not just of masculinity but also of male sexuality and eroticism (Ncube, 52).

An equally, if not more, essential element of social cohesion for the Arab-Muslim immigrant is obtaining legal residence as a sign of integration. The aforementioned characters speak of emigrating in order to find salvation and freedom. Rasa, in the *Clothesline Swing*, dissociates himself from the war in Syria and from the identity of refugee and embraces his identity as a Canadian citizen (Ramadan, *The Clothesline Swing*, 39), and Ramy, in *God in Pink*, goes as far as justifying the U.S. invasion of Iraq as a way to free gay Iraqis: "'Ever since America invaded our country, we hear more and more about sex, nudity, superficial values. And yes, *lotees* [Lotee/ Luti is an Arabic term used to describe an active homosexual man]. Before, these things didn't exist here.' / 'Why can't you see it as freedom?'" (Namir, 104) [emphasis included]. As for the *hakawati* in *Clothesline Swing*, he speaks of emigrating to Canada because he is not able to integrate in Lebanon and compares his future there to that of the many Palestinians who sought refuge in 1948 and still have not been granted Lebanese citizenship (Ramadan, *The Clothesline Swing*, 189). Criticizing the label "displaced persons," he describes himself as a lost key chain and speaks of his loss of trust in everyone and everything around him even in his religion: "We felt as if we were someone's keychain, and that person displaced us. They looked for us on the coffee table and under the kitchen sink; they searched for us in the pockets of jackets and pants. We were never found. We lost our faith in our owners, and we lost our faith in the gods who put us in this place to begin with (Ramadan, *The Clothesline Swing*, 189).

Similarly to Rasa in *The Clothesline Swing*—who recounts in detail the many sad events he has encountered in the Middle East and steers clear of mentioning any unfortunate memories of his life as a refugee in Vancouver, painting his experience as entirely positive and the country as a haven for all homosexual Arabs (Ramadan, *The Clothesline Swing*, 120–21)—Ramy paints the West as an escape, and his only chance at salvation from the horrors he would have to encounter as a gay man in Iraq (Namir, 10; 43). Trust is a key element in social cohesion, as expressed in both novels repeatedly. Ramy speaks of not being able to trust anyone in Iraq, not even his brother, and moving to another country and becoming a citizen of that country gives him a chance at trust. His trust, however, develops from a lack of trust in institutions, to a lack of trust in his society, to a lack of trust in the immediate people involved in his personal life (his friends and his family), to a lack of trust in religion and God. Seeking guidance from the local sheikh was his last attempt at maintaining the trust that would enable him to live and survive in Iraq. Ramy establishes early on that the Iraqi government is not to be trusted. The army and police are always shutting down clubs, and abusing gay and lesbian people. His last male lover, Sammy, is raped and killed by an Iraqi officer (Namir, 144), which drives Ramy to finally succumb and marry Jameela—and, ultimately, to father a son with her. His distrust of institutions is not exclusive to Iraq, as he describes on multiple occasions the rape of young gay men by Hebrew-speaking men: "Speaking in Hebrew, the boy yells at them. [. . .] One grabs the boy and cuffs his wrists together. The other rips the boy's robe off as he cries out. They push the boy's face against the wall. I shut my eyes and pray in silence" (Namir, 58). While it is safe to assume that the Iraqi protagonist's distrust of the Israeli government and institutions is not surprising, the placing of these scenes throughout the novel suggests that Ramy not only views his country as abused and corrupted but also the Arab world as a whole as abused and raped—and, as a result, weakened and corrupted. This seems to signal a distrust in Middle Eastern and Arab institutions as well. Ali, Ramy's first boyfriend, pleads with Ramy to go with him to Turkey: "I can't live here anymore. It's not safe for me" (Namir, 19). He tells Ramy that he is the only person he can trust. Ali sees emigration as a final salvation, which is why he commits suicide when Ramy refuses to run away with him (Namir, 20). This shows a deep sense of a need for trust by the Arab immigrant in order to feel a sense of cohesion within a society or culture.

Trust is "like an emotional inoculation against existential anxieties" (Kinnvall, 746). Trust is often used along with other terms such as safety, fairness, or reliability of institutions as well as individuals. It is clear in both novels that neither Ramy nor Rasa trust their Arab countries, their institutions, or people; instead, their trust has been relocated and is desperately placed in Western foreign systems and institutions. Erick Uslaner identifies three types of trust: strategic trust (between individuals concerning specific events), generalized trust (trust in a larger society), and particularized trust (ties to an ethnic or religious community) (Uslaner, 421). He concludes that what he calls "strategic trust" crucially shapes individuals' sense of belonging to a community/society. It occurs when an individual trusts that what they expect from another will be done. Although trust between individuals and institutions is not specifically related to social trust (trust between citizens), it directly affects the trust of the immigrant in their surroundings. The government of the country one immigrates to does not necessarily need to be a 'good government,' but an immigrant's mere trust that its state institutions will be fair and competent will result in a more positive integration experience for them, which will in turn aid the development of social solidarity and collective identity (Huysseune). In other words, individuals who show trust in a country's institutions also show trust in that country's larger society:

> [Trust] is what keeps us hopeful, what lets us sustain courage, what helps us go on. It is what gives stability to our insecure and unpredictable lives. Probably a more intriguing quality of its relationship with a sense of belonging, however, is that trust in larger society does not only seem to affect one's sense of belonging to that said society. It also

strengthens the individual's ties to [the ethnic or religious] community one might be identifying with. Individual experiences of inequalities and discrimination, family and network based differences as well as different ways of interpreting all this matter in building, maintaining or losing trust (Yorukoglu, 107).

For the Muslim protagonists in both novels, trust in the institution of religion—specifically, trust in Islam—while it does get shaken, does not break. When all other trust has failed, their trust in Islam survives. Perhaps this serves as an indication that for many gay Muslims immigrants in Europe, Canada, and the United States, their religion needs to remain part of their identity in order for them to survive in their new societies and cultures.

Masculinity and Cohesion in Today's Democratic Societies

The novels *God in Pink* by Hasan Namir and *The Clothesline Swing* by Ahmad Danny Ramadan show the social capital available to gay Arab men as they try to maintain membership in multiple social groups and construct models of queer Arab masculinity in diaspora. Older paradigms of 'assimilation' and 'integration' are being replaced in policy discourse with 'inclusion' and 'social cohesion,' with regard to Arab immigrants in diaspora. In Europe, Canada, and the United States today, 'liberal values,' which romanticize cohesion (Yorukoglu, 49), have placed Arab masculinity in an ambiguous and contradictory position. They position it between pious Islamic masculinity, seen as illiberal, and a modern liberal model of masculinity, which these discourses characterize by its tendencies toward Westernization. Within such liberal values, international human rights and gay rights have also become primary indicators of the progress of nations—and the acceptance of these rights, and especially gay rights, a mark of embracing modernity. This acceptance, however, frames Muslim and Arab immigrants to the West as traditional and backward (Puar; Butler). Arab masculinity is then positioned either as modern, if it accepts gay rights and liberal values, or traditional and backward if it does not. Because the only acceptable visible queer Arab in this paradigm is the victim as displayed by the main characters in both novels (and by Ahmad Danny Ramadan himself, as an outspoken example of a victimized Arab gay man), resistance to the image of the Arab male as victim often leads to the reproduction of stereotypical and heteropatriarchal Arab and Muslim norms that define masculinity as heterosexual.

Both novels, through an open broaching of male homosexuality, question the roles and performance of masculinity in predominantly

Arab-Muslim communities, and render Arab masculinity visible without having to deconstruct it. There is a common sense of pride in a male exploration of inner femininity that frames gay Arab masculinity in both novels, displayed by the sheikh in *God in Pink* and the *hakawati* in *The Clothesline Swing*. An equally emphasized element in the formation of diasporic Arab masculinity in *The Clothesline Swing* is the obtaining of legal residence as a sign of integration. Gay characters in both novels speak of immigrating as an attempt at freedom, and they regard the West as an escape from the dangers they would otherwise have to encounter as victimized gay men in their Muslim-majority, Arabic-speaking countries—although in *God in Pink*, Turkey is also presented as an option. A deep sense of need for trust by the gay Arab male immigrant is demanded in order to feel a sense of cohesion within a society or culture, but Arab masculinity here is impacted gravely by the lack of trust in Arab countries and their institutions and societies. The protagonist in Ramadan's novel instead places his trust in the Canadian system, laws, and institutions. The protagonist in Namir's novel constantly thinks about leaving the country but in the end chooses social cohesion with his family in Baghdad over expressing his gay identity, which is seen by Ramy and his friends as possible only outside the country. Both these novels seem invested in binaries, either/or visions of queer possibility. The definitions of cohesion—and, for that matter, definitions of identity—are fluid and open to the intricate assemblages of diverse facets of one's identifications, including those that seemingly contradict each other. Democracy demands relations of inclusion and exclusion owing to the formation of a specific group of citizens. This leads to a political other who is automatically excluded from "the borders of the sovereign unity of 'us'" (Yorukoglu, 58), and also leads to a cultural uniformity that enables individuals "like us" to be included within our society. That also gives room for hostility against people within society, as the "friendly enemy" as opposed to the enemy outside. Chantal Mouffe proposes that agonistic confrontation (what she defines as antagonism between adversaries, as opposed to enemies, creating paradoxical "friendly enemies") (Mouffe, 13) is democracy's very condition of existence (Mouffe, 103). The conflict that could result from such hostility could be very violent, altering one's relationship to 'home,' to land, to community, "possibly making 'here' become strange" (Ahmed, 160). The denial of conflict, ambiguity, antagonism, and anxiety in favor of idealized characteristics such as coherence, wholeness, and consistency has affected not only our sense of being with others but also the sense of our being among others. Ideally, cohesion must include acceptance, respect, and willingness to engage with difference. It must acknowledge and address inequality so as to maintain, or strive to maintain, social justice.

Notes

1   The Canadian federal government, for instance, has established a Social Cohesion Research Network that has become one of the most active research networks worldwide today (Stanley). The European Union and the Council of Europe have also focused on the issue of social cohesion through their public policies, as the EU's Cohesion Funds have become one of the best-funded programs annually (M. Sharon Jeannotte, cited in Chan et. al., 1). International organizations have also adopted the concept of social cohesion within their policies.

2   In the United Kingdom, the period a spouse is required to spend in the country before being granted settlement rights has increased from two years to five in an effort to promote community cohesion (Fabb).

Works Cited

AbuKhalil, As'ad. "Gender boundaries and sexual categories in the Arab world." *Feminist Issues* 15, no.1/2 (1997): 91–104.

Ahmed, Sara. *Queer Phenomenology: Orientations, Objects, Others*. Durham, NC: Duke University Press, 2006.

Amer, Sahar. "Medieval Arab Lesbians and Lesbian-Like Women." *Journal of the History of Sexuality* 18, no. 2 (2009): 215–36.

Baun, Michael J., and Dan Marek. *Cohesion Policy in the European Union*, first edition. London: Palgrave Macmillan, 2014.

Benbow, Heather Merle. *Marriage in Turkish German Popular Culture: States of Matrimony in the New Millenium*, first edition. Washington DC: Lexington Books, 2015.

Benhabib, Seyla, editor. *Democracy and Difference: Contesting the Boundaries of the Political*. Princeton, N.J.: Princeton University Press, 1996.

Blackledge, Adrian. "English Tests for Migrants Will Fail." *The Guardian*, October 30, 2009.

Bollen, Kenneth A., and Rick H. Hoyle. "Perceived Cohesion: A Conceptual and Empirical Examination." *Social Forces* 69, no. 2 (1990): 479–504.

Bosch, Marta. "The Representation of Fatherhood by the Arab Diaspora in the United States." *Lectora*, 14 (2008): 101–12.

Browne, Rachel. "Canada Accused of Obsessing over Sexuality of LGBT Refugees." *VICE News*, September 29, 2015.

Butler, Judith. "Sexuality Politics, Torture, and Secular Time." *British Journal of Sociology* 59, no. 1 (2008): 1–23.

Cartwright, Dorwin, and Alvin Zander. *Group Dynamics: Research and Theory*, first edition. London: Tavistock Publications, 1968.

Cervulle, Maxime and Nick Rees-Roberts. *Homo-Exoticus: Race, Classe et Critique Queer*. Paris: A. Collin, 2010.

Chan, Joseph, Ho-Pong To, and Elaine Chan. "Reconsidering Social Cohesion: Developing a Definition and Analytical Framework." *Empirical Research* 75, no. 2 (2006): 273–302.

Dryef, Zineb. "Maroc: Abdellah Taïa, l'homosexualité à visage découvert," Tetu.com, May 2009.

Dunne, Bruce. "Power and Sexuality in the Middle East." *Middle East Report* 28, no.1 (1998): 8–11.

Fabb, Richard. "How New UK Spouse Visa Rules Turned Me into an Englishman in Exile." *The Guardian*, July 8, 2013.

Friedkin, Noah E. "Social Cohesion." *Annual Review of Sociology* 30 (2004): 409–25.

Fromm, Erich. *Fear of Freedom*. London: Routledge, 1960.

Georgis, Dina. *The Better Story: Queer Affects from the Middle East*. Albany: SUNY, 2013.

———. "Thinking Past Pride: Queer Arab Shame in Bareed Mista3jil." *International Journal of Middle East Studies* 45, no. 2 (2013): 233–51.

Global News. "Nearly Half of Canadians View Islam Unfavourably, Survey Finds." *Global News*, April 4, 2017.

Goldberg, David Theo, *The Threat of Race: Reflections on Racial Neoliberalism*. Hoboken, NJ: Wiley-Blackwell, 2009.

Green, Andy, and J. Jamaat. *Regimes of Social Cohesion: Societies and the Crisis of Globalization*, first edition. London: Palgrave Macmillan, 2014.

Gross, N. and Martin, W. "On Group Cohesiveness." *American Journal of Sociology* 57 (1952): 533–46.

Habib, Samar. *Female Homosexuality in the Middle East: Histories and Representations*. New York: Routledge, 2007.

Hall, Stuart. *Cultural Studies 1983: A Theoretical History*, edited by Jennifer Daryl Slack and Lawrence Grossberg, first edition. Durham, NC: Duke University Press Books, 2006.

Haritaworn, Jin, Tamsila Tauqir, and Esra Erdem. "Gay Imperialism: Gender and Sexuality Discourse in the 'War on Terror.'" In *Out of Place: Interrogating Silences in Queerness/raciality*, edited by Adi Kuntsman and Esperanza Miyake, 71–95. York: Raw Nerve Books. Print, 2008.

Hearly, Mary. *Philosophical Perspectives on Social Cohesion: New Directions for Educational Policy*. London: Bloomsbury T&T Clark, 2015.

Heise, Lori L. "Violence, Sexuality, and Women's Lives." In *Conceiving Sexuality: Approaches to Sex Research in a Postmodern World*, edited by Richard G. Parket and John H. Gagnon, 109–34. New York: Routledge, 1995.

Holton, Robert. "Talcott Persons: Conservative Apologist or Irreplaceable Icon?" In *Handbook of Social Theory*, edited by Gorge Ritzer and Barry Smart, 152–63. Thousand Oaks, CA: Sage Publications, 2001.

Hudson, Alexandra. "One in 8 Germans would Join Anti-Muslim Marches: Poll." *Reuters*, January 1, 2015.

Huysseune, Michel. "Institutions and their Impact on Social Capital and Civic Culture: the Case of Italy." In *Generating Social Capital: Civil Society and Institutions in Comparative Perspective*, edited by M. Hooghe and D. Stolle, 113–22. New York: Palgrave Macmillan, 2003.

Jansen, Th., N. Chioncel, and H. Dekkers. "Social Cohesion and Integration: Learning Active Citizenship." *British Journal of Sociology of Education* 27, no. 2 (2006): 189–205.

Jenson, Jane. "Mapping Social Cohesion: The State of Canadian Research." *Canadian Policy Research Networks Inc.* Ottawa: Renouf Publishing Co. Ltd, 1998.

Johnson, Pat. "The Danger of Being Openly Gay in Syria." *Xtra News*, May 15, 2015

Junuzović, Azra, Deputy Head. Globalization, Diversity and Social Cohesion in Educational Settings. Paris, UNESCO.org, November 5, 2012.

Kennedy, Sean. "Learning English should Be Part of U.S. Experience." *CNN*, Cable News Network, September 17, 2015.

Kinnvall, Catarina. "Globalization and Religious Nationalism: Self, Identity, and the Search for Ontological Security." *Political Psychology* 25, no. 5 (2004): 741–67.

Kurl, Shachi. "Open-Door Policy? Majority Support Government Decision not to Increase 2017 Refugee Targets." Angus Reid Institute, August 22, 2017.

Lægaard, Sune. "Immigration, Social Cohesion, and Naturalization." *Ethnicities 10*, no. 4 (2010): 452–69.

Lagrange, Frederic, "Male Homosexuality in Modern Arabic Literature." In *Imagined Masculinities: Male Identity and Culture in the Modern Middle East*, edited by Ghoussoub, Mai and Sinclair-Webb, Emma. London: Saqi Books, 2000.

Lauter, David, and Brian Bennett. "Trump Frames Anti-Terrorism Fight as a Clash of Civilizations, Defending Western Culture against Enemies." *Los Angeles Times*, July 6, 2017.

Luibheid, Eithne. "Sexuality, Migration, and the Shifting Line between Legal and Illegal Status." *GLQ: A Journal of Lesbian and Gay Studies* 14, no. 2 (2008): 289–315.

Lysgard, Hans K. "The Definition of Culture in Culture-Based Urban Development Strategies: Antagonisms in the Construction of a Culture-Based Development Discourse." *International Journal of Cultural Policy* 19, no. 2 (2013): 182–200.

Mack, Mehammed. "Untranslatable Desire: Inter-Ethnic Relationships in Franco-Arab Literature." *Comparative Literature Studies* 51, no. 2 (2014): 321.

Maglaty, Jeanne. "When did Girls Start Wearing Pink?" Smithsonian.com, April 7, 2011.

Massad, Joseph A. *Desiring Arabs*. Chicago: University of Chicago Press, 2007.

Mayer, Margit. "Combating Social Exclusion with 'Activating' Policies." *The Urban Reinventors Online Journal* 3 (2009).

McGhee, Derek. "Queer Strangers: Lesbian and Gay Refugees." *Feminist Review* 73 (2003): 145–47.

Minsky, Amy. "Hate Crimes against Muslims in Canada Increase 253% over Four Years," Global News, June 13, 2017.

Monterescu, Daniel. "Stranger Masculinities: Gender and Politics in a Palestinian-Israeli 'Third Space.'" In *Islamic Masculinities*, edited by Lahouchine Ouzane, 123–43. London: Zed Press, 2007.

Mouffe, Chantal. *The Democratic Paradox*. London: Verso, 2005.

Mudrack, Peter E. "Defining Group Cohesiveness: A Legacy of Confusion?" *Sage Publications: University of Windsor* 20, no. 37 (1989): 37–49.

Murray, David. *Queering Borders: Language, Sexuality, and Migration*, first edition. Amsterdam: John Benjamins Publishing Company, 2016.

———. "Real Queer: 'Authentic' LGBT Refugee Claimants and Homonationalism in the Canadian Refugee System." *Anthropologica* 56, no. 1 (2014): 21.

Namir, Hasan. *God in Pink*, first edition. Vancouver, BC: Arsenal Pulp Press, 2015.

Nash, Geoffrey. *The Arab Writer in English: Arab Themes in a Metropolitan Language, 1908–1958*, first edition. Eastbourne: Sussex Academic Press, 2015.

Ncube, Gibson. "Arab-Muslim Masculinity on Trial: Gay Muslim Writers Broaching homosexuality." *Gender Forum* 47 (2014): 50–63.

Ouzgane, Lahoucine. *Islamic Masculinities*, first edition. London: Zed Books, 2006.

Puar, Jasbir K. *Terrorist Assemblages: Homonationalism in Queer Times*. Durham, NC: Duke University Press, 2007.

Ramadan, Ahmed Danny. *The Clothesline Swing*, first edition. Gibsons, BC: Nightwood Editions, 2017.

———. "Why I'm Proud to be Trump's Worst Nightmare." *Xtra*, November 17, 2016.

Ritchie, Jason. "How do you Say 'Come out of the Closet' in Arabic? Queer Activism and the politics of Visibility in Israel Palestine." *GLQ: A Journal of Lesbian and Gay Studies* 16, no. 4 (2010): 557–75.

Said, Edward W. *Orientalism*. New York: Pantheon Books, 1978.

Stanley, Dick. "What Do We Know about Social Cohesion: The Research Perspective of the Federal Government's Social Cohesion Research Network." *Canadian Journal of Sociology* 28, no. 1 (2003): 5–17.

Stychin, Carl F. "Same-Sex Sexualities and the Globalization of Human Rights Discourse." *McGill Law Journal* 49, no. 4 (2004): 951.

Takeuchi, Craig. "Syrian Gay Refugee Activist Ahmed Danny Ramadan is Proud to Call Vancouver Home." *Georgia Straight: Vancouver's News & Entertainment Weekly*, August 17, 2016

"Turks in Germany: Two Unamalgamated Worlds." *The Economist*, April 3, 2008.

Uslaner, Eric M. "Segregation, Mistrust and Minorities." *Ethnicities* 10, no. 4 (2010): 415–34.

Vasta, Ellie. "The Controllability of Difference: Social Cohesion and the New Politics of Solidarity." *Ethnicities* 10, no. 4 (2007): 503–21.

Williams, Raymond. *The Long Revolution*. New York: Columbia University Press, 1961.

Yorukoglu, Ilgin. "Acts of Belonging: Perceptions of Citizenship among Queer Turkish Women in Germany." PhD dissertation, City University of New York, 2014.

7

OF KNIVES, MUSTACHES AND HEADGEARS: THE FALL OF THE *QABADAY* IN ZAKARIYA TAMIR'S LATEST WORKS

Alessandro Columbu

Introduction

Born in Damascus in 1931, Zakariya Tamir is a renowned Syrian short-story writer, columnist, and the author of numerous books for children. He grew up in the central al-Bahsa district of the Syrian capital and received formal education until the age of thirteen when he was forced to leave school to work as a blacksmith. He emerged as a short-story writer in the second half of the 1950s and his self-taught, unusual literary figure gained prominence on the Syrian literary scene with works that, since the outset, have been characterized by a close focus on the vicissitudes of individuals and their struggle against social constraints. Patriarchy, intergenerational conflict, female sexuality and masculinity are also among the most recurrent themes that his stories address.

Tamir's first collection, *Sahil al-jawad al-abyad* (The Neighing of the White Steed), was published in Beirut in 1960, and since then he has published ten compilations of short stories, three collections of satirical articles, as well as numerous articles and essays in Arab periodicals. He gained international acclaim as a writer in the 1970s with his two most celebrated collections, *Dimashq al-hara'iq* (Damascus of Fires) and *al-Numur fi-l-yawm al-'ashir* (Tigers on the Tenth Day), both characterized by vivid and evocative allegorical depictions of life under dictatorship and authoritarianism.

In the early 1980s the state's censorship of his satirical articles and a general feeling of estrangement were among the factors that triggered Tamir's unexpected decision to leave Syria and move to London with his family. He returned to the literary scene only in 1994 with *Nida' Nuh* (Noah's Summon), followed by *Sanadhak* (We Shall Laugh) in 1998, *al-Hisrim* (Sour Grapes) in 2000, *Taksir rukab* (Breaking Knees) in 2002 and *al-Qunfudh* (The Hedgehog) in 2005, all published from his self-imposed exile in England.

This latest phase of Tamir's career, in particular, is characterized by significant transformations in the realms of gender, sexuality, and the representations of male and female characters equally. Focusing mostly on stories from three of Tamir's latest collections (*Sanadhak*, *al-Hisrim*, and *Taksir rukab*), this chapter explores the evolution and the transformations in the representations of masculinities and gender roles in the short stories of this writer, and looks at the literary devices and symbols employed to signal the decline of a traditionally strong and virile masculinity, and the emergence of a new male identity.

R.W. Connell's concepts of hegemonic masculinity equip us with the vocabulary and background to approach the evolution in the stories of this writer, making an original contribution to the study of contemporary Arabic literature. Connell's theory of hegemonic masculinity underpins the analysis of the main themes explored in this chapter: the political significance of gender roles and masculinities vis-à-vis a persistent authoritarian regime; the mutually informed representations of femininity and masculinity; as well as representations of homosexuality as complicity with and/or subversion of a patriarchal and authoritarian worldview (Connell).

The chapter explores how male protagonists and symbols associated with their masculinity in Tamir's trajectory have evolved from idealized figures that embody positive values in the context of increasing urbanization and class segregation to helpless and emasculated, delusional characters, as well as an object of derision and disdain in his most recent works. The text analyses this phenomenon in parallel with the end of totalizing ideologies and the fragmentation of the notion of unity in Arab nationalism suggested by Abu Deeb, as well as the collapse of a seemingly unchanging, ahistorical male protagonist (Abu Deeb). In addition, drawing inspiration from Georges Tarabishi's reflections on the relationship between nationalist ideology, patriarchy and masculinity in Arab cultural production this chapter looks at masculinity, the body and gender roles as inseparable from historical events and political discourse (Tarabishi, 5–20).

The following pages address *turath*, authoritarianism and patriarchy as elements shaping the subjectivity of Tamir's male protagonists, and examine the ways in which Tamir's protagonists have interpreted the highly polarized standards of behavior that patriarchy dictates for the male and the female, and the inextricable link between patriarchy and authoritarianism. The analysis of this theme in Tamir is motivated also by a desire to scrutinize the themes and the stylistic devices through which his works of this period retain a significant political charge, despite the supposedly diminished ideological charge that the decline of emancipatory ideologies has brought about.

Fragmentation and the Collapse of the Male

As Samira Aghacy argues in her study of masculinity in contemporary Arabic literature, the institutions of religious authority, family, and the authoritarian state in particular, exerting an "exaggerated and amplified power," exercise their influence and power on the individual to such an extent that addressing individual matters conversely offers insights into the changing nature of the patriarchal institutions. While the emergence of female Arab authors and their representations of female characters and their sexuality in Arabic literature has received considerable attention, the exploration of masculinities with regard to concurrent historical circumstances has remained a relatively unexplored subject (Aghacy, 9). In the specific case of Syria, a deep analysis is still required in order to construct the framework to address the political significance of masculinities in contemporary cultural production. One of the possible ways to approach the changing connotations assigned to the sexes looks at the distancing of Arabic cultural production from a traditional form of commitment to the causes of modernization and national liberation. The collapse of unifying ideologies of nationalism and socialism in parallel with the persistence of authoritarianism has reshaped the political dimension of cultural production, particularly with regard to the relationship between politics, gender roles, and sexuality—yet it has not resulted in an unambiguous separation between fiction and politics (Aghacy, 130).

Looking at Lebanese fiction writing from the postwar period, Aghacy argues for the increasingly significant transformations the war has brought about in the realm of gender roles. In particular, her study explores the new forms of male identities engendered by the trauma of war, exploring them as changing in accordance with the social, economic, and political events and changes in the region (Aghacy, 2). With regard to Syrian literature and to Tamir's works specifically, a similar approach can be pursued to assess the new configurations of masculinity that his works project in the context of the broader, albeit bloodless, political trauma represented by the collapse of consensus and of all notions of ideological and political unity. The gendered dimension that this process of collapse and defeat possesses entails a diminished degree of agency for the male as the primary actor in the political arena. In Tamir's early stories from the 1950s and 1960s the quest for emancipation and modernization, exemplified by the optimism of stories like "Rabi' fi-l-ramad" (Spring in the Ashes), as well as episodes characterized by uncertainty addressing disenfranchisement and marginalization, was typified by the central role of male characters and by the accessory presence of women. The failure of the project from which those stories derived their vitality and inspiration, and the persistence of authoritarian and arbitrary rule, have, similarly to the shock of the Lebanese Civil War, produced new gender identities in an author like Tamir, often associated with a sense of anxiety and uncertainty (Hafez, 270). Certainly, gender roles and the gendered nature of patriarchal authoritarianism have been a concern for this author since the early period. However, in the latest stories the sense of inadequacy that defeat and fragmentation have produced in male protagonists and the subaltern position to which authoritarianism relegates them present us with the opportunity to discuss the aesthetic strategies through which Tamir's stories reinvent masculinities in order to address these transformations.

Shaken Masculinity: Male Submissiveness to Authoritarianism and Women

While with female protagonists the object-to-subject transformation has engendered a process of empowerment through the assertion of the female sexual drive, in the case of male characters the stories of the author's latest period exhibit a different, contradictory development (Columbu, 22–27). In addition to the greater degree of subjectivity that female characters attain, the collapse of the male protagonist's supremacy in this period comes frequently as a consequence of internalized submissiveness. In the early 1960s and 1970s works that addressed and denounced the confrontation between citizens and the authoritarian state successfully exposed the overpowering role of the representatives of the state in crushing the helpless male citizen—who was acutely aware of his own integrity and manliness. This aspect contributed to heighten the significance of the state's emasculating practices and their effects not only on the single individual but also on the ideal of man. This idealized manliness, embodied by the male protagonists in Tamir's 1970s stories, serves as a useful term of comparison to trace the developments in the representations of male characters. Although the themes of arbitrary arrest and violence at the hands of the state's representatives remain present in the latest period, in the 1970s the lengthy descriptions of the protagonist's manly self-image and confidence in his own integrity accentuate the contrast between a positive model of traditional masculinity and the castrating force of the capricious authoritarian state (see for example "Layla min al-layali" from *al-Numur fi-l-yawm al-'ashir*, 47–62). In turn, while the connection between the protagonists' subjectivity and their sexuality remains a central aspect in the latest period, nonetheless, the oppressor/victim relationship is transformed as the male appears both as a victim of the emasculating state and as a self-emasculating figure. Men in these stories have internalized obedience to the extent that they become complicit in the brutal practices of the state. Together with the decline of nationalist, socialist, and emancipatory ideologies, the consolidation of authoritarian and patriarchal regimes across the Arab East during the 1980s/1990s normalized practices that put men in a feminine position in relation to the authoritarian state (Aghacy, 95). This aspect adds a further degree of complexity to evolving representations of male characters vis-à-vis the persistent authoritarian state, successfully exposing the nuances in the strategies of domination Syria's military regime—famously analyzed by Lisa Wedeen—uncovering the role complicity and outward loyalty play in reinforcing authoritarianism (Wedeen, 1999, 73–83). This view makes everyone complicit in self-enforcing strategies of domination, deconstructing a state-versus-citizens binary opposition but attributing an equal amount of responsibility to the state's practices of coercion and the citizens' continued, albeit hypocritical, acceptance. Farid al-Murabba', the protagonist of Story 58 from *Taksir rukab*, represents an example of this new obedient male: arrested in the early morning and taken to a makeshift prison, he is accused of refusing to take bribes by the interrogator. The protagonist goes on denying the accusation, proudly asserting his descent from a family in which no one would ever refuse "the blessing of a bribe" and extolling his easily bribable personality (Tamir, *Taksir rukab*, 147). After beating and torturing Farid for days for denying the accusation leveled against him, the interrogator agrees to release him, accepting Farid's offer of a monthly bribe and the prospect of increasing its amount every month. The protagonist's self-image and breakdown gradually deconstructs a conceptualization of patriarchal masculinity as ahistorical and unified, exposing it as a fragmented experience "both commanding and impotent, heroic and cowardly, central and marginal" (Aghacy, 3) In this and more prominently in other stories the humiliation the protagonist is subjected to exemplifies a process through which the authoritarian state performs what Connell defines as practices of authorization and marginalization, that is to say, the process of interplay of gender with the arbitrariness of the authoritarian state transforming men from dominant to subordinate (Connell, 80).

In addition to the male protagonist's own self-image and internalized submissiveness, the collapse of his supremacy in this period comes as a consequence of the greater degree of subjectivity that female characters attain, testimony to the mutually informing relationship of stronger femininity and weaker masculinity. The degradation of masculinity in Story 47 in *Taksir rukab* is rendered through the gradual fragmentation of the male protagonist Said as a result of his urge to please a "beautiful and daring young woman":

Said kissed the lips of a beautiful woman and daring young woman. She complemented him on his kiss, saying without embarrassment that she enjoyed it and would welcome more, but she found fault with his dense mustache, in which the stale odor of tobacco had taken root making it smell more like rotten fish. As soon as he reached home, Said rushed to the bathroom, paying no attention to his wife. He stood in front of the mirror and with a firm hand shaved his mustache (Tamir, *Taksir rukab*, 112).

Similarly to a variety of other devices the mustache in this story stands as a symbol of the male protagonist's masculinity and respectability. Said, the protagonist of the story, does not hesitate to shave it off to please his nameless, beautiful, and daring mistress. The consequences though are inevitable, and as Said looks at himself in the mirror he realizes he does not recognize his own reflection. The removal of the mustache as the symbol of masculinity introduces a process of gradual emasculation of the protagonist that amounts to a humiliation.

> He then looked into the mirror and saw there a man he did not recognize. "Who are you?" he asked.
> "My name is Raghid," said the man with the shaved mustache.
> Raghid then laughed a merry and mocking laugh and said to Said, "the moment you shaved your mustache you disappeared. You didn't exist any more."
> "Don't gloat or feel glad," said Said to Raghid. "In a few days my hair will grow back the way it was because it's very thick and has always giver barbers a hard time" (Tamir, *Taksir rukab*, 114).

Men's incapacity to stand up to women's demands results in their ideal, as well as physical, fragmentation and loss of identity. The competition that the attractive female protagonist induces in the different male characters pushes them to symbolically castrate themselves—by shaving off first their mustaches, and then their hair. Even Said's reflection splits, and sees itself reflected in the mirror as a different man who introduces himself as Walid. An argument erupts between the elements of the threefold contradicting personalities of the protagonist, exposing a process through which the male becomes incapable of pleasing the female. "I'm married to the beautiful and intelligent Amal who's impossible to please," argues Walid; "she only loves my mustache and considers it a sign of true manhood"; "She used to pass her hand through my hair and say it was the hair of a black stallion" (Tamir, *Taksir rukab*, 113). But upon finding out what Said has done, Amal asks him for an explanation—to which he replies first by lying that he has cancer. Contradicted by his two reflections in the mirror, he then claims to have been called up for the army. When Amal asks him to compensate her for the shock caused by his lie, the protagonist embraces her and engages in sexual intercourse, which the narrator describes as paying "whatever compensation he owed" (Tamir, *Taksir rukab*, 113).

In line with the trends examined by Aghacy in contemporary Arabic literature, transgressive imagery in Tamir's latest stories does not promote a liberation of sexual mores and free relations between men and women, but rather decries a diminished role for men in the public sphere (Aghacy, 183). Challenging and satirizing an idealized model of manliness, as well limiting the female's agency to the bodily dimension the sexual connotations attached to female protagonists in this and other stories reinforce the polarization of male versus female identities, and limit the female's scope of action and her agency to the sexual. Female characters accomplish their social and political dimension inside and outside the household exclusively through their bodies, but remain intellectually passive and insignificant, failing to truly penetrate the spaces assigned to men. What is more, Tamir's conceptualisation of female power appears all the more objectifying in the constant reference to female sexuality which, from being taboo and a subject the writer timidly hinted at in his early works, has become the sole element through which female protagonists articulate their subjectivity and impact the man's perception of his own masculinity and self-image.

Symbols of a Long-lost Manliness and Instruments of Satire in *al-Hisrim*: the *Qabaday*

The mustache is but one among the rich array of symbols of an ideal masculinity that populate the stories of *al-Hisrim* and *Taksir rukab*. Alongside the active role female characters play in shaping the male's identity and manipulating him for their own benefit, symbols charged with cultural and historical connotations intervene to reinforce the contrast with an ideal masculinity that Tamir's male protagonists seldom match. *Al-Hisrim* is a collection characterized mostly by the recurrence of stories depicting incommunicability between generations and the widespread detriments brought about by patriarchy in its various embodiments, as well as by the original reinvention of historical figures and varying religious traditions.

Khadar 'Allun, the protagonist of "al-Muharasha" (The Quarrel) and "Masra' khanjar" (Death of a Dagger), is an example of the original variety of concepts and roles performed by male protagonists, as well as of the historical and mythical symbols of masculinity that Tamir incorporates in the stories of this collection. Most of *al-Hisrim*'s stories are set in the microcosm of the popular al-Qawiq quarter, where the protagonists experience dependency and patronage. The narrator introduces al-Qawiq as "notorious for its wealthy, who would kill their mothers if that granted them more money" as well as "for its rude men, who would never say no to a bloody wrangle and would happily go to prison. Men such as Khaḍar 'Allun, who cut his left ear in court in front of the judge and ate it with great pleasure" (Tamir, al-Hisrim, 13). Without mentioning it directly the narrator outlines the protagonist's profile as a *qabaday*, a colloquial term used to this day in the Syrian vernacular to describe a generous and morally upright man, but which traditionally in Ottoman Syria was a real-life figure: a manly tough guy and an instrument of the local notables to ensure their control over areas of the city. As Philip Shoukri Khoury recounts, the *qabadayat* (plural for *qabaday*) were symbols and almost authorities in the popular quarters of Damascus, and an expression of the city's multiple traditions and customs. They were a prominent feature of life in the city, renowned for their strength and moral righteousness, with an intimate and loyal connection to those popular quarters (*al-harat al-sha'biya* in Arabic) to which the *qabadayat* belonged and whose honor they defended. Far from being simple role models, however, they also possessed a darker side in that they were usually violent unsophisticated instruments of power who used their physical prowess to serve the authority of the local notables, known as beys (*beyk* in Arabic). Although widely respected and revered, the *qabadayat* possessed no political or financial power and were usually under the protection of beys who employed them to run their patronage networks (Khoury, 153–59).

It is important to note how the narrator sets these two stories in contemporary times—an aspect the reader can infer from the occasional mention of cars, paved roads and plastic surgery, which did not form part of the urban landscape in Ottoman Syria. Nowadays the delusional and romanticized *qabaday* model of masculinity that Khadar represents—far from being ideal—becomes the object of ridicule in the second story ("Masra' khanjar"), eventually causing the male's own disenfranchisement and demise. The story begins with the protagonist, Khadar 'Allun, discussing with his mother the prospect of getting married and settling down, as well as that of receiving plastic surgery to get his ear fixed. His refusal to accept his mother's advice and the model of resilient virility he projects comes across as a delusional myth, modeled on the sixth-century Arab knightly poet and warrior 'Antara ibn Shaddad, as a symbol of a long-lost ideal of courage and integrity. The protagonist in fact entertains imaginary conversations with 'Antara, who functions almost as his consciousness, instructing him on everyday issues and on how to resist the feminization of society.

'Antara ibn Shaddad secretly accompanied Khadar day and night.
[. . .]

"It has become fashionable these days for men to emulate women,"
'Antara ibn Shaddad said to him, "and for women to emulate men. A few men are real men these days, and nobody understands them."

His mother was shocked to see her son laughing. He'd been frowning and looking so angry as though he were about to explode. She said to him impatiently: "May God help you and your twisted mind." After kissing his mother's hand Khadar left her house, and headed over to the local café. He sat down alone, smoking his shisha. 'Antara ibn Shaddad said to him:

"Don't smile. When men smile too much they become like coquettish women" (Tamir, *al-Hisrim*, 20–22).

What makes a true *qabaday* these days, in other words, is not his strength or his courage but rather his ability to distinguish himself from women. The role of 'Antara's myth becomes more relevant when the emasculating forces of the modern state intervene to deprive the male protagonist of his dagger, the token of his masculinity, which underpins his subjectivity and serves as a phallic metaphor. During an ordinary stop-and-search, two police constables confiscate Khadar's dagger, the dearest object he owns, symbolically castrating him and leaving him dumbfounded and the victim of 'Antara's reproach, because "[a] man who gives up on his knife isn't a man and he only deserves to sit among women," as 'Antara says to him (Tamir, *al-Hisrim*, 22). Khadar tries to retrieve his dagger with the help of Najib al-Baqqar, himself the remake of an equally important traditional Damascene figure, the Bey, to whom *qabadayat* were loyal and dependent. But al-Baqqar's intercession with the authorities remains unsuccessful, and to add insult to injury Khadar discovers that the police have sold his dagger to a foreign female tourist. Feeling weak and helpless by the story's closure, he is run over and killed by a car after wandering aimlessly in an affluent area away from his quarter.

In addition to inequality and dependence, Khadar's estrangement is also a consequence of his own delusion, and his resilient and delusional commitment to his knife, which ultimately serves as an instrument of the Bey's power, not his own. The historical figure of 'Antara and the imaginary conversations the protagonist entertains with him reinforce the contradictory nature of the latter's obstinacy and self-denial. The collective dimension of gender roles emerges particularly in the authority of the state, patronage, and wealth that rise above masculinity, deconstructing the protagonist's ideal of honor and respect embodied by his knife. The attempt made by Najib al-Baqqar to intercede for Khadar confirms masculinity and male solidarity as a façade behind which power relations and patronage hide, revealing them as the decisive factors that determine a man's position in society. The different connotations that the context and class identity attribute to masculinity successfully expose the performative nature of gender roles, acted out in accordance with socially constructed norms and patterns that make them pertinent or not—a product of class-bound gender ideologies and an overall repressive political atmosphere (Aghacy, 4).

"Al-Mutarbash": The Restaging of Historical Events as a Satire of Delusional Masculinity

Again from *al-Hisrim*, "al-Mutarbash" (from *tarbush*, Arabic for fez; *mutarbash*, someone who wears a fez) also revolves around a *qabaday*, Mansur al-Haf, another character embodying a mythical model of masculinity, whom the narrator introduces as " a man with the composure of a calm sea [...] who would gladly go to jail as though he was going to a summer resort, and when he was discharged he would say: 'only a stupid man would be happy to move from a small jail to a big one'" (Tamir, *al-Hisrim*, 161). His loyalty to his wife, Naziha, also highlights his *qabaday*-esque gallantry, but comes to an end when she asks him to take off his fez—which, in turn, causes their divorce and the subsequent expulsion of Naziha from the house. As the story unfolds the fez's symbolism is expanded to connote the protagonist's masculinity, as well as nationalism and resilience, and resistance against foreign occupation. The conflict between the protagonist and his wife takes an unexpected turn as the fez dispute acquires an international dimension, the moment the narrator reinvents an important moment in Syria's history.

> One day his wife said to him impatiently in an angry voice: "Either you divorce your fez, or you divorce me!" Mansur al-Haf was furious, but he didn't produce his dagger. He said to her: "Our house's door is wide enough for a camel to walk through it. Go, run to your family. You're divorced. You're divorced. You're divorced." Naziha left the house in shock, bareheaded, crying in a desperate voice: "Help!"
>
> A nosy, curious wind carried her lamentation to the ears of the French general Henri Gouraud, who set off to save her, and led his troops victoriously into Damascus, stained with the blood of the city's sons killed in Maysalun. Damascus received him with the desolation of a falcon trapped in a cage, deprived of its sky. However, a clique of dignitaries and their servants rushed to carry General Gouraud's car on their backs to express their warm reception to him (Tamir, *al-Hisrim*, 161).

The episode is loosely based on true events. In 1920, following the San Remo Resolution with Britain and a League of Nations mandate, France claimed control of the territories of today's Syria and Lebanon (McHugo, 70–71). General Henri Gouraud, mentioned in the story, was a real commander who led French troops against the Syrian nationalist resistance to occupation in the battle of Maysalun in July 1920, and was subsequently appointed France's high commissioner for Syria (McHugo, 67). The importance of these events and of the twenty-six-year-long French mandate for Syria's contemporary history cannot be overstated. French rule entailed a process of carving up the countries of Greater Syria, known in Arabic as Bilad al-Sham, a vast territory including today's Syria, Lebanon, and parts of Turkey and Palestine. Although Bilad al-Sham had never been a unified state, it existed under Ottoman rule for five centuries—and in Syrian collective memory it is considered a culturally and linguistically homogenous entity. The French proceeded to divide this whole into small sectarian-based, semi-independent entities, and by the time Syria gained its independence in 1946 the territories of Ottoman Bilad al-Sham had shrunk dramatically (Seale, 14–16).

Thus, in this story the connection between the wife's cry for help and the subsequent French expedition reinvents the significance of the Syrian defeat at Maysalun, using the male/female dynamics between Mansur and his wife to symbolize colonization at the hands of the imperial Western powers. After taking power in Damascus, General Henri Gouraud proceeds to ban the fez in the entire country—but Mansur refuses to remove it, and is arrested by the French authorities. Summoned as the only transgressor of the fez ban, the hero's defiant resilience arouses the irritation of the French general, who sentences him to decapitation.

The ironic twist to Mansur's heroism and resilience is provided by the ambiguous, symbolic value of the fez, a type of headgear originally from Morocco but popularized by Sultan Mahmud II in the Ottoman Empire (Deringil, 9). Simultaneously a symbol of past Ottoman imposition, a fetish that embodies the protagonist's resistance to the new occupiers, and a token of his masculinity, the fez's ambiguity serves to bring together core elements of Syria's collective memory. Syria had been part of the Ottoman Empire for over four centuries between 1516 and 1919, when the Syrian Arab Kingdom was established, being dissolved shortly afterward following the battle of Maysalun.

Similarly to the figure of 'Antara ibn Shaddad, this protagonist embodies a traditional model of masculinity in decline, and the contradictory nature of the headgear and its resonance in historical terms prove a powerful literary device to satirize a model of delusional masculinity. This is not the first time Tamir has satirized a peculiarly male stubborn and self-erasing attitude, this story being reminiscent of "al-Liha" (The beards), published originally in April 1967. Here the male inhabitants of an unspecified city, confronted by the prospect of annihilation at the hands of the Mongol Taymurlank, choose death before accepting having their beards shaved off (Tamir, *Shi'r*, 135–37). A dark irony surrounds the narrator's view of the protagonist's blind and illogical acceptance of sacrifice in "al-Liha," excluding simplistic and unequivocal interpretations (Hutcheon, 11). In addition, the multilayered and ambivalent style that pokes fun at elements of history and tradition while encouraging multiple viewpoints on the same story introduces elements of postmodern writing. As Ulrike Stehli-Werbeck observes, a parodic attitude toward elements of tradition reinvents the Arab *turath* in order to satirize a delusional worldview and a rigid notion of masculinity (Stehli-Werbeck, 228).

Still in such multilayered, evocative episodes the significantly more intense presence and agency that male characters still enjoy is evident. Although the roles assigned to male and female protagonists in these stories remain polarized, other examples show how, far from reinforcing patriarchy, the representations of male characters involve a satirical take on their virility that contributes to deconstructing men's apparent integrity and superiority over women. Intellectuallly sophisticated and politically charged subjectivities are interpreted exclusively by Tamir's male protagonists, these are also most frequently the victims of the narrator's sarcastic remarks. Although men retain a criticality that women achieve only through their bodily dimension, this element becomes a tool to satirize the male's supposed superiority, exposing the self-mutilating, delusional, and deceptive nature of a dominant and generally accepted notion of what is male/female. Tamir's male protagonists such as Mansur embody a political dimension that his female protagonists do not attain, but their soundness is hardly idealized and the interpretative effort that the style involves engages the reader to deconstruct the relationship between men and women.

Male Homosexuality as Decay and Humiliation

An examination of masculinity cannot overlook the role homosexuality plays in shaping its models. Applying this approach to Arabic literature and society in the introduction to *Imagined Masculinities*. Emma Sinclair-Webb suggests the idea that fiction too employs ideal models of masculinity, which are frequently constructed in opposition to deviant models and in relation to presumed characteristics of femininity (Ghossoub and Sinclair-Webb, 15).

Male characters have usually occupied the center of most stories since Tamir's very first collection, but especially in his early works the more realistic tone and the evidently *engagé* style resulted in stories charged with great symbolic and heroic connotations, with relatively little emphasis on their sexuality. As early as the 1970s aspects of an evolution in Tamir's style are manifest in works that render justice to a changing political and social reality and convey a more nuanced approach to social issues. In this sense, the denunciation of alienation and inequality became more often associated with gender identity and sexuality. In "Ard sulba saghira" (A Little Hard Land), a story from *Dimashq al-hara'iq*, the first signs of new and more complex masculinities emerge in the male protagonists' disquieting attitude toward the female body and sexuality, as well as, more relevantly, in the connection between their sexual deprivation and eventual turn to homosexual desire. The story equals an ambiguous snapshot of a friendship turned love relationship, albeit portrayed through a timid allusion, situated in a context of ethical and material sternness. The two protagonists, Ahmad and 'Isam, share the same room as lodgers in the house of a widow, whose attractive body they enjoy peeking at from their room's window while she does the laundry in the courtyard. The boys get easily aroused at the sight of the landlady's uncovered thighs as she is engrossed in her work, ostensibly heedless of the boys' attention. The protagonists' sexual imagination, however, is not one of love and affection, or even of lust for the object of their desire, but rather of violence and forced sexual intercourse. They dream at length of creeping into her room at night and tearing off her clothes, of gagging her mouth and enjoying her immobility, and the prospect of ending up in jail for rape does not seem to deter them from their plan, although it does not materialize. Once the landlady has completed the laundry, the two protagonists decide to leave the house. Yet before emerging from their room Ahmad thoughtfully, and in accordance with the local etiquette, knocks on the room door to warn the women in the house of their presence, that is to say, inviting women to conceal themselves. Outside, as they leave the house and walk, the protagonists come across a pretty girl looking agitated, who suddenly disappears from their sight when a handsome man in fancy clothes pulls up in a car and takes her away.

> They went silent again. They went down to a loud street, and made their way to a small restaurant. They ate monotonously, then went to a café they frequented, had tea and played cards keenly. 'Isam lost. They returned home as the sun was about to set, and lay down next to each other on one bed, while the other bed remained empty. (Tamir, *Dimashq al-hara'iq*, 129–34).

While the story does not explicitly depict a homosexual relationship this subtext can be inferred from the closure, and it denotes a significant development in the representations of male sexuality through the dyadic nature of the protagonists, which clearly alludes at something more than a simple friendship. The stark disparity between the heroic and manly gestures of the protagonist of "Rabi' fi-l-ramad" (Tamir, 1963) and the attitude toward women that men display in this story, signal the beginning of a process of fragmentation and crisis. The fact that stories dealing with homosexual desire and same-sex relationships in Tamir's early works were a rarity can be explained with the general reticence of modern Arabic literature to address the subject. As it is hard to imagine that an insightful observer of his environment as Tamir might have been unaware of the reality of homosexual relationships, it is safe to explain this reticence—at least in the early period of his career—with the normalization of male-female sexual relationships that modernity brought about in the Middle East after the eighteenth century. As Frédéric Lagrange explains in his essay, "Male Homosexuality in Modern Arabic Literature," while in classical Arabic literature the theme of male homosexuality was pervasive, contemporary fiction tends to obscure its nature and usually employs same-sex relationships to express malaise and decay, a trend that in Lagrange's essay transforms homosexuality in Arabic literature to "the invisible desire" (Lagrange, 199). In this story, the structure and imagery reinforce an idea of same-sex intercourse as a sign of disquiet, exemplified in the morbid approach to sex of the two protagonists, their social alienation as well as by the coincidence between the two boys' retreat to their bed and the twilight, an image often used by Tamir to connote violence and humiliation. While censorship remains certainly a possible explanation, it is also safe to argue that the disparity in the ways and the frequency with which Tamir brings to the stage heterosexual and homosexual desire is revealing of a moralism that advocates a form of normalized sexual equality between the two sexes. In the context of a split between literature and nationalist ideology, and in relation to the persistence of patriarchal authoritarianism, the pervasive role of sexuality reveals a lasting tendency to instrumentalize homosexuality to symbolise the demise of masculinity.

Syrian critic George Tarabishi significantly drew attention to subtexts that emphasize the phallic nature of political activism in works authored by both male and female writers across the Arab world (Tarabishi, 6). In this sense the fact that the Arabic novel conceived war, the liberation movement, and the political confrontation with imperialism as essentially male had in turn already been exposed by Tarabishi in his analysis of Arabic literary production before the 1980s. In Tarabishi's view a deeply patriarchal worldview shaped both nationalist ideologies and cultural production, which conceived manhood and womanhood as signifiers for the relationship between men and women and expanded their significance to apply it to the relationship between human beings and the outside world. Power relations between colonizers and colonized people came to also be conceived as dominant/dominated and, crucially, male/female (Tarabishi, 5–17). However, whereas Tarabishi explains this phenomenon in relation to the patriarchal ideology of a backwards society (Tarabishi, 5), the persistence of a male-centred view on society in Tamir's latest works also reflects a sense of pessimism at the persistence of authoritarianism and its normalization.

The story of the two boys as well as a few other stories of the same period capture a sense of male vulnerability and weakness, a process of questioning masculinity that has become characteristic of Tamir's latest works. Instances of this transformation become significantly apparent in *Sanadhak*, a collection published in 1998 and which introduces gender roles as a tool to exemplify decay projecting also a model of weak, unreliable masculinity once again through the restaging of historical events and personalities. In "Hamlat Nabulyun" (Napoleon's Campaign), the French Emperor's famous expedition to Egypt is reinvented in contemporary terms, set in today's Damascus, which Napoleon occupies, enjoying the submissive reception of the city's dignitaries and religious authorities. The story takes an unexpected turn to the sexual inverting the male/female relationship between colonial powers and colonized victims: Napoleon's wife, Joséphine, taints the emperor's reputation by engaging in repeated sexual intercourse and introducing "the young Damascenes to what they did not know"; the emperor's colonizing/phallic prowess on the other hand is reversed to represent him in homosexual terms. Sad and depressed about his wife's scandals, Napoleon seeks the advice of a local sheikh, who advises him to attend the city's hammams. There the Emperor finally finds gratification, "for being under the masseurs' bodies made him imagine his army conquering the entire world. Napoleon Bonaparte led a happy life in Damascus, but the French government sent someone to abduct him and bring him back to France where he spent the rest of his life sighing in sorrow and distress every time he recalled Damascus and its men" (Tamir, *Sanadhak*, 78). This reversal, and the 'revenge' of the feminized East on the male colonizer, confirms a conceptualization of the relationship between East and West that remains necessarily sexualized—one of strength and challenge, shaped by dichotomies such as activity/passivity and positivity/negativity. As Tarabishi explains, according to this view there can never possibly be room for two males. One of the two has to prove his manhood to provide evidence of the womanhood of the other (Tarabishi, 15).

In *Taksir rukab*, published in 2002, same-sex desire and intercourse appear more frequently albeit retaining the same negative connotations it possessed in his earlier stories. This collection exemplifies the changing nature of gender roles in Tamir's latest stories, representing the most significant transformation in this writer's career because of its transgressive, taboo-breaking themes and imagery. Throughout this collection sexuality features extensively in stories shaping an alternative view and exposing the hypocrisy of male supremacy, pushing the unmentionable to the limits of obscenity. The very first story in the collection serves as an introduction to this central theme which presents elements of transgression of social norms, yet reinforces gender hierarchies and a traditional view of sexuality and gender roles pointing, particularly in the closure, to male and female homosexual desire as the ultimate manifestation of decay.

> The rains were scant. People appealed for help to a saintly man whose prayers were often heard, and a strange, heavy rain fell such as had not been seen before. One drop falling on a man, made that which men have, but not women, grow bigger. And one drop falling on a woman made her breasts and buttocks swell. Women were happy, for the real thing was not like the artificial, and cosmetic surgery was very expensive. Men celebrated this correction, which made a trunk out of a branch, but some were not content with what they got for free. They asked for a rain that taught proper manners to any man stupid enough to think that size exempted him from having to rise for a woman. Women prayed for a sudden rain that would make them pregnant and able to give birth without men. Men became idle, and found only dismissal, contempt, and derision wherever they went. Women then fell upon women, and men upon men (Tamer, *Taksir rukab*, 1).

In relation to the evolution of the homosexuality theme other stories in this collection put forward an element of originality throught the skillful use of allegories in that they represent male same-sex intercourse in *Taksir rukab* as an internalized form of submissiveness of men to both women and authoritarianism. Men such as the inhabitants of the village of Dhaghbit (Story 24), who welcomed a nameless rapist into their homes and enjoyed being penetrated by him (Tamir, *Taksir rukab*, 57); or Taha the protagonist of Story 42 whom the narrator describes as "a man who enjoyed being submissive" and is pleased to receive his rapist's comments on his handsome looks (Tamir, *Taksir rukab*, 96). This aspect contributes to expand the connotations— almost exclusively negative—that homosexuality has traditionally attained in modern Arabic literature, in contrast with the undertones traditionally associated with male same-sex desire and intercourse. As Lagrange shows in modern Arabic literature has almost exclusively being represented as a pre-modern vice, a disease or an allegory for the humiliation of colonization, dispossession and expulsion at the hands of foreign occupiers (Lagrange, 185–89). Male same-sex intercourse in *Taksir rukab* shows inclination to employ a shaken and weakened type of male protagonist in order to lament the decadence and helplessness of a traditional strong type of manhood. Hence, changing the focus from the emasculating forces of the authoritarian state to the self-emasculating nature of the subdued and delusional male, homosexual desire serves to portray a compliant male as the victim of his own lack of masculinity and self-respect, denouncing submissiveness to authoritarian practices rather than denouncing oppression and tyranny.

Conclusions

Gender roles retain a decisive function in Tamir's latest collections with most stories putting forward a model of masculinity that is vulnerable, subordinate, and weak. Looking at gender configurations as mutually informed, instead of separate universes with disparate political significances, the collapse of the male protagonist's supremacy emerges as the consequence of the greater degree of female agency, as well as the man's own self-image. Although a new female subjectivity has emerged in the works of this period, the exclusively bodily and sexual role that these new female protagonists perform leaves male protagonists embodying multi-dimensional subjectivities, as opposed to the one-dimensional sexual female. In addition to the bodily and the libidinous elements, the male's disintegration and loss of subjectivity is articulated through the intellectual and the political as well as, relevantly, through a direct confrontation with the authoritarian state and its oppressive practices. Whereas the social and political dimension of the female comes to the front only through her sexuality, the disintegration of the male contains a larger variety of articulations. In other words the language inevitably reveals a conceptualization of men and women in society performing two strict, separate, and polarized subjectivities that are characteristic of patriarchy. The analysis of the symbols employed to signify masculinity and the feminization of the male characters, in contrast with the exclusively sexual dimension of the female protagonists, shows the greater relevance that the former still retain. This hardly amounts to male supremacism and the stylistic devices of irony and historical restaging serve to expose a dominant and virile type of masculinity as delusional.

In the latest phase of Tamir's career the representations of male sexuality also witness a transformation toward the provocative and the transgressive. Sex and gender relations become a suggestive means to denounce social decay through male protagonists characterised by sexual incapacity as well as by a form of homosexual desire that comes across as perversion and submissiveness. To clarify their relevance, it is necessary to situate these aesthetic and thematic developments in the context of nationalism and patriarchy, cornerstones of Syrian authoritarianism containing a normative gendered and sexual dimension. This allows us into an alley of interpretation that deciphers this new and somehow crippled male that has emerged in the context of fragmentation and defeat, as an attack against the symbology of power in Syria, as well as a disappointed look on the deterioration of the male. Akin to the representations of female protagonists' confidently performing their sexuality, homosexuality also functions as a device to expose the male's diminished self-worth and to denounce authoritarian practices as the result of an internalized form of submission to abuse.

Works Cited

Abu Deeb, Kamal. "The Collapse of Totalizing Discourse and the Rise of Marginalized/Minority Discourses." In *Tradition, Modernity and Postmodernity in Arabic Literature—Essays in Honour of Professor Issa J. Boullata*, edited by Wael Hallaq and Kamal Abdel-Malek, 335–66. Leiden–Boston, MA–Cologne: Brill, 2000.

Aghacy, Samira. *Masculine Identity in the Fiction of the Arab East Since 1967*. Syracuse, NY: Syracuse University Press, 2009.

Columbu, Alessandro. "Representations of Female Eroticism in Zakariyya Tamir: The Women's Revolution from Object to Subject," *La Rivista di ArabLit* 7, no. 12 (2016): 7–27.

Connell, R.W. *Masculinities*. Second edition. Berkeley, CA: University of California Press, 2005.

Deringil, Selim. "The Invention of Tradition as Public Image in the Late Ottoman Empire, 1808 to 1908." *Comparative Studies in Society and History* 35, no. 1 (1993): 3–29.

Ghoussoub, Mai, and Emma Sinclair-Webb, eds. *Imagined Masculinities: Male Identity and Culture in the Middle East*. London: Saqi Books, 2000.

Hafez Sabry. "The Modern Arabic Short Story." In *Modern Arabic Literature*, edited by Mustafa M. Badawi, 270– 28. Cambridge: Cambridge University Press, 1992.

Hutcheon, Linda. *Irony's Edge: The Theory and Politics of Irony*. London: Routledge, 2005.

Khoury, Philip Shoukri. "Abu Ali al-Kilawi: a Damascus Qabaday." In *Struggle and Survival in the Modern Middle East*, edited by Edmund Burke III and David N. Yaghoubian, 153–59. Berkeley, CA: University of California Press, 2006.

Lagrange, Frédéric. "Male Homosexuality in Modern Arabic Literature." In *Imagined Masculinities: Male Identity and Culture in the Middle East*, edited by Mai Ghoussoub and Emma Sinclair-Webb, 169–98. London: Saqi Books, 2000.

McHugo, John. *Syria: A Recent History*. London: Saqi Books, 2014.

Seale, Patrick. *Asad of Syria: The Struggle for the Middle East*. London: I.B.Tauris, 1988.

Stehli-Werbeck, Urlicke. "The poet of the Arabic short story: Zakariyya Tamir." In *Arabic Literature: Postmodern Perspectives*, edited by Angelika Neuwirth, Andreas Pflitsch, and Barbara Winckler, 220–30. London: Saqi Books, 2010.

Tamir, Zakariya. *Breaking Knees*, translated by Ibrahim Muhawi. Reading: Garnet Books, 2008.

———. *Taksir rukab*. London: Riyad el-Rayyes Books, 2002.

———. *al-Hisrim*. London: Riyad el-Rayyes Books, 2000.

———. *Sanadhak*. London: Riyad el-Rayyes Books, 1998.

———.. *Dimashq al-hara'iq*. Ittihad al-Kuttab al-'Arab, 1973.

———. "al-Liha." Damascus: *Shi'r*, 33: 135–37, 1967.

Tarabishi, George. *Sharq wa gharb: rujula wa unutha, dirasa fi azmat al-jins wa-l-hadara fi-l-riwaya al-'arabiya*, Beirut: Dar al-Tali'a, 1977.

Wedeen, Lisa. *Ambiguities of Domination: Politics, Rhetoric, and Symbols in Contemporary Syria*. Chicago: Chicago University Press, 1999.

8

ROMANCING MIDDLE EASTERN MEN IN NORTH AND SOUTH AMERICA: TWO MID-CENTURY TEXTS

John Tofik Karam

M iddle Easterners work the imagined rural landscapes of the Americas. This chapter juxtaposes the mid-twentieth-century fictive construction of Middle Eastern men in the U.S. and Brazilian countrysides. My focus is on the characters Ali Hakim in Richard Rodgers and Oscar Hammerstein's musical film *Oklahoma!* (1955) and seu Nacib (Mr. Nacib) in Jorge Amado's novel *Gabriela, Cravo e Canela* (1958; English translation: *Gabriela, Clove and Cinammon*, 1962).[1] Both figures are depicted in similar economic terms, as petty merchants, but their ethnicity is sexualized in distinct ways. As sly traders in bucolic towns, Ali Hakim and seu Nacib become sexually involved with (non-Middle Eastern) local women. However, Ali Hakim is portrayed as a sleazy ethnic who must be sexually contained and forced to marry in the U.S. while his counterpart seu Nacib comes to epitomize a 'civilized' ethnic who does not need to marry, but only sexually mix, in Brazil.

Oklahoma! and *Gabriela, Cravo e Canela* are 'narrations,' which, in Homi Bhabha's words, are "internally marked by cultural difference and the heterogeneous histories of contending peoples" (Bhabha, 299). Attentive to the ways in which heteronormative sexuality serves as a key metaphor for national crisis and containment, I focus on how each narration is marked by Middle Eastern men. *Oklahoma!* hypersexualizes Ali Hakim as constantly philandering with U.S. women, and he is shunned by locals for doing so. After marrying a white farm girl, he is neutralized in the U.S. narrative. Conversely, in *Gabriela*, seu Nacib is briefly married to a 'mulata' who commits adultery and undermines his standing. When Nacib annuls his marriage to the 'mulata Gabriela' and returns to being her patron and lover, he is validated in the Brazilian narrative. At the same time each Middle Eastern man reproduces U.S. and Brazilian hierarchies of race, class, and gender,

Ali Hakim is sexualized in an ethnically subordinate position and seu Nacib in an ethnically dominant one, within distinct national narratives.

Oklahoma! and *Gabriela, Cravo e Canela*[2] are national narratives wherein the U.S. and Brazilian peoples emerge as both "pedagogical objects" and "performative subjects" (Bhabha, 297). Set in the late nineteenth century, *Oklahoma!* narrates two love triangles in which the farm girls Laurey and Ado Annie are courted by the white cowboys Curly and Will. These respective suitors win out over their competitors, the farmhand Jud and the Persian peddler Ali Hakim, and settle down as husbands and farmers. Performing an organic and assimilating nation, the musical film reifies and romanticizes the occupation and incorporation of the Oklahoma territory by white farmers just before it becomes part of the United States. Set in the early twentieth century, Jorge Amado's novel focuses on the 'mulata Gabriela,' who fled drought from the Sertão backlands only to enter into liaisons with three masculine embodiments of 'underdevelopment' on the northeastern Brazilian coast: the Syrian merchant Nacib, the outlaw Fagundes, and the womanizer Tonico. The novel ends with Gabriela as the cook and mistress of Nacib, an ambivalent performance of the 'mixing' of the Brazilian people. In both 'foundational fictions,' marriage and sexuality are key metaphors for belonging in the U.S. and Brazilian nations.

Such dynamics of inclusion and exclusion revolve around not only gender and sexuality but also race and ethnicity. While Sarah Gualtieri explores how early and mid-twentieth-century Middle Eastern, and mostly male, migrant elites lobbied to become white in order to become U.S. American, my own work looks at the ways that Middle Eastern men claimed to mix, or miscegenate, in order to become Brazilian (Gualtieri; Karam). In producing ambiguous and contested Middle Eastern ethnic formations, these interlocking hierarchies of gender, sexuality, and race underlie both *Oklahoma!* and *Gabriela*. While the Middle Eastern man is contained by marriage with a rural white woman in the U.S. narrative, his sexuality must be exercised with a mulatta mistress in order to belong in the Brazilian narrative. In both cases, Middle Eastern men confirm their place in the nation, but only by reproducing the hierarchies of ethnicity, race, gender, and class that ignore Middle Eastern women and work against non-elite women.

Middle Eastern Peddlers in the U.S. and Brazil

Mostly departing from present-day Lebanon, Palestine, and Syria, Middle Eastern immigrants numbered roughly 130,000 in the U.S. from the 1870s through the 1930s (Suleiman, 2) and 107,000 in Brazil during the same period (Lesser, 49). Quietly passing through U.S. and Brazilian ports of entry in the early years, these immigrants attained a striking presence in informal and petty commerce by the late nineteenth century. In New York City, over half engaged in peddling or shop owning (Khater, 74). In São Paulo, Arabs made up a significant number of *mascates* (peddlers) and small businesses (Knowlton, 113). Based in metropolises, Syrian–Lebanese trading nodes and networks spread deep into U.S. and Brazilian hinterlands. According to Akram Khater and Alixa Naff, the original Syrian colony on Washington Street in Brooklyn helped supply merchants who moved to cities and towns in the so-called heartland, such as Chicago and Cedar Rapids. These entrepôts were then used to branch into more distant territories, such as the Dakotas and Oklahoma. Likewise in Brazil, Syrian–Lebanese immigrants on the famous Rua 25 de Março in downtown São Paulo supplied their countrymen who peddled across settlements on coffee plantations in the south as well as on cacao plantations in the northeast.[3] Using novel railroad transportation in the U.S. and the newly constructed roadways in Brazil, Middle Eastern peddlers and petty merchants reached all forty-eight U.S. states and Indian territories by 1910 (Naff, 82), and all Brazilian states and territories by 1920 (Knowlton, 67).

Middle Easterners, however, were often viewed as pariahs by dominant U.S. and Brazilian elites. A U.S. government report in 1899 stated "this class of Syrians realize the worst attributes of the parasite . . . fawningly servile to . . . all those from whom he considers there is something to be gained" (cited in Naff, 220). The U.S. sociologist Edward Ross also observed in 1914 that "at a time when our retail commerce has happily come to the 'one price' system, the lustrous-eyed peddlers from the Levant bring in again the odious haggling trade with its deceit and trickery" (Ross, 193). Likewise in Brazil, a participant in a 1926 National Society of Agriculture meeting remarked, "we should also do everything to make difficult the immigration of Syrian elements which, far from benefiting agriculture, parasitically exploit[s] it in the profession of false businessmen" (Sociedade Nacional de Agricultura, 359). Another member of the Brazilian elite wrote that "the type of immigration required by the country's needs is that of agricultural workers and the Syrians are not classified in this category," being rather "dedicated to commerce and speculative activities" (cited in Junior, 39, 41–42). Embodiments of ostensibly uneven exchange, Middle Easterners were hardly embraced in this hemisphere's heartlands.

But their economic roles shored up national narratives. In 1931, a Syrian peddler appears in Lynn Riggs's play critical of Oklahoma's absorption into the U.S., *Green Grow the Lilacs*. According to one Oklahoman blogger, migrants from the southern Lebanese town of Marjeyoun first came as peddlers during the so-called 'Land Rush' and they established the St.

Anthony's Orthodox Church in Tulsa. Sol Bayouth was one of the founders of the parish. He was friends with Lynn Riggs, who used Sol "as a template for a character in his story 'Green Grow the Lilacs.'" [4] In his notes, Riggs describes the Syrian peddler as "wiry," "swarthy," and "very cunning," and one of the farm-girl characters alleges that he has "wives in ever' state in the union" (Riggs, 46–7). When this play was turned into the musical *Oklahoma!* by Rodgers and Hammerstein in 1943, the Syrian became the Persian Ali Hakim (Baringer, 452). A Syrian peddler also briefly shows up in Jorge Amado's *São Jorge de Ilhéus*, published in 1945. With peculiar gestures and a textualized accent, the character convinces a reluctant Brazilian peasant to purchase a necklace with fake gems, clinching the deal through a "daily theatrical representation that was his business": crying crocodile tears, raising his hands to God, and swearing that he lost money in the transaction. This novel takes place in the Bahian town of Ilhéus, the setting for Amado's later novel *Gabriela*. Though disparaged as an economic drain on U.S. and Brazilian societies in earlier times, the Middle Eastern male peddler is more pedagogical and performative in theatrical and literary works of the 1930s and 1940s.

Middle Eastern migrants were racialized in different ways by U.S. and Brazilian officials and policies. In the U.S., 'Syrian' was classified as part of the 'Caucasian' race in the late nineteenth century, but came under racial scrutiny from 1909 onward (Gualtieri, 53; Naff, 108; Samhan, 216–17). Due to anti-Asian naturalization laws in the following decade and a half, several U.S. courts denied citizenship to Syrians and all alleged Asians. In a 1924 court ruling, Syrians were again classified as white—and, ambivalently, become U.S. American. Though not construing Middle Easterners as 'Asians,' Brazilian immigration authorities viewed them as inferior to Europeans but assumed that their inadequacy could be solved through miscegenation. Inaugurated with the publication of Gilberto Freyre's *Casa-Grande e Senzala* in 1933, the idea of miscegenation between the Amerindian, African, and Portuguese became a bastion of Brazilian nationalism. Freyre claimed that interracial sexual relations created a unique Brazilian race that was free from rigid racial divisions and 'mixed,' culturally and physically. Gauged by marriage data, Middle Easterners were questioned for alleged propensity to avoid 'mixture' through the 1940s (Araújo, Souza, Viana). But by the early 1950s, they were commended for allegedly high rates of miscegenation (Guimarães), though white elites were hardly expected to do the same (Lesser). Middle Easterners needed to become white in order to become U.S. American, but they needed to mix in order to become Brazilian. These distinct incorporations of Middle Eastern-ness appear in the scripts of *Oklahoma!* and *Gabriela*. While the Middle Eastern man must marry into a rural white family in the U.S. narrative, he only needs to maintain a mulatta mistress in the Brazilian narrative.

Taming the Itinerant Sexuality of Ali Hakim in *Oklahoma*!

Heading toward the Skidmore farm in *Oklahoma!*, Ali Hakim first appears with a young woman, Ado Annie, seated on his horse and buggy. "The peddler man," locals call him. Aunt Eller, the farm owner, descends from the porch to scold him about a past purchase. Ali Hakim tries to pacify her with a gift. He pulls out one silk garter, "from Persia," free of charge. Aunt Eller covetously stares at it, and asks him for the other to complete the pair. The second garter, the peddler informs her, costs fifty cents. Aunt Eller roars with anger, calmed by the arrival of her niece, Laurie, and Ado Annie. With three women in his midst, Ali announces "now that all you ladies are here, let me show you some pretty do-dads." He pulls out lace-trimmed slips, but his female clients are indifferent. Ali becomes frustrated: "don't no one want to buy something?" Turning to Aunt Eller's niece, he asks "And what about you miss Laurie?" Dreamy-eyed, the blonde protagonist lists a series of intangible wishes. Ali has just the thing: "the elixir of Egypt," which, in his words, is "a secret formula that belonged to the Pharaoh's daughter." Aunt Eller interjects "it's smellin' salts," and Ali adds "a special kind of smellin' salts. Just take a deep breath and you see everything clear." Laurie is bedazzled and Ali makes a sale for two bits. As a foreigner peddling intimate wear and accessories to young and old women, Ali Hakim borders the masculine and feminine.

The Persian 'peddler man' also seems to pursue multiple sexual partners, including the farm girl Ado Annie. In the first scene on his horse and buggy, Ali woos the girl: "ah! Ado Annie. I can ride with you like this till the end of the world!" But Annie misconstrues his figure of speech as a marriage proposal. She previously tells her friend Laurie that she is going to marry Ali Hakim, but Laurie warns that the peddler man is not interested in marriage. When left alone with her presumed suitor in front of Aunt Eller's homestead, Annie asks what Ali means by such "purty talk." The Persian man explains that the end of the world is the hotel in the nearby city where they can experience paradise. Annie is perplexed. Paradise in a hotel? She thinks there are just rooms inside. Ali answers, "nah, for you and me baby, paradise." In misconstruing Ali's sexual advances as a marital commitment, the farm girl appears chaste and naive, and the Middle Eastern man astute and libidinous—the standard markings of an orientalist 'rescue fantasy,' critiqued first by Ella Shohat and Robert Stam and more recently by Amira Jarmakani.

But their exchange is cut short by the arrival of the white cowboy Will Parker, Ado Annie's other suitor, who has already proposed to her. Will relates to Ado Annie that he won fifty dollars at the county fair, meeting the stipulations of Mr. Carnes, Ado Annie's father, who demanded that Will save fifty dollars before asking for his daughter's hand in marriage. Will the white cowboy rescue Ado Annie from the peddler man who only wants to have sex, and not marry her? As a sly Persian, Ali Hakim is temporarily relieved and congratulates Annie and Will on their marital commitment: "It's a wonderful thing to be married. I got a brother in Persia who's got six wives." Ali goes on: "I got another brother with one wife. He's a bachelor." As a comical antagonist in this subtextual rescue fantasy, the Persian man's exaggerated sexuality reinforces an allegedly familiar and wholesome Oklahoman community.

But Ali does not get off so easily. Within the next few scenes, he becomes maritally entangled with Ado Annie once again—but this time in the presence of her gun-carrying father, Mr. Carnes. Having just learned that Will Parker won fifty dollars, Mr. Carnes fears that this dumb cowman might now marry his daughter. As a farmer, the father prefers a clever Persian peddler to a stupid local cowman, epitomizing the racial ambiguity of Middle Easterners and their potential to fold into whiteness. Mr. Carnes asks Ado Annie about her relationship with the peddler man. Ado Annie relates that the two had been strolling by the lake under the moonlight on the previous night when Ali Hakim called her a "Persian kitten because they's the cats with the soft brown tails." Learning of his daughter's sexually charged romance, Mr. Carnes cocks the gun in his hands and states in no uncertain terms to the peddler man, "in this part of the country mister, that better be a proposal of marriage." The Persian man cringes.

All is not lost for the astute Ali Hakim, however. He consistently endeavors to help Will Parker win Ado Annie's hand in marriage and gain her father's permission to do so. Will needs all the help he can get. Despite winning fifty dollars at the county fair, which he intended to use to earn the respect of Ado Annie's father and the right to marry his daughter, Will unwittingly spends the money on gifts for Ado Annie. But Ali Hakim ends up buying the gifts from Will for fifty dollars, so as to provide the cowboy with the money needed to win the farmer's daughter. The Persian peddler spends more money from his own pocket for the same purpose later. Although a shrewd money handler, Ali Hakim spends his cash not only to help Will win over Annie and her father but also to evade marrying a local woman. To the father's dismay, Ali succeeds in bringing together the two Oklahoman natives. At the end of the musical film, Will and Annie are engaged and ready to wed.

At the finale of the film, however, Ali Hakim is forced into marriage with another local girl, Gertie Cummings, the irritating daughter of a store owner from a nearby town. Gertie suddenly appears with a ring on her finger right after the wedding ceremony of the musical's two protagonists, Laurey and Curly. She attracts everyone's attention. The Oklahoman white girls are curious. Who would ever marry the annoying Gertie Cummings? Happy as can be, Gertie points to a visibly depressed Ali Hakim who edges into view. Ado Annie approaches the Persian man, asking if he really wanted to wed the unpopular Gertie. Ali Hakim explains, "I wanted to marry her when I saw the moonlight shining on the barrel of her father's shotgun. Thought it'd be better be alive but now I'm not so sure." Emblematic of his roving sexuality, the peddling profession of Ali Hakim will come to a definitive end. He will now help his wife's father run the county store. The Middle Easterner's exaggerated sexuality is contained by forcing him to marry a U.S. farm girl. As in the "desert romances" critiqued by Jarmakani, "heterosexual bourgeois marriage" is the "resolution" for such seemingly dangerous liaisons.

Virtuous Virility: seu Nacib as the 'Civilized Man' in Bahia

Unlike his peddling counterpart who is forced to settle down as a store owner in the U.S., seu Nacib makes his appearance in Jorge Amado's novel as the already established proprietor of a small bar named Vesúvio in the Bahian town of Ilhéus. His father, Aziz Saad, had been a peddler, and made the necessary bribes to a local official to naturalize his son when he arrived as a toddler from Ottoman-governed Syria. In the many years that have since passed, Nacib recalls not even distant memories of his Syrian homeland. Acquaintances and best friends nonetheless call him *turco* (Turk), but more as an "expression of caring, of intimacy," Amado qualifies (Amado, *Gabriela*, 61). Indeed, Amado notes in a later novel that the unflattering label of 'Turk' is used "without the intention to offend" because it is "part of the squabble, of the bargaining, of the pleasure of buying and selling" (Amado, *Tocaia Grande*, 39–40). Nonetheless, Nacib takes offense at the label and retorts, "Brasileiro" (Brazilian) . . . "filho de sírios, graças a Deus" (son of Syrians, thank God). To a degree of contrast with Ali Hakim's foreign status, seu Nacib's naturalization and national self-declaration introduces Middle Eastern difference within the Brazilian nationalist narrative.

In his younger days, Nacib worked alongside his father and uncle in what presumably was the family-owned textile shop, "measuring cloth" (Amado, *Gabriela*, 73). After the death of his father, Nacib grew impatient with his lazy uncle and sold his own share of the business. Using the profits to buy and sell cacao with volatile price fluctuations, Nacib equally tired of the wheeling and dealing. He eventually acquires the Vesúvio bar, some blocks away from the town's main commercial thoroughfare. Nacib attracts an increasing number of patrons with his easygoing demeanor and intriguing stories from "Syria, the land of my father." What also helps business, Amado notes, is watering down drinks and slightly inflating the monthly bar tabs of certain customers (Amado, *Gabriela*, 163). Though portrayed as an honest bar owner, seu Nacib exercises the shrewd bargaining sense imputed to so-called *turcos* as well.

Unlike Ali Hakim, who caters to female clients in the U.S., seu Nacib serves men who are thirsty for shots of *cachaça* (sugarcane rum), hungry for *salgadinhos* (finger foods) made by the cook Filomena, and who gamble at poker and darts. In this hypermasculine space, gossip about marital infidelity and sexual acts proves even more satisfying and entertaining than bar drinks and foods. Attracting much interest are stories of *coronéis* (political bosses) who massacre adulterous wives along with their lovers and, as a rule, are absolved by local officials. Upon hearing a very brutal tale, Nacib voices his own shock as orientalist hyperbole: "na Síria, terra de meus pais, era ainda mais terrível" (in Syria, land of my parents, it was even more terrible). If found to be unfaithful in Syria, Nacib explained, the wife was cut into little pieces and her lover, castrated. Brazilian men who condone local misogyny are horrified by such "strange customs." Orientalism in the southern hemisphere, like its counterparts in northern climes, evokes what Joseph Boone characterized as "the myth of the Arab male as more rugged and straightforward than other men—a myth of 'pure' unspoiled masculinity constructed out of late nineteenth century Anglo-European worries that its male population had become too civilized . . ." (Boone, 91).

However, Amado tells us that Nacib's "terrible stories from Syria" are *boca pra fora*, a put-on. Walking home from a bordello that night, Nacib cannot stop thinking of the young woman just killed by her brutal husband, the coronel Jesuíno. Of Nacib's remorseful thoughts, Amado writes, "this land of Ilhéus, his land, was far from being truly civilized. One would speak in terms of progress . . . but there continued ancient customs, that horror" (Amado, *Gabriela*, 161). Despite publicly presenting himself as more violently masculine than his Brazilian counterparts, Nacib privately yearns for a more "civilized" and, per Boone's approach, "feminized" community. Yet, as Amado writes, the "unspoken and cruel law" of the land (Amado, *Gabriela*, 420) enabled men to regain their honor after being betrayed by their wives. Whereas the Oklahoman town was romanticized as a chaste community that protected itself against sexual immoralities, Amado depicts this Bahian town with uncivilized—that is, "unspoiled"—masculinized norms, punctuated by a Middle Eastern man's own ambiguous relationship to it. Is Nacib a "real man," ready to defend his honor to the point of killing women? Or is he a "civilized man," taking a stand against gender violence?

The barbarity expected of men with adulterous wives in the rural Bahian town is in fact the main reason that Nacib hasn't married, despite his overwhelming desire to settle down with a woman. Working at the bar the entire day, his so-called "sentimental" affairs are limited to late evening hours spent with working women in the local bordellos. These sexual proclivities of the Middle Eastern man, however, are not ethnically marked as unique or aberrant. Amado portrays most Brazilian men—sons, fathers, husbands, and others—as avid clients of the cabaret, often arriving home at the break of dawn. Whereas Ali Hakim's ethnic difference intertwines with his sexual deviance in the putatively chaste rural U.S., Nacib's own sexual transgression is to quietly question the masculinist expectation of violence in rural Brazil. Given this key contrast, marriage in Jorge Amado's Brazil serves not as a sort of "resolution," as in the midwestern U.S., but rather as an observance of patriarchal rule and the "principle of power" upon which it rests—to use the words of Rafael Ramírez (Ramírez, 4). Mentioned earlier, Gilberto Freyre's *Casa-Grande e Senzala* notes the "sadism" of men over women, master over enslaved, and light-skinned over dark-skinned in rural northeast Brazil (Freyre, 76).

Epitomizing the Brazilian nationalist ideology of mixture, Gabriela is a cinnamon-skin-colored young woman with the scent of cloves in her hair. In contrast to the pale white Oklahoman woman staving off the advances of Ali Hakim, this brown Brazilian woman flirts with Nacib, calling him "a good looking young man!" Nacib subsequently agrees to take in Gabriela as a cook and, not long after, a lover. Her exquisite cooking skills are only surpassed by her sexual passion. In the kitchen and the bedroom, seu Nacib's appetites are fully satisfied. Such contentment, however, does not last long. Nacib becomes so enamored that he fears some man will seduce and steal Gabriela away. The "resolution," he initially decides, is marriage, despite the fact that Gabriela is not viewed by the town elites as a suitable wife. She is a poor itinerant laborer, and he an established and upwardly mobile merchant. Even Nacib's Brazilian male friends encourage him to keep Gabriela as a mistress, and marry another woman from high society. Nonetheless, the Middle Easterner weds Gabriela in a civil ceremony attended by a local Catholic priest. "Only then," Amado writes, "one knew that Nacib was Mahometan."[5] Unlike Ali Hakim, whose marriage is meant to neutralize difference, Nacib's consummation of marriage with Gabriela crosses and accentuates the boundaries of class, race, and religion.

But this was Ilhéus, a town between barbarity and civilization wherein the "quintessential way for a man to get screwed over," according to Sarah Hautzinger, "is for his wife to get sexually screwed by another man, rendering the husband a *corno* (cuckold)" (Hautzinger, 127). Nacib first gets wind of Gabriela's infidelity in an altercation with a hired hand he caught stealing from the bar's cash register. The thief first insults Nacib in ethnic and economic terms: "shitty Turk! Watering down drinks and robbing money," and then in sexual and marital ways: "why don't you take charge of your wife? Não sente os chifres doer? [You don't see you're a cuckold (figurative); you don't feel your horns hurt (literal)]." Nacib learns that each afternoon, his ostensible friend, Tonico Bastos, bids him farewell from the bar and heads straight to his house to sleep with Gabriela. Traumatized, Nacib needs to see it with his own eyes. So on the following day, after Tonico orders a quick shot at the bar and leaves, Nacib waits fifteen minutes, gets his revolver, and heads home. Another bar hand announced to the customers who all know of the affair, "Nacib has gone to kill Dona Gabriela e seu Tonico Bastos!" The institution of marriage, instead of a "resolution" as in Oklahoma, put men in Bahia at greater risk.

Upon entering his bedroom at home, Nacib bears witness to Gabriela lying naked in bed with Tonico. With a gun at his side, he has plenty of time to shoot and kill both of them, just as Colonel Jesuíno had done to his wife and her lover. Such is the "cruel and unspoken law" of the land. But as Amado recounts, "Não matara porque não era de sua natureza matar. Todas aquelas histórias terríveis da Síria que ele contava eram da boca para fora" [But he didn't kill because it wasn't in his nature to kill. All of those terrible stories from Syria that he used to tell were just a put-on] (Amado, *Gabriela*, 421). Tonico ends up fleeing half-naked. Gabriela, crying, is told to be gone by the time Nacib returned that evening. Shaken to the bone, Nacib later confides to a friend his intention to leave Ilhéus. If choosing to remain, he fears he will be ridiculed by others, having lost the "legitimacy of patriarchy" and fallen out of favor of what R.W. Connell calls "hegemonic masculinity" (Connell, 77). His friend, a lawyer, suggests another way to save face. On that same day, Nacib requests and is granted by the court a marriage annulment. Impressed with Nacib's legal recourse to handle threats to masculinity, Amado observes, the town of "Ilhéus possui, finalmente, um homem civilizado" [Ilhéus finally possesses a civilized man] (Amado, *Gabriela*, 427).

Other men call the Middle Eastern "the most civilized man of Ilhéus" (Amado, *Gabriela*, 477), but this does not matter much to Nacib. Although his heart is broken, he still longs for Gabriela despite her infidelity. Concerned with Nacib's depression, his lawyer-friend makes what seems to be another absurd suggestion: that he hire Gabriela as a cook once again. That very same day, Gabriela happily moves back to the maid's quarters in Nacib's home and the two rekindle their pre-marital relationship, in economic and sexual ways, as if nothing had happened. At the end of the novel, Nacib and Gabriela maintain their romance, not as husband and wife but as proprietor and cook/mistress. The Vesúvio bar prospers like never before, and its customers, in Amado's words, "praised the wisdom of Nacib, the way he knew how to get out of the labyrinth of complications . . . with honor and advantage" (Amado, *Gabriela*, 476). As a Middle Eastern man, seu Nacib confirms his ethnicity in the Brazilian nationalist ideology of mixture, but only by reproducing the hierarchies of race, gender, and class that repress poor women of color.

Conclusion

Tracing the ethnic difference that appears in U.S. and Brazilian narratives, this chapter suggests that Richard Rodger and Oscar Hammerstein's *Oklahoma!* and Jorge Amado's *Gabriela, Cravo e Canela* sexualize the ethnicity of two Middle Eastern migrant men in contrasting ways. Although both Middle Easterners are portrayed as sexually active traders who desire women in the country's heartland, Ali Hakim does not want to marry a U.S. woman and is forced to do so at the end of the story. Found to be morally perverse, if comical, by townspeople, Hakim's sexuality is forcibly contained by marriage and is greeted with laughing approval by Oklahoman locals. By way of the metaphor of marriage, Ali Hakim neutralizes his difference by wedding a white woman and agreeing to work for his white father-in-law in order to belong in the U.S. Instead, in Jorge Amado's *Gabriela*, the Middle Eastern Nacib wants to marry, and willingly marries, a Brazilian woman— but the town elites disapprove of the marriage, because the itinerant bride is viewed as lacking the necessary class distinction. After learning of Gabriela's infidelity, Nacib annuls their marriage instead of abiding by the "cruel and unspoken law" of the rural Brazilian town. He is not only considered a "civilized man" but, because of his "ingenious" reunion with Gabriela as his cook/mistress, is even called a "master of the good life" (Amado, *Gabriela*, 474). Seu Nacib must mix, not marry, in order to belong in Brazil.

Since their original release dates, the several remakes that these theatrical and literary productions have undergone tell us something about the persistence of the peoples they try to identify and the nations they try to narrate. First launched as a hit musical on Broadway in the mid-1940s, *Oklahoma!* was made into an award-winning movie in 1955 and has since been performed in small and large venues alike, most recently in the London revival that featured a relatively unknown Hugh Jackman (1998), which was repeated on Broadway (2002). Likewise, Jorge Amado's *Gabriela, Cravo e Canela* has been released in dozens of editions and languages. In the mid-1970s, it was made into a *telenovela* (television soap opera) as well as an internationally acclaimed film by Bruno Barreto in the early 1980s, and a more recent remake as a *telenovela* again (2012). As narratives about heartlands at two ends of the hemisphere, *Oklahoma!* and *Gabriela* continue to speak to U.S. and Brazilian publics. Yet, while the character of Ali Hakim is hardly acknowledged in the U.S., seu Nacib is a household name in Brazil. Orientalized and contained, Middle Eastern masculinity remains on the margins of the U.S. while its coveal 'civilizing process' earns a central place in Brazil.

Acknowledgements

This chapter is based on research that has been funded by a Fulbright-Hays Doctoral Dissertation Award from the U.S. Department of Education; the Center for Latin American Studies at the University of Florida, Gainesville; the Sultan Program of the Center for Middle Eastern Studies at the University of California, Berkeley; University Research Council grants from DePaul University; and the Conrad Humanities Award at the University of Illinois at Urbana-Champaign. I wish to thank Camila Fojas, Emily Gottreich, Waïl Hassan, and Lourdes Torres for their helpful comments and conversations along the way. I also wish to thank the organizers of this volume, Mohja Kahf and Nadine Sinno, whose interventions helped this piece immensely. All shortcomings are my own.

Notes

1 For other instances, see, Maud Hart Lovelace's *Betsy and Tacy Go Over the Big Hill* (1942) and Alice Christgau's *The Laugh Peddler* (1968) in the U.S., as well as Jorge Amado's *Tocaia Grande* (1981) and *O descobrimento da América pelos turcos* (1992).

2 From here on, Jorge Amado's novel is referred to as *Gabriela* in this chapter.

3 Others based in northern cities, such as Belém, Manaus, or Porto Velho had amassed sizeable fortunes through the grain and rubber trades in the Amazon (Karam, 23; Weinstein, 50–51, 259–60).

4 www.orthodox-okie.blogspot.com/2004_10_31_orthodox-okie_archive. html is no longer active. Last date accessed November 11, 2004. For more background on 'Sol' or Solomon Bayouth and the store that he opened in the town of Collinsville, just north of Tulsa around 1914, see: David Million, "Closing Time: Store Closes After 84 Years," *Tulsa World*, November 18, 1998, p. 1.

5 Although the inter-religious marriage could not be officially sanctioned by the Church, the Muslim groom Nacib and the priest agreed that the couple's future offspring would be baptized (Amado, *Gabriela*, 321).

Works Cited

Amado, Jorge. *Tocaia Grande: A Face Obscura*. Rio de Janeiro: Editora Record, 1981.

———. *Gabriela, Cravo e Canela*. Seventy-ninth edition. Rio de Janeiro: Editora Record, 1998.

Araújo, Oscar Egidio de. "Enquistamentos Étnicos." *Revista do Arquivo Municipal* 6, no. 65 (1940): 227–46.

Baringer, Sandra, Robert Hapgood, and Andrea Most. "Oklahoma! and Assimilation." *PMLA: Publications of the Modern Language Association of America* 113, no. 3 (1998): 452–55.

Bhabha, Homi, ed. *Nation and Narration*. London, New York: Routledge, 1990.

Boone, Joseph Allen. *The Homoerotics of Orientalism*. New York: Columbia University Press, 2014.

Connell, R.W. 2005. *Masculinities*. Cambridge: Polity Press, 1995.

Elias, Norbert. *The Civilizing Process* (1939), edited by Eric Dunning, Johan Goudsblom and Stephen Mennell. Oxford: Blackwell Publishing, 2000.

Freyre, Gilberto. *Casa-Grande e Senzala*. Rio de Janeiro: José Olympio Editora, 1977.

Gualtieri, Sarah M.A. *Between Arab and White: Race and Ethnicity in the Early Syrian American Diaspora*. Berkeley, CA: University of California Press, 2009.

Guimarães, Caio de Freitas. "A assimilação dos principais grupos estrangeiros, através das estatísticas dos casamentos e nascimentos, na população do município de São Paulo 1940–46." *Boletim do departmento de estatística do Estado de São Paulo* 14, no. 2 (1952): 81–114.

Hautzinger, Sarah. *Violence in the City of Women: Police and Batterers in Bahia, Brazil*. Berkeley, CA: University of California Press, 2007.

Jarmakani, Amira. *An Imperialist Love Story: Desert Romances and the War on Terror*. New York: New York University Press, 2015.

Junior, Amarilio. *As vantagens da imigração Syria no Brasil*. Rio de Janeiro: Off. Gr. da S.A.A Noite, 1935.

Karam, John Tofik. "Fios árabes, tecido brasileiro: desde o início do século, sírios, libaneses e palestinos exercem sua astúcia comercial nos quatro cantos do País," *Revista de História da Biblioteca Nacional* 4, no. 46 (2004): 22–24, Rio de Janeiro.

——— "Belly Dancing and the (En)Gendering of Ethnic Sexuality in the 'Mixed' Brazilian Nation." *Journal of Middle East Women's Studies* 6, no. 2 (2010): 86–114.

Khater, Akram Fouad. *Inventing Home: Emigration, Gender, and the Middle Class in Lebanon, 1870–1920*. Berkeley, CA: University of California Press, 2001.

Knowlton, Charles. *Sírios e Libaneses em São Paulo*. São Paulo: Editora Anhembi, 1961.

Lesser, Jeffrey. *Negotiating National Identity: Immigrants, Minorities, and the Struggle for Ethnicity in Brazil*. Durham, NC: Duke University Press, 1999.

Naff, Alixa. *Becoming American: The Early Arab Immigrant Experience*. Carbondale, IL: Southern Illinois University Press, 1985.

Ramírez, Rafael. *What It Means to Be a Man: Reflections on Puerto Rican Masculinity* translated by Rosa Casper. New Brunswick, NJ: Rutgers University Press, 1999.

Riggs, Lynn. *Green Grow the Lilacs: A Play*. London: Samuel French, 1931.

Ross, Edward. "The Lesser Immigrant Groups in America." *Century Magazine* 88, no. 6 (1914): 934–40.

Samhan, Helen Hatab. "Not Quite White: Race Classification and the Arab-American Experience." In *Arabs in America: Building a New Future*, edited by Michael Suleiman, 209–26. Philadelphia: Temple University Press, 1999.

Shohat, Ella, and Robert Stam. *Unthinking Eurocentrism: Multiculturalism and the Media*. New York: Routledge, 1994.

Sociedade Nacional de Agricultura. *Immigração: Inquérito promovido pela Sociedade Nacional de Agricultura*. Rio de Janeiro: Villani e Barbero, 1926.

Souza, Rafael Paula. "Contribuição á etnologia paulista." *Revista do Arquivo Municipal* 3 (1937): 95–105.

Suleiman, Michael. "Introduction: The Arab Immigrant Experience." In *Arabs in America: Building a New Future*, edited by Michael Suleiman, 1–22. Philadelphia, PA: Temple University Press, 1999.

Viana, Oliveira. *Raça e assimilação*. São Paulo: Companhia Editora Nacional, 1932.

Weinstein, Barbara. *The Amazon Rubber Boom*. Cambridge, MA: Harvard University Press, 1983.

9

TOUGH GUYS, MARTYRS, DANDIES, AND MARGINALIZED MEN: CHANGING MASCULINE ROLES IN IRANIAN CINEMA

Kaveh Bassiri

The social constructs of Iranian masculinity find their roots in pre-Islamic ideals of chivalry—the heroism of Rostam and other mythic warriors—and the Islamic values of martyrdom and sacrifice embodied by such spiritual models as Shi'a Imam Husayn ibn Ali.[1] In the twentieth century, traditional forms of masculinities faced the encroaching influences of modernity and Western cultures. Tensions between the demands for modernity and the resilient traditions of Iranian chivalry shaped different masculine identities. As hegemonic masculinities were reconfigured, filmmakers adapted their male stars to the changing cultural discourse, or participated in the forging of new gender identities. They gave the moviegoing public such colorful characters as the tough-guy hero *(luti)*, the revolutionary martyr *(shahid)*, and the Westernized dandy *(fokoli)*. The major sociocultural paradigm shifts that came with the Islamic Revolution also rewrote the normative discourses on male identity. In the films, neighborhood thugs were turned into Islamic heroes. Some filmmakers reinforced the new hegemonic masculinities, while others gave voices to marginalized or dissident masculinities. In this chapter, I track the changing roles of male subjectivity in Iranian cinema—from the valiant tough-guy of the pre-revolutionary period to the martyr of the Iran–Iraq War, from the lout of the lower class to the dandy of the middle or upper class, and from the impotent intellectual to the neglected veteran.

Iranian commercial cinema grew up during the Pahlavi dynasty (1925–79), when modernization became the focus of the nation. The Pahlavis saw vulnerability in Iran's lack of modernization and championed a Western model of hegemonic masculinity. Western knowledge became cultural capital, while traditional customs and religious knowledge were delegitimized and feminized. Outward appearance became an ideological battleground, as it served as an important measure of modernity and of a 'civilized' society. Reza Shah (r. 1925–41) even implemented a dress code. He banned tribal and traditional clothes, and, with the exception of the clergy, adult men were to be clean-shaven and wear Pahlavi hats with Western-style jackets and trousers. Iranian men continue to position themselves through these modernist discursive practices.

Most movie houses in Iran were built after the country's 1953 coup, while Mohammad Reza Shah (r. 1941–79) was consolidating power. As an instrument of modernization, cinema played a significant role in the discursive construction of modern Iranian masculinity. Though Iranian films traffic in many types of masculinity, we can trace a persistent reaction to the hegemonic form in the various archetypal male characters seen before and after the Islamic Revolution. Westernization was meant to help strengthen the role of modern men in society, but not to challenge the patriarchy or monarchy. In the 1950s and 1960s, the government encouraged historical adventure films with heroes like Rostam and Amir Arsalan, which entertained with romance, promoted a glorified past, and were loyal to the monarchy. These films advocated chivalry, unity, patriotism, justice, and Persian superiority. Meanwhile, a different kind of character, a *luti*, was becoming the dominant masculine star, highlighting the discord between the pro-Western vision of the ruling elite and the anti-Western popular culture of the masses. Critics labeled this tough guy with various names, such as *lumpen rouge* (Sadr, 111).[2]

Luti

The term *luti* goes back to the tenth century and is related to the word sodomy *(lavat)*. Some also believe the English word 'lout' comes from *luti* (Sadr, 111). In *Popular Iranian Cinema Before the Revolution: Family and Nation in Fīlmfārsī*, Pedram Partovi writes, "Suggestions of sexual corruption and dissipation . . . became a common appellation in Iran for those living on the margins of society" (Partovi, *Popular*, 58). The *luti*'s dominant role in his same-sex dealings is simply part of his tough-guy masculinity.

Over the centuries, the word *luti* became more closely associated with two marganized groups—"dervishes and entertainers"—and, more recently, "urban Robin Hood-type bandits," who "sometimes challenged oppressive governors, provided strong-arm support for local secular and religious leaders and bullied their fellow townsmen" (Floor). Many of the attributes of these groups—such as being an entertainer and abandoning worldly possessions, or fighting oppressors and defending the needy—are part of *luti* films.

*Luti*s are generally outsiders, on the fringe of society, acting either alone or in a gang. Their transgressive lives often come under attack, and they resort to fights in order to establish their masculine power and authority. They usually live in a homosocial community. The *luti* wrestles opponents in a traditional gymnasium known as the *zurkhaneh* ('house of strength') to become a *pahlavan* ('wrestler hero'). He follows the code of *javanmardi* ('young manliness'), the ancient principles of chivalry. These urban warriors are "to be truthful, to hold to their promises even when doing so was not in their own interest, to be wise, generous and full of esprit, and maintaining a broad-minded bohemian outlook on life" (Floor).

Neighborhood strongmen can be protectors or bullies, friends to the poor or thugs hired by the wealthy or the government to break rebellions. In the movies, the dual role manifests itself in the unique characters of the heroic *luti* and the villainous *lat*. The heroic *luti* follows the *javanmardi* code of honor, works alone, defends the weak and women, and respects elders. He is merciful, stoic, humble, chaste, loyal, and truthful. *Luti*s have an inner purity, and their cause is ennobled by spiritual righteousness. The villainous *lat*, on the other hand, is often boisterous and brags about his strength. He leads a criminal gang, bullies the weak, and can be hired as a mercenary. These two macho types become the clashing archetypal protagonist and antagonist of tough-guy films. But there is also a porous line dividing the behavior of a *luti* and a *lat*. For example, a *luti* can also engage in debauchery and brawl.

*Luti*s, like historical adventure heroes, hark back to past traditions and indigenous values. But unlike historic warriors, who are meant to affirm modern progress and loyalty to the monarchy, they represent the struggles and anxieties of the lower class in a changing society. They challenge Western values and bourgeois principles. In opposition to the modern Western-educated urban elite, the "honourable and lovable rogues of the *luti* tradition [stand] for all the forgotten and alienated victims of urban growth: vagabonds, smugglers, extortionists, blackmailers, dealers, cut-throats, gamblers and pickpockets" (Sadr, 117). *Luti* films were most popular with working-class male youths; the urban educated elite preferred American or European films and their version of masculine heroes.

As Fariba Adelkhah writes in *Being Modern in Iran*, "[t]he ethic of the *javânmard* cannot be understood only as a traditional legacy, but rather as a permanent improvisation according to a given mode in the musical sense" (Adelkhah, 4). For the young male viewer, tough-guy movies articulated the need for manliness and *javanmardi*—so fighting for tradition and honor, which meant fighting against modernization and consumerism, became the new mode of *javanmardi* in these films.

*Luti*s appeared in the 1960s melodramas derogatorily called *film-e abgushti*—what Hamid Naficy, in *A Social History of Iranian Cinema*, translates as "stewpot films" (Naficy, 2: 197).[3] These are not tough-guy movies, but their characters exhibit *javanmardi* qualities. Mohammad-Ali Fardin a handsome, former world-class wrestler often played a happy-go-lucky working-class character who is chivalrous and supportive of anyone in need. In popular movies such as *Aghay-e Gharn-e Bistom* (Mr. Twentieth Century, 1964) and *Ganj-e Qarun* (Croesus' Treasure, 1965) by Siamak Yasami, Fardin finds himself helping rich women in trouble—accidents that turn into romances and possibilities for breaking the class barrier. These films spoke to the dreams of the lower class as well as to their economic struggles and attachments to traditional beliefs. They glorify the poor as simple, honest, and authentic while ridiculing the wealthy as unhappy, materialistic, and corrupt. But, as with many early *luti* films, they ascribe problems to personal weaknesses or faith and not to sociopolitical conditions. Despite their critique of the upper class and exaltation of the working poor, the stewpot *luti*s ultimately subscribe to political conformity. Everyone belongs to their own class. For many critics, the films fail to seriously engage issues of class struggle and the inequality or injustice in society. There is no sign of suffering or protest. Instead, Hamid Reza Sadr in *Iranian Cinema: A Political History* argues, "They ended up preaching conformity and submission by reducing the political to a mere personal problem and then even further to a simple moral dilemma" (Sadr, 124). For instance, in *Ganj-e Qarun*, Fardin sings the virtues of being poor and not ambitious. In fact, poverty is a sort of requirement for higher morality, authenticity, and happiness. He ends up entering upper-class society by having actually been the long-lost son of the tycoon Qarun. Only with the tough-guy genre in the 1970s did Iranian cinema introduce characters who take charge, rebel, and demand change.

Dash Mashti and *Jaheli*

The tough-guy *luti*s are the emblematic masculine heroes of pre-revolution cinema, and Naficy identifies two types of films in the tough-guy genre: *dash mashti* and *jaheli*. Both types address the changing society and the social challenges of modernity but from a different perspective and historical juncture. "The *dash mashti* films concerned premodern, rural toughs from the turn of the twentieth century. . . . On the other hand, the *jaheli* films . . . dealt with the life and times of modern toughs after the Second World War—more precisely, with post–White Revolution toughs" (Naficy, 2: 270).[4] Naficy argues that the "cinematic shift from *dash mashti* to *jaheli* accompanied a gradual shift of societal paradigms within society from religious traditionalism to secularism and Western-style modernism" (Naficy,

2: 294). He also associates the making of *dash mashti* films with the late 1950s and the *jaheli* with the early 1960s, although the timeline is in fact not so clear-cut (Naficy, 2: 270).

Heroes in *a dash mashti* film, such as *Dash Akol* (1971) by Masud Kimiai, follow a dress code that includes "a felt hat (*kolah namadi*), a long coat (*qaba*), a large handkerchief manufactured in Yazd (*dastmal-e Yazdi*), a machete (*qameh or qaddareh*), a brass bowl (*jam*), a chain (*zanjir*), and woven cotton shoes (*giveh Maleki*)" (Naficy, 2: 283).[5] The *dash mashti* goes to the *zurkhaneh* to exercise and hangs out in alleys and traditional coffeehouses. He displays the ascetic qualities of a dervish, such as renunciation of material possessions.

Jaheli films are the most popular and emblematic examples of the tough-guy genre. The movie-star system thrived with these movies and resulted in such superstars as Behrouz Vossoughi and Naser Malek Motiee. Whereas *dash mashti* movies are optimistic and see poverty as a virtue, *jaheli* films are pessimistic and see poverty as a vice. *Dash mashti* literally means "a brother from Mashad," the most holy city in Iran (home of the tomb of the eighth Shi'a Imam), whereas *jahel* means 'ignorant.' The values of *dash mashti* are closely tied to asceticism, piety, and the virtues of rural traditions. *Jahel*s, however, live in cities and are exposed to Western influences. Hamid Dabashi, in *Close Up: Iranian Cinema, Past, Present and Future*, describes *jahel*s as "a type of lumpen who embodied the most sordid traits of patriarchy" and "represented the basest manifestation of male chauvinism" (Dabashi, 26). They mimic the modern dress code of hegemonic masculinity, but they make the Western fedora hat, jacket, and pants their own. They wear the clothes loosely, keeping their thick mustaches, and they never wear a tie. They are even known for their velvet hats (*kolah makhmali*). *Jahel*s use slang and speak in vernacular. They do not have a real job and hang out in nightclubs, cafés, and restaurants. "The chief protagonists also shifted from generous *luti*s, who generally defended the weak, to selfish, revengeful hooligans and louts" (Naficy, 2: 295). This shift in *luti* characters also speaks to the growing urban working-class population with its distinct social plight.

By the late 1950s, the manufactured identity of *jahel* as a *luti* had already become such a recognizable form of masculinity that it was easy for anyone to take up the role. The prescribed dress code, speech, and behavior of a *jahel* confirm what Judith Butler, in *Gender Trouble: Feminism and the Subversion of Identity*, calls the performativity of gender. She argues that gender is "a set of repeated acts within a highly rigid regulatory frame that congeal over time to produce the appearance of substance, of a natural sort of being" (Butler, 43–44). Thus, when in *Zalem Bala* (The Naughty Girl, 1958) the celebrated singer Delkash decides to pose as a man, she begins speaking and behaving like a *jahel*—donning a mustache, a velvet hat, and a black suit. The female-to-male gender parodies and the buffoonish tough guys of 1960s commercial films reveal that the *jahel*'s masculinity is a performative fabrication and that there is "no ontological status apart from the various acts which constitute its reality" (Butler, 173).

Kimiai's *Qaisar* (1969), a major box office and critical success, is the quintessential *jaheli* film. Its cast became a 'who's who' of tough-guy movies, including Vossoughi and Malek Motiee. The opening sequence—crafted by Abbas Kiarostami, with tattooed images of pre-Islamic warriors from the Iranian epic *Shahnameh* and the sounds of the *zurkhaneh*—sets the tone of *javanmardi* by idealizing the past heroic tradition. *Qaisar* is a reaction to modernization and an elegy for the disappearance of the traditional values of chivalry and manliness. The film champions individualism, a hallmark of modernity and capitalism, but its individualism supports traditional values and advances an idealized view of the past. The tension between the past and present or modernity and tradition is embodied in the protagonist, Qaisar. He is an oil-field worker who is now going to enact, single-handedly, a tragic revenge to restore the honor of his family. One day, he goes to a Shi'a shrine to pray for guidance and support. The next day, he goes to the cabaret, drinks, and sleeps with the singer, who is the girlfriend of the person he wants to kill.

Qaisar has to fight alone against the deviant thugs responsible for the death of his sister and brother. With all his contradictions, he posits *javanmardi* as an answer to the pressure of modernity and the alienation of lower-class young men in pre-revolutionary times. By tapping into a manliness that is rooted in tribal identity, the martyrdom of Shi'a imams, and the mythic warriors of the pre-Islamic epics, he becomes an ideal model of masculinity.

In the 1960s and 1970s—a time when the Pahlavi government dissociated itself from *luti* groups, executed their leaders, and was alarmed by such antisocial behavior—the tough-guy film genre was growing in popularity. The *jahel*'s vigilante behavior, his lower-class background, and his anti-Western and traditional beliefs were the opposite of what the Pahlavi government promoted. The commercial heroes of the pre-revolution, which ran the gamut from the happy-go-lucky working-class hero to the angry young revolutionary, challenged the regime and its Western-educated masculine elite. Naficy writes, "The government, for its part, wanted to encourage neither the toughs' take-charge attitude via violence, nor the tough-guy films' condemnation of Westernization as corrupt, nor the portrayal of poverty and marginality as the norm in a modernizing Iran" (Naficy, 2: 310). Yet the tough-guy rebels supplied an answer to the anxiety and rage of men caught in the demands and pressures of modernity and the oppressive regime. The Pahlavi's White Revolution, which began in 1963, left many, especially lower-class men and peasants, behind. New family laws and land reform, which were subject to the opprobrium of the clergy and landlords, further weakened traditional patriarchal roles in society. In this context, characters like Qaisar were "the archetypal anti-hero of Iranian cinema and a manifestation of nonconformity" (Sadr, 137). Films like *Qaisar* constructed desires as well as codes of combative behavior that young men idolized and went to see over and over again. Qaisar, became a model for angry young men and an icon, like the leftist Latin American hero Che Guevara, which also foreshadowed the coming revolution. Naficy argues, "In the tough-guy movies of the 1970s, personal revenge and crimes of passion were coded as citizens' revenge against governmental or upper-class oppression" (Naficy, 2: 232). By 1971, the first guerrilla operation against the Pahlavi regime (the Siahkal incident) had also taken place.[6]

Qaisar was not made with a political message in mind, but critics and viewers read it as a national allegory. In his later films, such as *Ghavaznha* (The Deer, 1974) and *Safar-e Sang* (The Journey of the Stone, 1977), Kimiai's revolutionary message is more intentional and evident. Sadr writes that in *Ghavaznha*, for "the first time a central sympathetic character . . . had played the role of a quasi-guerrilla" (Sadr, 142). *Safar-e Sang*, with its religious overtones and a call for rebellion, is even more prescient of the coming Islamic Revolution.

Given the notions of *vatan* ('homeland') as a female body and *khak-i pak-i vatan* ('pure soil of the homeland'), it is also easy to see how protecting the chastity and purity of a woman can be politicized and extended to defending the 'pure soil' of the motherland. Qaisar, like other *luti* heroes, must defend the *namus* ('honor') of his sister. This personal fight against family dishonor brought about by an immoral outsider becomes the recurrent theme of many Iranian films. Since the law does not provide the proper protection and justice, it is the male hero who has to take on the responsibility of protecting and restoring inviolability. Afsaneh Najmabadi, in *Women with Mustaches and Men without Beards: Gender and Sexual Anxieties of Iranian Modernity*, writes, "If in the gendered construction of modernity the homeland was a female body, the military masculine was the protector of the female homeland" (Najmabadi, 89). Thus, the *luti* working to restore the honor of his family becomes the revolutionary who restores the honor of a country violated by an oppressive regime and its Western allies. Najmabadi points out that "[t]o fail in one's patriotic duty was equated with failing in duty toward one's mother, and in particular with a failure of male honor in defense of the mother's chastity" (Najmabadi, 116).

A recent example of a film that integrates the struggle for the homeland with the spirit of Qaisar is the high-grossing *Lottery* (2018) directed by Mohammad Hossein Mahdavian. In the film, Amir Ali, a young man of the postwar generation, goes to Dubai to get revenge against the villainous Arabs who are responsible for the deception, violation, and suicide of his fiancée. Amir Ali is aided by Haj Musa, a pious and brave veteran of the Islamic Revolution and Iran–Iraq War. *Lottery* brings together masculine archetypes of the post- and pre-revolution like father and son, with Haj Musa and Amir Ali fighting on their own for the honor of not just the loved ones but also the nation.[7]

Shahid

The revolution arrived in 1979 with the overthrow of the Pahlavi dynasty and the ascent of Ayatollah Khomeini, who established the Islamic Republic. Many things perceived to be 'Western' were considered contrary to Islam. Even though many of the values of the tough-guy genre were similar to those endorsed by the new Islamic Republic, the regime did not want to be associated with the commercial cinema of pre-revolution years and its public display of sexuality. Minoo Moallem, in *Between Warrior Brother and Veiled Sister: Islamic Fundamentalism and Politics of Patriarchy in Iran*, raises the issue of the "emasculation of Muslim men produced by neocolonial modernity and the remasculinization permitted by nationalist and fundamentalist political movements," which helped shape the Muslim male hero of the revolution (Moallem, 24).

The government, as part of its unifying Muslim ideology, decided to promote an Islamic citizen as hero and to produce revolutionary films that would be an antidote to what it regarded as the immoral and decadent output of Hollywood and the Pahlavi era. After Iraq's invasion of Iran in 1980, the cinema—now funded by the regime instead of the box office—was to carry a spiritual and revolutionary dimension as 'sacred defense.' Films were to be unsentimental and simple—and without pretense, Western heroism, or the wish to entertain like Hollywood movies. By the end of the war, directors such as Ebrahim Hatamikia and Rasool Mollagholipoor—inspired by their mentor, Morteza Avini, and his documentary films—made what are heralded as the representative fictional examples of the cinema of sacred defense. Parviz Parastui also became the first iconic star of this genre. In the mid-1990s, around a quarter of Iran's films were about war (Naficy, 4:7). These films have been subject to various studies by such scholars as Pedram Khosronejad and Roxanne Varzi.

In the films, a new masculine protagonist combined *javanmardi* with innocent youth, spirituality, and self-sacrifice. He was modeled after the real war heroes whose pictures were plastered everywhere; streets, alley-ways, and freeways were named after them and their honorific, *shahid* ('martyr'). The revenge and revolt of tough guys were replaced with self-sacrifice and martyrdom.[8] *Shahid*s were not meant to be superstars, but ordinary men who were raised to a higher purpose by their Islamic calling.

Their characters were also to be distinguished from the leftist pro-letarians or Marxist revolutionaries who had played a significant role in the revolution. For example, in the recent film *Sianor* (Potassium Cyanide, 2016) by Behrooz Shoeibi, the pre-revolution schism between the Muslim and the Marxist members of the guerrilla group Mojahedin-e Khalq-e Iran ('People's Mujahedin of Iran') is presented as the struggle between pious and principled Muslims and extreme, deceitful leftists who kill and betray their own people. Hatamikia's recent film about Mostafa Chamran, the revolutionary commander and first defense minister of post-revolutionary Iran, is another example. The title, *Che* (2014), the first Persian letter of Chamran's last name, alludes to Chamran as a Muslim revolutionary ver-sion of Che Guevara.

The Muslim martyr heroes were honest, innocent, humble, gener-ous, selfless, faithful, fearless, and righteous. Their dress code replaced the Western hat and clothes of earlier masculine films with a khaki military uniform, shaggy hair, a beard, a gun, and a bandanna often emblazoned with Qur'anic text. During the 1980s, women were absent from the screen—and when they later appeared, their veiled presence further differentiated the sexes. For the cinema of sacred defense, the fight for God and the brother-hood of men replaced the defense of the honor of women and family. The battlefront took the place of the *zurkhaneh* gym, as the *shahid*s confronted a corrupt, heretical Iraqi enemy who used the latest technology and was clean-shaven and arrogant. Yet these war films did not have the pro-nation-alist and anti-Arab sentiments of the Pahlavi era.

In the movies of sacred defense, a mystical dimension was added, based on the Sufi narrative wherein, on the path to enlightenment, the *nafs* ('ego-self') is annihilated in order to persist in God. The word *Islam*, meaning 'submission,' applies to both the collective Muslim identity and to the will of God. For example, in *Deede-ban* (The Scout, 1990), directed by Hat-amikia and edited by Mohsen Makhmalbaf, an ordinary scout, played by a non-professional actor, has lost everything—including his motorbike. He slowly gains confidence, and begins to march alone in a sort of melancholic joy toward his destiny. The echoing sound of footsteps as he proceeds gives the impression that he is marching along with other soldiers. In his essay "Iranian Sacred Defence Cinema and the Ambivalent Consequences of Globalization," Shahab Esfandiary writes that the scene "may be a reference to verses of the Quran, where the Prophet Mohammed is informed that thousands of angels accompanied the small army of Muslim soldiers (in the war of Badr) when they succeeded in fighting back a large army of enemies" (Esfandiary 66). The scout's pilgrimage is to join the besieged soldiers and to enact his devotion by sacrificing himself for the *Basij* ('a paramilitary volunteer militia'), the nation, and Islam.

The spiritual journey in these films is twofold. On the one hand, we have a communal story of a jihad to spread justice against imperialism and oppression. The goal is to reject the modernist notions of self, secularism, capitalism, and consumerism. The martyr is to sacrifice himself for the collective subjectivity—a hyper-masculine, homoerotic brotherhood of soldiers who are often volunteer *basiji*. The dissolution of the hero's ego-self results in his immersion in the utopian *umma* ('the unified Muslim community'). On the other hand, the movies are also spiritual journeys of self-realization—a jihad of self against internal and external temptations. To purify his soul, the soldier renounces worldly possessions and carnal desires, and follows the path of love straight to God. Khomeini could be the beloved *murshid* ('the spiritual guide') who helps the *murid* ('committed one') find the right path—the way mystic Shams Tabrizi, the mentor and spiritual instructor, changed the life of the poet Rumi. The goal of this servant of God is to let God's love speak through his actions and to join Him through martyrdom.

The audience is meant to witness this journey from mundane to sacred, going through a spiritual transformation alongside the film's hero. (In fact, *shahid*, a Qur'anic word, means 'to witness'). The hero, the audience, and even the movie's actor and crew all go through this transformative spiritual experience, reconfirming the spiritual values of the nation. During the production, the crew enacts a sacred ritual similar to a *ta'zieh* (a Shi'a passion play). The experience of the martyrs is recorded as a testament. On the screen, the hero becomes a witness, a martyr to the will of God. Partovi, in "Martyrdom and the 'Good Life' in the Iranian Cinema of Sacred Defense," writes that "the films themselves are *shahadat* or testimony in revealing the divine presence through the heroes' performance of His will. . . . The audience is a *shahid*, or witness, to the divine presence too" (Partovi, "Martyrdom," 521). As in an Islamic *dhikr* ('remembrance'), viewers are inculcated in becoming *shahid*s.

Another transformation that took place in post-revolution films was the conversion of *luti*s into Muslim heroes, what Naficy calls the "Islamicate tough guy" (Naficy, 2: 310). Early on, those involved in the pre-revolution commercial cinema tried to refashion themselves as pious revolutionaries and martyrs. They made "[f]ilms that paid lip service to the armed resistance movement but in reality merely continued the traditions of the action genre" (Sadr, 174–75). With the biggest box-office sales up to that time, *Barzakhiha* (The Imperiled, 1982) by Iraj Ghaderi is a good example of a commercial movie co-opting revolutionary zeal. Played by leading pre-revolution commercial actors such as Fardin and Malek Motiee, a group of convicts escape prison and try to leave the country, but they have a change of heart after Iraq's invasion. They decide to stay and sacrifice their lives for their country. The movie's success prompted negative reactions from the conservative press and government, who questioned the credibility and sincerity of the pre-revolution artists behind it. As a result, many Pahlavi-era filmmakers and actors were banned from the film industry.

But the idea of converting thugs into Islamic heroes did not stop with *Barzakhiha*. Nor did it start there. It has long been part of Persian Shi'a tradition—as can be seen, for instance, in the conversion of the Umayyad commander al-Hurr ibn Yazid in the *ta'zieh* passion play. As with *ta'zieh*, the transformations on screen are also meant to interpolate the viewers—to have "not merely a cathartic but also a conversionary effect" (Partovi, "Martyrdom," 523). *Ekhrajiha* (The Outcasts, 2007) by veteran Masoud Dehnamaki is another successful example that broke box-office records. In Dehnamaki's comedy, a *luti* thug named Majid is reformed into a real man in the process of becoming a *shahid*. As in many Sufi stories, the change begins with the demands of earthly love. To get his girl and prove his man-liness, Majid goes to the battlefront and learns the true Islamic *javanmardi* value of self-sacrifice. He also ends up with the higher love of God.

Fokoli

Moallem writes, "In the modernist Pahlavi regime, the boundaries of tradi-tion and modernity were rigidly drawn, so that moving from one world to the other required particular strategies of copying, passing, and mimick-ing" (Moallem, 3). The *fokoli* is an example of a dandy who crosses these boundaries.[9] *Fokoli* derives from the French *faux-col*, meaning 'detached collar.' Sivan Balslev, in "Dressed for Success: Hegemonic Masculinity, Elite Men and Westernisation in Iran, c. 1900–40," identifies the earliest mention of the word "in the satirical magazine *Majaleh-ye Estebdad* from 1907" (Balslev, 554). *Fokoli* refers pejoratively to a man who is pretending to be modern by wearing a tie. Naficy describes his Western clothes as "short coats, vests, trousers, hats, sunglasses, watch fobs, leather shoes, ties, scarves, and cravats" (Naficy, 1: 279). Especially in the 1960s and 1970s—when Western pop culture, fashion, and media were omnipresent—*fokolis* highlighted the pressures of modernity and authenticity. They epitomized the critiques of artists, intellectuals, and clergy who saw the cause of Iran's social ills in the passive reception of Western values and the loss of Iranian identity. *Fokoli*s are usually portrayed as weak, ineffectual, and effeminate. They lampoon poor imitations of Western ideas. A leading intellectual, Jalal Al-i Ahmad, in his influential work *Gharbzadegi* (translated as 'Occidentosis' or 'Weststruckness'), defined these infatuated men stricken by the disease of "Westernization" as passive and "effeminate" (Al-i Ahmad, 96).[10] Their "effeminacy marks the surplus homoeroticism that escaped society's hetcronormative preferences" (Naficy, 1: 301). Ultimately, the subordination and feminization of the *fokoli* legitimizes hegemonic masculinity and the tough-guy hero.

The role of the dandy has been understood by scholars in different ways. Some, such as Sayyed Fakhr-al-Din Shadman and Sivan Balslev, describe *fokoli* as the negative manifestation of the authentic modern intellectual. Shadman sees him as the enemy of Persian culture who impedes true progress. The *fokoli*, then, allows intellectual elites to divert criticism of their own Westernization and Western-educated hegemonic masculinity onto those who are not properly educated or actually modern. Balslev writes, "The *fokoli*, constructed as an antitype of 'properly' westernized men, allowed men of the western-educated elite to deflate criticism of their own westernization and direct it toward men who did not enjoy the benefits of prolonged western education." (Balslev, 547). Just as the *lat* is the antithesis of the archetypal positive *luti*, the *fokoli* is the antithesis of the dominant hegemonic masculinity. *Lat*s are seen as the lumpenproletarians and a malady of the lower class, while *fokoli*s are the bourgeoisie and the malady of the upper and middle classes. Others, such as Naficy, consider that the *fokoli*'s performative acts "threatened the Islamic, patriarchal, secular, and heteronormal orders" by mimicry (Naficy, 1: 277). Naficy describes this mimicry—similar to the way Homi Bhabha uses the term—as a form of resistance that, in its excessive and inappropriate behavior, problematizes both Western ideals and Iranian traditional values. Naficy argues, "Westernized dandies were third-world subjects who struck back at the West by turning themselves into fabulous chimeras, social monsters, or inappropriate Others" (Naficy, 1: 295). In cinema, a further challenge from this gender-bending ambivalence and hybridity can be seen in the performative behavior of cross-dressing.

A dandy plays a supporting role in the first Iranian feature film, Ovanes Ohanian's *Haji Agha, Actor-e Cinema* (Haji Agha, the Cinema Actor, 1933), and *fokoli*s have long appeared opposite *luti*s, helping to define *mardanegi* ('men's virility')—as in Hossein Madani's *Jahelha va Zhigoloha* (Tough Guys and Gigolos, 1965).[11] While the lower-class *luti* advocates traditional values, the *fokoli* favors Western modernity. Usually, the *fokoli* does not have a proper job or a wife. Sometimes he competes with the *luti* hero for the same girl or even tries to lead her astray, but the *luti* wins in the end. Although the films ultimately reinforce marriage and compulsory heterosexuality, there is a degree of latent homosexuality evident in the *fokoli*'s behavior. *Jahel* is the active strong male, while *fokoli* is the passive weak male. Naficy writes, "Suppressed homosociality and homosexuality formed important undercurrents of dandy and *luti* movies" (Naficy, 1: 301). For *luti*s, their male social bond creates a homosocial environment, while the *fokoli*s' effeminate behavior encourages a homosexual reading of their character.

Parviz Sayyad's popular pre-revolution television series *Sarkar Ostovar* (The Sergeant) and his later 1970s movies based on the same characters provide a different take on the conflict of *luti*s and *fokoli*s. In some of these works, a naive country boy named Samad, played by Sayyad, competes with Einullah—a variation on a *fokoli*—for the love of Laila. Einullah has gone to the city for a few years and come back superficially modern, pretending to be educated and civilized. Unlike everyone in the village, he wears a suit and tie. Where Samad is strong and willful, Einullah is effeminate and lazy. His clothes do not even fit him properly, his tie is too big, and he is always trying to gain the respect of others. Laila loves Samad, but her village-chief father refuses to give her away to a lowly yokel. He has promised her to Einullah, whose wealthier father is his friend. In the end, Einullah loses to Samad and never marries Laila. In Sayyad's films, the values of the tough-guy movies were applied to a rural setting. They championed poor native villagers and their customs as honest and authentic, and rejected the rich and Western-influenced urban dwellers as materialistic and phony.

A *fokoli* may be re-masculinized into a *jahel* through the power of love and marriage. One example occurs in Reza Safai's *Jooje Fokoli* (Baby Dandy, 1974), which harks back to *Qaisar* as the hero, Feraidun, is meant to be the son of Qaisar's murdered brother. Although he has studied medicine, Feraidun has become a Westernized hippie and a rock musician who needs to be restored as a real man. By falling in love and going to a made-up shoddy Jaheli Institute, he takes his rightful place as his father's son, reinforcing the patriarchal masculine identity. The transformation is both *biruni* ('external') and *daruni* ('internal'). He cuts his long hair, changes his beard to a *jaheli* mustache, wears a *jaheli* suit and fedora hat, and begins talking like a tough guy. "The dandies became appropriate citizens . . . through their transformation from sexually ambiguous, effeminate, shady, Weststruck characters into honest, authentic, manly, and strong tough guys" (Naficy, 1: 301). An example of a parallel off-screen transformation is that of the actor Malek Motiee from a modern, irresponsible gigolo in 1950s movies into the tough-guy hero of the 1960s and 1970s. *Fokoli*s continued to appear in movies after the revolution, such as in Ali Hatami's *Jafar Khan az Farang Bargashte* (Jafar Khan Has Returned from Europe, 1985) or Saman Moghadam's *Maxx* (2005). But in recent decades, dandies have become just a subset of deviant, corrupt, and inauthentic Westernized characters or shallow and ill-fated expatriates.

The Marginalized Man

Masculinity is a configuration of dynamic social and cultural discursive practices. While a site of power, it is also unevenly allocated among men. There is a hierarchy. In *Masculinities*, R.W. Connell describes four types of masculinities: hegemonic, complicit, subordinate, and marginalized. Complicit, subordinated, and marginalized masculinities have to position themselves against hegemonic masculinities, but they also influence dominant norms. Ordinary men have to negotiate and perform these masculinities. In his essay, "Mullahs, Martyrs and Men: Conceptualizing Masculinity in the Islamic Republic of Iran," Shahin Germani describes the rubrics of ordinary Iranian men as those, who while benefiting from the law are paying greatly through "[h]igh unemployment, inflation, oppression, and rampant drug abuse" (Germani, 257). The films discussed here depict the complex hierarchies and negotiations of these masculinities.

In the cinema of the years before and after the revolution, the *jahel* and *shahid* became the standards against which other masculinities were measured. But these hyper-masculine films have been subject to frequent criticism. Secular intellectuals and conservative clergy alike denigrated the *luti* films, as trite or degenerate. Iranian war films often failed at the box office, and critics derided them as formulaic and clichéd. Here, I would like to briefly look at a few other types of masculinities in Iranian cinema.

In the late 1960s, along with *Qaisar* and the tough-guy movies, an alternative new-wave cinema with films like Dariush Mehrjui's *Gav* (Cow, 1969) was born that presented different types of Iranian men. Modernity, Westernization, and urbanization—as well as the changing role of women—had destabilized the patriarchy. Pahlavi's 1963 White Revolution had granted women's suffrage, and more women became involved in the public and private sectors.[12] The traditional solutions and behaviors no longer proved adequate or realistic. Men had a hard time adjusting to the changes both at home and in public. This situation continues today.

The new-wave films addressed this crisis. They portray a common man, often an antihero, with his insecurities and vulnerabilities. These are subaltern men forgotten by society; men searching for their identity and place in society; men who are unable to live up to the standards of dominant masculinity, or to fulfill their patriarchal role; men with conflicting and contradictory wishes. Examples of such pre-revolutionary films include Mehrjui's *Postchi* (The Postman, 1972), Bahram Beyzaie's *Ragbar* (Downpour, 1972), Naser Taghvai's *Aramesh dar Hozur Deegaran* (Tranquility in the Presence of Others, 1973), Bahman Farmanara's *Shazdeh Ehtejab* (Prince Ehtejab, 1974), Sohrab Shahid-Saless's *Tabiate Bijan* (Still Life, 1974), and Kiarostami's *Gozaresh* (The Report, 1977). These films give voice to the anxieties, insecurities, disappointments, and frustrations that brought about the Islamic Revolution. Similar new-wave films continue to depict different masculinities in post-revolution, with examples such as Kiarostami's *Nema-ye Nazdik* (Close-up, 1990), Saman Salur's *Chand Kilo Khorma Baraye Marassem-e Tadfin* (A Few Kilos of Dates for a Funeral, 2006), Mohsen Amiryoussefi's *Atashkar* (Fire Keeper, 2009), and Majid Barzegar's *Parviz* (2012).

After the revolution, and especially during the Iran–Iraq War, critical or dark films could not be made. But by the 1990s, during the 'reconstruction' period, filmmakers again challenged the narrow discourse of masculinity that was imposed by the government and the cinema of sacred defense. Iranian men paid greatly in the devastating eight-year war with Iraq, which had ended in a stalemate. After the war, and with the death of Khomeini in 1989, the country was looking for a new start and wondering whether this protracted conflict had been worth it. The need to present a male hero as a military warrior was also less relevant. Yet hundreds of thousands of returning veterans had neither accomplished their goal nor adjusted to the changing civil society that had been exhausted by the war. Directors such as Hatamikia and Makhmalbaf, who had promoted the cinema of sacred defense, expanded the realm of the genre by turning to the problems of veterans and what they saw as the hypocrisy of society. Their films depict not the idealistic *shahids* but veterans suffering from physical disabilities, post-traumatic stress disorder (PTSD), or the effects of chemical warfare. They cannot find jobs or pay for their medical requirements. They are sometimes estranged from their wives and families. In films like Makhmalbaf's *Arousi-ye Khouban* (Marriage of the Blessed, 1989) or Hatamikia's *Ajans-e Shisheh-i* (Glass Agency, 1998), veterans become the forgotten men, forewarning a society that was losing its revolutionary ideals. During a speech at his wedding ceremony, Haji, the veteran groom in *Arousi-ye Khouban*, chides the guests, chanting, "Eat. . . . Eating *haram* ['the forbidden'] is delicious." These films depict a country that is turning materialistic, corrupt, and bureaucratic. They question the war and the treatment of the soldiers not just by secular society but also by the government. Just as Kimiai had become a leading director of the tough-guy genre, Hatamikia became one of the foremost directors of the sacred-defense genre. Both are preoccupied with masculinity and heroic men, and their movies have adapted to the changing discourse in Iranian society. Kimiai, too, dealt with issues of war and veterans in movies such as *Dandan-e Mar* (Snake Fang, 1989). Even postwar new-wave directors, such as Jafar Panahi in *Talaye Sork* (Crimson Gold, 2003), have turned their camera on the plight of Iran's veterans.

The actor Parastui is continuing to redefine masculinity in different roles as a war veteran. In *Emrouz* (Today, 2014), directed by Reza Mirkarimi, he is a taciturn cab driver who, instead of saving the life of another soldier or veteran, is helping a lone, troubled pregnant woman in need of hospital care. Nacim Pak-Shiraz, in "Shooting the Isolation and Marginality of Masculinities in Iranian Cinema," argues that Mirkarimi "presents . . . marginal masculinity as the forgotten hero of Iranian values and ideas rather than as the victim of the dominant masculinities" (Pak-Shiraz, 955). Parastui becomes a new hero "out of the dejected masculinity" (Pak-Shiraz, 964) that is "neither the hypermasculine hero of pre-Revolutionary commercial cinema nor the conflicted man negotiating between the contradicting demands of tradition and modernity" (Pak-Shiraz, 953).

The secular middle-class intellectual—who, before the revolution, was part of the hegemonic masculinity either supporting the Pahlavi regime or the leftist opposition—also became a disenfranchised, forgotten man. He may have endorsed the revolution but now could not find a place for himself in the Islamic Republic. While not portrayed as a *fokoli* on screen, he was still weak, incompetent, confused, oversensitive, and ineffective. Sadr defines the character of intellectuals with four traits: "deep insecurity, political cynicism, personal mistrust, and self-destruction" (Sadr, 253). Mehrjui's *Hamoun* (1990), a popular and influential film, was the first major Iranian movie to present a genuine representation of intellectuals after the revolution.[13] Hamoun, the protagonist, is in a mid-life crisis, caught in the conflicts between the lower and middle classes as well as between modern and traditional values. The actor Khosrow Shakibai "was to define this type of personality in the early 1990s" (Sadr, 254). Other films about the struggles of intellectuals include Kiarostami's *Ta'm-e Gilas* (Taste of Cherry, 1997) and Farmanara's *Bu-ye Kafur, Atr-e Yas* (The Smell of Camphor, the Fragrance of Jasmine, 2000).

By the end of the century, a new generation who grew up after the revolution and did not participate in the war was changing Iran's social landscape. Based on 1996 national census figures, around 68 percent of the Iranian population was under thirty years of age with over 20 percent between eleven and twenty-five.[14] This maturing young generation wanted freedom, modernity, and prosperity. They were not interested in ideology, austerity, or traditional customs. The tension and clash between such young men and their veteran fathers became the motif of a number of Iranian films, such as Saman Moghadam's *Siavash* (1998) and Hatamikia's *Moj-e Morde* (Dead Wave, 2001). Shahram Khosravi, in *Young and Defiant in Tehran*, writes, "Identifying themselves as victims of the Revolution and calling themselves a 'burned generation' (*nasl-e sokhte*), they blame not only the official ideologies but also the cultural norms of their parental genera-tion" (Khosravi, 8).[15]

The increasing numbers of rebellious young men and women seized the attention of the media and popular culture. The government portrayed these youths as "self-alienated, unauthentic, *bidard* (without pain), and *biar-man* (without ideology)"—a source of "an 'ethical crisis' (*bouhran-e akhlaqi*) in the society" (Khosravi, 5). Iranian student protests of July 1999 furthered the conflict and mistrust between the conservative establishment and this new generation. Khosravi argues that the disparaging description of the wealthier youths of northern Tehran as *bidard* harks back to the negative use of *fokoli* (Khosravi, 78). The conservatives considered them as deviant, immoral, effeminate, and Weststruck.

It was this new generation of aspiring and defiant young men, who were also a major part of Mohammad Khatami's landslide 1997 and 2001 presidential wins, that came to be a new face of masculinity in such mov-ies as Kimiai's *Mercedes* (1998), Mirkarimi's *Koudak va Sarbaz* (The Child and the Soldier, 2000), and Parviz Shahbazi's *Nafas-e Amigh* (Deep Breath, 2003). Some films portray this new generation and their demands as a threat, whereas others look for a more authentic depiction of youth's hopes and disillusionments. In these films as in the society, young men are stuck in 'guyland' limbo—unable to grow into true adults or to fulfill the social expectations of the patriarchal system. They are vulnerable to peer pressure and their environment is sexually charged. They cannot find jobs, leave home, or raise families. Their situation is bleak. Running away and suicide are common. They go around aimlessly, getting involved with sex, drugs, alcohol, underground parties, or petty crime.

The modest hopes of young voters were derailed after Khatami was unable to fulfill his promises. They felt that society had neglected them. They became disaffected rebels who had lost hope—rebels without a cause. For many young men of the time, "[m]anliness was defined in terms of rebellion and defiance of all moral ties to others" (Sadr, 250). Their anti-social behavior was a resistance that was seen as a warning sign, with tragic consequences. More recent examples since the Iranian Green Movement—which began as a protest of the 2009 election results, another seminal time when the nation's youth engaged with the political system—include Shahram Mokri's *Mahi va Gorbeh* (Fish and Cat, 2013), Reza Dormishian's

Asabani Nistam! (I'm Not Angry, 2014), and Shahbazi's *Malaria* (2016). These films underline the youth's anxiety for the future and sense of disconnect from the past.

As mentioned earlier, throughout his career, Kimiai has adapted the masculinities portrayed on screen to the changing cultural discourse in society. In 2000, he introduced a pro-reformist hero in *Eteraz* (Protest), which was a response to his earlier film *Qaisar*. It is as if, disheartened with his early masculine remedy of the revolutionary tough guy, Kimia needed a new model and Khatami's reformist movement provided an alternative. In *Reform Cinema in Iran: Film and Political Change in the Islamic Republic*, Blake Atwood argues that *Eteraz* "announces the death of the tough-guy genre in Iranian cinema, a death initiated not by revolution but rather by the rise of Mohammad Khatami's reformist movement" (Atwood, 137). A comparison of *Qaisar* and *Eteraz* tells us a great deal about the radical change that Iranian masculinity has undergone in the past few decades.

Eteraz's Amir, who has been in prison for an honor killing, represents the *jaheli* values of *Qaisar*. Amir's motto, "if I wouldn't have done it, you would have," echoes Qaisar's saying, "if you don't get them, they will get you." But *Eteraz* "relocates those values underground and represents them as inhumane," with terrible consequences (Atwood, 159). Amir, once a hero in jail, finds himself a stranger in the city. He is later hired and integrated by the regime as a thug to attack students, such as his brother Reza's friends. Reza, by contrast, is practical, compassionate, and rational. He tries to convince Amir that there is no place for acts such as honor killings in the new progressive society. He enumerates the terrible consequence of Amir's actions, insisting, "I want us to talk rationally. . . . The days of such reactions have passed." Reza doesn't believe violence and rebellion are solutions. Instead, he upholds law, justice, and democracy. Mohammad-Reza Foroutan, who played Reza, has become an example for a new generation of actors. Sadr writes that Foroutan "brought to the cinema of the late 1990s the image of a more sensitive male" (Sadr, 251).

Unlike the action-driven *Qaisar*, *Eteraz* is about dialogue and reason. Reza is not above the law and does not work alone like Qaisar. With the college students, he spends a great deal of time debating the role of being a citizen and the current political situation in Iran. They discuss key figures like Khatami, Ata'ollah Mohajerani, and Akbar Ganji, who can be seen as potential new heroes. *Eteraz* is about now and the future. *Qaisar* begins with the naked body of *zurkhaneh* wrestlers and their tattoos of pre-Islamic warriors, while *Eteraz* begins with Amir picturing himself interrogating his victim and justifying his action. *Eteraz*'s past is recent, going back to the time of Qaisar, while the past of *Qaisar* is mythic and imaginary.[16]

In the end, Amir dies tragically—but for Reza there is still hope. The new generation of men need not resort to bygone traditions to define their identity. Films like *Eteraz* show that, even with all their difficulties and uncertainties, Iranian men have a chance to refashion themselves in a world that has stepped out of the shadow of *luti*, *shahid*, and *fokoli* stereotypes.

The past century's social transformations, brought about by such forces as modernization and Islamic revolution, have shaped the discursive construction of gender identity in Iranian society, as traditional male identities faced crises with the introduction of new urban societies, family structures, and performative masculinities. In the 1960s and 1970s, Iranian cinema often stood in opposition to the Westernized masculine model that the Shah wanted to reinforce. *Fokoli*s satirized the naive wholesale adaptation of Western ideas, while tough-guy *luti*s defended traditional values and advanced the concerns of the working class. Even the country's new-wave cinema problematized the idealized male image promoted by the regime. Meanwhile, the happy-go-lucky *luti*, who turned into the tough-guy *jahel*, became a revolutionary. Iran's post-revolution cinema, however, both endorsed and questioned the portrayal of an idealized Muslim male subject. Subsidized films eulogized the warrior *shahids* and converted thugs into Islamic heroes. On the other hand, many filmmakers began to portray subordinate and dissident masculinities from the rebellious youth to the forgotten veteran, bringing new male identities to the screen.

Notes

1 An earlier, shorter version of this chapter was written for the Global Encyclopedia of Lesbian, Gay, Bisexual, Transgender and Queer History, 1E. © 2019 Gale, a part of Cengage, Inc. Reproduced with permission.

2 Influenced by Marxism and writers such as Ali Akbar Akbari, the early critics often scathingly refer to *luti*s and *jahel*s as lumpen. These characters, however, were not always reconcilable with the Marxist understanding of lumpen.

3 "Stewpot" refers to the traditional Iranian stew *abgusht* that was relished by *luti*s in films such as *Ganj-e Qarun* (Croesus' Treasure).

4 The White Revolution refers to the sweeping social, economic, and legal reform that was launched by Mohammad Reza Pahlavi in the 1960s in order to modernize Iran.

5 *Dash Akol* is based on Sadeq Hedayat's short story of the same name. In the story, the character Dash Akol is described as "kind" and "benevolent" (Hedayat, 76), wearing "a velvet vest, loose trousers, and a felt hat" (Hedayat, 77).

6 During the Siahkal incident, Marxist guerrillas boldly attacked a gendarmerie post at Siahkal in Gilan province in order to rescue their comrades.

The men, who were later arrested and executed, became martyred revolutionary heroes.

7   While Amir Ali reminds viewers of Qaisar, Haj Musa recalls the heroes of
    Ebrahim Hatamikia's films, such as Haj Kazam in *Ajans-e Shisheh-i* (*Glass
    Agency*, 1998).

8   The character of a young martyr also echoes the frequent and popular
    appearance of a heroic lover who dies young in the movies of 1970s, such
    as *Dar Emtedad-e Shab* (Into the Night, 1978), *Salaam Tehran* (1977), and
    Mahiha dar Khak Mimirand (The Fish Die on the Land, 1977). More po-
    litical variation of a hero dying young appears in movies such as Kimiai's
    Ghavaznha (The Deer, 1974).

9   *Fokoli* characters also appear in Persian literature. An early example of
    such a character can be found in the 1921 short story *Farsi Shekar Hast*
    (Persian Is Sugar) by Mohammad-Ali Jamalzadeh.

10 Although the English translation for the book referenced here uses
    the spelling 'Al-i Ahmad,' the name is more commonly spelled as
    'Al-e Ahmad.'

11 Early on, Madani had popularized the character of *Jahel* in a satirical
    serial written in 1953 for the journal *Sepid va Seyah* (Black and White)
    under the title of "Esmal dar New York" (Esmal in New York). The series
    was later published as a book.

12 This chapter has not addressed the important relationship of masculinity
    and women in films, mainly because its complexity requires a full chapter
    in itself.

13 Male characters in Mehrjui's films, from both before and after the revolu-
    tion, are usually weak, vulnerable, lost, confused, and emasculated.

14 From *Sarshomari Omomi Nofus va Maskan* (National Population and
    Housing Census), released by Markaz-e Amar-e Iran (Statistical Center
    of Iran). Census figures can also be found online at Iran Data Portal.

15 There is a complex relationship between fathers and sons in Iranian
    culture and cinema that is not addressed in this chapter.

16 Amir, after being released from prison, also drives away with his family in
    an old 1968 Ford (from the time of *Qaisar*).

Works Cited

Adelkhah, Fariba. *Being Modern in Iran*, translated by Jonathan Derrick.
    New York: Columbia University Press, 2000.

Akbari, Ali Akbar. *Lompanism* [Lumpanism] Tehran, Markaz-e Nashr-e
    Sipihr, 1973.

Al-i Ahmad, Jalal. *Occidentosis: A Plague from the West*, translated by R.
    Campbell. Berkeley, CA: Mizan Press, 1984.

Atwood, Blake. *Reform Cinema in Iran: Film and Political Change in the Islamic Republic*. New York: Columbia University Press, 2016.

Balslev, Sivan. "Dressed for Success: Hegemonic Masculinity, Elite Men and Westernisation in Iran, c. 1900–40." *Gender & History* 26, no. 3 (2014): 545–64.

Bhabha, Homi K. *The Location of Culture*. London and New York: Routledge, 2004.

Butler, Judith. *Gender Trouble: Feminism and the Subversion of Identity*, second edition. London and New York: Routledge, 1999.

Connell, R.W. *Masculinities*, second edition. Berkeley, CA: University of California Press, 2005.

Dabashi, Hamid. *Close Up: Iranian Cinema, Past, Present and Future*. London: Verso, 2001.

Esfandiary, Shahab. "Iranian Sacred Defence Cinema and the Ambivalent Consequences of Globalization: A Study of the Films of Ebrahim Hatamikia" In *Iranian Sacred Defence Cinema: Religion, Martyrdom and National Identity*, edited by Pedram Khosronejad, 59–98. Canon Pyon, UK: Sean Kingston Publishing, 2012.

Floor, Willem. 2010. "Luṭi." *Encyclopædia Iranica*, online edition. January 15, 2020.

Gerami, Shahin. "Mullahs, Martyrs and Men: Conceptualizing Masculinity in the Islamic Republic of Iran." *Men and Masculinities* 5, no. 3 (2003): 257–74.

Gheissari, Ali. "Shadman, Sayyed Fakhr-al-Din." *Encyclopædia Iranica*, online edition. January 15, 2020.

Hedayat, Sadeq. *Three Drops of Blood*, translated by Deborah Miller Mostaghel. Surrey, UK: Alma Classics, 2008.

Jamalzadeh, M.A. *Once Upon a Time*, translated by Heshmat Moayyad and Paul Sparchman. New York: Bibliotheca Persica, 1985.

Khosravi, Shahram. *Young and Defiant in Tehran*. Philadelphia, PA: University of Pennsylvania Press, 2009.

Khosronejad, Pedram, ed. *Iranian Sacred Defence Cinema: Religion, Martyrdom and National Identity*. Canon Pyon, UK: Sean Kingston Publishing, 2012.

Kimmel, Michael S. *Guyland: The Perilous World Where Boys Become Men*. New York: HarperCollins, 2009.

Moallem, Minoo. *Between Warrior Brother and Veiled Sister: Islamic Fundamentalism and the Politics of Patriarchy in Iran*. Berkeley, CA: University of California Press, 2005.

Naficy, Hamid. *A Social History of Iranian Cinema*. 4 volumes. Durham, NC: Duke University Press, 2011–12.

Najmabadi, Afsaneh. *Women with Mustaches and Men without Beards: Gender and Sexual Anxieties of Iranian Modernity*. Berkeley, CA: University of California Press, 2010.

Pak-Shiraz, Nacim. "Shooting the Isolation and Marginality of Masculinities in Iranian Cinema." *Iranian Studies* 50, no. 6 (2017): 945–67.

Partovi, Pedram. *Popular Iranian Cinema Before the Revolution: Family and Nation in Fīlmfārsī*. London and New York: Routledge, 2017.

———. "Martyrdom and the 'Good Life' in the Iranian Cinema of Sacred Defense." *Comparative Studies of South Asia, Africa and the Middle East* 28, no. 3 (2008): 513–32.

Sadr, Hamid Reza. *Iranian Cinema: A Political History*. London: I.B.Tauris, 2006.

Varzi, Roxanne. *Warring Souls: Youth, Media, and Martyrdom in Post-Revolution Iran*. Durham, NC: Duke University Press, 2006.

Zakeri, Mohsen. "Javānmardi." *Encyclopædia Iranica*, online edition. January 15, 2020.

10

MEN AND MODERNITY IN
POSTCOLONIAL TUNISIAN CINEMA

Nouri Gana

> I think it is important to drive a wedge in, early and often and if possi-
> ble conclusively, between the two topics, masculinity and men, whose
> relation to one another it is so difficult not to presume.
>   —Eve Kosofsky Sedgwick (12)

In Arabic, *dhukura* (masculinity) is oceans apart from *rujula* (manhood).
Etymologically, *dhukura* comes from *dhakar* (male), which refers also
to the male sexual organ.[1] *Dhukura* is thus an accented sexual category,
while *rujula* is a neutered cultural construction. Its connotative reach is not
reducible to the sexual binaries of *dhukura* and *unutha* (femininity), with the
caveat that these two categories might interchangeably pertain to men and
women alike. Without diminishing the etymological polysemy of *rujula*,[2]
it is important to stress its cultural polyvalence and difference from both
masculinity and femininity. In French, by contrast, there is no distinctive
word for *manhood* apart from *masculinité* (which is an offshoot of *masculin*—
the French word for sexual, not gender, differentiation). Reconfiguration
of the problematic in terms of a distinction between masculinity and manhood is more attuned to the logic of the Arabic language. This linguistic
distinction between masculinity and manhood is, in no small measure, a
locus of modernity. Yet there is a disavowal, in most Arabic-speaking societies, of the Arabic language's differentiation between masculinity and
manhood—as well as between sexuality and gender. In an Arabic-speaking
world increasingly alienated from the subtleties of its linguistic heritage
and unsettled by the encroachments of Western cultural hegemony, it is
alarming that the ahistoricity of Arab contemporaneity has come to *converge*
with resistance to cultural imperialism. The impulse to counter imperialist Western feminism, for instance, has encouraged carelessness about the

initially promising status of women under Islam, to which scholars from Qasim Amin (1863–1908) through Tahar Haddad (1899–1935) to Leila Ahmed (b. 1940) have drawn attention. In this climate of fear of cultural contamination, the proximity between forgotten moments of modernity in Arab history and Western cultural modernity has been overlooked. As Arab poet Adonis observes, "I find no paradox in declaring that it was recent Western modernity which led me to discover our own, older, modernity outside our 'modern' politico-cultural system established on a Western model" (Adonis, 81).

Apart from the long Ottoman interim, no factor played a more detrimental role in smothering otherwise incipient Arab Muslim modernity than European and American imperialism.

The legacy of colonialism continues to weigh heavily on Arabs, unsettling their otherwise deeply entrenched sense of identity and their historically proven capacity for coexistence (in al-Andalus, for instance)— all the more so given the ongoing occupation of Palestine, with the support of Europe and the United States. Colonialism's legacy influenced the systems set up in Tunisia after its independence from France, during the era of Tunisia's president-for-life Habib Bourgiba (1956–1987). Bourgiba's emphasis on embracing modernity may have brought about positive changes in terms of laws (particularly with regard to women's rights), but remains entrenched in patriarchal worldviews and perceptions—including Bourguiba's own domination as the father figure of the postcolonial nation, creating a generation of Tunisian men stranded in a specifically modern, postcolonial neopatriarchy. It is important to make connections early and often between the two topics, Arab men and empire, whose ties to one another are so difficult to presume for Orientalist scholars. There follows a series of topics—Arab men and nation, Arab men and modernity, Arab men and Arab women, Arab men and Arab presidents-for-life—whose relationships to one another inform my approach to a number of modern Tunisian films that exemplify the sociopolitical and psychoaffective complexities of postcolonial and neocolonial Arab contemporaneity. These films are Moufida Tlatli's *Les silences du palais* (Silences of the Palace, 1994) and *La saison des hommes* (The Season of Men, 2000), Nadia Fares's *Miel et cendres* (Honey and Ashes, 1996), and Nouri Bouzid's *L'homme de cendre* (Man of Ashes, 1986). Through analysis of these Tunisian films, which unsettle hegemonic masculinity, I discuss the cultural and political constellations that produce the particular psychoaffective dispositions that Arab men come to inhabit. I contextualize the anxieties and contradictions of contemporary Tunisian masculinity by discussing the neopatriarchy of the postcolonial generation of men we might call 'Bourguiba's sons.'

Postcolonial Tunisia and the Leap into Modernity

> Our collective consciousness is indeed marked by a double mutila-
> tion, alienation vis-à-vis what is foreign, and alienation vis-à-vis what
> is past, the mimicry of modernity and the mimicry of tradition.
>
> —Aziz Krichen (8)

Tunisia in 1956—unlike any other country in the Arab world, not
exempting Egypt in 1954 or Algeria in 1962—is the exemplum of a country
wasting no time in gradualism but willing to leap briskly into modernity.
After serving as a French protectorate, following the 1881 Treaty of Bardo,
for almost three quarters of a century, Tunisia gained full independence
on March 20, 1956. Pride of place in Tunisian national memory is also
given to August 13, 1956. On that day, the *majallat al-ahwal al-shakhsiya*,
or Personal Status Code (PSC), was promulgated by Neo-Destur Party
leader Habib Bourguiba. The Tunisian Code was unmatched in the Muslim world, except perhaps by the 1924 Turkish Civil Code, and has come to
be synonymous with Tunisia's leap into modernity. The PSC's reforms are
predicated on the principle of equality between men and women (although
this principle is yet to be extended to the area of inheritance). The Code
requires mutual consent of spouses prior to marriage; interdicts marriage
before spouses reach puberty; prohibits polygyny; abolishes repudiation
(unilateral divorce initiated by the husband), by decreeing that divorce outside a court of law is without legal effect; and permits either spouse to file
for divorce (Anderson; Curtiss).

Not unexpectedly, the PSC met opposition from the *'ulama'*, or jurists
of Islamic law, as well as from remnants of the 1920 Old Destur Party.
Attentive to the political agenda of the opposition, Bourguiba hammered
home his vision of modern Tunisia—gaining the support of esteemed
jurists, including the head of Zaytuna Mosque and Muhammed Ju'ayit,
Sheikh al-Islam. Bourguiba challenged his detractors' assertion that the
abolition of polygyny deviates from the Qur'an, which he deemed himself
qualified to interpret in view of the sociopolitical urgencies of modernity.
He was clearly influenced by Tahar Haddad, a progressive Zaytuna intellectual who, in a pioneering work about the emancipation of women, laments
that "had not the practice of polygyny continued after the revelation of
this verse, this would have been the most frank call for its complete abolition" (Haddad, 55). This refers to verse 4:129 in the Qur'an, which states
that it is impossible for a husband to be equitable to all his wives, read in
conjunction with verse 4:3, which says that polygyny is allowable only if the
husband can treat his wives equitably, which is impossible.

In the moment of birth of the postcolonial nation, Bourguiba's effort was twofold: to neutralize political opposition and to conciliate a discontented population, abruptly alienated from practices hitherto thought beyond human intervention. Bourguiba sought to weaken the centers from which these practices derived their authority, such as the Zaytuna Mosque—the prestigious bastion of Islamic learning in Tunisia—which in 1956 was placed under the Ministry of Education before being absorbed into the University of Tunis by 1961. Bourguiba's efforts to secularize the nation morphed, however, into a raid on the observance of such pillars of Islam as the fast of Ramadan; one Ramadan day, the president drank a glass of orange juice on public television to urge Tunisians to quit fasting (quoted in Hopwood, 140). He argued "that Tunisia's involvement in a *jihad* against underdevelopment absolved its citizens from fasting, just as warriors in a *jihad* in defense of Islam were exempted" (Perkins, 141).

Bourguiba's reforms were perceived as masking a neocolonial form of modernity that denied Tunisia its sociocultural specificity. Such views gained momentum as he accented the linkages between modernity and French language and culture, presenting himself as exemplar. Bourguiba had married a French woman, Mathilde Louvain, in 1927. He said of himself, "This Arab is Frenchified to the tips of his fingers, a living example of assimilation" (quoted in Hopwood, 142). He refuted accusations of complicity with neocolonialism mainly by sitting on his laurels: "Having struggled most of my life against the colonial régime, having freed my country of its after-effects, I need not take lessons from anyone about colonialism" (Bourguiba, "The Tunisian Way," 486).

Parallel to this project of modernity, which boasts of gender equality and socioeconomic advancement, there emerges in Bourguiba's story a more gendered and male-biased narrative of nationhood. In a series of lectures he gave in the early 1970s at the Institut de Presse et des Sciences de l'Information, Bourguiba reminded his audience that the Tunisian nation was his creation. He said, with typical lack of humility, "I hope you get to know better the history of our country by listening to the person who made it" (Bourguiba, *Ma vie*, 75). While Bourguiba uses the plural possessive in referring to "our country," he claims to have forged it himself. This blending of the narrative of the nation with his own image reached its zenith in 1975 when he proclaimed himself president for life. "If Bourguiba had taken to heart lessons from French history his favorite must have been Louis XIV's *l'état c'est moi*. He did not distinguish any longer where he ended and where the state began" (Hopwood, 84). By "selving" the nation and anointing himself "Supreme Combatant" *(al-mujahid al-akbar)*, Bourguiba painted a male-biased picture of the nationalist project of modernity despite his enthusiasm for the emancipation of women. His 1960s campaign against women's veiling may even be read retrospectively as an attempt to enhance the privilege of the male gaze. During the anticolonial struggle, Bourguiba had opposed unveiling—at that time, deeming the veil the last frontier against assimilation to French culture.

Hardly respectful of the democratic conventions he initiated, and opting for heavy-handed methods, Bourgiba ruled an overawed population. He imposed an "etatist patriarchy" (Sharabi, 65) or a sort of "nationalitarisme" (Béji, 19), which blended the rhetoric of nationalism, the instrument of resistance under colonial rule, with repression, the instrument of cultivating postcolonial nationhood. It is as if Tunisians had forsaken the right to challenge the ideology of state nationalism as soon as they committed to it in their collective struggle for independencehence, the sense of *désenchantement national* of which Hélé Béji speaks. Bourguiba's cult of personality insinuated itself into the national imaginary and became synonymous with Tunisian nationalism. More than a psychological prop or a crude expression of self-glorification, this personality worship became an extension of the political system he instituted after Tunisia's independence from France in 1956. It magnified his personal will, elevated his ideas to the status of oracular infallibility, and gave him limitless executive powers. While it is all too common that leaders of newly decolonized nations apply to their own peoples the same colonial practices to which they once submitted at the hands of European powers, Bourguiba's case beggars the imagination. A Sorbonne graduate, he wrote against colonialism in newspapers such as *La Voix du Tunisien* before launching his own newspaper in 1932, founded the Neo-Destur party on socialist-communist models, and engaged in a decolonial struggle which resulted in his imprisonment and exile. His cult of personhood imperiled for generations the postcolonial liberation of men and women alike from the matrix of neopatriarchy.

Bourguiba's deformed ideology of postcolonial nationhood—which demanded and manipulated the tacit commitment of every Tunisian to the collective imperative of '*tunisianité*,' or '*Tunisianness*'—symptomized the persistence of the patriarchal impulse underneath the modernist project he spearheaded. The result might be called, following Hisham Sharabi, "a bastardized form of modernization," which produced a "modernized" patriarchy—a "neopatriarchy." Being a combination of colonial paternalism and state bureaucracy, neopatriarchy thrives on contradictions such that the more entrenched it is, the more exaggerated its contradictions become. As Sharabi observes, "[i]n this type of polity the gap between appearance and reality took on exaggerated forms. . . . Stark contradictions between verbal and actual behavior produced no problematic tensions for consciousness"

(Sharabi, 66). Sited in contradictions, Bourguiba's project of modernity was very much in the gravitational pull of neopatriarchy.

Bourguiba's rule over Tunisia (1956–87) produced a breed of men who might be aptly called 'Bourguiba's sons.' The contradictions and ambivalences of Bourguiba's sons is a measure of their filial relation to him as well as their acute disorientation. Not a homogenous group, they have been able neither to come to terms with the challenges of modernity, of which gender equality is part and parcel, nor to relinquish fully the shelter of traditional patriarchy. Modern Tunisian cinema is invested in unraveling the ways in which Tunisian men are stranded in the pull of neopatriarchy even while attempting, timidly or defiantly, to break from its confines. Like Bourguiba, while they can be enlightened about the workings of patriarchy they nonetheless perpetuate it—ferociously at times. The affective apparatus that sustains such psychosocial behavior can be called *melancholite* because it straddles, consciously or unconsciously, two contradictory logics—the logic of modernity and the logic of patriarchy, or the logic of gender equality and the logic of male privilege.

Undoing Manhood

> It bears repeating, there is a gap currently between the emancipation of women and that of men, a discrepancy between theory and practice, between tradition and modernity. Laws exist but are they capable of removing mental blocks? And yet, I would like to believe that cinema can, in its own way, help change things.
> —Moufida Tlatli (11) 1994, *African Screen*

The National Union of Tunisian Women was founded in 1956, shortly after the promulgation of the PSC, with a mission to improve the status of women by ensuring that the new reforms were respected. The Union's foundation signaled an anticipated disjunction between legal reform and social practice, which Moufida Tlatli evokes in the above epigraph. It is a mistake "to understand all the ways in which gender is regulated in terms of those empirical legal instances [here, the PSC] because the norms that govern those regulations exceed the very instances in which they are embodied" (Butler, *Undoing Gender*, 40). Sociocultural forces that regulate gender roles often override the top-down imposition of new rules of engagement.

There is perhaps no other artistic medium in postcolonial Tunisia more insistent on the urgency of closing this gulf between legal reforms and societal behavior than cinema. A series of postcolonial films from male directors—ranging roughly from Omar Khlifi's *Hurlements* (Screams,

1972), Abdellatif Ben Ammar's *Sejnane* (1973) and *Aziza* (1980), Rachid Ferchiou's *Les enfants de l'ennui* (The Children of Boredom, 1975), and Sadok Ben Aïcha's *Le mannequin* (The Mannequin, 1978) to Khaled Ghorbal's *Fatma* (2001)—stage the sedimentations of the neopatriarchy and promote the modernist project of gender equality. Parallel to these are a number of feminist films, which pose bold questions about women's oppression, sexuality, and liberation while deconstructing the neopatriarchal hold on social behavior. These stretch from Selma Baccar's documentary *Fatma 75* (1978) and her feature film *Khochkhach* (Flower of Oblivion, 2006), as well as Nejia Ben Mabrouk's *La trace* (The Trace, completed 1982), Moufida Tlatli's *Les silences du palais* (Silences of the Palace, 1994) and *La saison des hommes* (The Season of Men, 2000), to Nadia Fares's *Miel et cendres* (Honey and Ashes, 1996) and Raja Amari's *Satin Rouge* (Red Satin, 2002) and *Anonymes* (Buried Secrets, 2009). While these films rely on the feminist wager to undo normative constructions of manhood, films by male directors such as Nouri Bouzid's films, from *L'homme de cendre* (Man of Ashes, 1986) to *Le dernier film* (Making of, 2006); Ferid Boughedir's *Halfaouine: l'enfant des terraces* (Halfaouine: Boy of the Terraces, 1990) and *Un été à la Goulette* (A Summer at La Goulette, 1995); Jilani Saadi's *Khorma, la bêtise* (Khorma, Stupidity, 2002) and *'Urs el-dhib* (Tender Is the Wolf, 2006)—as well as Abdellatif Kechiche's *La faute à Voltaire* (Blame It on Voltaire, 2000) and *La graine et le mulet* (The Secret of the Grain, 2007)—delve into the experiences of male characters to unravel the neopatriarchal modes of production of manhood. Films in the two latter categories show how female and male directors have, while focusing on seemingly dissimilar issues, constructed a narrative of melancholy manhood.

I understand this melancholy narrative of manhood in two distinct ways. One is *melancholite*, because it is shot with fetishistic nostalgia for neopatriarchy and gendered constellations of social intelligibility and psychoaffective sovereignty. The other is *melancholic* because it stakes a claim to a set of individual traumas (such as childhood molestation, rape, incarceration, torture, and other forms of human-rights abuses) that would have been thrust into oblivion were it not for melancholia's Janus-faced scrutiny of the past. Melancholia has creative potential to intuit injustices that the past might have assimilated en route to becoming recognizable as *past*. Melancholia, far from being counterproductive to forging livable futures, constitutes an incubational moment for the emergence of just futures— all the more so given melancholia's critical vigilance toward projects that seek to elide the past. It evokes psychoaffective dissidence from regulatory practices of mourning, offering a vantage point for any revisionary project of redress provided that the initial state of discomfiture comes to be transformed into critical investiture. Melancholia has, in short, the potential to bring the dignity of human recognition to those who had incurred injustices but have not yet been able to work through them via adequate measures of empathic witnessing.

Tlatli's *Silences of the Palace* (Samt al-qusur) and *The Season of Men* (Mawsim al-rijal) are not technically and thematically dissimilar. In both films, the director relies on flashbacks to underline how past experiences of female protagonists weigh on their present lives and to assess the extent to which post-independence reforms changed the conditions of Tunisian women. Tlatli's findings are disconcerting. Set in beylical Tunisia (Hussein Dynasty of Beys, 1705–1957), which is technically part of the Ottoman Empire but *de facto* a French protectorate, *Silences* stages an initially promising reversal of fortunes both for Tunisia and for women. The independence of the country from France promises to usher in the independence of women from patriarchal bondage. Lotfi assures Alia, "Things are going to change. A new future awaits us. You will be a great singer. Your voice will enchant everyone."[3] Such a reversal, however, hinges on whether beylical conceptions of manhood will shrink into obsolescence in postcolonial Tunisia. Gil Hochberg argues that *Silences* "invites" itself to be read as a national allegory yet "constantly undermines" such a reading in order to highlight "the disjunct between the 'national story' and Alia's 'personal story' as a woman" whose "own situation has not improved" in the wake of Tunisia's independence (Hochberg, 42–43). Tlatli implies that the effervescence of national liberation and the legal reforms that followed were not calibrated for genuine change; indeed, "consciousness of difference between women and men as an instance of social inequality . . . is not the automatic outcome of militancy in a decolonization movement" (Lazreg, 141).

Less patriarchal forms of manhood do not necessarily emerge when beylical manhood is disbanded. The Bey of Tunisia, Sidi Lamine, was deposed by the vote of the constituent assembly, which subsequently made the country a republic and Bourguiba president, but the postcolonial nation did not go any farther than promulgating the PSC to remove the sedimentations of beylical manhood. Consider the differences between the revolutionary nationalist Lotfi and the anti-nationalist Sidi el-Bechir—and, to a lesser extent, his brother, Sidi Ali, who remains caught in the trappings of beylical supremacy though he shows more sensitivity than his brother toward both nationalists and women servants. Discussing the protests against French colonialism and its beylical acolytes, Sidi el-Bechir traces the origins of such a state of emergency/emergence to the crisis of manhood in the Palace of the Beys:

Sidi el-Bechir: There are no more powerful men left in the palace
(ufet er-rjal esshah mil-qsar).

Sidi Ali: They are on the other side (esshah duhru fil-wajha lukhra).

Sidi el-Bechir: But they have no class (el-wahra); class cannot be
seized; it takes generations to nurture.

Sidi Ali: The country's had enough of us (el-bled feddit mil-wahra wil-
kbarat); we may end up facing the same sad fate as Farouk of
Egypt and you're still dreaming of greatness and bigness (el-
wahra wil-kbarat).

This dialogue highlights the clash between two constructions of manhood,
one associated with the beys and the other with the revolutionary nationalists.
The former, sustained by class, "greatness and bigness (el-wahra wil-kbarat),"
falters under the nationalist gaze, whose manhood relies on braving bullets
from French machine guns. Sidi el-Bechir takes umbrage at his brother's
remark that the powerful men (er-rjal esshah) are on the other side of the
conflict; to him, those men lack class and greatness, the touchstones of beylical manhood. When Khalti Hadda fears that the country would be lost if
the Bey left, a servant reassures her that "nothing would be lost, since the
men who expose their chests to bullets know what they are doing." Beylical manhood—long associated with wahra, economic privileges, and sexual
exploitation of female servants—trembles in these two scenes.

The film's undoing of beylical manhood is far from an endorsement of
revolutionary nationalist manhood, however. The latter fails to live up to
its promises of gender equality, as Lotfi's relationship with the adult Alia
attests. In urging Alia to abort her pregnancy, Lotfi reveals a dormant bey
in himself. While Alia is inspired by his nationalist zeal to summon up her
strength to sing the forbidden national anthem, and while he seems to offer
her the protection she needs after her escape from the palace the night her
mother dies during an abortion, Lotfi fails to offer her the family she longs
for in a free Tunisia. At the beginning of the film, Alia interrupts the playing of a song, "Amal hayati" (The Hope of my Life), by the famed singer
associated with Arab nationalism, Um Kulthum. This interruption evokes
the successive abortions Alia has been having and the ungrievable life she
has been living. Lotfi's first words in the film, "you're late," suggest the
belatedness with which postcolonial subjectivities are plagued at the outset.
Alia's later defiance of Lotfi, her decision to keep the child, constitutes her
next step on the ladder of individuation and a blow to the intransigence of
beylical manhood.

Tlatli also lays bare women's discomfiting complicity with beylical
manhood, saying in an interview, "Arab women are not oppressed by men;

it is women who perpetuate the tradition. The decrees are there, the laws are there, but women did not immediately assimilate the possibilities." Tlatli's sensitivity to the role women play in patriarchal and neopatriarchal practices contradicts the argument that women in *Silences* "become a non-patriarchal family within a patriarchal context" (Shohat, 303). While not to an equal degree, for Tlatli men and women alike are subjects *of* and *to* patriarchy and cannot therefore be freed from it separately.

The Season of Men (2000) is Tlatli's second feature film. It chronicles the lives of women on the Island of Djerba during the eleven-month absence and one-month presence of their husbands who own bazaar shops in Tunis, the capital of Tunisia. While *Silence* takes us to opulent palaces, *Season* is concerned with lower-middle-class women. It tackles the issue of *nuzuh* (internal migration, or rural exodus) of the males of Djerba in southern Tunisia to the capital city for work, leaving their wives to the despotic "*hama*," or mother-in-law, Oummi Sallouha. Mindful of the interdependence between the economic and social independence of women, Tlatli here explores gender oppression as perpetrated by women against women. Men in the film, whether the aged Am Ali or the two brothers who work in Tunis, seem to have little role to play in a system that is nevertheless acted out in their name. While this by no means contradicts the logic of normative power, which works by absence, it is important to see the confluence of the absence and presence of this patriarchal domination in the mother-in-law, the *hama*. She presides over the house and urges her son, Said, to make clear to his rebellious wife, Aicha, that no other person's word but hers must be followed.

Season dramatizes what Suad Joseph aptly calls "patriarchal connectivity." Joseph explains that

> [p]atriarchy has operated effectively in part because both men and women were socialized to view themselves relationally. Connectivity has held family together in part because men and women, adults and children internalized the psychological demands of compliance with gendered and aged hierarchies. Intertwined, patriarchy and connectivity have underwritten the crafting of relationally oriented selves, socialized to negotiate gendered and aged hierarchies and *locally* recognized as healthy, mature, and responsible (Joseph, 13–14, emphasis in original).

Patriarchal connectivity is a form of sociality in which males and females collaboratively internalize and produce the norms by which they are governed. These norms are shot through with transgenerational patriarchal psychodynamics.

Tlatli's film dramatizes the ironies of a male-worshipping society, setting in motion a choking-off of patriarchal connectivity. For Aicha, the key to earning the respect of her *hama*, the arch-matriarch-cum-mother-in-law, is to give birth to a male child. Aicha's husband, Said, exploits the situation: to rid himself of her pleading to join him in Tunis, he makes that conditional on her bearing him a son. There follows the anxiety over getting pregnant when the husband is absent eleven months a year—which does not curb the amazement of Aicha's mother at Aicha's inability to conceive: "How is it," her mother exclaims, "I want to understand, that you can't get pregnant?"

When Aicha finally gives birth to Aziz, the joys of the *hama*, husband, and extended family reach an unprecedented pitch. Although the family is finally able to move to Tunis, this joy proves short-lived. Aziz is an autistic and emotionally troubled child who is rejected by his father—the person who was so bent on having a son. The father wants to institutionalize him. Aicha opposes this, jeopardizing her marriage to Said, who moves to a separate apartment. It is ironic that Aicha, the last person to desire a son, is the only one who devotes her life to him. In an admixture of resignation and defiance, she moves back with him to the old house in Djerba, which she thought she left forever when Aziz was born. It is as if she realizes that "the profound hopelessness of the struggle" to undo patriarchal connectivity is as taxing as "the still more profound hopelessness of its abandonment" (Lukács, 86). Her dedication to her autistic child exposes the anomalies of male-worshipping patriarchy. Relinquishing the child to a psychiatric institution, from a Foucauldian perspective, is further acquiescence to the regulatory machinery of patriarchy. Holding fast to a sick child underlines the poor health of patriarchal logic, its façade-like identification resting with sanity rather than with the compassion that ought to govern family ties. The opening scene of *Season* dramatizes Aziz's refusal to take a bath, a refusal to undergo a ritual of cleanliness connected by the film to patriarchy when the women bathe to prepare for the one-month season of men back home. *Season* concludes with a close-up of Aziz at the loom, trying clumsily to weave a woof of thin red threads. Aziz, by reenacting his mother's household craft, undoes what Pierre Bourdieu calls "the fear of the female, firstly in oneself" (Bourdieu, 53). The final fade-out evokes him in the melancholy impasse of patriarchal manhood with its regulatory repression.

Regulatory repression is the performative confluence between normative power and its actualizations by complicit or regulated subjectivities. While I understand that subjects are products of norms of which they become active perpetuators, I do not subscribe to the idea of the unbreakable circularity of regulatory power. Neither do I subscribe to a revolutionary dialectic of reversibility whereby norms could be simply supplanted, as in Bourguiba's vision of Tunisian modernity. The ineluctability of submitting to regulatory power matches only the force with which this power is paradoxically reproduced, challenged, and ultimately mutated through localized exercises of critical wakefulness to the workings of power relations. Regulatory power, scanned through a span of time, is neither immune to mutability nor exempt from radical transformation. The *hama*'s presidency for life, as it were, over the household is inextricably tied to the transgenerational fact that she in turn once submitted to her own mother-in-law, as Aicha's mother explains to her daughter. The *hama* applies to her daughter-in-law the same patriarchal practices to which she once submitted at the hands of her own *hama*. The circularity of regulatory power within patriarchal connectivity owes a greater debt to the dialectics of primary vulnerability than the functioning of the system allows us to see.

Regulatory repression is an attempt to surpass a scene of primary vulnerability that cannot be fully mourned, only compulsively acted out in spectacles of invulnerability. This is the *melancholite* side of patriarchal manhood that Nadia Fares's *Honey and Ashes* (1996) critiques. It is *melancholite* not so much because of its disavowal of primary vulnerability but because of its elegiac pursuit of the fantasy of invulnerability. *Melancholites* fail to transform the apprehension of profound vulnerability into a condition of sociality.

Fares's undoing of *melancholite* patriarchal manhood begins by scandalizing its material effects: scenes of abusive male behavior toward women such as beating, harassment, and rape punctuate the film. Fares does not offer alternative models of meaningful gender relations, forcing viewers to leave the theater with thought-provoking outrage. Such an emotion has potential critical valence yet risks being vitiated by the film's failure to offer male viewers any characters with whom they can identify—such as Sami in Tlatli's *Season*. Yet, perhaps Fares deserves credit for not offering a reassuring model of manhood, which might rationalize the *melancholite* violence inflicted by her eclectically chosen male characters on her eclectically chosen female characters.

Fares's *Honey and Ashes* relies on shocking scenes of aggression against women to underscore the compulsive violence with which feminist challenges to patriarchy are met. It also drives a wedge between masculinity and patriarchal manhood by inserting a matriarchal figure, reminiscent of Tlatli's *hama* character, who coerces her son Hasan into an arranged marriage. She disallows his marrying the girl he loves, Leila, who then runs away from her father's house and takes up secret prostitution to cover the costs of her studies. Just when Leila decides to quit, Idris, a fellow student madly in love with her, finds out her secret. Idris tries to rape her; she stabs him dead. Leila's court case draws the attention of Naima, a single mother who once fled to Russia to avoid an arranged marriage. Naima is a doctor; she treats a patient by the name of Amina for injuries inflicted by her abusive husband, and offers Amina her solidarity.

This film is about the intersecting struggles of three women against patriarchy; concomitantly, it constructs a narrative of manhood and weaves a continuum between matriarchal and masculinist mentalities. By reproducing the psychodynamics of extreme male violence and extreme male powerlessness, Fares paints a complex picture of 'Bourguiba's sons' suspended in Tunisia's modernist project, unable to reconcile themselves to the logistics of gender equality and to the demands of patriarchal mores. Her tapestry of male characters includes insanely jealous men, *hazzara*, drunken machismos, prostitution clients, and sanctimonious peasants. I examine the three major characters: Hasan, Leila's boyfriend; Idris, Leila's fellow student; and Moha, Amina's husband. While these characters are different, they can be seen as miniatures of one modern Tunisian man caught in the disorienting incongruities of an arranged marriage between tradition and modernity and between theory and practice. Hasan, in love with Leila, proves gutless before his mother who forces him to marry his cousin. His behavior is typical of a mama's boy *(weld-ummu)*, the aberrant example of weakness that patriarchal manhood exploits in order to enforce its regulatory rationale.

The film's prologue presents women's voices discussing male–female relations. One woman declares that she cannot tolerate a man's weakness while another maintains that weakness *(faiblesse)* in a man can be touching ("La faiblesse chez un homme, ça peut être quelque chose de touchant aussi"). In either case, weakness in a man is codetermined by the desires and aspirations of both men *and* women within patriarchy. Otherwise, how can we understand the logic that drives Naima to decline an arranged marriage and Hasan to succumb to one? Such a scenario is the measure of the film's attempt to pry apart the sociocultural attributes of manhood from biological differences between masculinity and femininity. Without romanticizing the weakness of Hasan and the courage of Naima, I argue that a combination of both casts a melancholy pall on patriarchal manhood—a manhood that feeds on the unacknowledged rift between masculinity and men.

Patriarchal manhood paradoxically depends on and defends against weakness. Whether Hasan is a victim of male powerlessness or of matriarchal supremacy, the latter is only an effect of the former. Consider Idris's attempt to rape Leila when he discovers she is a prostitute using the name Theresa. While Idris is indubitably in love with Leila, he is so only to the extent that she is a function of his own manhood. Such manhood is founded, as Abdelwahab Bouhdiba propounds, on the "kingdom of mothers," according to which the respect and idealization of the mother-imago is directly transferred onto the woman one loves. "Hence," Bouhdiba propounds, an "excessive idealization of [a] woman [is] inevitably followed by disappointment" (Bouhdiba, 224), because the loved woman would fall short of supplanting the mother-imago. Bouhdiba goes on to add, "Respect of our mothers prevents us from flying with our own wings. We have to see the mother, that is to say the truth, in her complete nakedness, face to face, without blenching, without accepting the slightest veil" (Bouhdiba, 227). This echoes Assia Djebar in *Ombre Sultane* (A Sister to Scheherazade): "Are men ever really naked? You are never free of fetters, you are bound fast by fears of the tribe, swathed in all the anxieties handed down to you by frustrated mothers. . . . Show me one really naked man on this earth, and I will leave you for that man!" (Djebar, 86). Bouhdiba and Djebar point toward the necessity of rechanneling matriarchal–patriarchal reflexes into uninhibited projects of selfhood. Enchanted by the mother-imago, Idris tells his friend that it is sinful *(e-hram)* to sleep with prostitutes, then tries to rape Leila while threatening to denounce her. Unbeknownst to him, she had already given up prostitution. Idris's attempt to rape Leila is a *melancholite* attempt to suture the narcissistic wound of his manhood—demarcated by the dominance of the mother-imago as well as by the all-too-human defenselessness against suffering that accompanies falling in love with another person. The inevitability of suffering structures libidinal encounters, so that love is unthinkable outside the parameters of mourning. Idris's injured ego, however, is blind to the vulnerabilities that inaugurate libidinal ties and seeks instead a fantasy of mastery over his love-object, Leila.

By refusing to prostitute herself for him, Leila denies him a vehicle for staging the foundational vulnerability of having been in love (with a mother-imago). She exposes the vulnerability of his patriarchal manhood. If Leila were to give herself to him, not only would she have thwarted his healing process ("lies don't heal," says Naima) but she would also become an accomplice in the repertory of lies that sustains patriarchal manhood. Although she stabs him with a knife, she says, "I killed him with the truth, not with a knife" (Quand je l'ai tué, je l'ai fait avec la vérité, pas avec un couteau).

Every time Moha—a former professor not only of his wife, Amina, but of Idris and Leila too—beats Amina, he tells their daughter, Safiya, and the doctor (who happens to be the know-it-all Naima) that she fell down the stairs. Only lies close the gap between traditional manhood and modern liberalism—that is, between being a wife beater at home and a professor of French at the university. Insofar as "the most extreme idealism . . . could co-exist, without conscious contradiction, with everyday social cynical practice" in neopatriarchal societies (Sharabi, 66), Moha is the prototype of Bourguiba's sons. The task of modernity becomes a mask of traditionalism in neopatriarchy. Although he claims to be the only person who could make Amina "happy and free," he sees no contradiction between such idealism and his male-worshipping mentality: "If you had really loved me," he tells Amina, "you would have given me a son." Furthermore, even though he once offered Amina one volume of Michel Foucault's *Dits et écrits*, and might be aware of Foucault's insights into regulatory power, he fails to integrate an element of self-scrutiny as he navigates the private and public spheres of his life as husband, father, and professor. In the classroom, he seems to maintain a gendered sensibility in his relationship with his students, assigning research topics about love to female students and about money to male students. In sum, Moha is as Frenchified (to use Bourguiba's word) a modern Tunisian as he can aspire to be within the citadels of neopatriarchy.

There is a moment in *Honey and Ashes* when Moha is crying alone by his desk. No sooner does Amina enter than he stops, and masks what could have been a homeopathic experience of mourning with bristling anger. *Honey and Ashes* deconstructs the *melancholite* recourse of Bourguiba's sons to masks of invulnerability in order for them to continue to command the credibility of patriarchal manhood. In this respect, the riddle *(tshanshina)* that young Safiya plays with her mother is suggestive. Safiya asks her mother who she thinks is the "biggest" and "strongest" of all; when her mother, Amina, interrupts halfway, "I know—God" *(e'raftu—Rabbi)*, Safiya corrects her: "No, it isn't God, it's Papa!" It is this kind of knowledge, instilled in girls at an early age that contributes to the perpetuation of the linkage between masculinity and male supremacy in modern Tunisian society. Tlatli's and Fares's films expose the disavowed chasm between masculinity and manhood through feminist lenses. By conferring on their female characters attributes traditionally assigned to manhood (courage, defiance, and perseverance), they undo the premises of the patriarchal collective unconscious and its hold on the forms of sociality and intelligibility that govern relations between Tunisian men and women.

Manhood Undone

Generally, the image people have in their heads is one which has to be favorable; they can't imagine anyone presenting an unfavorable image of themselves to them. So I almost rape them with my images so that they shan't be raped elsewhere.

—Nouri Bouzid ("On Inspiration," 56)

While Tlatli and Fares undo the "genderational" (Berkley)[4] premises of patriarchal manhood by confronting it with economized feminist challenges, Férid Boughedir and Nouri Bouzid provide a rationale for comprehending the "undoing effects" of manhood—whether by constructing its passage rites (Boughedir) or discerning the heterosexist biases on which it is predicated (Bouzid). In 'usfur estah (Halfaouine: Boy of the Terraces, 1990), Boughedir maps the different stages that the twelve-year-old protagonist, Noura, goes through in the process of being socially instituted and masculinized. The film offers a visual assemblage of signals attesting to rituals of virilization (and, simultaneously, defeminization) that mark a child's crossing of the threshold of the male world. These start with circumcision, which Noura re-experiences vicariously during his brother's circumcision ceremony. They range from Noura's sexual curiosity and banishment from the women's *hammam* (public bathhouse) after being caught trying to steal the underwear of a local beauty, to his first sexual encounter with an orphan-girl servant and his eventual rebellion against his father, Si Azzouz, which signifies his triumphant resolution of the oedipal struggle/complex. The making of Noura's manhood throughout the film parallels the unmaking of his father's authority—underscoring the transgenerational transmission of patriarchal order and, conversely, the vulnerability of patriarchy, its susceptibility to transformation. While Boughedir's film details the challenges and pleasures of Noura's initiation into manhood—and of the seamless collapsibility of masculinity, manhood, and heterosexual practices—Bouzid's *Rih essed* (Man of Ashes, 1986) enacts manhood as the site of infantile trauma and acute anxiety. If Boughedir's film documents various social incitements to manhood, Bouzid's directorial debut accents the process of "becoming undone" (Butler, *Undoing*, 1) in the very trajectory of becoming a man.

Man of Ashes chronicles the crisis of manhood that Hachemi experiences when preparations for his arranged marriage are underway, a time of social expectations of virility. The crisis is provoked by the circulating rumor about the alleged lack of manhood of Farfat, his childhood friend. Graffiti on street walls announcing that *Farfat mush rajil* (Farfat is not a man) provoke a series of traumatic flashbacks or *screen scenes* of childhood rape. The viewer realizes that when they were young carpentry apprentices, Hachemi and Farfat were molested by their mentor, Ameur, and grew up marked by this closet trauma even though it is an open secret. While both suffered sexual assaults, Farfat seems to bear the burden of its public disclosure. Hachemi sustains an intact reputation, untarnished by his intense homosocial relationship with Farfat. Director Nouri Bouzid insists, however, that Farfat is Hachemi's "double, the other side of the coin," who would have no qualms in saying to society, "Get stuffed, I will do what I like" (Bouzid, "On Inspiration," 50). As the double, Farfat personifies the 'internal' drama within Hachemi's psyche and lifts up a corner of the veil on the heterosexist unconscious of society. He implicates the viewer as witness to the stressful conditions of patriarchal manhood. It is via Farfat that the film brings in verities that would prove hard to swallow for most beneficiaries of patriarchal manhood: child molestation, homophobia, and erotic vengeance. By the end, Hachemi releases Farfat from his hold, as if letting loose a pent-up desire for vengeance; he kills the pederast Ameur by stabbing him in the groin.

The protagonist and his double struggle with the psychosocially daunting task of being (validated as) *men*—of being, paradoxically, members of a rigid community they can neither fully join nor leave behind. Farfat's fantasy of departure from Sfax to Tunis animates his rebelliousness against his biological father and ultimately against his father figure—mentor-cum-molester, Ameur. *Melancholite* anxieties of male supremacy (of which the gendered construction of manhood is a product) are augmented by heterosexist fears of emasculation, effeminacy, and homosexuality. Manhood in this community is "an eminently *relational* notion, constructed in front of and for other men and against femininity [and, I would add, queerness], in a kind of *fear* of the female [and the queer], firstly in oneself" (Bourdieu, 53, original italics). Like other docile members of their community, Hachemi and Farfat are already undone by the heterosexist norms of intelligibility of patriarchal manhood. At the level of personal history, they are more profoundly undone by the sexual assaults of their mentor-cum-molester— assaults that remain unspeakable, not least because they carry the taint of homosexuality or of what is commonly referred to in Tunisian pejorative parlance as *wabna* (coitus *a tergo* between men). Being victims of pederasty, Hachemi and Farfat grow up to be victims of homophobia in a community hypocritically bent on shaming victims and glorifying rapists. Consider, for instance, "Ameur's standing in the community as a respected family man who, naturally, will be invited to the wedding" (Stollery, 53) at the same time that Farfat is banished from his father's house, vilified by his childhood friend Azaiez as less than a man. This suggests that the tragedy of child molestation, far from being ethically and therapeutically addressed, is displaced by the scapegoating and blackmailing of homosexual shaming rituals, in which aggressors are associated with male power while the aggressed against are cast aside as effeminate weaklings. It is as if patriarchal manhood cannot appreciate the pain, let alone denounce the crime, of child molestation unless as a defamatory scandal of homosexuality. Such cruelty is symptomatic of the vulnerability that drives melancholites into prophylactic bonds of 'real men' and melancholics into careful re-examinations of the all-too-familiar cognitive modalities that inhibit *melancholites* from extending human solidarity to the victims of cisgender habitus.

Few things are worse than suffering from the long shadow of a childhood trauma in a culture marked by the foreclosure of conventions that would initiate the reparative work of mourning necessary for the treatment of such trauma. While the trauma of child molestation is disavowed, its effects (for example, the public invalidation of Farfat's manhood) are disseminated as entertainment items. The distance between the tragedy/injustice of child molestation and the scandal/stigma of homosexuality is the measure of the *melancholite* disposition of the patriarchal apparatus of manhood—its sadistic, Manichean, and *heteroimmunitary* pursuit of the myth or fantasy of invulnerability. *Heteroimmunitary* refers here to frantic reinvestments in the heteronormative patriarchal orders of manhood in the wake of global gay and transgender challenges to conventional forms of sexuality and gender identities. *Heteroimmunization* is what *melancholites* do to preserve the spurious familiarity that binds them to their patriarchal habitus. I reserve the term *melancholite* to describe the defensiveness with which the beneficiaries of patriarchal manhood guard against the encroachments of feminist challenges of gender equality. Encroachments come also from the challenges of new sexualities, new masculinities, and transgendered identities. In its *melancholite* form, manhood is a fragile repository of psychoaffective and sociocultural dispositions, fears, and anxieties, whose beneficiaries confer on it the power to command credibility. I distinguish this from the more retrospective/introspective melancholic form of manhood, which is grounded in an unequivocal historical injustice—or, as is the case with Hachemi and Farfat, in a traumatic experience of rape that can neither be forgotten nor openly confronted in the public sphere without further reactionary complications (for example stigmatization) from *melancholites* at large. Melancholic manhood in *Man of Ashes* becomes a necessary tool to denaturalize the familiarity that binds *melancholites* to phallocentric modes of behavior embedded in the sexist ideology of patriarchy.

Farfat's own public disclosure that he is "not a man" is symptomatic of his melancholic insurgency—his "insistent communicativeness which finds satisfaction in self-exposure," self-flagellation, and ego-impoverishments (Freud, 255). It is hard to determine whether melancholia is all suffering or perverse pleasure—whether Farfat is masochistically emptying his ego or luxuriating in his symptoms via his self-engineered claim that he is not a man. Robert Lang and Maher Ben Moussa (2001) exaggerate Farfat's turn against society and against its constrictive strictures of manhood, overlooking his struggle to reintegrate himself into the community. Farfat's melancholic diminution of self-regard cannot be understood separately from the absence of any conventional strategy that would help him process his trauma of childhood rape. Along with the coercive violence of hetero-sexist manhood, the lack of a socially honored framework of mourning renders the injuries of trauma ungrievable and thereby explains the "circuitous route by which the psyche accuses itself of its own worthlessness" (Butler, *Psychic Life*, 184). Yet, is not this self-inflicted violence "a refracted indictment of the social forms that have made certain kinds of losses ungrievable?" (Butler, *Psychic Life*, 185). Farfat's public disclosure that he is "not a man" is a tactical move from a solitary suffering of trauma to implication of his entourage in such a process of suffering and public shaming. Suffering stops being solitary when it is witnessed by community members. Farfat is, in denouncing himself, engineering witnesses—whether or not they prove empathic enough to bring him what Peter Shabad calls the "dignity of recognition" (Shabad, 210). His melancholia expresses a hybrid strategy of resisting patriarchal manhood while enduring it.

By implicating the community, Farfat is implicating us all in his suffering because we cannot deny what his experience entails for us symbolically (as Tunisians and Arabs) living in the aftermath of 1967. Bouzid avers that he "wanted to approach what makes up our present situation of crisis, the bankruptcy of our society. Thus, my first film [*Man of Ashes*] addresses childhood, not exactly mine but rather my generation's, how we were 'broken' from the beginning, how we suffered from adult violence" (quoted in Shafik, 194). The director's remarks take on a specific historical and political dimension in the context of *Man of Ashes*. There is no gainsaying the importance of the political allegory of European colonial and neocolonial rape, or of Israel's ongoing occupation of Arab lands following the 1967 war. Both are at the origin of the malaise of postcolonial nationhood and the current counterrevolutionary turn against the Arab uprisings. Both are key to understanding the political context in which the crisis of Arab manhood has been artistically inscribed through impotence, castration, or suicide. Bouzid's film is concerned, conversely, with the material and psychoaffective effects of these transnational Arab crises as they manifest—in condensed, indirect form—at the level of individual history. At the same time, it is crucial not to overemploy the allegorical mode of reading since it may diffuse the specificities of the cases at hand into the grand narratives of colonialism, postcolonialism, and globalization.

The importance of Bouzid's *Man of Ashes* lies in the severity of its critique of the allegorical continuum between patriarchal manhood and Bourguiba's brand of Tunisian nationhood. Hachemi and Farfat renounce identification with their biological fathers and their mentor-cum-molester.

For Hachemi, the only remaining model of manhood is represented by Monsieur Lévy, the old Tunisian Jew, but he dies just when Hachemi starts telling him about his trauma. The fact that by the end of the film Hachemi seeks but is not granted refuge in the brothel run by the old procuress Sejra expresses how the play of identifications in this scene is mobilized to recast the nets of fatherhood, motherhood, and manhood. Manhood is wrested away from patriarchal normativity throughout the film. Take the opening scene of a slaughtered red cockerel gasping its last breath. Far from being an allegorical emasculation, it is a performative trope of the melancholic predicament of manhood—its traumatic survival after the loss of virility. The slaughtered cockerel, a symbol of virility/masculinity, does not so much conjure up the fear of castration as the imperative to pry virility/masculinity apart from manhood. From the outset, the film deploys what might have been a castrating historical situation of colonial rape or child molestation in order to prod the viewer to rethink manhood beyond the fallacies of virility and masculinity. As long as the Arab world continues to be unfree from European, American, and Zionist incursions—and unfree from postcolonial presidents-for-life (against which the Arab uprisings struggle)—the everyday fetishization of virility/masculinity can only breed *melancholites* but not foster a collective consciousness of the melancholic predicament of manhood. Without such collective consciousness, not even the potentially redemptory valences of melancholia can be redirected into the critique of empire.

Man of Ashes punctures the fantasy of *melancholite* invulnerability and introduces us instead to the structural and historical condition of powerlessness that marks the melancholic condition of manhood in the Arab world. There is something politically redemptive in Bouzid's pre-occupation with staging broken individuals in a society unable to take stock of its failures. "Defeat" is one of the director's keywords—or, more precisely, the drama that follows from the disavowal of defeat in a world traversed by a "pair of contradictions—greatness and impotence" (Bouzid, "On Inspiration," 54). For Bouzid, the task of the filmmaker is to deal a rude awakening to the viewer, rape him out of his world of fantasy "so that he shan't be raped elsewhere" (Bouzid, "On Inspiration," 56). His preoccupation with defeated individuals whose manhood has already been undone explores the transformative valences of aestheticizing failure—hammering home melancholic men, and "melancholicizing" the spectators in the process. In a similar context, Rey Chow observes that "the powerless provides a means of aesthetic transaction through which a certain emotional stability arises from *observing* the powerless as a spectacle" (Chow, 135, emphasis in original). Through the chiasmus of proximity and distance, of identification and disidentification with the powerless, the viewer becomes cognizant of the imperiling structures of manhood in which he is involved; of the melancholic and *melancholite* anxieties attendant upon such structures; and of the necessity of reconfiguring manhood as a locus of cultural malleability, unbundled from heteroimmunitary exit strategies.

Conclusion

Habib Bourguiba's neopatriarchal cult of personhood informs the *melancholite* proclivity of men portrayed in modern Tunisian film. Bourguiba's autocratic rule was, in turn, informed by the history of French colonialism as well as by the trials of Arab nationalism against Zionist settler colonialism and Western imperialism. Both Bourguiba and sons are related to a historical condition that contributes to their de-formation and continues to exert pressure on their survival.

As these films demonstrate, modern Tunisian cinema has wagered on exploring the contradictions of Tunisian men in the pull of neopatriarchy. Surely, the encroachments of new forms of masculinity and new sexualities have challenged traditional conceptions of manhood, but they have not fully eradicated the patriarchal sensibilities that sustain them and from which they have yet to break free. Melancholy manhood is born when a loss or crisis of old conceptions of manhood has taken place but has not been accompanied by the parallel and adequate psychosocial and hermeneutic readjustment necessary for its resolution. Were Bourguiba's modernity not parachuted into an already entrenched patriarchal apparatus, but rather flowed from within its rhythms, generations of Tunisian men and women might have developed the psychic wherewithal with which to participate in modernity in ways that would surely redound to their own and others' benefit.

Notes

1   A version of this argument, much revised since, was previously published in the Journal of North African Studies 15.1 (2010): 105–26.

2   See *Lisan al-Arab*, entry *rajala*. For further definitions, see *Qamoos* online. Translations are the author's own unless otherwise indicated.

3   For more on the correlation between Tunisian independence and the liberation of women, see Naaman (2000), Sherzer (2000), Stollery (2001), Slawy-Sutton (2002), Gauch (2007), and Moore (2008).

4   This neologism is used by Anthony R. Berkley to refer to the overlap between gender and generation in Maya society. It is used here to stress the transgenerational transmission of gender discrimination in patriarchy.

Works Cited

Adonis. *An Introduction to Arab Poetics*, translated by C. Cobham. London: Saqi Books, 1990.

Adorno, Theodor. *Minima Moralia*, translated by E.F.N. Jephcott. London: Verso, 1984.

Ahmed, Leila. *Women and Gender in Islam: Historical Roots of a Modern Debate.* New Haven, CT: Yale University Press, 1992.

Amin, Qasim. *The Liberation of Women and the New Woman: Two Documents in the History of Egyptian Feminism*, translated by Samiha Sidhom Peterson. Cairo: The American University in Cairo Press, 2001.

Anderson, J.N.D. "The Tunisian Law of Personal Status." *International and Comparative Law Quarterly*, 7, no. 2 (1958): 262–79.

Armes, Roy. *Postcolonial Images: Studies in North African Film*. Bloomington, IN: Indiana University Press, 2005.

Béji, Hélé. *Désenchantement national: Essai sur la décolonisation*. Paris: François Maspero, 1982.

Berkley, Anthony R. "Respecting Maya Language Revitalization." *Linguistics and Education* 12, no. 3 (2001): 345–66.

Borowiec, Andrew. *Modern Tunisia: A Democratic Apprenticeship*. Westport, CT: Praeger, 1998.

Boughedir, Férid (Director). *Halfaouine: Boy of the Terraces*. France/Tunisia: Ciné Télé Tilms & Scarabée Films, 1990.

Bouhdiba, Abdelwahab. *Sexuality in Islam*, translated by A. Sheridan. Boston, MA: Routledge & Kegan Paul, 1985.

Bourdieu, Pierre. *The Masculine Domination*, translated by Richard Nice. Stanford, CA: Stanford University Press, 2001.

Bourguiba, Habib. *Ma vie, mes idées, mon combat*. Tunis: Ministère de l'Information, 1977.

———. "The Tunisian Way." *Foreign Affairs*, 44, no. 3 (1966): 480–88.

Bouzid, Nouri. "On Inspiration." In *African Experiences of Cinema*, edited by I. Bakari and M. Cham, 48–59. London: British Film Institute, 1996.

———, director. *Man of Ashes*. Tunisia/France: Ciné Télé Films & La Médiathèque des Trois Mondes, 1986.

Butler, Judith. *Undoing Gender*. New York: Routledge, 2004.

———. *The Psychic Life of Power: Theories in subjection*. Stanford, CA: Stanford University Press, 1997.

Camau, Michel, and Geisser, Vincent. *Le Syndrome autoritaire*. Paris: Presses de Sciences Po., 2003.

Chow, Rey. *Primitive Passions: Visuality, Sexuality, Ethnography, and Contemporary Chinese Cinema*. New York: Columbia University Press, 1995.

Curtiss, R.H. "Women's Rights an Affair of State for Tunisia." *Washington Report on Middle East Affairs* 50 (September/October 1993).

Djebar, Assia. *A Sister to Scheherazade*. Portsmouth, NH: Heineman, 1987.

Fares, N. (Director). *Honey and Ashes*. Switzerland/Tunisia: Dschoint Ventschr AG and CTV Services, 1996.

Freud, Sigmund. "Mourning and Melancholia." In *On Metapsychology: The Theory of Psychoanalysis*, translated by J. Strachey, edited by A. Richards, 245–69. London: Penguin, 1991.

Gauch, Suzanne. *Liberating Shahrazad: Feminism, Postcolonialism, and Islam*. Minneapolis, MN: University of Minnesota Press, 2007.

Haddad, Tahir. *Imra'atuna fi-l-shari'a wa-l-mujtama'* [Our Woman in Islamic Law and Society]. Sousse: Dar al-Ma'arif, 1930.

Hochberg, Gil. "National Allegories and the Emergence of Female Voice in Moufida Tlatli's *Les Silences du palais*." *Third Text* 14, no. 50 (2000): 33–44.

Hopwood, Derek. *Habib Bourguiba of Tunisia: The Tragedy of Longevity*. London: Macmillan, 1992.

Joseph, Suad, ed. *Intimate Selving in Arab Families*. Syracuse, NY: Syracuse University Press, 1999.

Joyce, James. *Ulysses*, edited by Declan Kiberd. New York: Penguin, 1992.

Krichen, Aziz. *Le Syndrome Bourguiba*. Tunis: Cérès Productions, 1992.

Lang, Robert, and Maher B. Moussa. "Choosing to Be 'Not a Man': Masculine Anxiety in Nouri Bouzid's *Rih Essed/Man of Ashes*." In *Masculinity: Bodies, Movies, Culture*, edited by Peter Lehman, 81–94. New York: Routledge, 2001.

Lazreg, Marnia. *The Eloquence of Silence: Algerian Women in Question*. New York: Routledge, 1994.

Lukács, Georg. *The Theory of the Novel*, translated by Anna Bostock. Cambridge, MA: MIT Press, 1971.

MacKinnon, Kenneth. *Love, Tears, and the Male Spectator*. Madison, NJ: Fairleigh Dickinson University Press, 2002.

Ibn Manzur, Abul Fadl Djamal al-Din Muhammad ibn Makram. *Lisan al-'Arab*. Beirut: Dar Al-Jeel, 1988.

Massad, Joseph. "Re-Orienting Desire: The Gay International and the Arab World." *Public Culture* 14, no. 2 (2002): 361–85.

Mernissi, Fatima. *Scheherazade Goes West: Different Cultures, Different Harems*. New York: Washington Square Press, 2001.

Moore, C.H. *Tunisia Since Independence: The Dynamics of One-Party Government*. Westport, CT: Greenwood Press, 1965.

Moore, Lindsey. *Arab, Muslim, Woman: Voice and vision in postcolonial literature and Film*. London and New York: Routledge, 2008.

Naaman, Dorit. "Woman/Nation: A Postcolonial Look at Female Subjectivity." *Quarterly Review of Film and Video* 17, no. 4 (2000): 333–42.

Perkins, Kenneth. *A History of Modern Tunisia*. New York: Cambridge University Press.

Qamoos online, 2004.

Quran, The, translated by M.H. Shakir. New York: Tahrike Tarsile Qur'an, 2002.

Sedgwick, E.K. "Gosh, Boy George, You Must be Awfully Secure in Your Masculinity." In *Constructing Masculinity*, edited by M. Berger, B. Walls, and S. Watson, 11–20. New York: Routledge, 1995.

Shabad, Peter. "The Most Intimate of Creations: Symptoms as Memorials to One's Lonely Suffering." In *Symbolic Loss: The Ambiguity of Mourning and Memory at Century's End*, edited by Peter Homans and Julia Stern, 197–212. Charlottesville, VA and London: University Press of Virginia, 2000.

Shafik, Viola. *Arab Cinema: History and Cultural Identity*. Cairo: The American University in Cairo Press, 1998.

Sharabi, Hisham. *Neopatriarchy: A Theory of Distorted Change in Arab Society*. New York: Oxford University Press, 1988.

Sherzer, Dina. "Remembrance of Things Past: *Les Silences du palais* by Moufida Tlatli." *South Central Review*, 17, no. 3 (2000): 50–59.

Shohat, Ella. *Taboo Memories, Diasporic Voices*. Durham, NC: Duke University Press, 2006.

Slawy-Sutton, Catherine. "*Outremer* and *The Silences of the Palace*: Feminist Allegories of Two Countries in Transition." *Pacific Coast Philology* 37 (2002): 85–104.

Stollery, Martin. "Masculinities, Generations, and Cultural Transformation in Contemporary Tunisian Cinema." *Screen* 42, no. 1 (2001): 49–63.

Tlatli, Moufida. "Moufida Tlatli Showcases the Inner World of Women's Emancipation."

Magharebia: The News & Views of the Maghreb, 2005.

———. (Director). *The Season of Men*. France/Tunisia: Les Films du Losange and Maghreb Films Carthage, 2000.

———. "Une affaire de femmes/Stories of Women." *Ecrans d'Afriques* 8, second quarter (1994): 811.

———, director. *The silences of the palace*. Tunisia/France: Ciné Télé Films and Mat Films, 1994.

11

CONSTRUCTIONS OF MASCULINITY
IN PALESTINIAN FILM

Sarah Hudson

Like the relationship between nationalism and masculinity in general, the relationship between the struggle for Palestinian national recognition and hegemonic Palestinian masculinity are inextricably intertwined (Massad) and have become more so over time. The extended Israeli occupation and its prolonged prevention of the development of an independent Palestinian nation has contributed to distinct changes in the performance of masculinity for Palestinian men in the West Bank and Gaza (Peteet). Support for Palestinian nationalism and unwavering resistance to the Israeli occupation have become significant components of Palestinian pride and honor in general, both of which are critical elements of traditional Palestinian masculinity (Peteet). Because of this enmeshment, the prolonged struggle for concrete, acknowledged national identity—and its continual blockage by Israel—has also resulted in a near impossibility for men living in the Occupied Territories to fully emulate traditional Palestinian masculine ideals such as the ability to protect the honor of the family and community (Spielberg, Dajani, and Abdallah, 274). Because of the inability to adhere to traditional Palestinian masculine standards, Palestinians in Israel and the Occupied Territories alike have incorporated performances of resistance to the occupation as a crucial component of masculinity and the achievement of "manhood" (Peteet). The extended occupation and resistance to it have altered the construct of Palestinian masculinity in ways that challenge traditional components of the masculine construct, such as hierarchies of age and maturity. The occupation and resistance has also complicated other components of the masculine construct such as gender hierarchies, which were disrupted during the first intifada but reinforced during the second intifada (Johnson and Kuttab), and added new facets such as the role of prison and public beatings in achieving "manhood" (Peteet, Male Gender and Rituals of Resistance) to the construct.

These changes are frequently highlighted and complicated in Palestinian fictional film, but not at the expense of endangering the concept of Palestinian resistance's moral superiority to the Israeli occupation. A number of Palestinian fictional films chart the intricate relationship between recent constructs of Palestinian masculinity and performances of nationalism through father–son relationships, highlighting the shifts in masculine performance between the generations. Michel Khleifi, Hany Abu Assad, and Elia Suleiman frequently incorporate competing performances of masculinity between fathers and sons as a central conflict in their films. Through the incorporation of such themes, these directors often critique the matter of modern Palestinian masculinity while simultaneously reconstituting the Palestinian moral self in relation to Israel and the occupation.

Nationalism, Masculinity, and Palestine

There is a fairly substantial body of literature describing the connections between nationalism and gender. According to Anne McClintock, "all nationalisms are gendered, all are invented and all are dangerous . . . in the sense that they represent relations to political power and to the technologies of violence" (McClintock, 352). Since their inception, national projects have, almost without exception, been conceived as primarily masculine endeavors (Nagel, "Masculinity," 244); however, the performance of specific gender roles also figures prominently in the imagining of nations. In *Race, Ethnicity and Sexuality*, Joane Nagel explains that nations develop moral economies in which nationalism

> is gendered, sexualized and racialized. National moral economies provide specific places for women and men in the nation, identify desirable and undesirable members by creating gender, sexual, and ethnic boundaries and hierarchies within nations, establish criteria for judging good and bad performances of nationalist masculinity and femininity, and define threats to national moral and sexual integrity (Nagel, *Race, Ethnicity and Sexuality*, 146).

According to McClintock, men typically represent the active agents of nationalism in these economies. Men symbolize forward progress, modernity, and revolutionary change, whereas women represent continuity and the embodiment and reproduction of the nation itself (McClintock, 359). It is, of course, important to note that no two nations or nationalisms develop identically and that, in practice, there is great variation in gender roles and moral economies between and within nations. Though overgeneralizing nationalist masculinities or femininities may be methodologically suspect, a number of scholars have argued that a hegemonic, dominant masculinity that sets the standards for male thought, comportment, and attitude can be identified in a given time and location (Nagel, "Masculinity," 247). The role of these hegemonic masculinities in national movements can become paramount as defining features during times of nationalist crisis, conflict, or uncertainty—but what happens when men cannot perform gender roles according to traditional expectations due to external forces? Expectations adapt to the circumstances, and, as a result, men begin to incorporate those adapted expectations into their performance of masculinity.

The Palestinian case provides a particularly complex example of the intertwined and ever-evolving relationship between masculine gender roles and nationalist discourse. In their attempts to become an independent, internationally recognized, sovereign nation, the Palestinian people have been thwarted again and again. Despite some development and influence from Arab nationalism prior to the 1960s "and, of course, earlier developments in Palestinian national identity during the late Ottoman era and the British mandate" (Khalidi; Swedenburg), the Palestinian national movement is generally agreed to have begun, as a unified movement, with the rise of Fatah in the late 1960s (Baumgarten; Khalidi). Though Fatah remains in power in the West Bank, its nationalist message has evolved substantially in its nearly fifty years in power. By the late 1980s, it had moved away from its original message of armed struggle as the only means of liberating Palestine to one that was more focused on politics and diplomacy (Baumgarten, 36). Hamas subsequently took up the banner of armed nationalist resistance, using much more extreme rhetoric and methods than Fatah. Despite its long-standing popularity, the longer Fatah remained in power with few results to show for it the more its popular support began to erode, and its inability to control Hamas after the first intifada damaged its legitimacy even further (Khalidi, 152). Though Fatah and Hammas encourage distinct forms of masculinity, their notions of the concept share a number of common traits that could be said to comprise modern hegemonic Palestinian masculinity.

Masculinity in the Occupied Territories was traditionally fairly similar to other flavors of Arab masculinity. According to Julie Peteet, "Arab masculinity (*rujulah*) is acquired, verified, and played out in the brave deed, in risk-taking, and in expressions of fearlessness and assertiveness. It is attained by constant vigilance and willingness to defend honor (*sharaf*), face (*wajh*), kin, and community from external aggression and to uphold and protect cultural definitions of gender specific propriety" (Peteet, "Male Gender," 34).

She also adds that virility and paternity are important factors in hegemonic Arab masculinity (Peteet, "Male Gender," 34). David McDonald explains that attaining *rujula* in Palestine can be thought of as a process that combines life-cycle events like circumcision and marriage with the successful performance of deeds that are in keeping with communal values of "chivalry (*marwa'a*), honour/pride (*fakhr/sharaf*), personal sacrifice and generosity (*karam*)" (McDonald, 194). These values also require putting the needs of the community—family, tribe, or nation—above one's own needs; respecting traditional hierarchies; and maintaining proper gender-specific norms of modesty (McDonald, 194). Though many of these expectations and rituals of masculinity have remained relatively unchanged over the years of the Israeli occupation, as national movements shifted and resistance became routinized, traditional hegemonic masculinity became increasingly difficult for Palestinians living under occupation to fully achieve.

In the Occupied Territories, work has grown increasingly scarce, mobility has become more limited, and community has proved impossible to successfully defend. As a result, many of the characteristics of hegemonic Arab masculinity have become subsumed by resistance activities in the Palestinian context. Joseph Massad claims that

> struggling against the Israeli occupiers and colonizers is not only an affirmation of Palestinian nationalist agency, it is also a masculinizing act enabling the concrete pairing of nationalist agency and masculinity (the two being always already paired conceptually) and their logical inseparability within the discourse of nationalism. Resisting occupation therefore can be used to stage masculine acts as it performs nationalist ones. Through this national anti-colonial resistance, a new figuration of masculine bodies is mapped out on the terrain of the national struggle, one that becomes the model for Palestinian nationalist agency itself (Massad, 51 XX).

Through resistance, a young Palestinian man can maintain his honor, defend his family, and make personal sacrifices for his community, all critical components of achieving *rujula*. Peteet articulates the way in which public beatings and imprisonment have become enmeshed with Palestinian masculinity to the point that they are now a rite of passage. She explains that public beatings have become common as a means of humiliating Palestinian men but, contrary to the hopes of the Israeli Defense Forces (IDF), "the meaning of the beating has been appropriated by the subject in a dialectical and agential manner" (Peteet, "Male Gender," 37). She argues that "in emerging from the beating unbowed and remaining committed to resistance activities, young men exhibit generosity to the point of sacrifice that asserts and validates a masculine self" (Peteet, "Male Gender," 40). Prison stints are another area of resistance practices that have been incorporated into hegemonic masculinity for Palestinian men in the Occupied Territories. Unlike public beatings or other resistance activities, surviving a stay in an Israeli prison can actually upend the traditional masculine hierarchy in which age denotes wisdom and respect for elders is paramount. Peteet demonstrates that many young men find themselves in unexpected positions of leadership after being released from prison and that, often, "young men circulate between prison and leadership positions" (Peteet, "Male Gender," 38–39). Tim Kennedy explains that, "Many adult males have been systematically reduced to a state of compliance by confinement and repression, and women have taken on the burden of daily struggle and survival. It is the young who then begin to assume a major role in maintaining Palestinian national identity" (Kennedy, 44). This new performance of masculinity, in which nationalist fervor and resistance to occupation is crucial, frequently creates an intergenerational conflict between the younger and older generations of Palestinian men that can be seen in a number of Palestinian fictional films.

Performances of Intergenerational Conflicts in Masculinities

Most Palestinian feature-length fictional films encompass a father–son relationship of some sort, often one grounded in conflict. The conflict in these father–son tropes is almost always centered on the occupation and resistance to it. Typically, the younger generation seeks a more active role in the resistance than the older generation. In Michel Khleifi's 'Urs al-Jaleel (Wedding in Galilee), Adil cannot bear the humiliation that he feels his father has brought upon the family by inviting the military governor to his wedding. As a result, Adil loses his ability to consummate his marriage—his primary masculine duty that day. In Hany Abu Assad's al-Jannah al-'an (Paradise Now), Said's father is dead, but Said continues to make choices in an effort to mitigate the humiliation he feels from his father's collaboration with Israel. Elia Sulieman's Yad ilahiya (Divine Intervention), which is predominantly set in Israel, presents another type of father–son relationship and slightly different view of the challenges to Palestinian masculinity. These differences are due to a number of factors, but the primary reasons are the structural format of Suleiman's film, which comprises a series of vignettes with a very loose narrative strand, and the characters' subject position as Palestinians living in internal exile within the state of Israel. Though this father–son relationship is less troubled than that of Adil and his father or Said and his, the film depicts both ES, Suleiman's loosely autobiographical protagonist, and his father suffering humiliations as the result of occupation and second-class citizenry in

Israel. Though each of these films depicts father–son relationships and the development and consequences of modern Palestinian masculinity, there is also a suggestion of impotence and sterility that underscores their depictions of modern hegemonic Palestinian masculinity. Adil cannot consummate his marriage; ES loses his girlfriend; and Said chooses to reproduce the resistance with his death rather than the nation through life, marriage, and children. Thus, like Palestinian nationalism and the official Palestinian state, Palestinian hegemonic masculinity is stuck, blocked, in the face of a seemingly never-ending occupation.

Wedding in Galilee

Michele Khleifi's *Wedding in Galilee* is generally considered to be the first feature-length Palestinian film. Released in 1987, its filming and creation preceded the first intifada (Palestinian uprising); however, the struggle between traditional Palestinian masculine ideals and modern concepts of Palestinian masculinity were already at play and can be seen in Khleifi's film. Its plotline centers around Adil's wedding. His father, Abu Adil, the patriarch and *mukhtar* (village leader), is determined to have a traditional Palestinian wedding despite the military curfew placed on the village. In order to gain permission for the celebration, he must invite the military governor to the festivities. Despite this capitulation, Abu Adil sees the wedding as a way to consolidate his local power over more militant youths in the village and as a means to "regenerate a set of traditional Palestinian values tied to agriculture and the land, gender roles, and religion" (Yaqub, "The Palestinian," 60). According to Anna Ball, the *mukhtar's* need to ask permission for such an important cultural event serves to emasculate the village leader (Ball, 7). However, masculinity, as an overdetermined social construct, is never static and possesses a multitude of meanings—and the central conflict of masculinity in this film circulates around those different meanings. Abu Adil chooses to view his capitulation to the military governor as a mode of self-sacrifice in which he is putting the concerns of his family and village above his own pride (Ball, 7). As previously mentioned, self-sacrifice and the primacy of family and community are important markers of hegemonic Palestinian masculinity. However, Abu Adil's concessions can also be interpreted as "a compromise of cultural tradition and a failure to resist the Israeli governor's own manly authority" (Ball, 7). The younger generation of Palestinians in Abu Adil's village, including his own son, interpret the *mukhtar's* compromise in the latter light. Through this interpretative conflict, Khleifi casts *rujula* as contested and ambivalent. For the younger generation, resistance to the Israeli officials has already become paramount in their conceptions of masculinity.

The intergenerational conflict is continued and heightened later in the film, when Adil is left with his bride in order to consummate the marriage. As a result of his father's capitulation, Adil is rendered incapable of performing sexually. According to Ball, "Adel recognizes that his father's complicity with the structures of occupation serves to emasculate him within the paradigms of Palestinian maleness; his marriage no longer signifies an affirmation of tradition, but rather the defeat of Palestinian autonomy" (Ball, 8). For Adil, the elision of Palestinian national autonomy with masculinity and sexuality has become so deeply ingrained that he cannot perform in one arena if he has suffered an affront in another. Unlike his father, who views the wedding as a means of bringing the community together for a cultural celebration, Adil can only see the presence of the Israelis as an affront to his masculinity. Interestingly, it is Samia, the bride, who preserves at least the outward appearance of cultural tradition as well as Adil's masculine pride by taking her own virginity. Throughout the bedroom scene, Samia is the active agent; the camera follows her movements, and she occupies the majority of the shots. Adil, meanwhile, is lessened in the camera's view. He is still, quiet, and retreats into the background of the camera frame. This character placement and movement within the camera frame further emphasizes that Adil has been rendered weak and humiliated by his father's capitulation to the military governor and is no longer capable of performing his conception of modern Palestinian masculinity.

Through this father–son relationship, Khleifi demonstrates the multivocal nature of Palestinian masculinity and offers an internal critique of Palestinian masculinity that results in an absence. Mary Layoun explains, "The film itself as a narrative representation of the fulfillment of national and sexual desire is equally a trenchant suggestion of an absence or lack that cannot be made present" (Layoun, 96). Though the modern hegemonic Palestinian masculinity, which prizes nationalism and resistance above all, dominates the film—the *mukhtar* is presented as an anachronistic relic, desperately clinging to past traditions and ideals throughout (Yaqub, "The Palestinian," 60)—this masculinity is also presented as fragile and impotent because its violation is, in many ways, beyond the men's control. Kennedy argues that "the simultaneous emasculation of the *mukhtar* and Adel is profoundly linked to the intimate intrusion of Israelis into the villagers' space" (Kennedy, 44). Though the *mukhtar* technically invited this intrusion, he did so only in exchange for the ability to practice a cultural tradition—so his decision was not freely made. Adil, on the other hand, had no say in the matter, and his sense of masculine pride is completely undone by the presence of the Israelis. According to Ball, the film "induces a sense of metaphorical and literal impotence in national and male-psyche alike"

(Ball, 8). Although, thanks to his bride, Adil's outward appearance of masculinity remains intact, his sense of nationalism and masculinity are presented as deeply intertwined and equally sterile and impotent.

Paradise Now

In *Paradise Now*, Hany Abu Assad presents a more extreme version of a problematic father–son relationship through the protagonist, Said, and his father who was executed for collaborating with Israel. Like Adil in *Wedding in Galilee*, Said feels his personal and familial honor has been stained by his father's shameful behavior. By the time of *Paradise Now*'s creation, 2005, the Palestinian people had enacted two intifadas in the Occupied Territories, and the notion of achieving *rujula* through resistance activities was firmly cemented into hegemonic Palestinian masculinity. Economic decline and increased restrictions on movement had also created a sense of hopelessness for many there. Many young men were no longer able to work consistently or for high enough wages, making achieving markers of traditional Palestinian masculinity difficult. As Said claims toward the end of the film, the occupation has culpability in creating the conditions for its continued existence; it produces collaborators and suicide bombers alike, in part by severely limiting the ability to achieve non-violent forms of hegemonic Palestinian masculinity and to progress and choose a different future. The resulting futility fuels feelings of impotence in Palestinian males, who then turn to suicide bombing (or collaboration) as their only means of changing the status quo and expressing specific elements of hegemonic masculinity. Said's father's nationalist failure results in his failure to perform hegemonic Palestinian masculinity—it prevents him from caring for his family in an honorable manner and is a demonstration of his failure to uphold honorable behavior. One of the most important factors that influences Said's decision to complete his suicide mission is the desire to mitigate his father's failure and restore honor to his family. Said's family honor has been sullied at the hands of his father, and according to hegemonic Palestinian masculinity, norms the duty to restore that honor rests with the oldest male of the household. For Said—who has been thwarted time and again in his attempts to improve his situation and who sees no light at the end of the tunnel—the ability to achieve the masculine ideal has become inextricably tied to Palestinian national resistance. The occupation leads to his father's failure and stands in the way of Said's attempts to undo his family's humiliation. In Said's mind, it is only through violent resistance that he is able to restore the honor of his family and become a 'real' man.

However, in so doing he also sacrifices his ability to conform to other aspects of Palestinian masculinity—namely, completing the process of *rujula* through a potential marriage to Suha and the reproduction of the family unit. According to McDonald, the official passage into manhood for Palestinian youth happens upon marriage and reproduction (McDonald, 194). Said rejects this option when he rejects Suha and instead can be said to have 'married' the resistance to the occupation through his self-sacrifice, through which he helps to reproduce the resistance. Said's decisions at first appear to contrast traditional hegemonic Palestinian masculinity and its focus on marriage and reproducing the family, with the modern conception of hegemonic Palestinian masculinity and its emphasis on nationalism. Under modern hegemonic Palestinian masculinity, Said's self-sacrifice can be read as the ultimate masculine act in the same way that a marriage ceremony is the chrysalis from which boys emerge as men, according to traditional masculine ideals. Said and Khaled, Said's best friend and fellow suicide bomber, go through a number of funeral rites before they are affixed with their bombing vests. However, because the men are alive while undergoing this process, the rites bear a striking resemblance to wedding rituals—cleaning, dressing, dinner among friends/the resistance family, and others. In the film, Said's suicide is portrayed as a type of wedding in and of itself—a wedding to the nationalist cause with the end goal of reproducing the resistance, even when that reproduction seems somewhat futile on the surface. In this way, self-sacrifice for the nation represents a different incarnation of the same masculine ideals as marriage and with starkly different results.

Whereas the optimal end result of marriage in Palestinian culture is conception of children and, therefore, the continued reproduction of the family (and, by extension, the nation), the end result of Said's 'marriage' to the resistance is death and a continuation of the status quo. Yaqub explains that "Suha and Said's failed relationship is a manifestation of the sterility of the community from which Palestinian culture and politics should (but cannot) arise" (Yaqub, "Paradise Now," 223). Said chooses to reproduce the resistance rather than culture and non-violent political paths. The impotence and sterility of his choice are exemplified in Abu Assad's refusal to visually depict Said's violent end. Nouri Gana describes this refusal as a "collapse of the spectacle," and claims that Abu Assad first builds desire in the viewer for the spectacle of death but then denies that desire by ending the film as Said presses the detonator (Gana, 36). The viewer is never allowed to see the consummation of Said's mission or, more precisely, only sees a blank screen as evidence of the mission's completion. Though violent resistance has been thoroughly incorporated into hegemonic Palestinian masculinity, Abu Assad denies the visual representation of this violence, suggesting that the result of the merging of nationalism and masculinity is an absence; *Paradise Now* indicates that the most extreme forms of modern Palestinian masculinity, like the violent national movements with which they are frequently allied, are sterile and impotent.

Divine Intervention

Elia Suleiman's *Divine Intervention* represents an interesting departure from hegemonic masculinity in the Occupied Territories because it primarily deals with how the Palestinian crisis in masculinity manifests itself in those who live in internal exile in Israel. While Palestinians in the Occupied Territories have incorporated resistance into the performance of hegemonic masculinity, their counterparts living in Israel are limited in their ability to actively resist the occupation or their own ill-treatment. According to Amalia Sa'ar and Taghreedn Yahia-Younis, the blocked paths to masculine expression have resulted in an inwardly turned wave of violence within Arab communities in Israel. They argue that

> [o]n the one hand, militaristic-heroic masculinity, which surrounds them through the practices of Palestinians in the PA [Palestinian Authority] and of Israeli Jews, is a path not available to them. On the other hand non-violent forms of productive patriarchal masculinity, notably the possibilities to accrue political and economic power, are also largely limited, because of class and national discrimination against them" (Sa'ar and Yahia-Younis, 308).

Divine Intervention—in its predominantly non-narrative format, which blurs elements of fiction and documentary—demonstrates how violence within the Palestinian communities in Israel is, at least in part, the result of an inability to adequately perform either traditional or modern hegemonic masculinity. However, it is important to note that masculinity is not a dominant theme in Suleiman's work. Rather, the struggles with masculinity in his films are predominantly a by-product of depicting the tensions of Palestinian life in general through ES's observations of his father and Palestinian society in Nazareth and Jerusalem. This tension can be seen through both ES's narrative line and that of his father.

One of the most noteworthy features of Elia Suleiman's films is their insistence on silence—or at least a lack of dialogue. The protagonist, ES, is always a mute observer of goings-on as he returns to his homeland from abroad. In the context of Palestinian masculinity, this silence can be read as passivity or weakness in the sense that ES does not confront the injustice of occupation and discrimination directly and overtly. However, though his silence is often interpreted by scholars as passivity or a symptom of the stasis of Palestinian life, Linda Mokdad argues that Suleiman's films blur "the line between the 'impossibility of speaking as a Palestinian' and the *refusal* to speak as a Palestinian" (Mokdad, 195). She adds that this shift requires approaching Suleiman's films and the silence within them as "reflections of agency and activity" (Mokdad, 196). When ES's silence is read as an agential choice, it can be seen as an assertion of masculinity through one of the few options left to the filmmaker who no longer lives in Israel. As a Palestinian living in exile, ES has access to scripts of masculinity that are not available to his compatriots who remain in Israel and the Occupied Territories. He is able to pursue education and economic stability in a way that is unavailable to many Palestinians who remain in his hometown of Nazareth. Because ES no longer lives in Israel full-time, he chooses not to overtly speak for those Palestinians who do; rather, he observes, records, and reports. Acknowledging his privileged position, he *refuses* to speak for those who remain and allows his observations of Palestinian life to speak for themselves. When viewed as an active choice, ES's silence can no longer be interpreted as a weakness or failed masculinity. It becomes an act of resistance in and of itself.

The tensions in Palestinian masculinity can also be seen in ES's relationship with his girlfriend, who lives on the other side of the Green Line. Through this relationship, Suleiman turns expected gender roles on their heads to some degree. According to Dorit Naaman, "the filmmaker's girlfriend takes on numerous roles, from seductress/dominatrix of the soldiers (through her gaze only) to potential terrorist and ninja fighter. She 'stands in' for the nation—occupied but still resisting" (Naaman, 518). In terms of the relationship itself, ES is prevented from pursuing a 'normal' relationship with her because they live on opposite sides of the Green Line. Rather than going on dates at restaurants or cafés, the couple meet at the Al Ram checkpoint and hold hands in his car as they witness the daily humiliation of Palestinians trying to cross into Israel through the checkpoint. ES's ability to perform masculinity in this fictional setting is hindered by the IDF and checkpoints—and the juxtaposition of his attempts to develop a relationship with the humiliation of everyday Palestinians serves to underscore the unequal power differential between Israelis and Palestinians, which is a constant reminder of the inability to achieve traditional Palestinian masculinity under occupation.

When ES is finally able to overcome the border—not through direct confrontation, but through distraction and a battle of symbols—and sneak his girlfriend into Jerusalem, no happy ending awaits the couple. As she gazes out of the widow of his Jerusalem flat, she sees that he lives down the street from a collaborator whose house is the regular target of vandalism.

She observes a pleasant exchange between the neighbor and Israeli police forces in which the neighbor greets the police, shows them his car, and offers them tea. As she watches this interaction, stone-faced, ES is asleep in the bedroom. Finally, she can no longer watch the exchange and leaves the flat. As she walks past the police and the neighbor, she stares at both defiantly, and they return her gaze in stupefaction. ES, who has awoken, watches her leave from the window. Once again, his attempts at developing a relationship are thwarted by Israel, and he is now forced to suffer the humiliation of his girlfriend leaving him. Because he is unable to successfully perform Palestinian masculinity in his real life, his girlfriend becomes the subject of his fantasies—in which he is better able to achieve masculine ideals.

Because ES does not live in the Occupied Territories and only resides in Israel part-time, he is unable to participate in the same type of hegemonic Palestinian masculinity that operates in the territories. Like many Palestinians living in Israel, he is unable to express his masculinity through open physical or military resistance. In order to express these desires, however, ES resorts to the tools available to him as an artist: imagination and fantasy. *Divine Intervention* is scattered throughout with fantasy sequences in which ES is able to express his desires for resistance. In one notable fantasy scene, he tosses a fruit pit (a stone) out of his moving car window. When the pit hits an Israeli tank, the tank explodes. The act of tossing a grenade or stone has been a symbol of the continuity of resistance in Palestinian imagery since the 1960s (Salti, 49). In this single act, ES is able to connect not just with modern-day resistance but also with resistance movements from past decades. Most of these fantasy sequences also involve his girlfriend, dressed as a *fida'i*, a Palestinian freedom fighter. During these sequences, his desire for a relationship with her is elided with his desire for resistance to the Israeli occupation and a free Palestinian state. It is through these sequences that ES's longing for hegemonic Palestinian masculinity—and that masculinity's reliance on, and incorporation of, nationalism—are revealed. However, ES is only able to achieve this masculinity through fantasy. In his waking world, his desires for hegemonic Palestinian masculinity are routinely blocked by Israel. Like Adil's and Said's attempts to express hegemonic Palestinian masculinity, ES's masculine expression is similarly sterile. A successful relationship does not evolve from his efforts, and his fantasies are incapable of reproducing family or community in any concrete way.

While Suleiman's choices to remain silent and ES's story line demonstrate ways in which the director himself struggles with hegemonic Palestinian masculine ideals, his father's narrative demonstrates the struggle, even for older generations, of maintaining the Palestinian masculine ideal in the face of discrimination and injustice. The experiences of ES's father, Fuad, which are observed without commentary from his son, are emblematic of how the difficulties in achieving and maintaining the masculine ideal pervade Palestinian society for all men, not just those coming of age. His father's frustrations are the result of economic humiliations and intrusions on his private space. These frustrations manifest themselves as a diffuse anger and hostility toward the community.

Fuad's initial frustrations arise when he must close his auto repair shop. Though Fuad has spent his life successfully running the shop, it is no longer profitable, and he must shut it down. This loss of economic status and power can be read as a significant blow to his sense of masculinity. Where he once held a respectable position as a business owner, the economic decline in Nazareth—as a result of overcrowding and discriminatory Israeli policies—has now robbed him of one of his primary sources of masculine pride. In addition to having to close his business, Fuad is then subjected to the humiliation of having Israeli tax officials inventory his home. During this process, he stands quietly in the background watching a football match. Sports have long been discussed as a sublimation of masculine aggression, and according to Sa'ar and Yahia-Younis, they are one of the few non-militarized avenues available for Palestinians living in Israel to express hegemonic Palestinian masculinity. The authors explain that other, non-militarized, scripts for successful Palestinian masculinity include religious devotion, education and white-collar success, and playing football professionally (Sa'ar and Yahia-Younis, 313). Fuad, having been undermined in one of these areas—losing his status as a successful white-collar business owner—uses another, football, to escape his current unacceptable reality: the violation of his personal space by Israeli officials.

Fuad's frustrated masculinity is manifested in the film as a rage, simmering just below the surface of his everyday activities. The second scene of the film begins with him standing beside his car and then driving to work. Over the course of the drive, Fuad simultaneously waves to and curses almost everyone he drives past. He is not visibly upset or angry, but his words do not match his smile and waving hand. He is filmed from within the vehicle, which lends the scene a claustrophobic and restricted feeling. When paired with Sa'ar's and Yahia-Younis's analysis of increasing violence in Palestinian areas within Israel as the result of blocked paths to conventional masculine expression, this scene can be read as Fuad's expression of his frustrated masculinity. However, this is unlike that of the younger men's, whose frustrated masculinity and attempts to achieve hegemonic masculinity result in sterile alternatives. Fuad's frustrated masculinity, which is the result of a loss in masculine status rather than a failure to achieve hegemonic masculinity, is cannibalistic rather than sterile. It is turned on his fellow Palestinians in

Israel. Fuad is also not alone in this cannibalistic expression of frustrated masculinity. *Divine Intervention* depicts the entire male community as simmering with a similar emotion. The film suggests that when Palestinian masculinity and overt resistance endeavors are simultaneously blocked, the resulting frustration and destructive impulse turns inward, upon the community itself.

Conclusion

Palestinian fictional cinema demonstrates that scripts of Palestinian masculinity are intertwined with scripts of performances of Palestinian nationalism, highlighting the conflict this enmeshment has created both between generations and within certain segments of the Palestinian community in general. What this cinema reveals, however, is that the intertwining of Palestinian masculinity with Palestinian national endeavors has favored a masculine performance whose results are impotent and sterile. If masculinity is inextricably entwined with the state of the nation and the state of the nation is kept perpetually in limbo by Israel, then nationalist masculinities cannot bear fruit—as evidenced by the fates of the male characters in these films. It is important to note, however, that despite these films' problematizing the connections between masculinity and nationalism they also serve to underscore the victimhood and moral superiority of the Palestinian position, both in the Occupied Territories and in Israel proper. Palestinian nationalist masculinities may be presented as sterile and, in many ways, fruitless, but the Palestinian goals of nationhood and self-determination are not. By highlighting the difficulties of performing masculinity in Palestine and placing the blame for those difficulties at the feet of Israel and its occupation of the West Bank and Gaza, these directors are able to simultaneously critique Palestinian masculinity while also reaffirming the moral position of the Palestinian cause.

Works Cited

Abu Assad, Hany. *Paradise Now*. Burbank, CA: Warner Independent Pictures, 2005.

Ball, Anna. "Between a Postcolonial Nation and Fantasies of the Feminine: The Contested Visions of Palestinian Cinema." *Camera Obscura* 23, no. 3 (2008): 1–33.

Baumgarten, Helga. "The Three Faces/Phases of Palestinian Nationalism, 1948–2005." *Journal of Palestine Studies*, 34, no. 4 (2005): 25–48.

Gana, Nouri. "Reel Violence: *Paradise Now* and the Collapse of the Spectacle." *Comparative Studies of South Asia, Africa, and the Middle East* 28, no.1 (2008): 20–37.

Johnson, Penny, and Eileen Kuttab. "Where Have All the Women (and Men) Gone? Reflections on Gender and the Second Palestinian Intifada." *Feminist Review* 69 (2001): 21–43.

Kennedy, Tim. "*Wedding in Galilee (Urs al-Jalil)*." *Film Quarterly* 59, no. 4 (2006): 40–46.

Khalidi, Rashid. *Iron Cage*. Boston, MA: Beacon Press, 2006.

Khleifi, Michel. *Wedding in Galilee*. Kino International, 1987.

Layoun, Mary. "A Guest at the Wedding: Honor, Memory, and (National) Desire in Michel Khleifi's *Wedding in Galilee*." In *Between Woman and Nation: Nationalism, Transnational Feminisms and the State*, edited by Caren Kaplan, Norma Alarcón, and Minoo Moallem, 92–107. Durham, NC: Duke University Press, 1999.

Massad, Joseph. "Conceiving the Masculine: Gender and Palestinian Nationalism." *Middle East Journal* 49, no. 3 (1995): 467–83.

McClintock, Anne. "No Longer a Future in Heaven: Nationalism, Gender and Race." In Anne McClintock. *Imperial Leather: Race, Gender and Sexuality in the Colonial Contest*, 353–89. New York and Abingdon: Routledge, 2013.

McDonald, David. "Geographies of the Body: Music, Violence and Manhood in Palestine." *Ethnomusicology Forum* 19, no. 2 (2010): 191–214.

Mokdad, Linda. "The Reluctance to Narrate: Elia Suleiman's *Chronicle of a Disappearance* and *Divine Intervention*." In *Storytelling in World Cinemas*, edited by Lina Khatib, 192–204. New York: Wallflower Press, 2012.

Naaman, Dorit. "Elusive Frontiers: Borders in Israeli and Palestinian Cinema." *Third Text* 20, no. 3/4 (2006): 511–21.

Nagel, Joane. *Race, Ethnicity, and Sexuality*. New York: Oxford University Press.

———. 1998. "Masculinity and Nationalism: Gender and Sexuality in the Making of Nations." *Ethnic and Racial Studies* 21, no. 2 (2003): 242–69.

Peteet, Julie. "Nationalism and Sexuality in Palestine." In *Social Constructions of Nationalism in the Middle East*, edited by Fatma Muge Gocek, 141–66. Albany, NY: SUNY Press, 2002.

———. "Male Gender and Rituals of Resistance in the Palestinian 'Intifada': A Cultural Politcs of Violence." *American Ethnologist* 21, no. 1 (1994): 31–49.

Sa'ar Amalia and Taghreed Yahia-Younis. "Masculinity in Crisis: The Case of Palestinians in Israel." *British Journal of Middle Eastern Studies* 35, no. 3 (2008): 305–23.

Salti, Rasha. "From Resistance and Bearing Witness to the Power of the Fantastical." *Third Text* 24, no. 1 (2010): 39–52.

Spielberg, Warren, Khloud Jamal Khayyat Dajani, and Taisir Abdallah. "No-Man's Land: Hearing the Voices of Palestinian Young Men Residing in East Jerusalem." *Peace and Conflict: Journal of Peace Pyschology* 22, no. 3 (2016): 272–81.

Suleiman, Elia, director. *Divine Intervention*. Kino Lorber Films. DVD, 2003.

Swedenburg, Ted. *Memories of Revolt: The 1936–1939 Rebellion and the Palestinian National Past*. Fayetteville, AR: University of Arkansas Press, 2003.

Yaqub, Nadia. "*Paradise Now*: Narrating a Failed Politics." In *Film in the Middle East and North Africa: Creative Dissidence*, edited by Josef Gugler, 219–28. Austin, TX: University of Texas Press, 2011.

———. "The Palestinian Cinematic Wedding." *Journal of Middle East Women's Studies* 3, no. 2 (2007): 56–85.

12

GENDERED POLITICS IN LATE NINETEENTH-CENTURY EGYPTIAN NATIONALIST DISCOURSE

Matthew B. Parnell

A Crisis of Masculinity in the Struggle for Egypt, 1875–84

In the 1870s, a struggle erupted in Egypt for political, economic, and social hegemony. This development followed previous decades in which Egypt entered the European-dominated modern world system, and resulted in growing foreign interest and influence there. Earlier reforms modernizing the Egyptian state and its subjects facilitated the emergence of new indigenous social strata, which also took greater interest and roles in Egypt and its affairs. Crisis ensued during the spring of 1876, when Khedive Isma'il admitted bankruptcy following years of borrowing from foreign banks and lending houses. European countries, Great Britain in particular, worried over issues following this development related to the accessibility of Egypt's trade routes, its financial debt, and the potential unsettling of the regional power balance. The economic crisis also prompted the founding of an indigenous oppositional movement bound by their grievances against the khedive and foreign intervention in Egypt as well as their shared material interests, ethnic solidarity, and territorial patriotism. The struggle intensified following the forced abdication of Isma'il in favor of his son, Tawfiq, in 1879 and the intervention of the Egyptian military behind Colonel Ahmed 'Urabi in 1881 in government affairs. However, the so-called 'Urabi Revolt came to an abrupt end when the British landed troops in September 1882 and defeated 'Urabi at Tal al-Kabir. The defeat opened a new chapter in modern Egyptian history and ushered in a period of almost exclusive British control over the country.

In the years leading up to and following 1882, Great Britain's justifications for its invasion and occupation of Egypt derived from more than just economic and political concerns. The ascription of cultural meanings to British domination built a powerful legitimacy for Egypt's colonialization.

The new doctrine of progress convinced skeptics and advocates alike that Western intervention in 'less developed' societies ensured the maturation of these more primitive peoples toward modernity and civilization. Frequently, the British colonial discourse represented Egypt's rulers in gendered guises, symbolizing that they were not 'manly' enough to properly govern the lands around the Nile. The portrayal of Egypt experiencing a crisis of masculinity in the 1870s and 1880s proved a useful image justifying Britain's intervention and the formation of its 'Veiled Protectorate.'

Around the same time, Egypt's oppositional movement offered its own concepts and images concerning national development and progress as part of its struggle for hegemony. Hardly the primitive, inferior subjects of the British colonial imagination, early nationalists also often employed representations of Egypt's masculinity crisis to challenge the political status quo, promote collective solidarity, and mobilize Egyptians toward nationalist goals. Moreover, the images of Egypt's gendered troubles provided a means for nationalists to assert their own claims to patriarchal authority over the lands around the Nile.

This chapter addresses the gendered images found in popular British and Egyptian satirical journals that depicted the struggle for Egypt. I argue that these representations served to facilitate popular identification with imperial or nationalist projects and edify the public about colonial or nationalist ideology through culturally specific expressions of hegemonic masculinity. In both the British imperial and Egyptian nationalist case, the underscoring of gendered difference left the *Other* exposed, ridiculed, and defined. The deployment of satire by cartoonists in constructing their gendered representations had little to do with simply eliciting humor. Rather, the depictions served an allegoric or emblematic purpose whose function was to encourage interest, sympathy, and understanding. While others have noted that the struggle for Egypt in the 1870s and 1880s had roots in social, economic, and geostrategic concerns, the gendered politics of the struggle that I present below provided powerful, culturally relevant justifications for change—and its representations gave perhaps the longest-lasting impressions to the viewing audiences.

Portraying Isma'il and Egypt's Financial Crises, 1875–79

In the two decades following the signing of the Treaty of London in 1840, giving Muhammad 'Ali and his family dynastic powers in Egypt, successive British governments maintained in principle that the only condition warranting direct interference in Egyptian affairs would be an imminent French occupation (Mansfield, 3). However, British concerns grew in the early 1870s following several failed attempts by Egypt's khedive, Isma'il, to stave off financial ruin. Much of Egypt's dire financial situation was owed to its ruler, who increased the country's foreign debt from 3.3 million to 98.5 million Egyptian pounds between his accession to the throne in 1863 and 1876. Isma'il's indebtedness resulted from his desire to revitalize and modernize Egypt through urban and agrarian reforms, improve education, and transform consumption patterns. These developments required him to borrow beyond his means and to accept loans with interest rates anywhere between 12 and 26 percent (Mansfield, 5). Isma'il contributed to his debt by paying the Ottoman sultan handsomely for the title of khedive in 1867, along with the right to change the law of succession in Egypt. Moreover, he spent lavishly on building new palaces and hosting extravagant celebrations such as the one commemorating the opening of the Suez Canal in 1869.

In the early 1870s, Isma'il attempted to restructure his loans with foreign banks, revise Egyptian tax codes, and force landowners to expand the production of cotton for export. When these efforts failed to assuage Egypt's debt, the khedive sold off some of his and his family's royal estates. Nevertheless, in 1875 Egypt faced financial crisis, compelling Isma'il to sell off shares in the Suez Canal Company to Great Britain in order to stave off bankruptcy. While Britain had been reluctant to take on a more direct role in Egypt, its shipping through the Canal increased upward of 2,000,000 tonnes by 1875. Thus, the vital importance of the Canal and Egypt to British political and economic interests necessitated action (Kubicek, 252).

In the spring of 1876, Isma'il's insurmountable debts forced him to admit Egypt's bankruptcy leading to European power intervention with the formation of the Public Debt Commission on May 2, 1876. The Commission's responsibility was to supervise the Egyptian budget and economy. France and Great Britain appointed two controllers to oversee Egypt's state revenue and expenses, the 'Dual Control' as it came to be known. The new system meant Egypt effectively lost much of its political and economic independence, as the controllers oversaw much of the affairs of the state.

As the level of alarm stemming from Isma'il's financial predicament rose in the first half of 1876, the popular British satirical journal, *Judy*, marked the occasion by weighing in on these noteworthy developments. From this point forward, cartoonists represented Isma'il as an inferior, gendered subject.

In *Judy*'s April edition, "A Friend Very Much in Need" (Figure 12.1) provided a striking image of Isma'il as a beggar with empty pockets, a patch over his left knee, carrying a heavy load of "debt upon debt" and "ruinous interest" on his back. The khedive's expression connotes a naive bemusement at his condition. In the scene, Stephen Cave, who had returned to

12.1. "A Friend Very Much in Need." *Judy*, April 19, 1876.

London from Egypt in March after heading a mission to inquire upon Egypt's finances, asks for a restructuring of Isma'il's debts and assures Lord Derby, the secretary of foreign affairs, that Egypt could pay off its burdens if provided some relief. However, given the representation of Isma'il here it seems clear that his inability to control his financial affairs determined his position—thus justifying the khedive's subordinate depiction.

12.2. "Great Easterns. Down!" *Punch*, May 26, 1876.

Once negotiations concerning the Anglo–French Dual Control and Egypt's total debt charges concluded in the latter half of 1876, cartoonists continued to characterize the khedive with depictions formulating an inferior, gendered representation. In the caricature, "Great Easterns. 'Down!'" (Figure 12.2), *Punch* expressed British frustration in the face of John Bull who

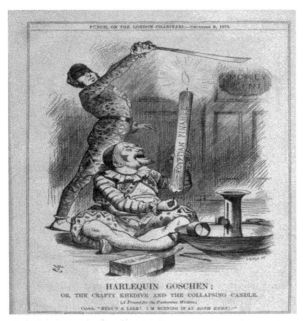

12.3. "Harlequin Goschen." *Punch*, December 9, 1876.

appears clearly irritated by Isma'il and the Ottoman sultan Abdul Aziz. The journal mocked the two rulers as sponge and balloon sellers, provoking the ire of Bull who had "quite enough" of their antics. In December of the same year, *Punch's* "Harlequin Goschen" (Figure 12.3) advanced the image of a knavish Isma'il, mischievously burning Egypt's finances from both ends of the candle, a lark to ruinous effect on his country.

As a new political dynamic in Egypt emerged after 1876, British satirical journals continued to include visual depictions of the country's unfolding troubles. The panic in Britain following Isma'il's appointment of a new cabinet in 1879 occasioned reactions from the satirical press, beginning in March with *Punch's* "Fast and Loose" (Figure 12.4). The journal left no doubt as to who was responsible for Egypt's precarious position, depicting the khedive bound tightly by ropes labeled "ministerial responsibility" and "financial control." *Punch* repeated a similar theme in April's "Poor Fellah!"— caricaturing Isma'il riding an overburdened

12.4. "Fast and Loose." *Punch*, March 8, 1879.

12.5. "Poor Fellah!" *Punch*, April 19, 1879.

donkey symbolizing the Egyptian *fellahin* (Figure 12.5). The burdened beast was meant to signify the plight of Egypt's peasants—beaten with taxation and weighed down with debt, insolvency, and a profligate Isma'il. The citation of khedival extravagance and corruption was nothing new for *Punch*, but in depicting the beaten-down Egyptian *fellahin* the journal broke new ground in representing the Egyptian nation. From this point forward, the depiction of a non-personified, impoverished nation in the form of an animal became more commonplace. Likewise, cartoonists rendered Isma'il with new traits to denote his unmanly character according to Victorian-era British standards. He no longer simply symbolized a shrewd or a lark; he now represented an unjust, immoral, and wasteful ruler too.

'Taming the Crocodile' to Caring for 'Baby' Egypt: The British Invasion and Occupation, 1879–84

As political developments in Egypt unfolded, European officials scrambled to decide their next course of action. In May 1879, Germany, Great Britain, and France sought out Ottoman sultan Abdulhamid II (r. 1876–1908), demanding he force Isma'il to abdicate the throne. Abdulhamid acquiesced to these demands in June by ordering the deposition of the khedive in favor of his son, Tawfiq. European political and financial figures viewed the new khedive as malleable and thus more suitable to rule Egypt compared with his father. The British specifically viewed Tawfiq's appointment as khedive as a safeguard to London's political and economic interests. While Tawfiq did not represent a significant threat to the British, his proclivities toward a more constitutional, liberal-styled government appeased those in Great Britain calling for reform in order to enable Egypt's development as a modern, independent nation (Marsot 1969, 4–10).

From the time Tawfiq took power to the British invasion of Egypt in 1882, the struggle for power pitted the interests of the new khedive against a collection of oppositional parties in Egypt made up of landowners, army officers, and government officials. From this time, British politicians and observers alike called for direct European intervention in Egypt based on the perception that instability and chaos threatened the country's political and economic institutions. Following these developments, popular British satirical journals covered Egypt's affairs at an increasing rate. In fact, *Punch*, *Judy*, and the newly established *Fun* published collectively over sixty images with Egypt as the subject between 1882 and 1884—compared with twenty-one in the previous decade.

Depictions of Egypt in popular British satirical journals during the latter half of the 1870s generally utilized images of the khedives Isma'il and Tawfiq as representative models of Egypt to encapsulate developments there for British viewers. These visions emphasized physiognomic characteristics to reflect on and persuade public opinion on the reasonings behind Egypt's financial crisis or why Isma'il had been forced to abdicate his throne. Following developments between June and August 1882, British satirical journals rendered Egypt in crisis again—but this time around, the most common image was that of the country as an untamed crocodile. In addition, we find a notable transformation in the representation of Tawfiq. From this point forward, the khedive was portrayed in clearly gendered representations whether as an emasculated or a child-like figure.

In July 1882, Egypt reached boiling point following Tawfiq's decision to take refuge in Alexandria and the sultan's refusal to stand against the leader of the nationalist movement, Ahmed 'Urabi. When the Egyptian government refused a British ultimatum on July 10 to stop work on military defenses in Alexandria, the British fleet bombarded the city the following day. *Fun* greeted British prime minister William Ewart Gladstone and his government's actions with "Taming the Crocodile" (Figure 12.6). The basic narrative of the image shows Gladstone taking a stand, aiming his revolver into the mouth of the Egyptian nation imaged as a crocodile pleading for its life. The metaphor of Gladstone's stand proved of significant importance, showing a willingness and power to face the Egyptian nation alone as the French Marianne and German chancellor Bismarck watched behind a screen after other European countries refused to contribute troops to the invasion. The image of Egypt's ruler certainly no longer connoted a hegemonic or even respectable position. Tawfiq haplessly hung on by the narrowest of margins while the British prime minister conveyed a dominant, masculine status.

12.6. "Taming the Crocodile." *Fun*, July 26, 1882.

12.7. "The Egyptian Baby." *Fun*, October 11, 1882.

On August 20, the British landed troops at Port Said and quickly secured the Suez Canal before moving inland. The war for Egypt ended abruptly on September 13 at Tal al-Kabir, where the British defeated Ahmed 'Urabi and his forces. The resolution of the 'Urabi Revolt spelled the beginning the British occupation of Egypt and an opportunity for British satirical journals to remark on the situation. A new British policy began to be shaped in November 1882, when Lord Dufferin was dispatched to Egypt by Gladstone to investigate the political condition of the country and submit a report to London (British National Archives, Dufferin's Report and Correspondences FO 78/3454 and 78/3455). Up to the time of Dufferin's mission, the British cabinet mulled over what to do with Egypt—disagreeing over outright annexation, establishing a paramount British influence in Egypt, immediately turning the reins of government back over to the khedive, or maintaining a force in the country to safeguard European interests in the Suez Canal (Marsot, *Egypt and Cromer*, 27–30). Dufferin's recommendations to the British government would go on to serve as the foundation on which British rule in Egypt would eventually unfold and the parameters determining Britain's exit (Hurewitz, 197). As such, British involvement in Egypt subsequently expanded to meet new two purposes: pacification of the country and reform of its political institutions.

Dufferin's report defined a new relationship between Great Britain and Egypt based upon what has been called a "policy of ambiguous policy," through which the decision to stay or go could be legitimated (Pollard, 85). While a debate on the merits of Egypt's occupation was waged in parliament and in the British political discourse through the end of 1884, cartoons and caricatures reflecting on Britain's presence in Egypt employed images that left no doubt about the new power relationship in Egypt after 'Urabi's defeat. No longer a threat *per se*, the image of the Egyptian nation as an animal was largely dropped from this point forward. In its place, cartoonists portrayed a dominant British figure opposite Egypt depicted as an effeminate subject, or a British figure caring for an infantilized khedive in order to display the gendered relations that characterized the struggle for hegemony.

The representations of this new power dynamic proved to have staying power, cementing the patriarchal politics of the British presence for years to come. *Fun* commented on the new relations by depicting

12.8. "On the Way to Westminster." *Fun*, October 18, 1882.

Gladstone in "The Egyptian Baby" (Figure 12.7) as a father figure to Tawfiq, who had come to rescue the khedive and coddle him following the sultan's neglect. The very next week, *Fun's* "On the Way to Westminster" (Figure 12.8) employed a similar gender and age dichotomy to ridicule the Grand Old Man (as Gladstone was widely known by then) and his children, Egypt and Ireland. Over the next two years, gender and age difference continued to symbolize colonial power relations as referenced by *Punch* in "Nurse Gladstone" (Figure 12.9)

12.9. "Nurse Gladstone." *Punch*, August 25, 1883.

from August 1883 and repeated by *Fun* in "'Dual Control,' or the Egyptian Infant" (Figure 12.10) in January 1884.

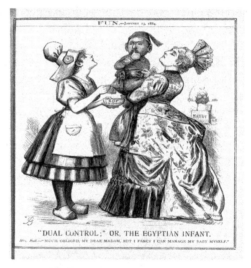

12.10. "Dual Control." *Fun*, January 23, 1884.

The Development of Egypt's Nationalist Movement and a National Consciousness

In the middle decades of the nineteenth century, Egypt experienced unprecedented institutional and infrastructural transformation as Muhammad 'Ali (r. 1805–48) consolidated power and established a modern centralized state with expanding state institutions. He also founded state-sponsored schools to meet the demands of his expanding military and bureaucracy.

These schools offered indigenous Egyptians a path of upward mobility through state service or employment in the liberal professions—a more direct path than that provided by older, traditional forms of education such as private tutoring or the religious *kuttab* schools. Isma'il expanded Egypt's educational system following years of abandonment and neglect under his predecessors 'Abbas (r. 1848–54) and Sa'id. During Isma'il's reign (1863–79), tens of thousands of Egyptian students entered the burgeoning state-school system to feed Egypt's government bureaucracy and institutions (Heyworth-Dunne, 330–92). These developments ultimately played a significant role in differentiating Egypt politically, socioeconomically, and culturally from Istanbul, introducing a sense of Egyptian national identity to the growing ranks of the country's middle and upper social strata.

By the late 1870s, the changes described above had created ideal conditions for social conflict and the emergence of a protonationalist struggle once Egypt's political and economic crises intensified. At that time, an oppositional movement emerged in Egypt and demanded a share of power with the older dominant elite, while also voicing its discontent at growing European influence. Participants in this movement were united not only behind their material interests but also in their sense of ethnic solidarity and territorial patriotism. Once Colonel Ahmed 'Urabi and members of the Egyptian Army led a military demonstration to 'Abdin Palace in September 1881, diverse social forces united and mobilized mass support for the 'Urabist movement under the slogan "Egypt for the Egyptians."

The indigenous printed press's ability to reach both a literate and illiterate audience supplied Egypt's masses with a sense of collective participation in current national events and stimulated protonational awareness (Fahmy, 59–60). Inasmuch as print media served to focus public attention on economic inequalities, political corruption, and foreign intervention, the images and rhetoric found in the popular discourse delivered potent nationalist symbols and messages to a wide mass of Egyptians who were entertained and shaped by their meanings. Under Isma'il, the Egyptian press underwent a major transition from exclusively featuring official administrative, economic, and judicial items of information to becoming overtly politicized and stylized. Isma'il's enthusiasm for the press derived from his general approach toward Egypt's westernization and modernization. The khedive encouraged, funded, and protected journalists and writers who hailed from Egypt and other parts of the Islamic world (Ayalon, 39–46). Isma'il's approach stimulated the establishment of presses around Egypt, but other long-term factors—such as Egypt's increasing urbanization, the burgeoning new educational system, rising public literacy, and further development of the communication and transportation infrastructure—expanded the market for private journalism. At the end of Isma'il's reign in 1879, Egyptians and non-Egyptians alike published sixteen journals/newspapers, ten of which were written in Arabic (Kelidar, 3). Estimated circulation statistics reflect the incredible growth Egypt saw in the number of publications: readership of Arabic newspapers was virtually nonexistent in 1860, but by 1881 circulation had risen into the tens of thousands (Cole, 126).

The political crises of the late 1870s and early 1880s boosted demand among newspaper readership as contributors began to relate political matters to a range of issues from Islamic reformism to Egypt's Westernization and foreign encroachment, Isma'il's extravagance and autocratic rule to demands for increased political participation. These converging factors defined the beginning of an era referred to as the Nahda (literally, 'leaping up') or 'Renaissance,' which also contributed to the revival of Arabic literary culture and the formulation of new kinds of national consciousness. The imposition of the Dual Control in 1876 ignited fierce criticism of Isma'il from local journalists calling for constitutional rule in Egypt and the cessation of European interference in Egyptian affairs. The press's dissemination of political grievances increased with the removal of Isma'il and the ascension of his son Tawfiq to the Egyptian throne in 1879. Over the next three years, journalists attacked the new khedive for his willingness to cooperate with the European controllers as well as publishing repeated calls for reform and greater participation of Arabophone Egyptians in politics. Tawfiq reacted to this criticism by issuing the Press Law of 1881, which enhanced the government's powers to suppress or shut down any publication in the interest of public order or propriety.

Despite the risks, publishers and their journalists continued issuing sharp condemnations of Tawfiq, his government, and the growing European influence in Egypt. The most outspoken publications contributing to the protest movement in the year before the British invasion included those edited by the Syrian Christians Adib Ishaq *(Misr al-fatat)* and Salim Naqqash *(al-Mahrusa* and *al-'Asr al-jadid)*; the Egyptian Christian Mikha'il 'Abd al-Sayid *(al-Watan)*; and Muslims Hasan al-Shamsi *(al-Mufid)*, Hamza Fathalla *(al-Burhan)*, and 'Abdullah Nadim *(al-Ta'if)*. In the months prior to the British invasion the press provided a crucial aid to the 'Urabist uprising, informing its audience on the political events of the period while putting an "anti-Establishment spin on the news" (Cole, 244). Indeed, the Egyptian intelligentsia exercised significant power and influence through its publications and thus wielded a menacing weapon against the khedive and the British. Its ability to voice dissent, shape collective consciousness, and spur popular mobilization through print did not go unnoticed by Tawfiq and his supporters. Following the British victory at Tal al-Kabir in September

1882, the regime moved quickly to take into custody 'rebels' associated with the nationalist movement; members of the intelligentsia comprised 78 percent of those arrested (Cole, 241–49).

The Childish Khedives and Manly Heroes of Egypt, 1879–82

Publishers and journalists utilized an array of rhetoric and images to criticize the khedival regime and European intervention in Egypt as well as to promote the ideals of the nascent nationalist movement. Frequently, the press adopted tropes of masculine crisis to ridicule Isma'il and Tawfiq in ways that were similar to the images from British satirical journals discussed above. These representations in the Egyptian press insinuated about the incompetence of Egypt's rulers and demonstrated their powerlessness in the face of more dominant European encroachment and nationalist upsurge.

Among the most popular and outspoken journals at the time, Yaqub Sannu''s, *Abu naddara zarqa'* (The Man with the Blue Glasses) frequently employed gendered images to level scathing criticism against the khedives, members of the khedival government and household, and representatives of European nations in Egypt. In contrast, ordinary Egyptians (whether members of the urban working classes or peasants), officers in the army, and notables in the Chamber of Delegates were often cast in scenes lamenting the paucity of their involvement in politics, defying khedival and European hegemony, and heralding their support for constitutional rule. Sannu' posed arguments in favor of Isma'il's rival for Egypt's throne—the khedive's uncle, Muhammad 'Abd al-Halim Pasha—as well as Ahmed 'Urabi and his fellow army officers.

Sannu''s journal first appeared in Egypt in 1877, but it was after his forced exile to Paris in June 1878 that its popularity grew immensely around Egypt. The editor's adept usage of colloquial Egyptian Arabic and satirical illustrations in *Abu naddara* facilitated the accessibility and impact of the journal across the literacy/illiteracy divide. In fact, the English writer and journalist Blanchard Jerrold who was traveling in Egypt at the time, likened *Abu naddara* to the British *Punch*—even calling the journal the "Arab Charivari" (Jerrold, 218). Sannu' claimed to have achieved a circulation of 10,000 copies of *Abu naddara* in 1879, but this figure is questionable when compared with estimates for other newspapers (Cole, 123). Nevertheless, Swiss traveler and writer John Ninet remarked at the time on *Abu naddara*, "there was hardly a donkey boy of Cairo, or of any of the provincial towns, who had not heard them read, if he could not read them himself; and in the villages I can testify to their influence" (Ninet, 127–28). Jerrold added, "The satire was so thoroughly to the taste of the public, that the paper was sold in immense quantities. It was in every barrack, in every government office. In every town and village it was read with the liveliest delight" (Jerrold, 218–19).

Sannu' often displayed his strong support for the nationalist movement in *Abu naddara* through iconic representations of politics, gender, and age. In contrast to the depictions ridiculing khedival effeminacy or childishness, he produced images of 'Abd al-Halim Pasha and 'Urabi in social scenes inscribed with culturally recognized characteristics of idealized masculinity such as strength, courage, honor, and benevolence as well as the novel trait of devotion to the Egyptian nation. Moreover, Sannu' frequently employed images and textual labels connoting familial relations, representing the nation as a family unit. As such, the criteria formulating the ideal masculine subject included the conception of fatherhood or patriarchal authority determined by devotion to and patronage of the Egyptian nation. Thus, Sannu''s illustrations in *Abu naddara* imparted a unique negotiation of cultural concepts with Egyptian nationalist ideology, rendering constructs of gender as symbolic of the struggle for political hegemony in Egypt.

Sannu''s exile to Paris in 1878 posed little hindrance to his ability to stay informed about events and developments in Egypt (Gendzier, 73–76). He published bold attacks against Isma'il at the time of Egypt's financial crisis and during the period in which Tawfiq ascended to the khedival throne. In June 1879, the editor issued his first caricature employing the symbolism of the country's crisis of masculinity to ridicule Isma'il (Figure 12.11). The image captures the former khedive exposing his bare buttocks as a figure resembling the German chancellor Bismarck spanks him. Meanwhile, Tawfiq and his European audience watch on as an Egyptian peasant *(fellah)* holds Isma'il's feet. The Arabic caption reads, "The *fellah* says: Punish him with a belt. Give him one on his arse. He's a disobedient boy. He doesn't listen to what our leader says." The scene conveyed Egypt's new power dynamic with Isma'il portrayed as an inferior, infantilized subject put in his place by the dominant parties who orchestrated his abdication.

Tawfiq's image would suffer a similar fate in the August 19 edition of *Abu naddara*, imagining the new khedive as a baby nursing at the breast of his prime minister, Muhammad Sharif Pasha (Figure 12.12). The French caption states that Sharif "offers his master the milk of knowledge." The Arabic caption reads, "Sharif the wet nurse offers his teat to the little Pharaoh. The great nations have brought him toys, which they use to satisfy him upon the arrival of the *firman*. The sons of Egypt witness this and are agonized." It is quite clear that Sannu' intended to point out the political risk to Tawfiq and the nationalist movement due to European interference in Egypt. His representation of the khedive as a baby provides a fitting metaphor to depict Tawfiq's impressionability and powerlessness in the

12.11. "Punish him with a belt." *Abu Naddara*, June 24, 1879.

12.12. "The milk of knowledge." *Abu Naddara*, August 19, 1879.

face of European pressure. While Sannu' does not give the impression that baby Tawfiq had been weaned from the care of Sharif yet, the agony of the nation's sons connotes an ominous future ahead for Egypt.

Sannu' initially held back on the level of vitriol extended toward Isma'il in his depictions of Tawfiq early in the new khedive's reign. However, in late summer 1879 Tawfiq's decision to establish a collaborative cabinet and reinvigorate the powers of the Dual Control signaled to the country's constitutionalists that the political improvements they hoped for would not come to fruition. With khedival authoritarianism reestablished, the editor issued direct statements in opposition to the regime and in support of a rival to the throne, Muhammad 'Abd al-Halim Pasha. The December 1879 issue of *Abu naddara* again referenced gender and kinship metaphors to ridicule the regime (Figure 12.13), but this time

12.13. "Father Halim, Egypt's darling." *Abu Naddara*, December 9, 1879.

12.14. "The Little Pharaoh." *Abu Naddara*, January 15, 1880.

Sannu' elevates the representation of 'Abd al-Halim to the status of patriarchal authority as he stands atop the smoldering ruins of Egypt beating away Isma'il and his 'children,' who are portrayed as omens of calamity in the form of owls (Homerin, 165–84). The editor conveys a clear political message through the gendered dichotomy of the images. 'Abd al-Halim, the heroic, masculine savior contrasts with the depiction of Isma'il and his cronies, who are charged with responsibility for the nation's ill-fated existence. Sannu' communicates a rich symbolism in this caricature through the interplay of visual and textual components. The Arabic caption proclaims, "Father al-Halim, Egypt's darling, drives out the owl [Isma'il] and his children for joyfully ruining the land while gratuitously dividing it up among themselves." *Abu naddara*'s editor skillful representation of 'Abd al-Halim communicates a close relationship between patriarchal authority within the family and the nation. On this point, the image infers that the regime carried the responsibility for the nation's misfortune because it violates the covenant of the nation and family while 'Abd al-Halim deserves the loyalty of Egyptians as a fatherly protector due to his devotion to and defense of the nation. We may surmise the reader/viewer would have been able to relate to the duty of the father as well as his children. Combined, these characteristics formulated the essence of legitimate patriarchal authority.

In the next issue of *Abu naddara*, from January 1880, Sannu' again emphasized the symbolism of patriarchal authority and family bonds by depicting Tawfiq's childishness and his illegitimacy to rule as being based upon his refusal to take the "medicine made of the love of the people and the nation" (Figure 12.14). Here, we find Tawfiq sitting on his chamber pot pointing to his preferred remedy, the large syringe held by Isma'il. The captions demean Tawfiq as "the little Pharaoh" (*Le petite Pharaon*, French) and "the boy" (*al-wad*, Arabic), associating the new khedive's childishness and inability to rule with his rejection of the nation. Here too, it seems Sannu' emphasizes the violation of the nation–family covenant—and thus legitimate authority.

Sannu' repeated this formulation in February 1881, depicting "Father" 'Abd al-Halim ascending to the top of a pyramid with the assistance of the "honorable sons of Egypt" (Figure 12.15). The cartoon invokes thoughts of the modern game of "King of the Hill" or "Tom Tiddler's Ground," in which the object of the activity is to climb to the top of a mound, hill, or pile of stones. In this zero-sum game, occupation of the top spot confers dominant status upon the occupier; winning is determined by one's ability to prevent other competitors from reaching the top. Sannu''s positioning of 'Abd al-Halim near the top of the pyramid signifies his hierarchical

12.15. "Aiding Prince Halim to the top." *Abu Naddara*, February 5, 1881.

The Childish Khedives and Manly Heroes of Egypt, 1879–82   253 standing in relation to Tawfiq—but, more importantly, the support of the nation validates his patriarchal status and hence the label "father."

Sannu's admiration and support of 'Abd al-Halim in *Abu naddara* continued, but political developments in Cairo during the early months of 1881 inspired him to champion new masculine heroes of the nationalist cause: the Egyptian Army and its junior officers. In January 1881, Colonels Ahmed 'Urabi, 'Abdallah al-Hilmi, and 'Ali Fahmi received word that the Turkish minister of war, 'Uthman Rifqi, planned to introduce measures to replace officers of Egyptian *fellah* origin in the army with Circassian (Ottoman-Egyptian) officers. Already agitated by measures introduced the previous year by Rifqi, the colonels perceived these plans as further evidence of discrimination against Arabophone Egyptian officers. In opposition to the conspiracy, the army officers issued a petition to Egypt's Council of Ministers on January 17 calling for the removal of Rifqi. After careful deliberation between Tawfiq and his government, it was decided that 'Urabi, al-Hilmi, and Fahmi were to be arrested and court-martialed. On February 1, the colonels were summoned to Qasr al-Nil barracks to be tried—but Egyptian officers and their regiments intervened to rescue them. Following this, Tawfiq could not resist the rebellious army units and thus reinstated the three colonels, dismissed Rifqi, and appointed Mahmud Sami al-Barudi, a known sympathizer of 'Urabi, as minister of war (Schölch, 135–43).

Over the next year and a half, Sannu' published multiple cartoons advocating the nationalist cause and praising military involvement on its behalf (Gendzier, 80). In May 1881, he issued a vivid denunciation of French and British involvement in Egypt with Egyptian soldiers playing the idealized role as the nation's saviors (Figure 12.16). The caricature depicts the French consul, M. de Bligniéres, blessing the wedding of John

12.16. "Bligniéres blessing the wedding of Mr. Bull to Miss Riazina."
Abu Naddara, May 1881.

Bull to Egyptian prime minister Riyad Pasha, "Miss Riazina," whose dowry was the key to the Nile Valley. However, Egyptian soldiers interrupt the proceedings to rescue Egypt from this fate, seemingly enacting a masculine prerogative to protect and defend the nation. In the background, an Egyptian soldier kicks a childish Tawfiq, shown as too preoccupied with a toy to notice what is going on. The textual commentary further ridicules Tawfiq by labeling him as the "child Khedive" (French) and the "dimwitted boy" (al-wad al-'ahbal, Arabic). It should be noted that from this point forward Sannu' used these terms consistently to reference the khedive, demonstrating Abu naddara's continued reliance upon gendered representations to delineate notions of superiority and inferiority.

The military demonstrations of September 9, 1881 allied the nationalist movement and the military in an unprecedented fashion against Riyad Pasha. On that day, Colonel Ahmed 'Urabi and other junior officers led their largely fellah-origin regiments to the square in front of 'Abdin Palace to confront the khedive. There 'Urabi demanded from Tawfiq the dismissal of Riyad Pasha's cabinet, reconvening of the Chamber of Delegates, and restoration of the army to 18,000 men (Reid, 226). Tawfiq had little choice but to acquiesce given the show of force by the army and the attendance of many Cairenes, who surrounded the square in support of 'Urabi. In the aftermath, the khedive responded by dismissing Riyad Pasha and calling for Muhammad Sharif to form a cabinet once again.

Thereafter, public interest in 'Urabi soared, much to the credit and delight of the nationalist press that promoted him as a national hero. Sannu' seized the moment to represent 'Urabi as an ideal masculine subject in a November 1881 caricature depicting him as guarding the door to Egypt, now visualized as a paradise in contrast to its image of ruin two years earlier (Figure 12.17). The French caption reads, "'Urabi says to John Bull, 'As long as I guard the door of the paradise of the Nile, you will not step foot in it. Only a prince chosen by God can enter. Egypt is for the Egyptians.' John Bull is frightened while the powers applaud 'Urabi's dissent." Once again, Sannu' repeats gendered characteristics to distinguish 'Urabi as a dominant masculine subject. These include courage, strength, dignity, and devotion to the nation. Equally striking, the cartoonist portrays John Bull taken aback by 'Urabi's show of strength—thus, for the first time in Abu naddara, conveying the British as the inferior subject.

12.17. "The Door of Paradise." *Abu Naddara*, November 1881.

12.18. "Egypt for the Egyptians." *Abu Naddara*, February 17, 1882.

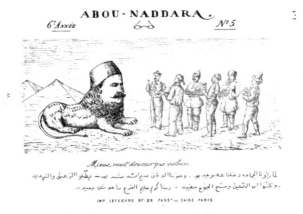

12.19. "Better tenderness than violence." *Abu Naddara*, March 4, 1882.

'Urabi's ascendancy continued following the subsequent dismissal of Muhammad Sharif as Egypt's prime minister and the appointment of Mahmud Sami al-Barudi and his cabinet in February 1882, including the colonel as the new minister of war. These political developments inspired Sannu' to publish caricatures in consecutive issues of *Abu naddara* further embodying 'Urabi as the nationalists' masculine hero. The February 1882 issue depicts 'Urabi in the foreground standing at attention while holding his sword in one hand and in the other hand a flag emblazoned with "Egypt for the Egyptians" (Figure 12.18). Behind him, his fellow officers clean up the mess personified by the former prime minister, Muhammad Sharif, and Khedive Tawfiq. Sannu' describes the scene in Arabic, stating, "'Urabi, the leader of the Arabs, says that Egypt is for the Egyptians amid Abdullah sweeping out the dimwitted boy [Tawfiq] and Fahmi using incense to purify the area as Baba Sharif steps out." The next issue of *Abu naddara* shows 'Urabi as a mythical sphinx guarding Egypt while figures representing the Great Powers bring him food and drink, presumably to conciliate Egypt's powerful guardian (see Figure 12.19). It is important to note that these presents contrast strikingly with the toys shown being brought to baby Tawfiq three years earlier.

Conclusion

The optimism of Egypt's nationalists reached new heights in the first half of 1882; however, their hopes were dashed as riots unfolded in Alexandria in June of that year followed by the British bombardment of the city the next month. The revolution ended with Great Britain's invasion of Egypt in September, the defeat of 'Urabi and the Egyptian Army at Tal al-Kabir, and the surrender of Cairo shortly thereafter. These events proved pivotal in modern Egyptian history: as a result, the country's nationalist movement suffered a decade of relative hibernation as the British established their authority over Egypt.

Despite these historical transformations, the representation of Egypt's crisis of masculinity continued to inform the political and popular discourse into the twentieth century. Western arguments associated the British colonial presence with themes involving tutelage, progress, and reform of a 'young' Egypt guided by mature, masculine British officials. Once a new generation of Egyptian nationalists emerged in the 1890s, they contested British colonial-style rule and articulated new visions of Egypt, Egyptians, and 'Egyptian-ness' that linked national transformation and independence to the cultivation of new men, women, children, families, and homes. Moreover, as the British continued to claim their 'Veiled Protectorate,' meant to guide a child-like Egypt, these new nationalists cited the nation's youth and youthfulness as the keys to regenerating Egypt and securing its independence.

Works Cited

Abu naddara zurqa'. Cairo and Paris, 1978–1910.

Ayalon, Ami. *The Press in the Arab Middle East, a History*. Oxford: Oxford University Press, 1995.

British National Archives. Dufferin's Report and Correspondences. Foreign Office Files 78/3454 and 78/3455, 1882–84.

Cole, Juan R.I. *Colonialism and Revolution in the Middle East: Social and Cultural Origins of Egypt's 'Urabi Movement*. Cairo: The American University in Cairo Press, 1999.

Ellegard, Alvar. September. "The Readership of the Periodical Press in Mid-Victorian Britain: II. Directory." *Victorian Periodicals* 13, no. 3 (1971): 3–22.

Fahmy, Ziad. *Ordinary Egyptians: Creating the Modern Nation Through Popular Culture*. Stanford, CA: Stanford University Press, 2011.

Fun. London, 1861–1901.

Gendzier, Irene. *The Practical Visions of Ya'qub Sannu'*. Cambridge, MA: Harvard University Press, 1966.

Heyworth-Dunne, James. *An Introduction to the History of Education in Modern Egypt*. London: Frank Cass, 1968.

Homerin, T. Emil. "Echoes of a Thirsty Owl: Death and Afterlife in Pre-Islamic Arabic Poetry." *Journal of Near Eastern Studies* 44, no. 3 (1985): 165–84.

Hurewitz, J.C. *Diplomacy in the Near and Middle East: A Documentary Record: 1535–1914*, vol. I. New York: D. Van Nostrand Company, Inc., 1956.

Jerrold, Blanchard. *Egypt under Ismail Pacha: Being Some Chapters of Contemporary History*. London: Samuel Tinsley, 1879.

Judy, or the London Serio-Comic Journal. London, 1867–1907.

Kelidar, Abbas. "The Political Press in Egypt, 1882–1914." In *Contemporary Egypt: through Egyptian Eyes*, edited by Charles Tripp. London and New York: Routledge, 1993.

Kemnitz, Thomas Milton. "The Cartoon as a Historical Source." *Journal of Interdisciplinary History* 4, no. 1 (1973): 81–93.

Kubicek, Robert. "British Expansion, Empire and Technological Change." *The Oxford History of the British Empire vol. III, The Nineteenth Century*, edited by Andrew Porter, 247–69. New York: Oxford University Press, 1999.

MacKenzie, John M. *Propaganda and Empire: The Manipulation of British Public Opinion, 1880–1960*. Manchester: Manchester University Press, 1984.

Mansfield, Peter. *The British in Egypt*. New York: Holt, Rinehart, and Winston, 1971.

Marsot, Afaf Lutfi al-Sayyid. *Egypt in the Reign of Muhammad 'Ali*. Cambridge: Cambridge University Press, 1984.

———. *Egypt and Cromer: A Study in Anglo-Egyptian Relations*. Westport, CT: Praeger, 1969.

Ninet, John. "Origins of the National Party." *The Nineteenth Century* 13 (1883): 127–28.

Pollard, Lisa. *Nurturing the Nation: The Family Politics of Modernizing, Colonizing, and Liberating Egypt, 1805–1923*. Berkeley, CA: University of California Press, 2005.

Punch, or the London Charivari. London, 1841–1992.

Reid, Donald M. "The 'Urabi Revolution and the British Conquest, 1879–1882." In *Cambridge History of Egypt vol. II*, edited by M.W. Daily, 217–38. Cambridge: Cambridge University Press, 1998.

Schölch, Alexander. *Egypt for the Egyptians: The Social-Political Crisis in Egypt, 1878–1882*. Reading: Ithaca Press, 1981.

13

MEN AT WORK: THE POLITICS OF PROFESSIONAL PRIDE IN OTTOMAN BEIRUT

Kathryn Kalemkerian

> Where are the poets? Where are the physicians? Where are the ora-
> tors? . . . Where are the philosophers? Where are the engineers?
> Where are the historians? Where are the astronomers? Where are
> the learned scholars?"
>
> —Butrus al-Bustani, 1859.[1]

In the second half of the nineteenth century, a young professional class of men was forming in Beirut, the city that was en route to becoming the provincial capital of the *vilayet* of Ottoman Syria. Their rise was due to multiple factors (Hanssen; Watenpaugh; Zachs), but part of it, which has hitherto been alluded to but not explored in depth, was an evolving discourse on men's work. Locally in Beirut, this discourse stood in response to the perception, addressed above by Butros al-Bustani (1819–1883),[2] that men were no longer partaking in careers that would ensure a modern and progressive society—or, in other words, a perception that society had fallen from a status of *mutamaddin* (civilized) and it was, literally, a man's job to fix it. It also stood in response to the regional rise of Ottoman bureaucratic culture, stemming from the mid-century *Tanzimat* reforms, which created jobs and opened a career in the civil service for many Ottoman men. Fur-ther, the rise of this group was tied to a wider, global imperial phenomenon of honor systems, which ranked imperial male subjects according to the state's predetermined notions of 'achievement.' This global connection was marked in material culture, through the decoration of imperial male sub-jects with orders and medals. By the turn of the century, awarding orders had become popular in imperial cities all over the world. In Beirut, thirty separate announcements of bestowments in 1900 were printed in the local newspaper, *Lisan al-hal*, some of which included up to six or seven bestowed men at one time. Just a few years later, in 1904, announcements in *Lisan al-hal* had dropped to one or two per month, and continued to dwindle until the outbreak of World War I in 1914.

The sudden decline of this nineteenth-century phenomenon was part of a wider questioning of how this professional class, which had risen so quickly in the previous century, was to survive and move forward as the Age of Empire (Hobsbawm)[3] was drawing to a close. By tracing the trajectory of this class through the example of imperial orders, this chapter links the politics of masculinity with class formation. Imperial orders were a specifically gendered object of material history that I show were connected to trans-imperialism and Ottoman history as well as provincial, in this case Beiruti, debates. These overlapping contexts reveal a narrative of the professionalization of men, showing that at least one element of masculine identity—men and work—was already being debated before World War I. Elizabeth Thompson, in her work *Colonial Citizens*, has argued that a "crisis of paternity" unfolded in the 1920s and 1930s—by which point Ottoman Syria was divided into Syria and Lebanon, and governed under French mandates. By focusing on the prewar years, therefore, I argue that debates over a man's profession, as revealed through changes in material culture, pre-empted part of the gender struggles that unfolded after the war. This new professional class of men found themselves at a crossroads during the prewar period, which was part of setting the stage for gendered tensions that came later.

In considering the terms of a 'crisis' of masculinity, this chapter draws on Mary Louise Roberts's work on rethinking the use of the term when examining gender transformation (Roberts).[4] Roberts critiques the reification of the crisis trope, saying that it occludes an analysis of exactly which norms of masculinity were being questioned. To understand gender transformation in a more constructive way, she argues, we need to reject the traditional narrative of a crisis equalling the breakdown and reconstruction of a set of dominant norms, and instead understand how "articulations of masculinity are set within complex historical contexts, and are constantly frustrated and re-imagined" (Roberts, 363). Roberts offers the idea of "gender damage" as an alternative concept, because "damage" does not assume the existence of stability beforehand in the way "crisis" does (Roberts, 362). By drawing out men and work as one specific narrative, it becomes clear that this particular transformation was tied to a distinct history of class formation, which I show did suffer something more aligned with "damage" than "crisis." I show how men's professional life, and thus the class that rose with this professionalization, went through change and instability in the prewar years, when the imperial world was entering uncertain territory and previous representations of the modern, idealized, male citizen were being cast as outdated.

From the turn of the century up until the end of World War I, dramatic historical change took place in the Ottoman Empire; the 1908 Young Turk Revolution brought an end to real sultanic rule and established a new triumvirate leadership; World War I came and went, bringing intensified conscription, a catastrophic famine, and ending with the collapse of the Ottoman Empire; Ottoman Syria was divided in two, establishing the French mandates of Lebanon and Syria. Amid these historical events came wider ideological shifts between Ottomanism, Turkism, and Arabism. Despite much scholarly dedication to these years of change, gendered analysis has received minimal attention. With regard to Ottoman Syria, Thompson was the first to thoroughly conduct a gender analysis of the period. The narrative of the crisis of paternity that she identifies goes as follows: The prewar years (1880–1914) constituted a socially and economic stable and prosperous period in Ottoman Syria due to Ottoman reforms, whereby urban and rural communities benefited.[5] This auspicious situation came crashing down with the outbreak of World War I, which ushered in the crippling period known as the *safarbarlik*—whereby the traumatic effects of war, coupled with a devastating famine, caused an estimated 18 percent of the population of Greater Syria to perish. Such devastation gave rise to "shattered households and the crisis of paternity" (Thompson, 23). Rural and urban women stepped into the workforce as men were sent to war. For rural women, this work included labor on farms and selling goods in the market; in the case of urban women, it involved organizing relief aid, and trading on the black market.[6] A sentiment of 'male guilt' soon became apparent, as men were perceived as unable to protect women; often they did not return from the war, and when they did they were usually destitute or handicapped. Women were becoming heads of households, children were orphaned, and family networks dissolved.[7]

In the postwar decades, mandate Syria and Lebanon continued to struggle economically due to the collapse of the silk industry, the increase in foreign imports, a wide gap between rich and poor, and the swelling of urban cities. Lower-class and upper-class families were impacted differently, but with the same result: women's roles in the workplace shifted within both classes, the 'gender anxiety' intensified, and the rumbling crisis of paternity finally broke to the surface. For poorer communities, these pressures meant that men were often unable to provide for their families. Women lost their prewar jobs in cottage industries and the silk and textile trades, and turned to seek extra family income through seasonal wage work and domestic help. Although more wealthy families had the resources to ride the tide of the postwar economic situation, change was still affected through calls for an increase in women's education and work possibilities. Formal schooling became increasingly popular for daughters of elite and middle-class families, and many went on to find work after receiving an education—becoming teachers, typists, shopkeepers, and hotelkeepers in the 1920s, and doctors and lawyers by the 1930s. Women started to move out of the family home, marry later, and have fewer children. The male patriarchal household was therefore shaken in all classes. Strain had been placed on the social order, and this sharply threatened male authority (Thompson, 30–38). The French played an important role in the crisis too, by challenging the authority of local elites and seeking to assert their own paternalistic control over the civil order.[8]

Thompson's work was influential, and reference to a "crisis of paternity" as well as a "crisis of masculinity" in Lebanon and Syria appears frequently in scholarship (Hanssen, 211 and 268; Tanielian, 62–82; Totah, 137; Watenpaugh, 128). Yet discussion on whether, or how, elements of this crisis were rooted in the Ottoman period has been less attended to. Considering that much of the argument is based on gendered change in the workplace, a better understanding of men's working lives in the prewar period can help further situate the postwar struggles historically. Although the prewar period of 1880–1914 was economically stable, financial security did not necessarily translate into security in terms of one's role in the latter years of the empire or the shifting political landscape. A detailed examination of the role of work in the prewar years shows that there was an important class component to changes in men's roles in the workplace that was new and was itself undergoing waves of instability. These waves brought questions of what idealized, middle-class masculinity was, and thus constitued a change that was specific to the rising professional milieu in Beiruti-Ottoman society.

In the historiography of the modern Middle East, scholarship focusing on women has provided an important, steady discussion on the role of women and work.[9] This body of scholarship often highlights how calls for women to enter the workplace were rhetorical—used in colonial and national contexts to invoke national aspirations as "mothers of the nation," which stood as a vision for a modern future, and to serve as a qualification for independence in the face of the colonial powers (Baron; Booth; Pollard; Tucker).[10] While men's work is often referenced when it comes to the context of economic history (Rafeq),[11] there exists much less discussion on the subject in terms of gender politics, and how such analysis could shed light on the sociopolitical situation of the time. This occlusion occurs partly because men do not symbolize the nation to the same extent as women, who were elevated as "mothers of the nation" in nationalist rhetoric. It is also partly because women had not hitherto been the subject of historical work, and scholars were rightly concerned with drawing women's history into focus. Scholarship has not yet substantially explored the place of masculinity amid the wide-ranging ideologies of Ottomanism, Arabism, and regional nationalism, nor how these ideologies intersect within the history of work and masculinity. Notions of distinctly 'male' work were certainly there; they had political underpinnings, and were part of the way in which gendered norms, and the power attached to them, were established. In the historiography of Ottoman Syria specifically, this omission is a glaring gap in the historical narrative—especially considering that even a cursory glance at sources such as newspapers, periodicals, portraits, and photographs shows that a man's profession was frequently referenced, both textually and visually, and was starkly attached to specific male virtues and attributes. The repetition of virtues and attributes as attached to professionalism evidences the existence of a shared discourse on men and work that circulated and was understood across empires, as well as taking on particular local meanings.

We know from Thompson's study that the situation of women and work in Ottoman Syria changed dramatically during the Great War. In looking at what came before, Reilly points to the existence of a prewar tension regarding gender and work in his article on Damascene women at the turn of the nineteenth century. He says that reforms and economic change during the stable period of 1880–1914, despite bringing prosperity, impacted women's work due to the beginnings of modernization and professionalization—both of which were male-dominated transformations. Previous forms of work in which women partook—such as investing, leasing and selling commercial and agricultural property, production work in the textile industry, cigarette manufacturing, domestic services, and services concerning childbirth and childcare—were not only impacted, mostly negatively, by Ottoman reforms, commercialization, and capitalist transformations but were also devalued in the wake of this professionalization of men. Their skills were perceived as "backward and embarrassing" (Reilly, 104) rather than modern and professional. Women were therefore being marginalized in the workforce in general, in the prewar period.

Reilly highlights the rise of a cultural bourgeoisie of professionalized men as one of the main forces in this shift, saying that it ended up causing "a larger gap of culture and comprehension between women and urban educated men in the late-nineteenth and early twentieth century than before or since" (Reilly, 104). It was only "after a generation or two [that] women from the middle and upper classes gained access to modern education and professions, overcoming this gap between themselves and their menfolk" (Reilly, 104). According to Thompson's thesis, it was exactly this closing of the gap that was part of the paternal crisis. This point can also be taken as evidence that debates over gender and work were being drawn out in the pre-war period. Notions of 'men's work' versus 'women's work' were sharpened, which in turn put more emphasis on how a man could distinguish himself as embodying a particular form of masculinity through his work. Profession, therefore, had become an important part of self-identification as a modern man.

Although Reilly's example pertains to Damascus, the general narrative of the rise in a professionalized class of men can also be found in late-Ottoman Beirut—perhaps even more so considering it was a main urban hub and provincial capital. In the Beiruti press, and in the works of *nahdawi* intellectuals such as Butrus al-Bustani, women and their place in society were frequently discussed. This theme became entangled in *nahdawi* writings about becoming *mutamaddin* (civilized); women were perceived as in need of rescuing from "degeneration" and elevated from their "uncivilized" state by being educated and reformed, but by no means should they challenge the patriarchal order. As al-Bustani said in a lecture in 1849, "the civilized woman" should be useful to society but "a woman's place in comparison to a man's is known and she should not cross the line or circumvent it under any circumstances" (quoted in Zachs and Halevi, 3). Women were not the only ones who measured societies' level of *tamaddun* (civilization), however. Men's career choices were also incorporated into the discourse and pointed to as part of the problem. In a lecture ten years later, quoted at the opening of this chapter, al-Bustani criticizes men for the Arab world losing its state of glory of the fourteenth century because Arab [men] were no longer partaking in "civilizing" work. Clearly, a focus on men's work was seen as a recourse to, and marker of, achieving modernization and civilization.

Much of the reshaping of men's work was tied to the structural upheaval of the Ottoman bureaucratic machine during the mid-nineteenth century reforms, which replaced the old Ottoman *kalemiye* (scribal service) with the *mülkiye* (civil officialdom) (Findley). The *kalemiye* system—made up of scribes who were in charge of writing correspondence, logging finances, and recording land tenure for the government—had formed a "ruling elite" in the eighteenth century (Findley, 6). This elite, as one author states, "were seen as servants of the ruler, not free men who had accepted a contractually limited obligation to serve the state" (Findley, 7). Scribes were not salaried but paid in the form of compensation in the right to collect revenues, and promotion was often based on nepotism and favoritism.[12] They were a small group, numbering around 2,000 men, who mostly served—and had mostly been born—in Istanbul. Besides some translators, they were all Muslim (Findley, 47). There was a system of promotion through the various positions from the entry point of apprentice to the highest point of grand vizier (Findley, 67–68), whereby a man would enter the system as an *effendi* and could rise to the rank of *pasha*. This goal was achieved only by a small handful, however, and the majority of scribes spent years working in a clerkship without managing to enter a higher office (Findley, 69-70).

The *Tanzimat* reforms of the mid-century changed this system vastly, by bringing in new government offices and new forms of recruitment and establishing the beginnings of a type of 'civil service,' which became a new and popular source for men to find employment. Historian Carter Vaughn Findley distinguishes the changes that this system brought. Non-Muslims were integrated to a much larger extent than they were in the *kalemiye* (Findley, 92). Muslim employees were divided into traditional Muslims, referring to those educated in the traditionalist system, and modern Muslims, who were educated in the modernist system (Findley, 93). Officials were no longer appointed on the basis of being the son of an official and a system of promotion based on merit was introduced, replacing nepotistic methods of advancement. The secretarial skills that predominated the old system grew less important, and the positions that opened up included local administrators, diplomats, treasurers, inspectors, statisticians, and magistrates. Specific training was offered in preparation for these careers, and young men could prepare for them by enrolling at the *Mülkiye Mektebi* (Ottoman School of Civil Administration), founded by Abdülmecîd in 1859 and reformed by Abdülhamid II in 1887 (Fortna, 209–13). Rather than seen as being slavish to the sultan, as was the norm in the old system, these men were encouraged to value and take pride in their work as part of a modern Ottoman world. Thus, a whole new process had been developed—the result of which was the rise of civil officialdom and a new idea of professionalism, which led to the formation of an urban, professionalized class of bureaucrats. This new class of men soon began to get a reputation as being respectable and modern. They appeared in Ottoman Turkish political culture, and took on a particular masculine identity of the new, modern, Ottoman man. Contemporary Ottoman Turkish novels, for example, began to feature "handsome young officials" as leading characters (Findley, 12).

This trend was not unique to the Ottoman context, and similar bureaucratic reform was happening in other imperial settings. Nor was professionalization limited to bureaucratic roles. Rather, the Age of Empire had given rise in general to a class of 'white-collar' male workers, who were responsible for making empires tick. The new professionalized class was therefore part of a wider change in imperial history, which linked together ideas of masculinity, work, pride, progress and empire. It was a trend that was also not restricted to imperial centres but fanned out across the provinces. Fruma Zachs has discussed the rise of this group in Ottoman Syria. She identifies the group as comprising two halves: merchants who set up local enterprises, and white-collar professionals such as doctors, lawyers, writers, translators, linguists, journalists, engineers, and teachers (Zachs, 59).

In exploring the entanglement of masculinity within this narrative, Zachs and Sharon Halevi discuss how new gendered identities emerged through this class, and formed two models of masculinity—one of the old generation and one of the new generation (Zachs and Halevi, 79). This distinction is also in line with Findley's identification, mentioned above, of civil servants as being those educated in either traditional or modern schools. The authors, Zachs and Halevi, say that these models were in competition with each other in the second part of the nineteenth century. The need to articulate a model of the modern Arab man, they claim, was due to the unease over Western influence on women, and concern that it would damage Arab society and culture. As a result, anxiety over how to distinguish the modern Arab man and avoid being subordinated to a Western model arose, along with a tension between the old and the new generation regarding how to overcome this. Their argument shows how this tension was mitigated in novels through the use of the pre-Islamic concept of *muru'a*, meaning manly virtue, which was given new significance and positioned as a model for modern Arab masculinity (Zachs and Halevi, 67). Wealth and family status no longer served as a linchpin of masculinity and marriageability for the newer generation. Rather, the new man was formed "by cultivating (his) character and advancing through merit." The authors conclude that a discourse on the "new man" began much earlier than the crisis identified by Thompson, which stemmed from the socio-economic changes of the late nineteenth century and was imbedded in the debates over the role of women and modernization.

By using literary texts as their sources, Zachs and Halevi open up a window onto the intellectual debates over this formation of masculinity. While I argue for a similar point, that masculinity was being debated and worked out in the prewar period, I am concerned more with what exactly this idea of 'merit' entailed and how it molded a gendered dimension of this professionalization of men in terms of attributes and virtues. Zachs and Halevi's work helps to identify a local Syrian debate over masculinity, which was in line with the Nahdawi project of transforming traditional society in a way that was not confined to imitating the West. However, being a specifically middle-class debate, in the prewar years merit and masculinity were also connected to the professionalization of men working for the Ottoman Empire, as seen with the changes to Ottoman bureaucracy from the *kalemiye* to the *mülkiye* and the rise in white-collar work across imperial centers in the Age of Empire in general. The question over the merit of a man was therefore embedded in a local discourse of the Nahda, in terms of what forms of work and what attributes were classed as *mutamaddin*, the Ottoman context of reform and modernization, as well as a nineteenth-century trans-imperial communication whereby empires were shaping modern imperial male subjects by encouraging new professions based on associated virtues and attributes. Thus, discourse over masculinity was not initially connected only to nationalism or colonialism but arose as a topic of trans-imperial dialogue that involved notions of modernization and imparted class formation in the *fin de siècle* imperial world, and simultaneously took on local formations and meanings.

In the Ottoman Empire, changes in material culture paralleled this rise of professional men, and can offer added information on the politics behind what this meant in terms of concepts of modern masculinity. One object that stood at the heart of the rise in professionalism, pride, and merit was imperial orders, bestowed on men by imperial powers. Honor systems and the decoration of men had become a phenomenon of material culture across empires, and exemplified the urge for men to present themselves as hardworking; successful in modern professions; and, essentially, the ideal imperial subject. A serious analysis of these orders also takes male professionalism to an extra level of meaning. Orders brought with them specific adjectives of virtues and attributes connected to merit, and made them distinct markers of masculine pride.

Orders emerged as part of the expansion of imperial systems of honor, which rose and peaked in empires across the world during of the Age of Empire. They were class based and gendered: generally not awarded to the poor, they instead marked either membership of the urban middle stratum, a high position in the military, or membership of the ruling elite. They were overwhelmingly androcentric, being almost exclusively bestowed on men for most of the nineteenth century. Exemptions in which women were bestowed were often in the context of an imperial ruler, such as Britain's Queen Victoria (r. 1837–1901) or Isabella II of Spain (r. 1833–68). Women were often nominally incorporated into honors systems, though it did not mean that in reality they were esteemed for merit in the way that men were. As such, men managed to establish broadly recognized traits of what stood out as a general understanding of 'imperial masculinity.' This masculinity encouraged men to distinguish themselves as exemplifying a model male citizen, and set up a connection between male pride and notable acts of merit. Across empires, the connotations associated with these distinguishing acts included loyalty, bravery, and legitimacy, which in the eighteenth and first half of the twentieth century were mostly for military purposes. By the turn of the nineteenth century, orders across the world started to shift from their military origins toward marking acts of civilian merit. Sometimes they would be awarded for an act of bravery, such as saving someone's life, but most often they were used to mark a man's success within his profession. By wearing an order, a man was therefore recognized in imperial settings across the world—and this connected men visually, forming a type of 'international men's club' of the decorated.

By ranking individual men in terms of their qualities and merit, orders held political power. In the Ottoman context, a system of honoring men who worked for the Ottoman state did previously exist. In the old Ottoman scribal service, for example, advancement to the position of *hacegân* (bureau chief) was considered an outstanding achievement, and was honored with a special robe *(hil'at)*. However, orders shifted the politics of honoring through their trans-imperial dimension. They put masculine traits in competition with one another globally, as imperial powers sought to lay claim to their men as being the most worthy, valued, and modern subjects. This competition intensified at the turn of the nineteenth century, when empires were vying for power and looking to construct a hegemonic masculinity which would be recognized globally and position themselves at the top. The British and French, for example, sought out Ottoman orders but were reluctant to reciprocate and award their own orders to Ottomans.

Despite their global connection, orders had multilayered meanings and the more specific definition of what determined 'achievement' was decided by the imperial state. In the nineteenth-century Ottoman case, they became incorporated into the evolving professional class in a similar way to wider changes in clothing. The rise of this class could therefore be *seen* through changes in fashion that began in the mid-nineteenth century, when white-collar professionals began to merge Western and local fashions. This change was the beginning of a new 'look' that ended up representing their class and a new idea of the modern professional man, which started to form in the mid-century during the time of reform. Initially, it consisted of the traditional *sirwal* (Ottoman pantaloons), a *qumbaz* (men's gown, which was held together with a sash belt at the waist and left open at the front), and a *lastiq* (cashmere waistcoat), topped off with the maroon Ottoman fez. If an order had been issued, it was either seen hanging from the neck or pinned to the chest. By the end of the century, a distinct civil servants' uniform had branched off of the above and comprised a tailcoat with a banded collar, sometimes with heavy embroidery down the front, to which imperial orders were usually pinned; tighter tailor-made trousers; sometimes a bow tie; and, again, almost always the fez. Facial hair was also a prominent feature, and a common example was either a trimmed beard or a clipped mustache. The change in clothing has a wider Ottoman context dating to the *Tanzimat* reform period, the politics of which has been discussed as such (Quataert, 403–25; Zachs, 39–85; Jana). Indeed, clothing in general—and particularly headgear—had a political place in the history of the Ottoman Empire and was used as a means of "disciplining behaviour" (Quataert, 406), with legislation changing from the eighteenth century in correspondence with political change. Most relevant to this discussion were the 1829 new clothing laws introduced by Sultan Mahmoud II (r. 1808–1839) which, as Donald Quataert has argued, was part of a broader history of elite formation, centralization, and state building.

Headgear was a main feature in these changes. The turban along with the wide range of other previous existing examples—which varied from community to community and occupation to occupation, and which represented rank in the Ottoman court—was replaced with the overarching Ottoman fez (Quataert, 403 and 414). The law changing headgear, then, was designed not only to homogenize Ottoman subjects as one community but to also eliminate signs of occupational difference between men. Yet it did end up distinguishing one man from another, as the introduction of the fez became a visual facilitator to identify belonging to the new class that was coming into formation. Those who wore the fez included non-Muslim merchants, Ottoman ministers and officials, and those in training for a professional life—such as students of the new military, civil administration, and medical schools. However, Ottoman workers—such as artisans, servicemen, and tradesmen—rejected wearing it solo, and wrapped it with material to form a turban. Quataert suggests that keeping a partial turban was partly to distinguish themselves as Muslim as well as a rejection of Mahmud II's reforms, which tried to dismantle the guild system to which they belonged (Quataert, 414). Considering that these workers included Muslims and non-Muslims alike,[13] I view their decision to be mostly concerned with marking themselves as workers. Headgear and clothing had for so long been a part of distinguishing one's occupation, implying that there must have been an element of pride that they took in being recognized as a tradesman. Although the turban with the fez represented a lower social class, it does not mean to say that a sense of pride in their trade was not felt. As Quataert says, Ottoman workers took "their identity from their workplace [and] rejected the state's alternative" (Quataert, 420). Indeed, they may have not wanted to be marked as working for the wider machine of Ottoman bureaucracy, and instead valued being marked as local workers who were providing a service and working within networks of their own local area.

The case of the fez is an example of how the imperial state used material culture to promote *Osmanlılık* ideology—or, in other words, a means to override ethnic and religious differences and to bond subjects through a shared loyalty to the empire. The terms of this loyalty were not necessarily constant, however; loyalty vacillated between that to the sultan and that toward a shared Ottoman Islamic heritage. Nevertheless, both the fez and orders ended up being tied to markers of this new class of men, which did indeed transcend religious and ethnic identities. Although most career bureaucrats were Istanbulites, the professional 'look' described above and the distribution of orders were not limited to the imperial capital, but spread to other provincial cities. Many officials were stationed in Ottoman Syria, and so interacted with, had relations with, and often intermarried with the local population—particularly the notables (Hanssen, 62)—and had a visible impact in Beiruti life. It is therefore true, as historian Jens Hanssen states with regard to late-Ottoman Beirut, that the bureaucratic attire was part and parcel of the formation of a visible social hierarchy and that decorated civil servants reflected the popularity of the elaborate Ottoman—as well as the wider trans-imperial—ranking system (Hanssen, 63). Bureaucrats took pride in distinguishing themselves in Beirut by showing off their ranking and wearing their orders at official events, to denote their "status, integrity, and achievement" (Hanssen, 63).

More than any element of attire, however, orders worked as a symbol to connect profession, modernity, status, and national or imperial identity with perceived masculine attributes. Many different orders were incorporated into the Ottoman honors system throughout the nineteenth century.[14] The two most prestigious were the *Mecîdî* (*Majidiya* in Arabic), and the *Osmânî* ('*Usmaniya* in Arabic). The *Mecîdî* was established by Sultan Abdülmecîd I (r. 1839–61). It was designed with his *tughra* (sultanic stamp) in the centre; surrounded by dark-red enamel; and inscribed with the words *Hamiyyet* (Devotion), *Gayret* (Effort), and *Sadâkat* (Loyalty). The design therefore emphasizes the centrality of loyalty and devotion to both sultan and empire, for which the order was awarded, as well as the three main virtues that were being honored. The *Osmânî* was issued by Sultan Abdülaziz I (r. 1861–76) to replace the *Mecîdî* as the highest-ranking Ottoman decoration, though the latter retained its popularity and prestige. The new order did, however, mark a shift from the *Mecîdî*'s emphasis on loyalty to the sultan to constructing a sense of Ottoman legitimacy combined with an Islamic identity.

Despite the introduction of the *Osmânî* in the late nineteenth and early twentieth century, the *Mecîdî*, which held five rankings, was the most frequently bestowed order in the Arab provinces. Like most orders of the nineteenth-century imperial world, it took the shape of an eight-pointed star—but what made orders distinct was their inscriptions, which was where the honored virtues were stated. The acts which corresponded to the *Mecîdî*'s engraved virtues of *Hamiyyet*, *Gayret*, and *Sadâkat* changed over time, reflecting shifts in what the state felt necessary to highlight and award. Such shifts of course had sociopolitical underpinnings, which impacted the way in which the state tried to shape ideals of masculine virtue. For example, when Abdülmecîd initially established the order it was to award military men—and therefore initially espoused a notion of heroic, military masculinity, which was strategic and of political importance at the time since the empire was fighting the Crimean War (1853–56). Military acts signified loyalty, effort, and patriotism, and wearing the order worked as a visual means of marking such success. This connotation also corresponded to the military nature of bestowments within empires in general in the first half of the nineteenth century. However, a shift was emerging, and the last awards to be issued under Abdülmecîd were not of a military nature. The Medal of Merit and the Medal for Talent, for example, supported the idea of civilian effort *(gayret)* now in the realms of "talent, science and skill" (Eldem, 239). By the end of the century, the *Mecîdî* order—the most prestigious military award—was issued for non-military purposes, and marked success in an occupation.

It was not just orders for men that reflected the tie between orders, honor, work, merit, and gender. Amid this shift to awarding civilians to mark merit, women were incorporated into the honors system for the first time. In 1878 the order of Şefkat, meaning 'compassion' or 'tenderness,' was created. In line with the trend mentioned above, it was also focused on rewarding a form of work—and thus played a role in determining what type of work elite women should be doing. It consigned elite women's work to the realm of humanitarian and charitable work, which would uphold certain virtues of compassion and tenderness, and the order was inscribed with the words "*Hamiyyet*" (Devotion), "İnsâniyyet" (Humanity), and *Muavenet* (Assistance) (Eldem, 258). In reality, however, this order was seldom issued to anyone outside of the palace. The majority of bestowals were for women living in the palace, such as imperial princesses and servants of the harem, or to foreign royal and aristocratic female visitors as a mark of having met the sultan. In rare instances of bestowments of orders on women outside of the palace, they were used to mark a woman as the wife or daughter of a prominent man.[15] As with other examples in imperial contexts, wearing a

Şefkat symbolized that the woman was connected either to the sultan or to another important male figure.[16] As with other calls for women's rights, the Şefkat paid mere lip service to the elevation of elite women and work. The indication of a rising class is therefore not apparent with women's orders as, unlike men's bestowments, they were reserved purely for the elite. What they did do, however, was further shape the system of honors into a gendered hierarchy of men and women and how they, albeit rhetorically in the case of women, should choose certain occupations to fulfill these virtues and attributes for the sake of the empire.

The shift from military bravery to civilian merit and professional success elevated certain careers to form a hierarchy of worthiness. The new Ottoman bureaucrats were at the top of this hierarchy, as they served the empire directly. Indeed, most images of these bureaucrats show the *Mecîdî* orders pinned to their uniforms. Orders were also widely issued to non-bureaucrats, who equally wore them proudly as a means of showing off their success and worth. Thus, although the rise of the professionalized man was sparked by Ottoman bureaucratic reform, this new class was not limited to those working within the Ottoman state. Professions that were awarded outside of the civil service were also marked as those that demonstrated the effort *(gayret)* that was considered a service to the empire, and thus were also placed high up in the hierarchy. These were mostly intellectuals, architects, engineers, and educators, though those awarded were often employed for specific state projects. Entrepreneurship and trading were also rewarded, and it was not unusual for merchants to receive the third rank of the *Mecîdî* order. In my research, I have not come across examples of orders being handed out to holders of blue-collar jobs. This does not mean that a sense of pride did not also exist among tradesmen and servicemen, as mentioned earlier through the example of headgear and the rejection of the fez. What it does emphasize is that there had developed a class-based manipulation of material culture with regard to pride and work, and that the state was trying to influence how this was to take shape.

One of the most striking aspects of the history of orders was that, like the fez, they were worn by a cross section of Ottomans in terms of ethnicity and religion, with photographic evidence existing of bestowed Armenians, Jews, Greeks, Christians, and Muslims. Their trans-communal appeal therefore wove together segments of Beiruti society that were often left unconnected in the history of Ottoman Syria and Lebanon, which is so often treated according to sectarian differences. Ideas of male pride were circulated, shared, and adhered to among this class of men, and orders were a means of visually proving the embodiment of it. At the same time, they also connected these minorities to a wider global phenomenon and their 'success' was often recognized outside of the empire. One example of a man whose story speaks to the prominence of career versus sectarian or ethnic origin in terms of identity and social status is that of Manouk Manoukian, also known as Beshara Mehendis. Born to Armenian parents in 1841, his Armenian name was Arabized. He inherited the nickname Beshara from his father, Yehia Manoukian, who was given the Arab name Elias Beshara by locals. His surname, however, came from his fame as a civil engineer, with 'Mehendis' meaning engineer in Arabic. In his youth, he accepted all kinds of employment—one of which was working on the Beirut–Damascus highway project in 1860. The Ottoman governor, Fuad Pasha, was impressed with his work and offered him a higher post in the Ottoman administration. He was assigned to work on the Trebizond–Erzurum road, and in 1870 he returned to Beirut where he continued to work as an engineer for the Ottoman government. There, he was involved in many projects, including building bridges and the Ottoman Bank, and was part of the project to modify the famous *grand serai* (governmental palace). He worked as an inspector of water pipes, and in 1890 took part in an archaeological dig in Saida that uncovered ancient burials and other artifacts. He received a multitude of awards for all this work, including five from the Ottomans, two from France, one from Germany, one from Italy, one from Austria, and one from Brazil. He was even invited to move to and work in Brazil by Emperor Don Pedro II (r. 1831–89), who offered him a high position in his imperial administration (Varjabedian, 183–91). Beshara Mehendis therefore marked the epitome of what a model, male, imperial subject should be. He engaged in work that offered him a high status and his achievements were recognized on a trans-imperial scale. Thus, rather than telling an especially 'Armenian' narrative, his biography speaks to how identity and status through being a known and successful member of the professionalized class transcended the prevalence of other ethnic or religious identities.

Beshara Mehendis received most of his awards when bestowment was at its peak in imperial contexts of the early twentieth century. He was therefore not an exception but part of a wider trend. Looking at further examples of the bestowed, the local press is a useful source and offers a sense of how widespread bestowment had become by the turn of the century, as well as information on who was awarded, for what purpose, what attributes it was meant to show, and how the public responded to bestowment. We know, for example, that at the turn of the century locals would go to the house of a newly decorated man to celebrate and read poetry ("Akhbar mahaliya," *Lisan al-hal*, January 19, 1900). In essence, the press offers an "on the ground" reading of how these orders were perceived and received. The local newspaper, *Lisan al-hal*, is the most useful example for this purpose.

From the turn of the century, its "Akhbar mahaliya" (local news) section started to become consistently full of announcements regarding which local men had been bestowed. The year 1900 offers an appropriate case study, as it saw the peak of the phenomenon. In January alone, there are twelve announcements of men being bestowed ("Akhbar mahaliya," *Lisan al-Hal*, January 4, 11, 17, 23, 24, 25, 26, 29 [two announcements], and 31 [three announcements], 1900). A typical example would often state who was bestowed, the rank of the order, and what it was awarded for. More detailed announcements would often list the attributes that went along with the award. A note of congratulations and good wishes followed all announcements. On January 11, 1900, for example, the paper announced that Taher Zadeh Rifaatlou Muhammad Sadwq Beyk, a merchant from Jaffa, was granted the "Third Order"[17] because he demonstrated *wajih* (elegance) and was *amthal* (an ideal model). The following week, on January 17, Muhammad Ezzat Effendi also received the "Third Order" for his work as a manager of the telegraph center at the court. He was rewarded for his *sidq* (sincerity) and *mazid* (activeness). On January 25, Mansour Beyk was given the *Osmânî* order for his work for the Ministry of Finance, to mark his *nazih* (unblemished record), *sidq*, and general dedication to the state. On January 31, Habib Beyk Assad was given the *Osmânî* order for his *shafqa wa insaniya* (sympathy and humanity), *sidq*, and true dedication and patriotism. Most orders bestowed were Ottoman, but there was also the frequent appearance of non-Ottoman bestowments—serving, again, as a reminder of the global nature of this phenomenon. On January 25, 1900, for example, Nakhla Beyk Outran was given the "*wisam* of knowledge" by the Iranian government, and on January 31, 1900, Girgis Effendi Kibba received the *medalliat al-sharaf* (medal of honor, possibly meaning the French Legion d'honnour) from the French for his work as the first translator of the French consul, and to mark his *istiqama* (truthfulness in service). The example of Ottoman subjects being awarded non-Ottoman awards, and the public announcement of their bestowments, highlights the inter-imperial nature of orders, and the wider promotion of idealized masculine virtues.

In a similar vein, the local-news section's announcements of administrative appointments and obituaries almost always contain the corresponding attributes of the man, regarding why he would be—or had been, in the case of obituaries—good at his job. On January 6, 1900, for example, the obituary of Effendi Qadan Shihab, states that he was *lami'* (intelligent), *tayib al-nasab* (of good stock), *'imad al-wajaha* (elegant), and spent "all of his life until the last breath serving the homeland" as a deputy board director of an unmentioned Ottoman institution. He was known for his love of peace, his clear conscience, and his good intentions. He must have been decorated, as it states that he received titles and blessings for his honesty and service to the Ottoman state. Five days later, an announcement appears detailing his replacement by Almeer Qablan Abi Alma', an effendi, though no further details are given. It can be assumed that he had yet to prove himself, as the entry also includes details of other appointments—this time for Sheikh Rashid al-Khazem to take care of the Metn district, who is described as *nazih* (having clean hands), and Selim Amoun who was to replace al-Khazem's original post, characterized as being *nashit* (active).

The same attributes are therefore repeated over again. Of great importance was honesty: a man had to be sincere, to show true dedication to his job and the state. He had to be strong mentally and physically, by demonstrating intelligence and activeness. Mannerisms were also important, as elegance in conduct was a cause for reward. All of the above molded a man's reputation, which was to be judged accordingly. Although family background was taken into account in terms of reputation, considering *tayib al-nasab* (of good stock) was cause for praise, a man could achieve a reputation for himself through *nazih*, attaining an unblemished record. Awards for such qualities can be read as guidelines for how to mold oneself in terms of both appearance and behavior as a man within this emerging professional class. Getting a professional job was not the only way to assure this status; one had to follow through by demonstrating the possession of these traits.

The issuing of these material symbols of pride through profession, which were so valued in the nineteenth century, came to a grinding halt after the first decade of the twentieth century. The uniform of Ottoman officials described earlier fell out of use and imperial orders no longer made an appearance on portraits and photographs, although they were still being awarded—albeit to a much lesser extent. Wider changes in fashion were the topic of much political satire in the late-Ottoman press. The adoption of European styles became a visual representation of the imitation of Western 'progress,' and had given rise to a heated debate within Ottoman society that targeted both men and women. European styles were ridiculed as farcical, shameful, anti-Islamic, or disrespectful to traditional Ottoman culture, and a marker of European dominance; to the contrary, for the expanding elite and professionalized class they were symbolic markers of success. Palmira Brummett discusses the use of fashion in detail in the Istanbul Ottoman press through political cartoons. She shows how fashion was used to comment on sexual honor through women's clothes, to connote the honor of the nation, or to demonstrate public morality. Ottoman *alafranga* (Europeanized) women connoted weakness, not only in the sense of the empire succumbing to the West but also as women subverting male authority in the household (Brummett, 232 and 233) and thus challenging masculine honor.

After the deposal of Sultan Abdülhamid II and the Young Turk Revolution in 1908, men's fashion came under fire as well—especially the bureaucratic attire that merely years before had been such a source of pride. Istanbul-based newspapers like *Kalem* and *Davul* ridiculed civil servants as "outcasts" and their uniforms as outdated because they were signs of the old authority. The civil servant had become, symbolically, obsolete. He was cast into a museum, displayed among the dinosaurs, and referred to as "fossils" in one image from *Kalem*, being viewed by the new generation, who are wearing simple tailored suits and fez hats, with no orders to be seen (Brummett, 121). In another image in *Kalem*, a "uniform sale" is on; embroidered jackets are displayed on mannequins, medals and orders are displayed in a case, and the Ottoman emblem hangs above them in the shop window with a "liquidation" sign next to it (Brummett, 256). This weakening in the perception of Ottoman officials paralleled the decrease in employment of civil servants after the Young Turk Revolution. For example, Findley shows that the number of officials working in the foreign ministry peaked in 1890 and then started dropping steadily until 1915 (Findley, 96).

The dramatic decline in the issuing of orders was not only connected to political change at the Ottoman state level but was also embedded in a wider sea change in global politics. It was symbolic of how the Age of Empire was shifting and coming to an end even before World War I. The 'imperial masculinity' of the late nineteenth century, which as I have shown was entwined with competition between empires, was crumbling and had to be configured into something new. In a reflection of these times, bestowment had peaked to such a degree that orders had reached a point of being over-issued, decreasing their value and disrupting the meaning of merit. As a result, orders transformed from a symbol of pride to one of ridicule in Ottoman and other imperial presses in the early twentieth century. In the Ottoman context, this change was taking place in the auspicious socioeconomic situation of the prewar period that Thompson describes. While there may have been stability economically, there was not necessarily stability in terms of social identities.

As the imperial world was weakening, imperial masculinity was reconfiguring into something more localized. In the Ottoman Empire, tensions were rising, resulting in the 1908 Young Turk Revolution and the establishment of a Committee of Union and Progress (CUP)-led government. The new state—and, in particular, the new imperial war minister, Enver Pasha—tried to steer the notion of an ideal masculine identity into the direction of military heroism (Akmeşe). As the CUP sought to cultivate a new male Ottoman subject based on militarism, the professional values of the previous years were overtaken by martial values. In other words, men's work was to be for the good of the nation; and with rising global tensions on the eve of World War I, this work had to be in line with a sense of duty toward the nation in preparation for war. The issuing of orders and medals to men changed in alignment according to this shift; they had come full circle, returning to their militarized beginnings and awarded for military merit. Attributes awarded therefore also returned to those associated with military bravery. The introduction of new conscription laws in 1908 made it mandatory for all male subjects between twenty and forty-five to serve in the military, forcing men out of their jobs to do so. The fact that the law was never properly implemented for non-Muslim men (Karakışla, 68–71) enabled some of them to continue with their professional lives, opening up a discrepancy between which subjects were and were not able to pursue a professionalized career, with the potential even to hold on to their jobs during the war period. This discrepancy thus broke up what had been the rise of a reasonably mixed ethnic and religious class of professionalized Ottoman men.

Without the previous signs and symbols of success that orders had offered, and with these larger political reconfigurations, members of the professionalized class had to seek other methods to prove themselves as outstanding men. In the provinces the new military approach to Ottoman-ism was communicated from the central government through the press, but did not necessarily catch on as broadly as the governing CUP had hoped. Rather than being replaced by one trend, several began to emerge. In Beirut, for example, one growing discussion over professionalism unfolded at the Syrian Protestant College, whereby doing "work" that was for the global good of humanity was classed as the most "heroic" (Kalbian, "Opportuni-ties"; Kalbian, "Heroism"). Simultaneously, the prewar years saw a rise in a new class marked by "dandyism," which in itself embodied a whole new set of symbolic meanings of success—embroiled in a new look that included the Western bowler hat, monocle, and cigarette (de Bustros, 13–19).

The politics of profession had therefore started to change, as it moved away from the context of trans-imperialism and nineteenth-century under-standing of *Osmanlık* ideology. Many members of the class of professional middle-class men were left high and dry as the prestige of bureaucratic posts shifted to one of ridicule, and the state was pushing a different mea-sure of modern masculinity that was based on militarism. Further, with conscription and the war career paths were interrupted, after which the mandate period brought in a new system to which these men had to inte-grate, re-establish themselves, and seek recognition. Some men, such as

Beshara Mehendis, were able to do this; the French recognized his pre-war career and achievements, and gave him a post as the head engineer in Lebanon, which he held until he retired. In the 1920s, they even awarded him the French Foreign Legion Cross. Indeed, in postwar colonial contexts governing powers tried to reignite the phenomenon of bestowments as a means of securing loyalty, though it never reached the level of popularity it had enjoyed at the turn of the century. Not many men were as lucky as Beshara, however, and most struggled to regain their prewar success.

Through an analysis of material history, this chapter has traced the evolution of one particular aspect of masculine identity: that of profession-alization. A crisis of masculinity often assumes that a consistent masculine identity or performativity was shattered or thrown into question. How-ever, by examining something as specific as work, which is tied so closely with class, the picture that emerges in the prewar years is not one of a consistent masculine identity that was called into question or ruptured. Rather, masculine identities formulated through profession were already evolving and shifting according to wider political currents. From the mid-nineteenth to early twentieth century, this formulation was based partly on a trans-imperial idea of masculinity and merit, but was simultaneously renegotiated according to both Ottoman and provincial politics and reali-ties. The struggle that ensued in the postwar period regarding men and work was therefore not only due to women stepping into the workplace. Mary Louise Roberts's use of the term "damage" is apt for this example. In the *Oxford English Dictionary*, "damage" is defined as when the value or usefulness of something is impaired. This chapter has shown that the value and usefulness of men's work was being questioned and forced to realign itself, even before the war, with the political currents of the time—globally, regionally and locally.

Notes

1   Al-Bustani, quoted in Fruma Zachs and Sharon Halevi 2015. *Gender-ing Culture in Greater Syria: Intellectuals and Ideology in the Late Ottoman Period*, 3. London: I.auris.

2   Butros al-Bustani was a Beiruti *nahdawi* (a member of the Nahda, a cul-tural movement, also referred to as the 'Arab Renaissance') intellectual. Much of his work concentrated on how to achieve *tamaddun* (civilization) in Syrian society.

3   Eric Hobsbawm identifies the period 1875–1914 as the Age of Empire, and as being the period that shaped modern society.

4   The author would like to thank Christine Lindner for drawing her atten-tion to Roberts's work.

5   Factors that propelled this situation included the booming of the silk industry; an increase in local markets; general favorable conditions in the world economy; and European investment in the development of transportation infrastructure, which increased merchant activity.

6   Thompson also points out that in the postwar period the roles of men's wartime experience versus women's were definite by male martyrs versus weak and impoverished women.

7   The collapse of family networks and increase in women-led households was especially impacted by the arrival of dislocated Armenian refugees, who were mostly women and children.

8   Note that this is not the only explanation given by Thompson. Another equally central part of her argument is that the establishment of the French mandate threatened the power of the local elites. See Thompson, 15–17.

9   This scholarship is usually concerned with highlighting the types of work that women were undertaking, which were often less visible jobs. See Abisaab; Joubin, 19–45; Semerdjian, 60–85; and Reilly, 75–106. The last-named is the most relevant to the present chapter. James Reilly lists illegal work such as prostitution, as well as dealings with property and *waqf*s; work that took place in the home, such as weaving and spinning; household labor in general, as well as move visible but still marginalized work such as cutting and packing in the Régie tobacco factory; and agricultural labor.

10 As the cited works demonstrate, scholarship on women and work is primarily based on the case of Egypt—thus, although headway has been made in historiography focused on women glaring gaps still remain, with a much smaller body of work being on the Mashriq and North Africa, and less still on the Gulf.

11 Abdul-Karim Rafeq discusses the functioning of guilds *(tawa'if)* their economic function, their social function in relation to sectarianism, and their response to industrialized Europe and the making of the middle class.

12 Scribes were often from the 'scribal household,' being the son or relative of a scribe, or having a patronage relationship with one. See Findley, chapter 2.

13 See figures 3 and 6 in Quataert "Clothing Laws" for Armenian workers wearing the wrapped fez.

14 Many orders were established under the rule of Abdülhamid II, including those of a military nature such as the Russian War Medal, the Lifesaving Medal, the Medal for Talent, and the Medal for Merit. For a full history of Ottoman orders, see Eldem.

15 A transparent example of this linkage to a male act is the bestowal of a second and third Şefkat to the wife of Grand Vizier Kâmil Pasha, Lâyıka Hanim, which were both given to her to honor her husband's qualities. See Eldem, 263–64.

16 The example of the Şefkat is also a reminder of how the honors system was class based, with poorer women having no access to it.

17 The entry does not indicate which order this was. The absence of the name, however, suggests that it was the *Mecîdî*, which was the most common.

Works Cited

Abisaab, Malek. *Militant Women of a Fragile Nation*. Syracuse, NY: Syracuse University Press, 2010.

"Akhbar mahaliya." *Lisan al-hal*, January 4, 11, 17, 19 23, 24, 25, 26, 29, and 31, 1900.

Akmeşe, Handan Nezir. *The Birth of Modern Turkey: The Ottoman Military and the March to World War*. London: I.B.Tauris, 2005.

Baron, Beth. *Egypt as a Woman: Nationalism, Gender and Politics*. Berkeley, CA: University of California Press, 2005.

Booth, Marilyn. *May Her Likes Be Multiplied: Biography and Gender Politics in Egypt*. Berkeley, CA and Los Angeles: University of California Press, 2001.

Brummett, Palmira. *Image and Imperialism in the Ottoman Revolutionary Press, 1908–1911*. Albany, NY: State University of New York Press, 2000.

al-Bustani, Butrus. "Khutba fi adab al-'arab." In Butrus al-Bustani. *al-Jam'iya al-suriya li-l-'ulum wa-l-funun 1847–1852*, 177. Beirut: Dar al-Hamra, 1990.

de Bustros, Nicolas. *Je me Souviens*. Beirut: Offset Doniguian, 1983.

Eldem, Edhem. *Pride and Privilege: A History of Ottoman Orders, Medals and Decorations*. Istanbul: Ottoman Bank Archives and Research Centre, 2005.

Findley, Carter Vaughn. *Ottoman Civil Officialdom: A Social History*. Princeton, NJ: Princeton University Press, 2014.

Fortna, Benjamin C. *Imperial Classroom: Islam, the State, and Education in the Late Ottoman Empire*. Oxford: Oxford University Press, 2002.

Hanssen, Jens. *Fin de Siècle Beirut: The Making of an Ottoman Provincial Capital*. Oxford: Oxford University Press, 2005.

Hobsbawm, Eric. *The Age of Empire, 1875–1914*. London: Abacus, 1994.

Jana, Katja. "Changing Heads and Hats: Nationalism and Modern Masculinities in the Ottoman Empire and the Republic of Turkey." In *Masculinities and the Nation in the Modern World: Between Hegemony and Marginalization*, edited by Pablo Dominguez Andersen et al., 217–42. New York: Palgrave Macmillan, 2015.

Joubin, Rebecca. "Creating a Modern Professional Housewife: Scientifically Based Advice Extended to Middle and Upper-Class Egyptian Women, 1920s–1930s." *Arab Studies Journal* 4, no. 2 (1996): 19–45.

Kalbian, Vahan. "Heroism in Medicine," speech, published in "The Commencement Exercises." *Al-Kulliyeh*, vol. V (June 1914): 256.

———. "Opportunities for Self Help in the S.P.C." *Al-Kulliyeh*, vol. IV, no. 2 (December 1912).

Karakışla, Yakuza Selim. *Women, War and Work in the Ottoman Empire: Society for the Employment of Ottoman Muslim Women (1916–1923)*. Istanbul: Libra Kitap, 2015.

Pollard, Lisa. *Nurturing the Nation: The Family Politics of Modernizing, Colonizing and Liberating Egypt (1805–1923)*. Berkley, CA and Los Angeles: University of California Press, 2005.

Quataert, Donald. "Clothing Laws, State, and Society in the Ottoman Empire, 1720–1829." *International Journal of Middle East Studies* 29 (1997): 403–25.

Rafeq, Abdul-Karim. "Craft Organization, Work Ethics, and the Strains of Change in Ottoman Syria." *Journal of the American Oriental Society*, vol. 111, no. 3 (1991): 495–511.

Reilly, James. "Women in the Economic Life of Late-Ottoman Damascus." *Arabica* 42, no. 1 (1995): 75–106.

Roberts, Mary Louise. "Beyond 'Crisis' in Understanding Gender Transformation." *Gender and History* 28, no. 2 (2016): 358–66.

Semerdjian, Elyse. "Sinful Professions: Illegal Occupations of Women in Ottoman Aleppo, Syria." *Hawwa* 1, no. 1 (2003): 60–85.

Tanielian, Melanie. "Politics of Wartime Relief in Ottoman Beirut (1914–1918)." *First World War Studies*, vol. 5, no. 1 (2014): 62–82.

Thompson, Elizabeth. *Colonial Citizens: Republican Rights, Paternal Privilege, and Gender in French Syria and Lebanon*. New York: Columbia University Press, 2000.

Totah, Faedah M. *Preserving the Old City of Damascus*. Syracuse, NY: Syracuse University Press, 2014.

Tucker, Judith. *Women in Nineteenth Century Egypt*. Cambridge; New York: New York University Press, 1985.

Varjabedian, Sisak Hagop. *Hayere Libanani Medj* [Armenians in Lebanon], vol. 1 Beirut: Hamaskaïne, 1951.

Watenpaugh, Keith. *Being Modern in the Middle East: Revolution, Nationalism, Colonialism, and the Arab Middle Class*. Princeton, NJ: Princeton University Press, 2006.

Zachs, Fruma. *The Making of a Syrian Identity: Intellectuals and Merchants in Nineteenth Century Beirut*. Leiden; Boston, MA: Brill, 2005.

Zachs, Fruma, and Sharon Halevi. *Gendering Culture in Greater Syria: Intellectuals and Ideology in the Late Ottoman Period*. London: I.B. Tauris, 2015.

14

"YOU ARE LIKE A VIRUS:" DANGEROUS BODIES AND MILITARY MEDICAL AUTHORITY IN TURKEY

Oyman Basaran

In Turkey, as in many countries, when called to military service, men are not interrogated about their sexual orientation.[1] Instead, draftees must request exemption from service by explicitly declaring that they are homosexual.[2] The Turkish military classifies homosexuality as a *psychosexual disorder* as defined by Article 302 of the American Psychological Association's manual, the *Diagnostic and Statistical Manual of Mental Disorders* (DSM II)—the 1968 edition, which is still in use in Turkey.[3] The military has recourse to medical expertise, and demands that exemption-seeking conscripts undergo medical inspections that may involve psychological tests (the Minnesota Multiphasic Personality Inventory [MMPI], the House-Tree-Person [HTP] test, and the Rotter Incomplete Sentence Blank test, as well as interviews and physical (rectal) examinations. Conscripts are also occasionally asked to bring along elders to confirm their declaration of homosexuality. Furthermore, some are asked for photos depicting sexual intercourse where the conscript can be seen as the passive partner. After completing these steps,[4] the ineligibility certificate—or "rotten report"[5]—is granted to those who have succeeded in convincing the military psychologists of their homosexuality.

In this article, I examine these medical inspections through which the Armed Forces protects and regulates the order of military service in Turkey. The inspections serve two functions, which remain in an irresolvable tension with each other: with the help of the inspections, on the one hand, the military attempts to exclude *feminine/dangerous* bodies threatening its order in the military service; on the other hand, through refining and proliferating surveillance mechanisms, the Turkish Armed Forces seeks to prevent conscripts from earning unjust exemption by pretending to be homosexual/feminine. In Turkey, as in some other parts of the world—for instance, in Caribbean and South American cultures (Murray)—the active/passive (penetrator/penetratee) binary correlates with the masculine/feminine binary regulating the dominant understanding of homosexuality (Biricik; Tapinc). In public culture, a gay person is stigmatized as effeminate and is assumed to be the passive party in sexual intercourse. Furthermore, according to the current Turkish Military Health Regulations, Article 17 on psychosexual disorders, "[i]n order to be included in this clause, the sexual abnormalities should be very *clearly evident* in every aspect of life, and should be reflected in feelings and behavior" (emphasis added) (Türk Silahlı Kuvvetleri Sağlık Yeteneği Yönetmeliği). The vagueness inherent in the abstract category of psychosexual disorder makes it possible for the military to incorporate the culturally specific notion of homosexuality into its classificatory framework. The Armed Forces constructs *gender inversion* (effeminacy in men) as a threat to the order of military service, which is based on male homosocial bonding in order to maintain the hegemonic masculinity and gender regime in Turkey.

As we shall see, along with the cultural stereotype of the homosexual body the figure of the *impostor* also proves crucial in understanding the complexity of the inspections. While conscripts constantly engage in performances that mimic the stereotype of homosexuality in order to receive exemption from military service, the surveillance mechanisms in these inspections are used to filter out the undeserving/pretending conscripts (in addition to the feminine/dangerous bodies). The performances of the conscripts—whether gay or not—bring about suspicion, mistrust, and fear on the part of the medical authority regarding the epistemic boundaries of dangerous bodies, and render the information that the experts glean from the conscripts questionable at best. In other words, the figure of the impostor, I suggest, destabilizes the medical authorities' efforts to delineate the boundary between eligible and ineligible bodies.

How do these two imagined figures—dangerous/feminine body and impostor—play themselves out in the medical inspections and, in turn, shape medical military authority? The last three decades have witnessed important works analyzing the complex connections between the military, gender, and sexuality in various contexts and locations (see, for instance, Enloe; Gill; Kaplan; Mosse). However, with the exception of a few notable projects (Açıksöz; Altınay; Biricik; Şen), the lack of academic studies examining these issues in Turkey comes as a surprise given the substantial role that the military has played in the construction and regulation of (gender) identities in the country. The Turkish military, medicine, and the cultural notion of homosexuality intersect in the inspections. They are designed to protect hegemonic masculinity and the boundaries of male homosocial bonding through excluding non-normative/dangerous bodies from military service. My analysis of the complex nature of medical authority in the inspections is informed by Michel Foucault's analysis of medicine's colonization of law and the moral status of medical experts. Medicine, Foucault argues, is one of the key apparatuses in modern societies, which consist of technologies of biopower that "brought life and its mechanisms into the realm of explicit calculations and made knowledge-power an agent of transformation of human life" (Foucault, *History of Sexuality*, 143). Crucial to the purpose of this chapter is his point that the introduction of medicine (its techniques, classifications, methods, and discourse of truth) into law establishes a new domain of knowledge and applicability for the latter and extends its hold on its subjects (Foucault, *Abnormal*). Foucault's analysis of the coupling of medicine and law informs my analysis of how discursive practices create dangerous bodies as objects of knowledge and exclusion in the medical inspections, which are constructed as simulacra of military service.

The domain of knowledge that the coupling of the military and medicine aims to delineate in assessing the dangerousness of the conscripts in the inspections is far from being fixed and secured. In fact, it is fragile and vulnerable to conscripts' counterstrategies. While Foucault, in his theoretical framework, not only makes room for counterstrategies and resistances but also sees them as a necessary component of power relations, he does not, in my opinion, pay enough attention to how these counterstrategies can, in turn, reshape the power mechanisms (Foucault, *Power/Knowledge*). This chapter thus goes beyond Foucault by incorporating into its analysis of the power technologies of medical authorities the conscript's counterstrategies—or, rather, the medical authorities' awareness of, and responses to, these strategies. Following the scholars who expand on the Foucauldian framework by attending to the failures, fears, obsessions, and uncertainties on the part of the authorities who deploy the rational technologies of power (scientific procedures, surveillance mechanisms, and writing techniques) (Aretxaga; Horn; Jeganathan; Redfield; Stoler), I also focus on the fragility of the moral status of the medical experts and discuss how their "epistemic anxieties" (Stoler, 19) about creating a clear-cut distinction between homosexual/dangerous and eligible/normal bodies—the anxieties that are projected onto the figure of the impostor—reshape medical authority in the inspections.

Following a brief section on the methodology of the study, this chapter has two main parts: in the first, I briefly discuss the political, social, and cultural importance of military service as well as the social and economic changes in the post-1980s period in Turkey in order to point out the historical and cultural background from which the concern of the Turkish military regarding dangerous bodies arises. The medical inspections are placed in a broader context to give an account of why the Turkish Armed Forces needs such a complex medical apparatus. In the second section, I take a more detailed look at the surveillance mechanisms and medical experts' discursive practices in relation to the performances of the conscripts during the inspections. By extending Foucault's analysis of the coupling of medicine and law, I aim to answer the question of how the interplay between the figures of the dangerous body and the impostor shapes military medical authority in Turkey.

The Study

This study is based on qualitative research conducted in Istanbul and composed of tape-recorded, face-to-face, and in-depth interviews. The interviewees are draftees who were seeking ineligibility certificates at the time of the interviews and the psychologists who were charged with conducting medical inspections to determine the draftees' ineligibility status. These psychologists consisted of both undergraduate- and graduate-level professionals—some licensed, some unlicensed. The psychological tests and psychologists' interpretation of them are also examined.

Until the 2006 publication of a groundbreaking work on homosexuality and bisexuality by the Turkish LGBTQI rights group Lambda-Istanbul (*Ne yanlışız ne de yalnızız: Bir alan çalışması, eşcinsel ve biseksüellerin sorunları* [We are neither wrong nor alone: A field research on homosexual and bisexual issues]), military health inspections had remained out of the public gaze. Considering the overwhelming power and presence of the military in Turkey, it was exceedingly difficult for me as a researcher to locate and contact psychologists and draftees who might agree to talk about their experiences. Due to both external and internal censorship mechanisms that the Turkish Armed Forces deploys to circumscribe the boundaries of what is and is not utterable, contacting the psychologists on the permanent staff at military hospitals was not an option. Instead, I interviewed five male psychologists who ranged in age between twenty-five and thirty. These psychologists worked in military hospitals in two large cities, Istanbul and Ankara, as part of their compulsory one-year military service; they were in charge of proctoring and evaluating the psychological tests and conducting interviews with the draftees. Their scientific training and credentials made them an invaluable part of the committee that approves or denies draftees' applications for exemption. In these interviews, I focused on the following questions: How do the psychologists evaluate the psychological tests and the interviews? What are the criteria that they use in granting exemption from military service? What are their scientific and moral assumptions regarding sexuality and gender? How do they perceive their own practices?

Draftees were understandably hesitant to let me conduct interviews for fear of getting into trouble with the authorities. Using a snowball sampling technique, I contacted some of them through mutual friends who assured them that I was not a journalist and would keep their identities confidential.[6] All twelve of the self-described gay men I interviewed had undergone medical inspections in the three largest cities in Turkey: Istanbul, Izmir and Ankara—the only cities with military hospitals available for medical inspections. The subjects' ages ranged from twenty-three to thirty-three, with most of them working for private companies and earning relatively high salaries. The class position of these interviewees should not be surprising given that modern gayness, as a self-described identity whose underlying principle is sexual orientation, has attracted only some segments of society in Turkey (Bereket and Adam; Özbay; Tapinc). The interviews were conducted at coffee shops or at interviewees' apartments. In these interviews, I was interested in obtaining more information about the medical inspections as well as in these gay men's interpretations of their own experiences.

Their reasons for requesting exemption from military service varied: Some feared they might be exposed to homophobic violence; some felt that the military glorified violence and obedience, which conflicted with their ideals; and one had just started a promising job and did not want to risk a career interruption. All of the interviewees were deemed exempt from military service without the need for additional observation with the exception of Salih, who was required to stay in a psychiatric ward because he was not perceived as "feminine" enough. Friends and internet research were their main sources of information about the medical inspection.

As mentioned in the introduction, in addition to "feminine" bodies, the Turkish military's other concern is impostors who, it is thought, can gain exemption undeservedly. During my research, subjects hinted that there were cases where heterosexual men received the ineligibility certificate by acting feminine. Unfortunately, despite my efforts, I could not reach any of them. However, it is crucial to note that we should not simply overlap the category of the impostor with that of heterosexual men, nor broaden the category and claim that there are gay pretenders as well. Instead, I suggest that the boundary of this category along with other categories such as "fit" and "unfit" is not natural but an *effect* of the power relations that also produce the subjects (psychologists and draftees) themselves, who work with these categories strategically. More specifically, in the remainder of this chapter I aim to clarify how the psychologists' efforts to classify the draftees as "fit" and "unfit" are destabilized by the looming figure of the impostor, and how the blurred boundary between authenticity and imitation complicates medical authority.

Military Service and Masculinity in Turkey

Military service became compulsory for all men in 1927 as a means to expand the power of the new nation-state and to mold the subjects within the new gender regime (Altınay; Sirman 2005). The new regime defined men as independent and sovereign subjects who were now "able to enter into a formal relation with the state. Women, exalted as mothers, [were] citizens only to the extent that they fulfill[ed] their role as helpers and advisors" (Sirman 2005, 164). However, *masculine sovereignty* was promised to the young men only in exchange for an absolute obedience to the military discipline and authority of the state (Açiksöz, 7). Regarded as a culturally and legally sanctioned prerequisite for employment and marriage in Turkey (Sinclair-Webb, 74), military service has also functioned as a rite of passage in men's lives, similarly to countries such as Israel and Bolivia (Gill; Kaplan). In military service, young men are educated and disciplined in accordance with the requirements of proper citizenship and are taught "proper" sanitation (Sirman, 1990, 33). In other words, the Turkish military has become one of the key institutions through which citizenship and state are gendered/masculinized (Altınay).

However, over the past three decades the appeal of military service has been dramatically waning in Turkey. With the intensification of the armed conflicts between the Turkish state and the Kurdistan Workers' Party (PKK) in the 1990s, there has been unprecedented growth in the number of men seeking loopholes in the recruitment procedures with the hope of dodging the draft. Proving the nationalist motto "Every Turk is born a soldier" wrong, the number of draft evaders has been growing since the outset of clashes between PKK and the Turkish Army (Mater, 2005). Furthermore, conscientious objectors began to make their refusal to serve public in the 1990s—which put them at risk of imprisonment and loss of citizenship rights. Middle- and upper-class draftees have also increasingly deployed their social and economic resources to delay the draft or to at least curtail the burden of military service by enrolling in college and graduate schools or paying for exemption from full-term military service.

Nevertheless, these conflicts were not the only reason for the growing reluctance of some segments of society—mainly members of the middle and upper classes—to join the army. Sweeping social, cultural, and political changes occurred in Turkey in the 1980s and 1990s, such as the economic transition to a liberalized market economy, the emergence of new axes of differentiation within society other than a rural/urban divide, the greater fragmentation of social identities, and increasing complexity in the expression of these identities (for example, consumerism) (Kandiyoti). These transformations restructured the class system in Turkey and destabilized the cultural significance of deep-rooted institutions, including military service for the young men of the middle and upper classes regardless of their sexual orientation. For them, military service was no longer the primary symbolic medium through which they expressed their masculinity. Moreover, the post-1980s period also produced new social groups and political actors that challenged the gendered and heterosexualized structure of the public domain and the parameters of politics in Turkey. Although a deeper analysis of these changes is beyond the scope of this study, for our purposes we should underline two important aspects of those years: the emergence of gay subcultures in metropolitan cities and, along with feminist and anti-war movements, the rise of the Lesbian, Gay, Bisexual, Transvestite, and Transgender (LGBTT) movement (Partog). As one of the consequences of globalization processes—more specifically, that of transnational flows of images and identities—in this period, more and more middle-class men incorporated a 'gay' (or *gey*, in Turkish) identity in large cities in Turkey (Bereket and Adam; Özyeğin). On the other hand, political organizations that articulate issues concerning not only gay men but other non-normative subjects have also become more powerful. These organizations have aimed to force the state to make legal, political, and administrative changes that would improve the citizenship status of these subjects.

It is no surprise that the visibility of gay and other non-normative identities has brought about public anxieties that have been vented in many forms of violence, ranging from physical to legal. And the Turkish military, a self-appointed guardian of the Turkish nation and hegemonic masculinity, is one of the most important state institutions that has responded to this rupture in the public sphere. Even before the LGBTQI movement began flourishing, the Turkish Armed Forces had taken harsh precautions against non-normative identities. In the days following the 1980 coup, when the Turkish military was terrorizing dissidents and was expanding its power within society through very harsh methods, trans individuals and "effeminate" gay men were expelled from the country's cities on the grounds that they were posing a danger to public order (Eşsiz). Similarly, the medical inspections that this chapter describes are but one of the mechanisms through which the Turkish Armed Forces aims to defend the moral and gendered imaginary of the nation. However, in the latter case, the military turns its surveying gaze inward, to military service.

The Turkish Armed Forces has subjected the order of military service to scrutiny and surveillance since the Turkish Military Penal Code came into effect in 1930 (Turkish Military Penal Code [Law no: 1632]). Article 153 of the Code specifies "immoral" acts/crimes ("Crimes against Soldiers' Dignity and Honor") that would not go unpunished in military service—including excessive drunkenness; wearing one's military uniform in a casino or brothel; marrying, or cohabiting with, an unchaste person (read 'prostitute'); or practicing *gayrıtabi mukarenet* (unnatural behaviors). The penalties range from short-term prison sentences to losing all rank and expulsion from the army (Eşsiz, 190).

The Turkish military-judicial apparatus brings same-sex sexual engagements, which are not criminalized by civil law in Turkey, under the catchall term *gayrıtabi mukarenet*, which calls for punitive mechanisms. These mechanisms classify and place the offences on a scale of severity, and correlate them with suitable penalties. On the part of the authorities, the determining factor, with the help of testimonies, is whether the accused person committed the alleged crime or not. The coupling of the military and medicine, on the other hand, introduces another discourse of truth and shifts the focus from "acts" to "status/conduct." What are to be categorized and known are no longer acts (sexual intercourse) but the pleasures; desires; dreams; life stories; and, more importantly, behaviors and appearances of the conscripts. In the following section, I look more deeply at experts' discursive practices in relation to the performances of the conscripts, which the culturally sanctioned stereotype of homosexuality underpins.

Medical Inspections

Although the medical procedures that the draftees who request exemption undergo vary between military hospitals, they share some similarities: to get the ineligibility certificate, a draftee must first appeal to the military recruiting office in the district he lives in and demand his transference to the psychiatry department at a military hospital. He is not required to declare his homosexuality at the recruiting office, but a psychologist will interrogate him about his complaint at the military hospital. Upon his declaration, he may be sent for psychological testing under the supervision of military psychologists. He will take the tests either alone or with other people who are at the facility for the same reason. The next time he comes to the hospital, he will receive the test results and bring them to the psychologist who may interview him. In some cases, he will then be sent to the general surgery department for a rectal examination. Here the surgeon checks for physical indications in the anus that are considered to be a sign of sexual intercourse, and writes a report. The draftee is then called back to the hospital to hear the committee's decision, waiting outside the committee room with those who suffer from mental health issues, including schizophrenics, psychotics, and paranoiacs. The conscripts are then called individually into the room, where the committee members sit around a U-shaped table with the psychiatry and general-surgery reports in front of them. After reading the reports aloud and attentively observing the draftee's posture, affect, and gait, they may ask the same questions previously posed by the psychologist. Typically, the inspections culminate in one of three ways: the draftee's request is denied, his military service is suspended for a year (in this case he has to go through the same procedure the following year), or he is granted the ineligibility certificate.

As part of the inspections, draftees may be required to take up to three psychological tests: the Minnesota Multiphasic Personality Inventory (MMPI), the Rotter Incomplete Sentence Blank (RISB) test, or the House-Tree-Person (HTP) test. The HTP test consists of two phases: in the first phase, which is non-verbal and creative, the testee is asked to draw a house, a tree, and a person; in the second phase, which is verbal and apperceptive, the testee is asked to reflect on what they have drawn (Buck; Burns). Hasan, one of the psychologists I interviewed, explained how they interpret the test:

> The fact that the leaves have fallen off, for instance, or that there are only a few leaves on the branch, are symptoms of hopelessness, melancholy, or depression. A broken branch tells us a traumatic story. . . . It says something about the self-perception of the person. Or, let's say, you draw a house. . . . The chimney is the phallic object in the analysis. Whether there is a chimney or not . . . its presence or non-presence makes a huge difference.
>
> Interviewer: What does the absence of the chimney stand for?
>
> The man has trouble identifying with his own sex. There should be one, normally.
>
> Interviewer: So it [the absence of the chimney] is an indicative of homosexuality?
>
> Yes, it is a sign.

Although the psychologists interviewed emphasized that the tests were designed to assess general psycho-pathological disposition and personality structure rather than reveal homosexual inclinations, the results of these tests are used to bolster military psychologists' decisions. Certain psychological dispositions covered by the notion of "feminine"—such as melancholia, depression, vulnerability, lack of self-control, and trauma—are cast as signifiers of homosexuality. The consistent presence of gender inversion increases the odds of the draftees receiving a "rotten report."

Another component of the medical inspections is the interview. In the interviews, as in the psychological tests, failures in the identification process (for instance, attachment with one's mother rather than father) and traumatic childhood events come to be seen as decisive factors in the orientation of the conscripts toward homosexuality. Aiming to identify pathologies (for example, traumas, rape, and abuse) in the lives of the draftees as children, the psychologists repeatedly ask them if such life-altering experiences occurred. The draftees are also encouraged to talk about their lifestyles; first sexual experiences; and desires, pleasures, and feelings—promiscuity is also cast as a signifier of homosexuality. The military psychologists seek to determine if the candidate's homosexuality is a temporary state of "deviance" that may result from poor economic conditions or short-lived fantasies, which would decrease the likelihood of assigning an ineligibility certificate.

The intertwining of morality and medicine in the inspections becomes salient in the physical examination of the conscripts. According to modern cultural norms in Turkey, a male homosexual is stigmatized as 'effeminate' and the 'passive' party in sexual intercourse—a target of public scorn, humiliation, and ridicule. Thus, unsurprisingly, in some cases the draftees' anuses are checked for physical indicators, the presence of which confers a better likelihood of being deemed ineligible. The strong tie between homosexuality and the receptive role allows no room for cases that do not obey the binary logic of gender. If the draftee is the active party in a same-sex relationship, the military psychologists are skeptical: one of them asked, "If he is active, why not women?"

Though less common, the active/passive dichotomy informs another practice in the medical inspections: examining photographs. Despite the psychologists' claims to the contrary, some conscripts are asked for photographs of themselves taken during sexual intercourse where they are seen as passive/the penetratee. One of the men that I interviewed brought such a photo to the attention of the psychologists during his inspections in the hope of expediting a process that, he said, was already humiliating. He made sure that his face and the act of intercourse were clearly seen in the photo, with the intent of preventing any suspicion of deception on the part of the psychologists. Photos indicate how far the medical gaze, or "scientific scopophilia" (Terry 139), can permeate into the bodies of the conscripts.

Through medical and non-medical techniques—the tests, interviews, physical exam, and photographs—the military psychologists formulate intelligence about the draftees; as informed by the culturally specific stereotype of homosexuality, what poses a problem for the military is the consistent presence of femininity in men. In their answers to the questions in the tests and interviews, the draftees thus insist on the impression that their homosexuality fits the stereotype so that they can increase their chances of ineligibility.

However, I was frequently told that the test results, the responses in the interviews, and the anal indications do not carry as much weight in the psychologists' deliberations as behavior and manners. One of the psychologists even emphasized that the psychological tests are done only so that they appear in the applicant's file. In the following section, I point out the reasons behind this movement of the psychologists' focus toward the exterior self.

Dangerous Bodies

> You trust his sincerity. He brings over documents indicating his affiliation with homosexual organizations. Yet, he is a normal, masculine man.... He does not have any definitive characteristics of homosexuality.... He is not feminine.... He is normal. If you met him on the street, you wouldn't think of him as homosexual at all. I mean, you would say, homosexuals have a general thing, you know, they walk coquettishly. Well, some of them are really feminine, but this guy behaves in a masculine way, walks in a masculine style, and he says, "I am homosexual." Well, okay, fine; but if we decided in his favor, we would be in trouble.... Thus the most important criterion is *behavior* (emphasis added).

As the comments of this military psychologist indicate, one of the primary goals of the medical inspections is to find out whether a draftee's gayness will cause any problem during military service. It is thought that overt femininity is troublesome because it provokes and seduces other men and disrupts the military order. The importance of outward manifestations of femininity is so prevalent that even if signs of feminine homosexuality (passivity, vulnerability, and childishness) are not found in a draftee's tests, gender inversion in appearance and manners may be sufficient to prove homosexuality. On the other hand, it is highly unlikely for a masculine-looking man to qualify for the ineligibility certificate. When determining a draftee's ineligibility status, the psychologists thus ask themselves, "Would he provoke or seduce other men? Is his homosexuality noticeable? Is he feminine enough?"

The surveillance techniques that are mobilized to answer these questions in the military can be so invasive that draftees even find themselves in prison-like settings. A candidate may be placed in a psychiatric ward to be monitored for several days if the psychologists have not come to a conclusive decision during the regular inspections. Salih, one of the interviewees, who was considered "not feminine enough," was put into such a ward for further observation in 2003. He stayed there for ten days with soldiers who had been transferred from their military units for severe psychological problems. During his stay, he constructed an image in accord with that of the stereotypical effeminate homosexual:

> After your possessions are taken at the entrance, you are placed into the same cells with the people who have experienced disassociation in military service. There were two male prostitutes who were in the same situation as me. They kept drawing attention to themselves. They were sure that they would get the exemption certificate by trying to seduce the soldiers. I could not act like that. You face a quandary there. The soldiers try to find a way to get to you. Some guy said to me, "Let's come inside the room" in a nonchalant manner—which means "Wouldn't you want to sleep with me?" Because every day you wake up and put on some make-up; or, you know, it is apparent that you are different. It is apparent that you are not like the other people who are under therapy for alcoholism or have experienced mental breakdown. But you have to stand out among other soldiers since there are psychologists above too.
>
> Interviewer: Above?
>
> Behind the windows on the upper floor. Actually, think of that place like an arena or a zoo. They release people in there and the psychologists observe them constantly. I think that they try to find out how much you can affect the system. You are like a virus. If you infect the computer and break it, then they cannot let you into the system.

The medico-panoptic gaze turns the bodies of the draftees into objects of surveillance and knowledge. Through concerted efforts, various actors (psychologists, nurses, and medical personnel) monitor and record every move of the draftees. The goal is to observe consistency in the draftees' moves in an effort to glean definite evidence of their homosexuality/femininity and to determine whether or not the person would be compatible with military service. Within military service in Turkey, certain forms of exchange, interaction, and intimacy among men/soldiers—homosocial bonding practices (for instance, friendship, comradeship, solidarity, and sacrifice for your peers)—are normalized, encouraged, and deemed necessary for keeping the soldiers together and sustaining military order. The coupling of medicine and the military seeks to protect this order through assessing the dangerousness of the conscripts, thereby excluding certain bodies (effeminate men) that are feared to disrupt the dynamics inherent in male homosocial bonding in military service by provoking or seducing other soldiers.

But how should we analyze the medical experts' discursive practices in the inspections? What are the characteristics of the object—dangerous bodies—that emerge in these inspections? Here, Foucault's analysis of abnormality can help us to understand the production of dangerous bodies and its implications for the medical authorities in these sites.

Foucault examines the implications of medicine's colonization of law for medical authority in detail in his lectures on abnormality (Foucault, *Abnormal*). He focuses on experts' inquiries into whether the abnormalities of an individual character create a mental disorder that affects his penal responsibility. He analyzes how psychiatry constitutes itself as an authority responsible for the control of abnormal/dangerous individuals by producing a psychological-moral double of the offense and of the psychologists themselves. The experts double the offense by producing knowledge about the motivations, causes, and origins of the offense and the character of its author. In their statements, notions such as "psychological immaturity," "poorly structured personality," "serious emotional disturbance," or "profound affective balance" emerge as twins of the offense itself such that each one resembles the offense without being qualified as an offense itself (that is, there is no law against being "psychologically immature" or having a "poorly structured personality"). They resemble the offense because they can explain why the individual committed the crime, if indeed they did. Here, the focus has shifted from the criminal act to the potentiality for criminality. Along with the offense, the position of the expert is also split: they now become a doctor-judge as they analyze and assess traits and forms of conduct based on the question of whether or not the conduct will breach the law in future (Foucault, *Abnormal*, 22).

In accordance with Foucault, I argue that the discursive practices in the inspections examined in this chapter are characterized by a series of "doublings." The inspections are imagined as the simulacra of military service and the offense (that is, the disruption of order) is doubled with the performances of the conscripts (that is, feminine behavior and manners), which resemble the offense by being potentially dangerous for the military order. The psychologists establish an arbitrary yet culturally defined threshold for being feminine/dangerous *enough*. The object to which they address themselves is not the act (sexual intercourse) but feminine conducts and ways of being. Here, what is considered to be under threat is not the military's law prohibiting same-sex intercourse but the entire body of military service. The psychologists imagine a state of disorder, and their calculative reasoning aims to estimate the probability of the conscripts' causing disorder in the future through constantly scanning their bodies for signs of femininity. In other words, along with the offense the position of the psychologists is also doubled: the experts scientifically analyze and pre-emptively judge the conscript's conduct in terms of *dangerousness* and exclude certain bodies from the military.

However, "Is he feminine enough?" is not the only question the psychologists ask. Another crucial, yet unsettling, question that underlies their efforts is "Am I being fooled?" The psychologists' attempt to turn the candidates into objects to be known, thereby evaluating whether they are dangerous or not, is undermined, and partly fueled, by the experts' suspicion that candidates may be pretending. In the following section, I discuss how the figure of the *impostor* reshapes medical authority by destabilizing the psychologists' boundary-making practices based on the notion of a dangerous body.

Impostors

> On a daily basis, I don't dress like that. That is a way you conform to the image of homosexuality that already exists in the society. It feels really bad, because, you know, you are gay and normally you don't live like that. . . . And you speak in front of the psychologists in a coquettish manner. You cross your legs. But I am not such a person; I don't speak like that but in order to prove my sexual preference, I have to exhibit myself in the way they want to see and believe, something that I am not.

These comments by Kerem show that the draftees develop self-fashioning strategies through which they convey impeccable feminine impressions in order to reconstruct their bodies as feminine/dangerous enough. With the assistance of hints available online and through other networks, they put a great deal of effort into how they look, act, and sound. This kind of "negative idealization" (Goffman, 40) requires them to exaggerate, dramatize, or create certain actions while concealing those that are inconsistent with their front. On the other hand, the gnawing suspicion of possible cases in which what some psychologists call "malicious" people can manipulate the inspections forces the psychologists to continually modify and improve their surveillance and control techniques. For instance, one of the psychologists did not want to tell me the questions they ask in the tests in case I shared them with one of those malicious people. After I reminded him that the questions were in circulation on the Internet, he told me that he kept changing them. Through refining and proliferating the surveillance mechanisms, the psychologists aim to detect inconsistency in the performances of the conscripts—which, they think, would prove their lack of honesty.

The figure of dangerous body thus accounts for only part of what guides the medical and non-medical practices in these medical inspections. The morally devalued stereotype of homosexuality goes hand in hand with another figure—that is, the *impostor*—who is also seen as morally repugnant in Turkey. In the public imagination, similar to homosexuality, a person's unjust exemption undermines his dignity, masculinity and devotion to the nation. This is so because the pact between state and men is grounded on the assumption that men are willing to obey the state's authority unconditionally and be ready to kill and die for the nation—particularly in a war. From this perspective, impostors who evade their duty undeservedly short-circuit the economy of sacrifice of the Turkish military and threaten the very foundation of the military, which is manpower.

Medical experts' epistemic anxieties about their classification endeavors intersect with the Turkish military's concern regarding its own preservation. In order to restore their categorizing capacities and dispel the blurred boundary between authenticity and imitation, the psychologists' "will to knowledge" (Foucault, *History of Sexuality*) sometimes introduces other pathologies as criteria for exemption. One psychologist explained:

> The inspections are susceptible to abuse. You have to think whether he [the draftee] is cheating or not. But most of them are honest. They are really homosexual. Oh, and there are other cases . . . people who are afflicted with schizophrenia or borderline personality disorder. They do not know who they are. Their perceptions of reality and self are distorted. Even if he is not homosexual, since he cannot experience his own identity and cannot identify with his own sex, he thinks that he is homosexual.

Nevertheless, with the imagined, hovering figure of the impostor, such attempts never provide an absolute anchor that fixes the continuous flow of uncertainty in the inspections. The boundary of the category of psychosexual disorder is constantly destabilized, and the military's grip on the conscripts loosens as the conscripts, whether gay or not, engage in mimicking performances (counterstrategies), which causes suspicion on the parts of the experts (Is he faking? Are these photos real?). The figure of the impostor interrupts the future-oriented calculative reasoning of the experts and turns their will to knowledge into an obsession that relentlessly propels them to proliferate and refine the surveillance mechanisms in the very present—the mechanisms that paradoxically bring about more opacity and uncertainty. We can argue that the authority of the medical experts lies in their ability to catch the impostors as they construct themselves as *good judges of character*. The unsettling effects of suspicion are sometimes offset by a heightened sense of self-esteem accompanied by quasi-magical attributes, such as sense, as described by one of the psychologists:

> People who try to pretend cannot succeed. This is so because a doctor who has worked in a psychiatry clinic for as little as one year or two years would not buy the trick. You may ask how I detect the trick. Is it just by looking at his eyes? But it is really something like that. Spotting the trick is an issue of sentiments. There is the general expression in psychiatry, smell. So, it is based on the sense of smell. You smell and spot the deceit.

Conclusion

In this chapter, I have discussed the dynamics underlying medical authority in the inspections that draftees undergo in order to receive exemptions proving their homosexuality in Turkey. The medical inspections can be seen as the Turkish military's response to the growing visibility of non-normative bodies and the increasing reluctance of some segments of society to perform military service. Through the inspections, the Armed Forces can screen out the bodies that do not fit the noble imagery of the Turkish soldier/man. Moreover, the military can limit exemption from compulsory military service and maintain its manpower. Expanding on Foucault's analysis of medical power, I have examined how the Turkish military's double concern shapes the medical authority in their inspections.

As Foucault argues, the insertion of medicine into traditional forms of power creates a (seemingly) unique domain of objectivity that links the scientific discourse of truth, individualizing knowledge, and classifying power. The role of medical experts in this assemblage is to deploy technologies of power and produce knowledge about individuals in order to determine whether they pose a threat to the body of society or not. The coupling of medicine and the Turkish Army assigns psychologists a similar role in their medical inspections. In these inspections, homosexuality—or, more truly, *gender inversion* (effeminacy in men)—is seen as a threat to the gender regime based on the masculine/feminine binary, and is the ultimate criterion for exemption from military service. Through medical and surveillance techniques, the medical gaze scans bodies for signs of femininity and excludes those that, the experts fear, would shatter the homosocial bonding imagined in the military service by provoking or seducing other soldiers. Here, the experts' will to knowledge intersects with the Turkish military's desire to extend its hold on the male subjects and protect hegemonic masculinity in Turkey.

However, I also argue that the nature of the medical authority in these medical inspections is more complicated than this account allows, because the Turkish Armed Forces is concerned not only about dangerous bodies but also about "malicious" people who pretend to be homosexual in order to receive an exemption. In the medical inspections, the psychologists' practices of objectification are disturbed, and underpinned, by the imagined figure of the impostor—the figure that crystallizes the psychologists' awareness of the conscripts' counterstrategies. The affective investment that the psychologists make in the medical and non-medical mechanisms mostly derives from their desire to catch these "malicious" people—a desire that binds them to the military authorities as it overlaps with the latter's basic need to preserve their manpower. I therefore go beyond Foucault by taking into account the conscripts' counterstrategies and, more importantly, the medical authorities' responses to these strategies and how they reshape the medical authority in the inspections.

For a long time, these invasive medical inspections remained out of the public gaze in Turkey. However, with the efforts of progressive journalists and activists, they have recently received attention albeit minimal in national and international media.[7] Seeing these inspections as a human-rights violation, LGBTQI rights activists aim to alert the national and international public to the issue and the need for change surrounding the Turkish military's policies regarding sexual orientation. While it is hard to predict whether these efforts to end the inspections will be successful, there is one thing we can be sure of: considering that the Turkish state is very reluctant to remove its compulsory conscription system, the "rotten report" will remain an appealing option for some men regardless of the humiliation and frustration they will endure.

Notes

1 Women are excluded from military service in Turkey.
2 For details on the regulations for the conscription of LGBTQI individuals in several countries, see Gade, Segal, and Johnson. The Italian and U.S. armies in World War II are examples of militaries that demanded medical inspections in order to grant military exemption on the basis of homosexuality (Berube 1990; Canaday 2009 [on the U.S. Army]; Nuciari 1994 [on the Italian Army]).
3 The Turkish military continues to use the first printing of the DSM II, which was published in 1968. The American Psychological Association revised it in 1973 and removed homosexuality from the list of disorders. For details, see Conrad.
4 It is important to note that not all draftees are required to take every step. The process can vary from one city to another.

5   Although it is commonly known as the "rotten report," some of the draftees and all of the psychologists interviewed used the term "ineligibility certificate." In the remaining sections of the article "rotten report," "ineligibility certificate," or just "report" are used interchangeably.
6   Pseudonyms are used in this chapter to protect the anonymity of the informants.
7   For instance, the British radio channel BBC Radio 4 broadcast a documentary on this issue, Emre Azizlerli's *The Pink Certificate*, in 2012.

Works Cited

Açıksöz, Can. "Sacrificial Limbs of Sovereignty: Disabled Veterans, Masculinity and Nationalist Politics in Turkey." *Medical Anthropology Quarterly* 26 (2012): 4–25.

Altınay, Ayşegül. *The Myth of the Military Nation: Militarism, Gender, and Education in Turkey*. New York: Palgrave Macmillan, 2004.

Aretxaga, Begona. "Maddening States." In *States of Terror*, edited by Joseba Zulaika, 255–69. Reno, NV: Center for Basque Studies, University of Nevada, 2005.

Bereket, Tarık, and D. Barry Adam. "The Emergence of Gay Identities in Contemporary Turkey." *Sexualities* 9, no. 2 (2006): 131–51.

Berube, Allan. *Coming Out Under Fire: The History of Gay Men and Women in World War II*. Chapel Hill, NC: University of North Carolina Press, 1990.

Biricik, Alp. *Rotten Bodies/Idealized Masculinities: Reconstructing Hegemonic Masculinity through Militarized Medical Discourse in Turkey*. Saarbrücken: VDM Verlag, 2008.

Buck, John. "The H-T-P Test." *Journal of Clinical Psychology* 4 (1948): 151–59.

Burns, R.C. *Kinetic-House-Tree-Person drawings (K-H-T-P): An interpretative manual*. New York: Brunner/Mazel Publishers, 1987.

Canaday, Margot. *The Straight State: Sexuality and Citizenship in Twentieth-Century America*. Princeton, NJ and Oxford: Princeton University Press, 2009.

Conrad, Peter. *The Medicalization of Society: On the Transformation of Human Conditions into Treatable Disorders*. Baltimore, MD: Johns Hopkins University Press, 2007.

Enloe, Cynthia. *Bananas, Beaches and Bases: Making Feminist Sense of International Politics*. Berkley and Los Angeles, CA: University of California Press, 1990.

Eşsiz, Veysel. "Devletin eli, beli, sopası anlatılmamış sürgünden 'kabahatlere' Türkiye'de trans bedenin denetimi." In *Cinsellik muamması: Türkiye'de queer kültür ve muhalefe*, edited by Cüneyt Çakırlar and Serkan Delice, 185-220. Istanbul: Metis Yayınları, 2012.

Foucault, Michel. *Abnormal: Lectures at the College de France 1974–1975* [1999]. London: Verso, 2003.

———. *History of Sexuality: The Will to Knowledge* [1978]. London: Penguin Books, 1998.

———. *The Birth of the Clinic: An Archeology of Medical* Perception [1963]. New York: Vintage, 1994.

———. *Power/knowledge: Selected Interviews and Other Writings 1972–1977*, edited by Colin Gordon. New York: Pantheon Books, 1980.

———. *Discipline and Punish: The Birth of the Prison*. New York: Vintage, 1979.

Gade, Paul A., David R. Segal, and Edgar M. Johnson. "The Experiences of Foreign Militaries." In *Out in Force: Sexual Orientation and the Military*, edited by Gregory M. Herek, Jared B. Jobe, and Ralph M. Carney, 106–31. Chicago: University of Chicago Press, 1996.

Gill, Lesley. "Creating Citizens, Making Men: The Military and Masculinity in Bolivia." *Cultural Anthropology* 12, no. 4 (1997): 527–50.

Goffman, Erving. *The Presentation of Self in Everyday Life*. New York: Doubleday, 1959.

Horn, G. David. "Performing Criminal Anthropology: Science, Popular Wisdom and the Body." In *Anthropologies of modernity: Foucault, Governmentality, and Life Politics*, edited by Jonathan Xavier Inda, 135–58. Oxford: Blackwell Publishing, 2005.

Jeganathan, Pradeep. "Checkpoint: Anthropology, identity, and the state." In *Anthropology in the Margins of the State*, edited by Veena Das and Deborah Poole, 67–81. Santa Fe, NM: School of American Research, 2004.

Kandiyoti, Deniz. "Introduction: Fragments of culture: The Everyday Life of Modern Turkey," In *Fragments of culture: The Everyday Life of Modern Turkey*, edited by Deniz Kandiyoti and Ayse Saktanber, 1–25. London and New York: I.B.Tauris & Co. Publishers, 2002.

Kaplan, Danny. "The Military as a Second Bar Mitzvah: Combat Service as Initiation to Zionist Masculinity." In *Imagined Masculinities: Male Identity and Culture in the Modern Middle East*, edited by Mai Ghoussoub and Emma Sinclair-Webb, 127–43. London: Saqi Books, 2000.

Lambda-Istanbul. *Ne yanlışız ne de yalnızız: Bir alan çalışması, eşcinsel ve biseksüellerin sorunları* (We are neither wrong nor alone: Field research on homosexual and bisexual issues). Istanbul: Berdan Matbaacılık, 2006.

Mater, Nadire. *Voices from the Front: Turkish Soldiers on the War with the Kurdish Guerillas*, translated by Ayse Gul Altinay. New York: Palgrave Macmillan, 2005

Mosse, George L. *The Image of Man: The Creation of Modern Masculinity*. New York and Oxford: Oxford University Press, 1996.

Murray, Stephen O. "The 'Underdevelopment' of Modern/Gay Homosexuality in Mesoamerica." In *Modern Homosexualities: Fragments of Lesbian and Gay Experience*, edited by Ken Plummer, 29–39. London and New York: Routledge, 1992.

Nuciari, Marina. "Homosexuality and Armed Forces in Italy." In *Research Project: Comparative International Military Personnel Policies*, edited by Gwyn Harries-Jenkins, 169–86. Alexandria, VA: United States Army Research Institute for the Behavioural and Social Sciences, 1994.

Özbay, Cenk. "Nocturnal Queers: Rent Boys' Masculinity in Istanbul." *Sexualities* 13, no. 5 (2010): 645–63.

Özyeğin, Gül. "Reading the Closet through Connectivity." *Social Identities: Journal for the Study of Race, Nation and Culture* 18, no. 2 (2012): 201–22.

Partog, Erdal. *Queer teorisi bağlamında Türkiye LGBTT mücadelesinin siyasi çizgisi.* Istanbul: Metis Yayınları, 2012.

Redfield, Peter. "Foucault in the Tropics: Displacing the Panopticon." In *Anthropologies of Modernity: Foucault, Governmentality, and Life Politics*, edited by Jonathan Xavier Inda, 50–83. Oxford: Blackwell Publishing, 2005.

Şen, Şener. *Silahlı kuvvetler ve modernizm.* Istanbul: Nokta Kitap, 2005.

Sinclair-Webb, Emma. "'Our Bulent Is Now a Commando': Military Service and Manhood in Turkey." In *Imagined Masculinities: Male Identity and Culture in the Modern Middle East*, edited by Mai Ghoussoub and Emma Sinclair-Webb, 65–83. London: Saqi Books, 2000.

Sirman, Nükhet. "The Making of Familial Citizenship." In *Turkey in Citizenship in a Global World: European Questions and Turkish Experiences*, edited by E. Fuat Keyman and Ahmet İçduygu, 147–73. London: Routledge, 2005.

———. "State, Village and Gender in Western Turkey." In *Turkish State, Turkish Society*, edited by Andrew Finkel and Nükhet Sirman, ed., 21-51. London: Routledge, 1990.

Stoler, Laura Ann. *Along the Archival Grain: Epistemic Anxieties and Colonial Common Sense.* Princeton, NJ and Oxford: Princeton University Press, 2009.

———. "Developing Historical Negatives: Race and the (Modernist) Visions of a Colonial State." In *From the Margins: Historical Anthropology and Its Futures*, edited by Brian Axel, 156–89. Durham, NC: Duke University Press, 2002.

Tapinc, H. "Masculinity, Femininity and Turkish Male Homosexuality." In *Modern Homosexualities: Fragments of Lesbian and Gay Experience*, edited by Ken Plummer, 39–53. London and New York: Routledge, 1992.

Terry, Jennifer. "Anxious Slippages between 'Us' and 'Them:' A Brief History of the Scientific Search for Homosexual Bodies." In *Deviant Bodies: Critical Perspectives on Difference in Science and Popular Culture*, edited by Jennifer Terry and Jacqueline Urla, 129–69. Bloomington and Indianapolis, IN: Indiana University Press, 1995.

Turkish Military Penal Code (Law no: 1632), Pub.L.No. 1520, Publication Date in Official Gazette 6/15/1930 (passed 5/22/1930). www.mevzuat. gov.tr/mevzuatmetin/1.3.1632.pdf.

Türk Silahlı Kuvvetleri Sağlık Yeteneği Yönetmeliği [Health Regulation for Turkish Armed Forces, issued by the Council of Ministers, Pub.L.No.19291, Publication Date in Official Gazette 11/24/1986 (passed 10/8/1986).

15

GENDERED MEMORIES AND MASCULINITIES: KURDISH PESHMERGA ON THE ANFAL CAMPAIGN IN IRAQ

Andrea Fischer-Tahir

Male Resistance, Female Victimhood?

The Kurdish uprising in the aftermath of the Kuwait War (1990–91) and the Kurdistan parliamentary elections in May 1992 paved the way for the establishment of a "Kurdish quasi-state" (Natali) in northern Iraq (Keen; Cook; Stansfield).[1] Kurdish nationalist discourse shifted from practices of resistance to those of state building. In this context, the peshmerga as armed fighters—or, more precisely, those peshmerga who were killed and seen as martyrs—pervaded the public space in the form of iconographic paintings, sculptures, and memorials, and became a constant presence on radio and television and in commemorative rituals. In memoirs and specialized books by high- and middle-ranking politicians and decision makers from all political parties, the peshmerga became the cynosure of tales of bravery and martyrdom (Banîxelanî; Celal; Kerîm; Emîn, *Going around in Circles; From the Danube Bank to Nawzeng, Fingers Crushing Each Other*). The peshmerga represented decisiveness, strength, and heroism—and this image was male. As powerful symbols of the Kurdish liberation movement, peshmerga and martyrs served to legitimate the Kurdish government in Iraq (Fischer-Tahir, "Wir gaben viele Märtyrer"; Laizer).

During this period, the genocidal persecution sparked by the poison-gas attacks in Halabja and the Anfal campaign, both in 1988, took center stage in narratives on the collective Kurdish suffering of the past. As a symbol of the *karesat-î Enfal* (Anfal catastrophe),[2] the ruling parties introduced the image of rural women dressed in black, mourning the fate of their disappeared husbands and sons. Memoirs and sagas of heroic achievements, however, tended to marginalize the events of the Anfal campaign. When television programs or newspaper rubrics devoted to the life and death of the peshmerga touched on the events of 1988, the stories emphasized their

305

martyrdom. Withdrawal, confusion, and physical and mental suffering—all part of the collective peshmerga experience—grew dim in a manner Paul Connerton designates "forgetting as humiliated silence" (Connerton, 67). The topic of Anfal remained vague because the campaigns of 1988 had ended with the defeat of the peshmerga. The brave men had been overwhelmed by the Iraqi regime.

In addition, Anfal was difficult to narrate from a Kurdish nationalist point of view because some Kurds had supported the Iraqi regime. In January 1991, in an effort to win them over for an uprising in the same year, the Kurdish parties promulgated an amnesty for these supporters, many of whom went on to become Kurdish party allies in the militia war from 1994 to 1997. Not everyone was permitted to speak officially about these former regime supporters. Take the example of the book *Tûn-î merg* (Fire Chamber of Death, 1995), written by a low-ranking member of the ruling Patriotic Union of Kurdistan (PUK) under the pseudonym Ziyad 'Ebdurehman. *Tûn-î merg* was one of the rare publications devoted exclusively to the Anfal campaign. The author clearly addressed the involvement of Kurds in the process of extermination, and risked his life by contradicting the official narrative that claimed the regime's aim was to exterminate all Kurds. Ultimately, 'Ebdurehman left Kurdistan.

Whereas the Kurdish liberation movement was associated with the image of the "strong man," the Anfal catastrophe conjured up the "weak woman." Karin Mlodoch has shown that as early as the 1990s, rural women who had survived Anfal rejected the image of their envelopment in weakness and mourning ("With Anfal our lives disappeared"). On the contrary, they organized their social lives and constructed counter-narratives (Bhabha) that incorporated the complicity of former regime supporters (Mlodoch, "'We Want to be Remembered'"). But what did the peshmerga do? Was the Anfal narrative of male resistance and female victimhood shared by all below the decision-making level of the parties? In this chapter, I demonstrate that the peshmerga took different paths to remember Anfal. I compare the memoirs of a military leader who began to write in the late 1990s and a biographical interview I conducted in 1999 with a peshmerga of low rank. In dealing with memory, I understand the concept—with reference to Pierre Bourdieu's concept of "habitus" (Bourdieu, *Outline a Theory of Practice*, 72; *Homo Academicus*, 170)—as structured and structuring structures, and as practice shaped by schemes of perception, thought, and action. In so doing, I am aware of the "conceptual interference between memory and culture" that has been criticized by such scholars as David Berliner (203).[3] Although major differences exist between the memoirs and the interview, I exemplify both texts as expressions of masculinity—highlighting memories of harmed masculinity.[4] Since published memoirs and an interview conducted for academic purposes constitute two diverse forms of social action, the comparison will illustrate that masculinities as "configurations of practice . . . can differ according to the gender relations in a particular social setting" (Connell and Messerschmidt, 836).

Left a vague topic in the 1990s, the debate on and scientification of Anfal in Kurdistan has gathered momentum since the end of the Ba'th regime in April 2003. In this debate, the term 'genocide' became the principle concept used to describe Anfal. I will relate the debate to my two examples in order to draw attention to the different interpretations of the peshmerga defeat in 1988. In so doing, I argue that the scientification of Anfal contributes to the repression of memories of harmed masculinity.

The Peshmerga

The armed struggle as an integral part of the Kurdish movement in Iraq dates back to 1961, when the Kurdistan Democratic Party (KDP), led by Mulla Mustafa Barzani, rose up against the government of Abd al-Karim Qasim. Since then, Kurdistan has been in a perpetual state of war—interrupted only from 1970 to 1974, when the KDP attempted to negotiate a status of autonomy for Kurdistan in Iraq. The term peshmerga, literally meaning "those who face death," was adopted in 1945–46 during the Kurdish Republic of Mahabad (Ahmed 125).[5] The leading parties of the KDP (established in 1946), the PUK (splintered from the KDP, officially established in 1975), and the Kurdistan branch of the Iraqi Communist Party (ICP, established in 1934) operated peshmerga units—as did a number of smaller entities. The peshmerga was considered the protector and liberator of the Kurdish people, as well as the male guardian of a Kurdish soil imagined as female (Fischer-Tahir, *Brave Men*, 75).

Peshmerga units were based in rural, often mountainous, areas and in several sub-districts established their own authority. They carried out attacks against Iraqi soldiers, police stations, and Kurdish supporters of the regime. Supported by their clandestine city branches, they also engaged in militant actions in the urban centers. Party activists from the cities joined the peshmerga to receive ideological training, military instruction, and propaganda material and to attend party conferences. Many of them ended up as full-time peshmerga, either of their own volition or to avoid imprisonment at the hands of the police or the security forces. From a class perspective, the Armed Forces were made up of young men from the villages and from the urban middle- and lower-classes, while most of the party leaders came from an upper-class background and the old-established social, political, and religious elites that emerged before the second half of the twentieth century. The peshmerga constituted a "male homosocial world" (Lipman-Blumen, 19). Women stood at the margins of this world: a number of armed women served in the units of the ICP and PUK and many women joined their peshmerga husbands or fathers.

In the wake of the uprising in 1991, the Kurdish parties embellished streets, public squares, and buildings with paintings, statues, and memorials dedicated to the martyrs. When the militia war broke out in 1994, however, they made every effort to destroy the *lieux de mémoire* of other parties (Nora). Not unlike other post-revolutionary rulers, the KDP and PUK—as the governing parties since 1992—supported their members with land, pensions, and jobs in the party apparatus and state administration. Hence, among the social elites they privileged the peshmerga and their relatives, who claimed a reward for long-standing or prospective party support. Respect and a higher reputation for the peshmerga as promised by the dominant nationalist discourse did not, however, lead to a policy of granting privileges to the peshmerga as such. Only a handful of former peshmerga of lower-class origins were able to use their symbolic capital to assume leading political and administrative positions.

Like lower-class males, female peshmerga found themselves less privileged than upper-class men. The wives of 'famous men' constituted an exception here. Kafiya Suleiman, the only female minister in 1992, secretary-general of the PUK Women's Union—and wife of the former leading commander and influential politician Omer Fetah—is one example. Women who joined the peshmerga of their own accord, or those who belonged as wives or daughters, were positioned on a lower rung in the mythology of the Kurdish liberation movement. Almost twenty years after the uprising, the women in the first category are still fighting for the right to be fully recognized as peshmerga—and hence, distinguished from those in the second category. The latter, on the other hand, oppose this distinction as a further discounting of their efforts. For example, in an article published in the PUK daily *Kurdistan-î Nwê* on October 6, 2009, one of the wives called upon the (male) leader of the party to thwart these "unjust efforts" by female peshmerga (Sedîq, 13). Interestingly, numerous wives and daughters spent years with peshmerga units whereas a wide range of men who counted as peshmerga joined the units for a short period only, sometimes for no more than a few months. Far from addressing gender-based injustice as such and the PUK method of dealing with the past, this example reveals the competition between women at the margins of a male homosocial world. By competing rather than resisting, they support the persistence of what Pierre Bourdieu calls "masculine domination" (Bourdieu, *Masculine Domination*).

In general, few women are remembered in public space as martyrs or as women who were killed or committed suicide in protest against oppressors of the Kurds. At the same time, the mythology of the Kurdish movement recognizes as martyrs several men who were not killed in combat missions but, for example, died in car accidents before or after the uprising. It seems that if women are to be seen as martyrs, they must fulfill more criteria than men. The degree of value attached to martyrs depends on their position in relation to the top of the hierarchy, proving yet again that elite males are more privileged in collective memory than lower-class men and women. In terms of the men who control the construction of memory at quasi-state level, this phenomenon can be interpreted as hegemonic masculinity (Connell, *Masculinities, Gender and Power*), which is constituted through practices of distinction from and domination over socially inferior men and women (Meuser).

The Anfal Campaign and Men's Memories
Methodological Approach and Material
The Iraqi Ba'th regime carried out military campaigns against the peshmerga and its supporters in the rural areas of the country from February to September of 1988. The regime labeled these campaigns "al-Anfal" and stigmatized the peshmerga and its supporters as *mukharribin umala* (agent saboteurs), meaning the PUK, and as *saklili al-khiyana* (offspring of the betrayal), alluding to the KDP (Emîn, *Xûlanewe naw bazîne-da*, 207–10); both terms condemned the cooperation between the Kurdish parties and Tehran during the Iran–Iraq War of 1980–88.[6] Over the course of the military campaigns and with the aid of chemical weapons, the regime forced the peshmerga to retreat to Iran. Thousands of non-combatant villagers were captured by the Iraqi Army and the National Defense Battalions, which were composed of Kurdish men who supported the regime out of political conviction, for material gain, to escape regular military service, or because their tribal leaders did so. Most of the men captured were collectively killed and hastily buried in mass graves, while women, children, and the elderly endured months of imprisonment (Hardi; Mlodoch, "Mit Anfal ist auch unser Leben verschwunden"). In March 1988, the peshmerga, supported by Iranian troops, attempted to take control of the town of Halabja. The regime responded with massive poison-gas attacks on March 16, killing up to 5,000 people (Middle East Watch, xiv). After the uprising of 1991, Kurdish politicians claimed that 182,000 people had disappeared during the Anfal campaign (Middle East Watch, xviii).[7] Taking violence as a form of communication, it could be said that one message from the regime to the peshmerga was: you are not capable of protecting those you claim to be

your people. The question is whether the peshmerga interpreted the Anfal violence in the same way.

Let us begin with Awat Qaramanî's book, entitled *Narrow Ways. The Novel Biography of Awat Qaramanî. The Events of 1963–1999*.[8] Emerging from the historiographical wave in post-revolutionary Iraqi Kurdistan, it was first published in 2004 by the Kurdistan Ministry of Culture in the PUK-dominated city of Sulaimaniya and republished in a slightly revised version in 2009. Qaramanî was a peshmerga for about twenty-five years before migrating to the United Kingdom after Anfal. He occasionally visited Kurdistan in the 1990s but never returned permanently. Around 1999, he began to write a book, the preface to which was contributed by 'Ebdulla Kerîm Mehmûd—likewise a former PUK peshmerga, to whom I will return later.

The term *yadaşteroman* (novel biography) refers to a blend of memoir and fiction. In the book, Qaramanî deals with his own life as part of the Kurdish liberation movement. Literary descriptions of individuals, landscapes, and situations and dialogue precision seem to constitute the "novel" element. He begins his "novel biography" with an account of how he became a KDP peshmerga in 1963 after the first Ba'th coup. At the time he was fifteen years old. There is little information in the book about his family and early life. We learn only that he grew up in one of the Sulaimaniya *gerek-î şe'bî* (people's quarters) inhabited by migrants from the rural areas and the lower class. His name, Qaramanî (*qaremanî*: 'the brave'), refers to the village Berde-î Qareman/Baziyan to the northwest of Sulaimaniya, which is considered in local memory to be the site where Sheikh Mehmud Berzinji and his followers in 1919 resisted British occupation and struggled for an independent Kurdistan. In over four hundred pages, Qaramanî narrates the story of his involvement in the splintering away of the PUK from the KDP and its struggle against the regime and internal conflicts. He focuses on his time as a peshmerga in the sub-district of Qaradagh in the 1980s. The novel biography ends with Qaramanî's emigration to the United Kingdom and several grievances about living in exile. The account of what happened during the Anfal campaign constitutes about forty pages.

According to my observations in the region since 1993, books of this kind circulate among former peshmerga and young men from the milieu of the peshmerga parties. Men discuss them when they meet in teahouses, clubs, bars, and bookshops or on other informal occasions. The books are sometimes reviewed in the party media and frequently referred to by other authors from the same milieu. It can therefore be assumed that Qaramanî's book addresses the PUK milieu—in particular, the party's male members and their social environment. It is linked to knowledge production on the

Kurdish liberation movement, and the author seeks recognition for his efforts on behalf of the PUK. Hence, he corrects the memoirs of another peshmerga commander in the epilogue, insisting that it was he, Qaramanî, who was in command in place X in the year Y and not the "martyr Z" (Qaramanî, 378). The unusual compound novel biography indicates that the author seeks distinction from those who merely record their memories, as well as recognition as a writer.

Qaramanî argues with words and illustrations. The photographs presented in the appendix show him standing either in the company of leading politicians and martyrs or with the requisites of warfare. The only images that include women are a group photograph of twenty-nine men and one woman, presented as "the first peshmerga of the new revolution" in 1975, and a picture showing Qaramanî's wife sitting down to a meal with their three children. In sum, this former peshmerga knows how to present himself as the perfect man: both warrior and *xawen-î xêzan* (family owner).

The second case under investigation is the interview with Şoriş (a pseudonym meaning 'revolution'), conducted in 1999 within the context of my PhD research on resistance and life stories (Fischer-Tahir, "Wir gaben viele Märtyrer"). To prepare and complete the interview, I met Şoriş four times and recorded a total of six hours of material. Prompted by an open question, Şoriş began to speak, pausing only for further questions, for tea and cigarettes, and to sleep overnight. I adopted the methodological approach of "narration analysis of biographical self-presentation" (Fischer-Rosenthal and Rosenthal) to analyze this procedure, as well as numerous other life-story interviews with former political prisoners and with peshmerga from various parties.

Şoriş was born in Kirkuk in 1961. Similar to Qaramanî, he was the son of semi-urbanized lower-class rural migrants. Unlike Qaramanî, Şoriş benefited from the welfare policies of the 1970s and had the opportunity to attend university. He was a fellow of the PUK left-wing group Komele, became involved in student protests, refused to do military service, and was eventually obliged to flee the city. In a village under the control of the Kurdish liberation movement, he connected with the peshmerga from the Communist Party—eventually joining them. The section about Anfal takes up one-third of the interview transcript. In contrast to Qaramanî, Şoriş was addressing what he perceived to be a Western female researcher and expected his story to be read by a "Western" audience. He trusted me because we were introduced by one of his comrades and because my husband, as a peshmerga, was injured by poison gas in 1988. Yet, like Qaramanî, Şoriş wanted his experience to make sense and adopted a perspective that was simultaneously retrospective and prospective, thereby creating both consistencies and causalities. He did so only because I had asked him to talk about his life. The mode he selected derived from internalized schemes of perception, thought, and action but were also a result of the interview as a "social relationship," which "as such . . . can have an effect on the results obtained" (Bourdieu, "Understanding," 608).

Peshmerga Remembering Anfal

Qaramanî begins a new chapter when he comes to the events of 1988. (The previous chapter is dedicated to military clashes between PUK peshmerga and the Iraqi Army.) He writes,

> In February 1988, the Iraqi army attacked the area of Dol-î Cafetî [north of Sulaimaniya], which was along the way to the leadership base. Mam Jalal was abroad at the time. Kak Nawshirwan was there. I was at the leadership base a few days before the attacks began. . . . They asked for more forces. . . . That winter was the beginning of a very tough war. . . . The peshmerga forces resisted heroically. It was obvious that Iraq had planned to occupy this area (Qaramanî, 309–10).

"Mam Jalal" ("father-brother" Jalal) is the nickname given to Jalal Talabani, leader of the PUK since 1975. At that time, Nawshirwan Mustafa Amin ("Kak Nawshirwan") was head of the Komele.[9] Qaramanî refers to the first Anfal campaign of Bergelu-Sergelu, which targeted the PUK leadership. He portrays himself as having been close to the leadership and the highest decision-making level in his party. He goes on to chronicle combat missions, decision-making dialogues, and eventually his arrival in Iran, where the chapter ends. However, Şoriş's memories lack a distinct beginning and end. Instead, following a political analysis of the competition between the KDP and PUK in the 1980s, the PUK attack on the ICP in 1983, and the cooperation of the KDP and PUK with Iran (in his view, all acts showing a "lack of class-revolutionary consciousness"), the communist Şoriş says, "Finally, [in] 1988 . . . the Iran–Iraq War came to an end and the government turned against the Kurdish revolution. They tried to divide us. Three, four times they attacked us and tried to surround us, between Chamchamal (west of Sulaimaniya) and Sulaimaniya, between Kirkuk and Sulaimaniya." Şoriş refers to the fourth Anfal campaign of the Lesser Zab Valley in May 1988, and places Anfal in the wider context of the war. From discussing a general attack on the Kurdish revolution, he goes on to break down the events to his own immediate experience of them. Constantly skipping back and forth in time, he speaks about individual events he experienced and others he knows about. He pauses several times to explain the "mistakes made by the Kurdish parties" at that time and since the uprising in 1999. He explicitly addresses the Kurdish militia war and the alliance of the KDP and the Ba'th regime in the joint attack on Erbil, which was under PUK control, on August 31, 1996. Like Qaramanî, Şoriş ended up in Iran. He speaks about the uncertainty of exile (Iran did not welcome ICP fighters). Again, reflecting on what he calls the "mistakes" of the other parties he suddenly says, "And then, the uprising of 1991 broke out." Contrary to the interview sections dealing with his childhood in Kirkuk and the student protests against the Ba'th regime, Şoriş talks about Anfal in a somewhat disorganized manner.

There are several similarities between what Qaramanî writes and Şoriş says. First, both men address the Kurdish regime supporters and either mention or describe clashes with the *caş*. Meaning 'little donkey,' this is a pejorative term used to describe men who support the regime. As mentioned earlier, the political climate in the 1990s was not conducive to discussing the *caş* in public—a fact verified by the author of *Tûn-î merg*, one of the rare books on Anfal. However, Şoriş did not regard the interview as an official arena or useful to the Kurdish public, and Qaramanî wrote from the safety of exile.

Similarly to what I observed in the 1990s as common content of unofficial conversations among peshmerga, Qaramanî and Şoriş likewise focus on the third campaign in Germiyan in April 1988. The highest number of disappeared men and women come from the district of Germiyan (Middle East Watch, 129–66). Şoriş says, "And then Anfal came to Germiyan. The people there were very poor and exhausted. All of them were victims." And Qaramanî writes, "The people of Germiyan were prepared [to fight], every man and house. The Ba'th regime became incensed with the people of Germiyan, who were Anfalized to a savage degree, along with house and children, property and valuables" (Qaramanî, 326–7). The word "house" also signifies "wife." Qaramanî clearly means "men" when he writes "people." His sentences refer to imaginations of women as part of men's possessions (for example, children and material belongings), as dominant in social discourse (Fischer-Tahir, *Brave men*, 47). This is less conspicuous in Şoriş's statement. The striking difference between the two men, however, lies in what they emphasize. Qaramanî underlines the bravery of the people of Germiyan, while Şoriş stresses victimhood.

In terms of the purpose of Anfal, both men claim that it was the aim of the regime to destroy peshmerga resistance. Thus Şoriş says, "Our impression when we saw these events was that the government seeks to clean the area near the border in order to defend itself against Iran. We didn't believe the government would not allow any peshmerga to be here." Both men use the expression *pak kirdin* (to clean, to make something clean). The adjective *pak* (clean, pure) also refers to religious and moral purity, and is associated in social discourse with imaginations of honor (Fischer-Tahir, *Brave men*, 64). Raymond Jamous conceptualized honor as "the exercise of authority over domains that are 'forbidden' or *haram*"—such as territory, house or wife—by "exchanges of violence" (Jamous, 168). Of the phrase "in order to defend itself against Iran," it can be said that "clean" reflects views of a world ruled by men, whose struggle over forbidden domains such as soil and human or organizational bodies is considered legitimate if they acknowledge each other's honor.

There are other representations from the realm of hegemonic masculinity. Apart from the male martyr, Qaramanî and Şoriş frequently describe individuals or groups of men as *qareman* (brave, heroic). Although female peshmerga or the wives of peshmerga play a certain role in Qaramanî's novel biography, they are at most *aza* (strong). In this context he mentions Kafiya Suleiman, who "was stronger than the peshmerga"—she assisted the injured on the marches out of the Anfal areas. Interestingly, she is depicted as "Lady Kafiya, wife of Kak Omer [Fetah]" (Qaramanî, 243). Another significant example of hegemonic masculinity in both cases is the verb *pelamar birdin/pelamar dan*, which simply means 'to attack.' Kurds, on the other hand, frequently use it in the sense of 'to rape.' In addition, both Qaramanî and Şoriş highlight male decisiveness and decision-making. The former tells of tactical meetings where men make decisions and in several passages emphasizes his own decisions, and the latter recounts male decisions during the fighting. Regarding the overwhelming military power of the regime, Şoriş clarifies his own position: "I decided not to surrender"—in contrast to other peshmerga who did do so. Finally, the word *tole* (revenge) is often used. Qaramanî writes,

> It was terrible. Right in front of our eyes [the army] burnt down one village after another without a single gunshot. . . . Kak Qadir said: "We should take revenge for these villages right now." I said: "Alright." He spoke very carefully. I was glad and said: "Now we will pour out the burning pain in our hearts on this army and take revenge" (Qaramanî, 330).

These sentences are significant. Qaramanî stresses both his own and his comrades' readiness to respond to the challenge of the hostile male entity that had violated the peshmerga domain.

In Şoriş's representation, however, the word "revenge" is absent. Indeed, he initially speaks of readiness and decisiveness but soon remembers the overwhelming military power of the enemy, saying, for example,

And then came the Halabja catastrophe. The Halabja catastrophe! . . .
In the end the people were afraid. . . . There was no longer any trust,
because you can't resist chemical weapons. . . . Anfal produced insecurity
and chaos among the peshmerga. . . . A human being cannot assess a
situation like that . . . cannot think and cannot decide what to do.

Şoriş describes how the peshmerga, whose duty it was to protect and
liberate the people, gradually lost its strength and the ability to make the
right decisions. Şoriş mentions Halabja eighteen times in his account of
what happened in 1988, referring in part to the responsibility of the Kurdish nationalist parties: "It was the government of Iraq. However, we made
mistakes, too . . . because the revolution in Kurdistan had close relations
with Iran." The Kurdish nationalist discourse in the 1990s established Halabja as the most powerful symbol of collective suffering. It was seen as more
"qualified" for this role than Anfal, since in Halabja the regime had made
no distinction between enemies and its own supporters. Şoriş's statement is
not an isolated assessment. At the end of the 1990s, the counter-narrative
on "mistakes" made by the peshmerga with regard to Halabja was widespread among critics of the ruling parties and could be heard in informal
conversations of low-ranking peshmerga. A striking feature of Qaramanî's
text is the total absence of the name Halabja, although he writes about
poisonous attacks on PUK bases in the villages during the Anfal campaign
(Qaramanî, 318, 342).

Another aspect left out by Qaramanî but addressed by Şoriş, and other
peshmerga I interviewed in 1999, is the issue of guilt. Şoriş says,

The whole revolution was unable to assess the government's aims. As
a result, we sometimes played a negative role. When [one of the vil-
lagers] wanted to surrender, we turned against him and attacked him:
How you can say that? The opposite would have been better, because
we couldn't defend him.

Şoriş intimates that the villagers were forced to pay for the wrong
decisions of the peshmerga. He also hints at feelings of guilt when he talks
about his family, who lived in a village at that time. He had already left the
village on a combat mission when the Anfal campaign began: "I didn't know
what fate lay ahead of me, but their destiny was uncertain, too. . . . Eighty-
seven people were captured in our village, some of whom were my relatives.
They are still disappeared." This was one of the moments when the narrator had tears in his eyes and seemed nervous, something I assume he would
have suppressed had the interviewer been male or a Kurdish woman. Social

norms dictate that tears are tolerated in females, children, and elderly men but not in men of warrior age.

Qaramanî's text also deals with family concerns. In his case, however, his family and several relatives were part of peshmerga life. The two sentences on the destruction of the sub-district Qaradagh, where he had spent many years, are revealing. He writes, "For me, this was a catastrophe. It was the worst day of my peshmerga life" (Qaramanî, 335). Şoriş, in contrast, talks about "the villagers" during and after Anfal and is particularly concerned about "the women who were forced to bear the burden" after surviving Anfal. This statement is linked to the gender discourse in the ICP milieu. Since the 1940s, the communists had considered themselves the avant-garde in the struggle for women's rights. In the mid-1990s, the ICP was among those that showed concern for the Anfal survivors it felt had been forgotten in Kurdish politics and society. The statement also echoes the image of the female Anfal survivors as weak, one that was established by the ruling parties.

Apart from the Kurdish caş, Qaramanî and Şoriş construct three male groups as the inferior masculine Other. The first is the "betrayer": peshmerga who surrender and—under torture—provide the enemy with information. Şoriş, for example, says that this occurred among "the peshmerga of the PUK and KDP." However, "as ICP, we did not betray any side," neither their own peshmerga nor those of other parties. He attributes this discrepancy to "consciousness." The second masculine Other alludes to the weakness of other parties. In Qaramanî's text, it is the ICP. When it comes to leaving the areas occupied by the regime, the communists are represented as handicapped, since "among them were very old people who couldn't run" (Qaramanî, 341). The reader also learns that the KDP peshmerga "don't fight. They just hide" (Qaramanî, 331). The third masculine Other group refers to men from the village. A revealing aspect of Qaramanî's text is the description of the male population of the village where his unit halts on a march. "They were a defense unit of four-hundred with their own guns. When we were there, we did not need peshmerga. They were all organized as peshmerga. . . . [T]hey were very brave" (Qaramanî, 323). Şoriş represents male villagers in a slightly different light. Thus, he recollects, "[W]e wanted the tribal peasants to see that we were there. If we fought the government they would acknowledge us." Şoriş indicates that the peshmerga of the left-wing parties were expected to show bravery, since the "tribal peasants" would otherwise not listen to them or their "new ideas." Şoriş utters these sentences with an undertone of irony and detachment. He even laughs a little when alluding to the relationship between masculinity and social recognition. A similarity in both cases, however, is the representation of villagers as a faceless mass, to be considered as equals should they act according to peshmerga rules. In short, both represent villagers as a mass that was easily impressed by acts of physical strength and bravery, although Şoriş saw the policy of canvassing peasants in this manner as absurd.

In summary, both men are aware of the defeat they experienced. Qaramanî describes it by focusing on the loss of territory, and Şoriş explicitly addresses the inability to meet the requirements associated with the institution of the peshmerga. In order to symbolically re-establish their harmed masculinity, both men make a sharp distinction in their memories between their own masculine selves, on one hand, and the inferior masculine other and women, on the other hand. Because Qaramanî's audience is the male-dominated PUK milieu, these distinctions are also a prerequisite for recognition. Şoriş's case is slightly different. In the interaction with a Western woman, the social rules of mutually recognized honor have no bearing. Instead, the interview opened up space and time to address experience otherwise repressed by the memory policies pursued by the ruling parties in the 1990s. It also provided space and time for bodily expressions that would be typically perceived as unsuited to normative masculinity. The examples show that production of memory can be adjusted to the social relations that govern specific situations of it. Nonetheless, both men seek recognition through reference to physical strength and knowledge—although Şoriş indicates his inability to grasp and explain what happened in 1988. His synopsis is consequently, "It was a catastrophe. I can't compare it to anything else."

Harmed Masculinities and the Scientification of Anfal

Anfal was reduced to a symbol and a dense narrative in the 1990s nationalist discourse dominated by the ruling parties. This has changed as a result of the transition process in Iraq since 2003 and the Iraqi Tribunal, on the one hand, and the growing temporal distance to the events of 1988, on the other. Thus, ten years after Qaramanî began to write his novel biography and Şoriş spoke with me about his life, the topic of Anfal has gained considerable attention in the political and scientific field of Kurdistan. The scientific field witnesses discussions on Anfal from such diverse perspectives as sociology, historiography, political science, international law, psychology, religion, economic science, and literature. The ruling parties support this process of knowledge production on Anfal by funding conferences, journals, and book publications.

Kurdish authors tend to follow the narration of Anfal as provided by the Middle East Watch report *Genocide in Iraq: The Anfal Campaign against the Kurds*, which was translated into Kurdish in 1999–2000;[10] quotations from the report are frequently used, and its maps and documents reprinted. Compared with Qaramanî and Şoriş, the new narration of Anfal follows a strict chronology of events. This not only holds true for work in the scientific field but also for memoirs like Xelîl Serkanî's *Enfal le yadewarî pêşmergeyek-da* [Anfal in a peshmerga's memory, 2009], which contains a reproduction of the Middle East Watch report. Scientification also involves the quantification of spatial and material destruction, and of consequential damage at the level of social relations and health (Dizeyî; Mihemmed). Special attention is drawn to the women who survived Anfal, but there is the tendency to victimize these women ('Ezîz; Resûl; Salih). Also in sharp contrast to the 1990s, the topic of the former regime supporters, the *caş*, is broadly discussed. We find, however, a tendency to pathologize the *caş* as people who "came under the influence of the occupants [the Iraqi regime]" because of their "mental weakness" (Qeredaxî 8).

A great number of authors are former peshmerga. Instead of reflecting on their individual and group experience, they tend to write themselves out of the story. One such prominent example is 'Ebdulla Kerîm Mehmûd, who also wrote the preface to Qaramanî's "novel biography." He published, for example, two monographs, based on interviews with rural Anfal survivors (Mehmûd). When I asked him in an interview why he had begun to work on Anfal, he said, "I had read about the genocide of the Armenians, and that of the Jews. But nothing was available on the genocide of the Kurds."[11] Mehmûd's statement mirrors a central argument in the debate: Anfal was genocide similar to the annihilation of the Jews. Kurdish authors from all disciplines tend to refer to Raul Hilberg's Holocaust paradigm as presented in the Middle East Watch report (Hilberg; Middle East Watch, 7–8). Hence the term "catastrophe" is on the way to marginality, while "genocide," adapted as *cînosayd*, has become the principal concept in writing about Anfal. As I argue elsewhere, the comparison between Kurdish suffering and that of the European Jews has been used since 2003 by the political elite in Kurdistan to legitimize calls for international protection and to justify political and economical claims in the new Iraq (Fischer-Tahir, "The Concept of Genocide"). However, neither Qaramanî nor Şoriş use the term genocide in their representations. According to Şoriş, "It was a catastrophe. I can't compare it to anything else." The publisher and journalist 'Arif Qurbanî, who also made a significant contribution to the Anfal topic, offers an explanation for Şoriş's lack of adequate expression: "One of the reasons why the term genocide was missing in the 1990s was lack of interest in the topic by the media. And the ordinary peshmerga had never even heard of the term."[12] Due to the appropriation of the genocide concept and its circulation in science, politics, and the media, the term is now established and available to everybody. It is not only used to compare and legitimize political claims. The concept also seems to offer some form of mental relief to the former peshmerga insofar as it allows for an interpretion of the defeat of 1988 as something logical and unavoidable: of course we couldn't protect our people during Anfal, because resistance to genocide is futile. As a summary of the state of current knowledge production on Anfal in Kurdistan, this interpretation helps to repress memories of harmed masculinities.

Notes

1 This chapter was first published as "Gendered Memories and Masculinities: Kurdish Peshmerga and the Anfal Campaign" in The Journal of Middle East Women's Studies 8, no. 1: 92–114. © Association for Middle East Women's Studies. Reproduced by permission of the copyright holder and Duke University Press.

2 All translations are by the author.

3 On memory in Middle East and Islamic studies, see Humphreys, Davis, Makdisi and Silverstein, and Haugbolle. On repression, censorship, and amnesia, see Burke and Connerton. For a critical appraisal of the memory boom, see Gillis.

4 For masculinities in Middle Eastern and Islamic studies, see Ghoussoub and Sinclair-Webb, and Aghacy. On gender and Kurdistan, see Savelsberg, Hajo, and Borck; Mojab; and King.

5 On Iraqi history, see Batatu (1978); Farouk-Sluglett and Sluglett (1987); and Makiya, *Republic of Fear*. On the Kurdish movement, see Vanly and Chaliand, and McDowall.

6 Anfal (Qur'an, Sura 8, Spoils of War) is itself an allusion to the cooperation between the Peshmerga and Iran during the conflict, which was considered by the regime as betrayal. Thus the name Anfal linked imaginations of apostasy and its consequences (persecution, expropriation, death, refusal of an Islamic burial) to those of political betrayal as part of the Ba'th ideology (Makiya, *Cruelty and Silence*, 90).

7 On Anfal, see Human Rights Watch. On Halabja, see Hiltermann.

8 The English translation as stated on the back cover of the book.

9 Jalal Talabani became president of Iraq in 2005. Nawshirwan Mustafa Amin (Newşirwan Mistefa Emîn) broke away from the PUK and established the oppositional platform Goran (Change) in 2009.

10 The report was published by the PUK media company Xak in a translation by Siyamend Muftîzade in 1999, and in a translation by Cemal Mîrza 'Elî in 2000 by the Kurdish Diaspora Centre Havîbûn in Berlin.

11 Interview with 'Ebdulla Kerîm Mehmûd in Sulaimaniya, October 4, 2009.
12 Interview with 'Arif Qurbanî in Sulaimaniya, September 29, 2009.

Works Cited

Aghacy, Samira. *Masculine Identity in the Fiction of the Arab East since 1967*. New York: Syracuse University Press, 2000.

Ahmed, Fadil. *Die kurdische Befreiungsbewegung zwischen Stammeskultur und Erneuerung* [The Kurdish liberation movement between tribal culture and renewal]. Hildesheim: Internationales Kulturwerk, 1994.

Banîxelanî, Ehmed. *Bîrewerîyekan* [Memories]. Stockholm: Iraqi Communist Party, 1997.

Batatu, Hanna. *The Old Social Classes and the Revolutionary Movements of Iraq*. Princeton, NJ: Princeton University Press, 1978.

Berliner, David C. "The Abuses of Memory: Reflections on the Memory Boom in Anthropology." *Anthropological Quarterly* 78, no. 1 (2005): 197–211.

Bhabha, Homi. "DissemiNation: Time, narrative, and the margins of the modern nation." In *Nation and Narration*, edited by Homi Bhabha, 291–322. London, New York: Routledge.

Bourdieu, Pierre. 2007. *Masculine Domination*. Cambridge: Polity Press, 1990.

———. "Understanding." In *The Weight of the World: Social Suffering in Contemporary Society*, edited by Pierre Bourdieu et al., 607–26. Stanford, CA: Stanford University Press.

———. 1984. *Homo Academicus*. Paris: Minuit, 1999.

———. *Outline a Theory of Practice*. Cambridge: Cambridge University Press, 1977.

Burke, Peter. "History as Social Memory." In *Memory: History, Culture and the Mind*, edited by Thomas Butler, 97–113. Oxford: Basil Blackwell, 1989.

Celal, Îbrahîm.1998. *Xwarû-î Kurdistan-u šoṟiš-î eîlûl. 1961–1975* [South Kurdistan and the September Revolution, 1961–1975]. Berlin: Šênê.

Connell, R.W. *Masculinities*. Cambridge: Polity Press, 1995.

———. *Gender and Power: Society, the Person and Sexual Politics*. Cambridge: Polity Press, 1987.

Connell, R.W., and James W. Messerschmidt. "Hegemonic Masculinity: Rethinking the Concept." *Gender & Society* 19, no. 6 (2005): 829–59.

Connerton, Paul. "Seven Types of Forgetting." *Memory Studies* 1, no. 1 (2008): 59–71.

Cook, Helena. *The Safe Haven in Northern Iraq: International Responsibility for Iraqi Kurdistan*. Colchester: Human Rights Centre, University of Essex, 1995.

Davis. *Memoirs of State: Politics, History, and Collective Identity in Modern Iraq*. Berkely: University of California Press, 2005.

Dizeyî, Yusuf. *Enfal. Karesat, encam-u rebendekanî* [Anfal. Catastrophe, results and methods]. Erbil: Ministry of Education, 2001.

'Ebdurehman, Ziyad. *Tûn-î merg. Hêrişekan-î Enfal le belgenamekan-î rijêm-da* [Fire chamber of death. The Anfal attacks in regime documents]. Tewrêz: Author's edition, 1995.

Emîn, Newşirwan Mistefa. *Xûlanewe naw bazîne-da: Dîwe-î nawewe-î rûdawekan-î Kurdistan-î 'Iraq,* 1984-1988 [Going around in circles. The inside story of events in Iraqi Kurdistan, 1984-1988]. Berlin: Awdani, 1999.

———. *Le kenâr-î Danubewe bo xir-î Nauzeng.* 1975–1978 [From the Danube bank to Nawzeng valley, 1975-1978]. Berlin: Awadani, 1997.

———. *Pencekan yektrî eškênin.* 1979–1983 [Fingers crushing each other, 1979–1983]. Berlin: Awadani, 1997.

'Ezîz, Mihemmed Re'uf. *Enfal-u rehende sosiyolocîyekan* [Anfal and sociological methods], Sulaimaniya: Tîşk, 2005.

Farouk-Sluglett, Marion, and Peter Sluglett. *Iraq since 1958: From Revolution to Dictatorship.* London: KPI Ltd., 1987.

Fischer-Rosenthal, Wolfram, and Gabriele Rosenthal. "Narrationsanalyse biographischer Selbstpräsentation" [Narration analysis of biographical self-presentation]. In *Sozialwissenschaftliche Hermeneutik,* edited by Ronald Hitzler and Anne Honer, 33–57. Opladen: Leske and Budrich, 1997.

Fischer-Tahir, Andrea. *Brave men, pretty women? Gender and symbolic violence in Kurdish urban society.* Berlin: Europäisches Zentrum für Kurdische Studien, 2009.

———. "The Concept of Genocide as Part of Knowledge Production in Iraqi Kurdistan." In *Writing the History of Iraq: Historiographical and Political Challenges,* edited by Ricardo Bocco, Hamit Bozarslan, Peter Sluglett, and Jordi Tejel, 226–40. London: World Scientific Publishing and Imperial College Press, 2009.

———. "Wir gaben viele Märtyrer": Widerstand und kollektive Identitätsbildung in Irakisch-Kurdistan ["We gave many martyrs": Resistance and collective identity production in Iraqi Kurdistan]. Münster: UNRAST Verlag, 2003.

Ghoussoub, Mai, and Emma Sinclair-Web, editors. *Imagined Masculinities: Male Identity and Culture in the Modern Middle East.* London: Saqi Books, 2000.

Gillis, John. "Memory and Identity: The History of a Relationship." In *Commemorations: The Politics of National Identity,* edited by J. Gillis, 3–25. Princeton, NJ: Princeton University Press, 1994.

Hardi, Choman. *Gendered Experiences of Genocide: The Forgotten Women of Anfal in Iraq.* London: Ashgate, 2011.

Haugbolle, Sune. *War and Memory in Lebanon*. New York: Cambridge University Press, 2010.

Hilberg, Raul. *The Destruction of the European Jews*. New York: Holmes and Meier, 1985.

Hiltermann, Joost. *A Poisonous Affair: America, Iraq, and the Gassing of Halabja*. New York: Cambridge University Press, 2007.

Human Rights Watch. "Bureaucracy and Repression: The Iraqi Government in Its Own Words." Report. February 1994.

Humphreys, R. Stephen. *Between Memory and Desire. The Middle East in a Troubled Age*. Berkeley, CA: University of California Press, 1999.

Jamous, Raymond. "From the Death of Men to the Peace of God: Violence and PeaceMaking in the Rif." In *Honor and Grace in Anthropology*, edited by J.G. Peristiany and Julian Pitt-Rivers. Cambridge: Cambridge University Press, 1992.

Keen, David. *The Kurds in Iraq. How Safe is Their Haven now?* London: Save the Children, 1993.

Kerîm, Hikmet Mihemmed. *Şoriş-î Kurdistan-u goṟankarîyekan-î serdem. Xebat şaxekan yan ṟapeṟîn-î şarekan?* [Kurdistan revolution and contemporary changes. Struggle in the mountains or rebellion of the cities?]. Sweden (unknown publisher), 1993.

King, Diane E. May. "The Personal is Patrilineal: *Namus* as Sovereignty." *Identities: Global Studies in Culture and Power* 15, no. 3 (2008): 317–42.

Laizer, Sheri. *Martyrs, Traitors and Patriots: Kurdistan after the Gulf War*. London: Zed Books, 1996.

Lipman-Blumen, Jean. "Toward a Homosocial Theory of Sex Roles." *Signs* 1 (1976): 15–31.

Makdisi, Ussama, and Paul A. Silverstein, eds. *Memory and Violence in the Middle East and North Africa*. Bloomington, IN: Indiana University Press, 2006.

Makiya, Kanan (Samir al-Khalil). *Cruelty and Silence: War, Tyranny, Uprising, and the Arab World*. New York: Norton, 1994.

———. *Republic of Fear: The Politics of Modern Iraq*. Berkeley, CA: University of California Press, 1989.

McDowall, David. *A Modern History of the Kurds*. London; New York: I.B.Tauris, 1996.

Mehmûd, 'Ebdulla Kerîm. *Reṣeba-î jehr-u Enfal* [Poisonous storm and Anfal]. Volume I–II. Erbil / Sulaimaniya: Ministry of Culture, 2002–04.

Meuser, Michael. "Männerwelten: Zur kollektiven Konstruktion hegemonialer Männlichkeit" [Men's worlds: On the collective construction of hegemonic masculinity]. *Schriften des Essener Kollegs für Geschlechterforschung* 1 (2001): 5–32.

Middle East Watch. *Genocide in Iraq: The Anfal Campaign Against the Kurds.* New York: Human Rights Watch, 1993.

Mihemmed, Goran Mistefa. *Karîgerîye abûrîyekan-î prosekan-î cînosayd-î gel-î kurd le Germiyan-da, qeza-î Kelar wek nimûne* [The economic effects of the process of genocide of the Kurdish people in Germiyan. The example of the district of Kelar]. Erbil: Salahuddin University Press, 2009.

Mlodoch, Karin. "'We Want to be Remembered as Strong Women, Not as Shepherds': Women Anfal Survivors in Kurdistan-Iraq Struggling for Agency and Acknowledgement." *Journal of Middle East Women's Studies* 8, no. 1 (2012): 63–91.

———. "'Mit Anfal ist auch unser Leben verschwunden.' Zur psychosozialen Situation von Frauen in Germian, Kurdistan-Irak" ["With Anfal our lives disappeared." On the psycho-social situation of Anfal women in Germian, Iraqi Kurdistan]. Diploma thesis, Freie Universität Berlin, 2000.

Mojab, Shahrzad, ed. *Women of a Non-State Nation: The Kurds.* Costa Mesa, CA: Mazda Publishers, 2001.

Natali, Denise. *The Kurdish Quasi-State: Development and Dependency in Post-Gulf War Iraq.* Syracuse, NY: Syracuse University Press, 2010.

Nora, Pierre. *Les lieux de mémoire.* 7 volumes. Paris: Éditions Gallimard, 1984–92.

Qaramanî, Awat. *Rêga barîkekan. Yadaşteroman-î Awat Qaremanî.* Rûdawekan-î 1963–1999 [Narrow Ways. The Novel Biography of Awat Qaramani. The Events of 1963–1999]. Second edition. Sulaimaniya: Rehend, 2009.

Qeredaxî, Mehabad. "Karesat-î Enfal-u karîgerîye derûnîyekan-î leser komelge-î kurd" [The Anfal catastrophe and its psychological effects on Kurdish society]. Paper presented at the International Conference on Genocide against the Kurdish People, Erbil, January 26–28, 2008.

Qurbanî, 'Arif. *Şayethalekan-î Enfal* [Anfal eyewitnesses], vols. I–IV. Sulaimaniya: Asa.

Resûl, Şukrîye. "Helweşandin-î xêzan-î kurd le nêwan deselat-î Be's-u maf-î mirov" [The disintegration of the Kurdish family between Ba'th rule and human rights]. *Hawar-î Enfal* 1 (2002–2007): 28–50.

Salih, 'Edelet 'Omer. "Şalaw-î Enfal-u karîger-î leser bar-î abûrî-u derûn-î-u komelayetî-î afret-î be-cêmaw-î Enfal" [The Anfal campaigns and their impact on the economic, mental and social situation of Anfal women]. Paper presented at the International Conference on Genocide against the Kurdish People, Erbil, January 26–28, 2008.

Savelsberg, Eva, Siamend Hajo, and Carsten Borck, eds. *Kurdische Frauen und das Bild der Kurdischen Frau* [Kurdish women and the images of Kurdish woman]. Münster: LIT, 2000.

Sedîq, Pirşeng Mihemmed. "Pêşmerge-î jin-u jin-î pêşmerge, em naheqqîye bo?" [Woman peshmerga or peshmerga wife, why this injustice?]. *Kurdistan-î Nwê*, October 6, 2009.

Serkanî, Xelîl. *Enfal le yadewarî pêşmergeyek-da* [Anfal in a peshmerga's memory]. Sulaimaniya: Genc, 2009.

Stansfield, Gareth. *Iraqi Kurdistan: Political Development and Emergent Democracy*. London: Routledge Curzon, 2003.

Vanly, Ismet Chérif, and Gérard Chaliand, eds. *Les kurdes et le Kurdistan. La question nationale kurde au Proche-Orient* [The Kurds and Kurdistan. The Kurdish national question in the Middle East]. Paris: Maspero, 1978.

16

MILITARIST MASCULINITY, MILITARIST FEMININITY: A GENDERED ANALYSIS OF JORDAN'S WAR ON THE ISLAMIC STATE

Ebtihal Mahadeen

O n December 24, 2014, a Royal Jordanian Air Force pilot by the name of Muadh al-Kasasbeh was captured in Raqqa, Syria, after his F-16 fighter crashed in hostile territory. The so-called Islamic State (IS) published a video of his capture and subsequently engaged Jordanian authorities in negotiations for his release in return for freeing Sajidah al-Rishawi, a failed suicide bomber who was on death row for her involvement in the Amman hotel bombings in 2005. But despite attempts by Jordanian authorities to secure his release, on February 3, 2015, IS released a gruesome video showing al-Kasasbeh being burned alive. Jordanian media later claimed he was killed on January 3, 2015.

The unedited, uncensored twenty-two minute video of al-Kasasbeh's brutal murder was played countless times on Jordanian and Arab television—causing outrage and anger in Jordan, and condemnation and shock worldwide. The shocking content of the video was amplified by its high production values, leaving no doubt that it was engineered for remediation. And, much like the murder itself, the official and popular Jordanian response was highly mediated and sought to emphasize Jordan's resolve to fight terror and avenge al-Kasasbeh's death. But more importantly, this response was carefully constructed along very specific, gendered lines that glorified militarism and pointed to an ideal militarist masculinity capable of rising to the occasion. The discourses circulating in Jordanian media at this time reinforced a strong militarist masculinity that must exact revenge and attack the enemy, while venerating the king and the Armed Forces. On the one hand, the king—as head of state, supreme commander of the Armed Forces, and a military man himself—was presented as the epitome of this masculinity. On the other, the military itself was presented as a "factory of men," where this masculinity was manufactured and protected. But women also played a role in propping up this militarist masculinity through performing (or being made to perform) certain militarist femininities: two prominent types seen in the media at this time were female soldiers aiding the campaign but not directly taking part in it, and "the martyr's mother"—a symbol of motherhood and nationhood.

Yet it would be wrong to assume that the aforementioned militarist masculinity emerged solely as a response to al-Kasasbeh's death. This is because its construction has been ongoing for decades in Jordan. The traditional veneration of the Armed Forces and the king as a father figure and supreme commander are features of contemporary Jordanian sociopolitical life, and in a way are integral to the upholding of an otherwise fractured Jordanian identity. And while this militarist masculinity is dominant in peacetime, it comes to the fore—quite aggressively—as the masculinity that can respond to threats in times of local or regional tension. One need only think of the response to the Amman hotel bombings in 2005, which, much like the response to al-Kasasbeh's death, drew on gendered discourses to portray Amman as a fragile, weeping female on the one hand, and the (masculinized) Armed Forces and the king as her saviors and protectors on the other.

Gender, Militarism, and War

Despite their often reductionist and simplistic tendencies, attempts have been made by scholars in the Middle East to engage with masculinity since the 1970s (Saadawi; Tarabishi). Of course, an argument can be made that "the study of men has in fact been the traditional focus of most scholarship on the Middle East" (or anywhere else for that matter) due to the historic and ongoing disregard for (or ghettoization of) women's positions and roles within social, political, and historical dynamics (Sinclair-Webb, 8). But what I am concerned with here is not the reductive reading of masculinity as men, or as male-gendered individuals, but rather the critical view of it as an institution that is socially constituted through certain privileges, performances, and politics. In this sense, I acknowledge R.W. Connell's and James Messerschmidt's position that there is both a plurality and a hierarchy of masculinities (Connell and Messerschmidt, 846), but I focus solely on militarist masculinity and do not expand my analysis to other types.

More nuanced works on masculinities in the Middle East began to emerge rather recently (Ghoussoub and Sinclair-Webb; Amar; Inhorn). And significantly, a complementary and popular area of scholarly interest is that which explores the nexus of militarism, war, and women—such as Nadera Shalhoub-Kevorkian's work on the subject in Palestine (2009) and Nadje Al Ali's and Nicola Pratt's edited collection on women and war in the region (Al-Ali and Pratt). This underscores the importance of seeing masculinity and femininity as interlinked, particularly in analyses of militarism and war. Indeed, as Connell and Messerschmidt argue, "patterns of masculinity are socially defined in contradistinction from some model, whether real or imaginary, of femininity" (Connell and Messerschmidt, 848).

Militarism is defined here following feminist conceptualizations of it as an ideology that "encompasses the myriad political, economic, and social relationships, processes, and practices that are organised around, draw on, and support military values" (Khalid, n.p.). In Cynthia Enloe's engagement with the term, she delineates its components as including a belief in men as protectors; a belief that soldiers deserve praise, and that social hierarchies are normal; an acceptance of war/having enemies as inevitable; the valuing of physical force for conflict resolution; and a belief in the necessity of military power for mature states (Enloe, *Globalization and Militarism*). All of these components come together in the analysis of Jordanian militarism that follows.

Anti-war feminist thinking and activism have been distinctly transnational, social-constructivist, and focused on the embodied experiences of war and militarism (Cockburn). Critical scholarship argues that there is no direct or natural link between militarism and masculinity (Enloe, *Maneuvers: The International Politics of Militarizing Women's Lives*) but rather that states work hard to first shape social understandings of femininities and masculinities, and then to capitalize on these to fill their military ranks and to promote militarism in the service of the national security (Enloe, *Maneuvers: The International Politics of Militarizing Women's Lives*). In other words, "the military's masculinity has less to do with men's essential characteristics than with what they represent in relation to the military's mandate" (Higate, 6). The linking of masculinity with aggression and femininity with peace is therefore a result of essentialist readings of gender, and is not helpful for unpacking exactly how militarism and masculinity (and femininity) function in society. Significantly, in this context "national security" means protection from external enemies as much as it means maintaining the social order within the country itself (Enloe, *Does Khaki Become You?: The Militarisation of Women's Lives*, 11). It therefore uses militarist femininities and masculinities to sustain gendered power relations within the patriarchy.

Militarist masculinity has begun to be acknowledged in the literature of Middle Eastern studies. According to Paul Amar, "security masculinities" include "policing, security, and moral governance institutions and private security consulting firms [that] produce knowledge that defines Arab masculinities" (Amar, 40). On the other hand, Emma Sinclair-Webb is keen to emphasize that "militaries and militarism should not only be seen as sites where notions of masculinity are established to exclude women" (Sinclair-Webb, 87). This echoes wider feminist and critical approaches to militarism as impacting and responding to both masculinities and femininities.

Yet very few scholars have engaged with representations of masculinity or militarism in Arab media. What does exist, such as Walter Armbrust's analysis of Farid Shawqi's brand of masculinity (Armbrust) and Hazim Saghieh's exploration of Saddam Hussein's carefully crafted image (Saghieh), does not offer a systematic unpacking of the masculinities at play—nor does it necessarily deploy critical or feminist or masculinity theorization to make its contribution. This is not to say that these explorations are not useful but rather to point to the glaring gap in our understanding of the dynamics of mediated, militarist masculinity in the region.

This chapter attempts to address this gap by analyzing the mediated response to the killing of Jordanian Royal Air Force pilot Muadh al-Kasasbeh after his capture by the Islamic State, with a view to unpacking the elements of militarist masculinity in circulation as well as the role women played in perpetuating this masculinity by performing certain femininities. By viewing masculinity as a social institution, and militarism as an ideology that revolves around militaristic values (such as hierarchy, discipline, aggression, and so on), this chapter will illustrate the mediated construction of militarist masculinity and the functions it performs for a patriarchal society at a time of crisis. It relies on an analysis of media texts including Jordanian newspaper articles, press releases, televised reports, videos, and social-media posts. It also draws on Western (largely U.S. and British) media coverage of the events following al-Kasasbeh's killing. These texts are also drawn on for factual information where appropriate.

Masculinity and Militarism in Jordan

The Jordanian military is a pillar of regime stability and a key institution upholding the monarchy in Jordan. Alongside these roles, it has also traditionally performed social and economic functions—not least of which is the absorption of tens of thousands of young Jordanian men into its ranks, providing them with a source of income and establishing a network of beneficiaries in the process. According to Salam Al Mahadin, the events of September 1970 produced the conditions for the "Jordanisation of security apparatuses" (Al Mahadin, 109) and that, in turn, produced an inextricable link between national identity, masculinity, and militarism. What is interesting, however, is that this link goes beyond the confines of the military itself and seeps through into cultural productions as well. Al Mahadin maintains that it was the ascension of King Abdullah to the throne in 1999 that launched this trend, yet many of its elements can actually be traced back to the reign of King Hussein (r. 1953–99). This includes the valorization of the king as the supreme commander of the Armed Forces and as a father figure, as well as the conferring of considerable prestige on the military as a key political, social, and economic institution. On the cultural side, "patriotic" songs articulating what is marketed as an "authentic" Jordanian identity through the use of the Bedouin dialect, and multiple references to the king and the military as ideals of masculinity, also abounded at this time.

The mainstreaming of this brand of militarist masculinity has only accelerated with each crisis or threat facing Jordan. This brand has become so ubiquitous that patriotic songs are played, and danced to, at weddings and other social celebrations as a matter of course. The mainstreaming of songs that praise the Jordanian Army and threaten violence against enemies (one such song promises that "we will gouge out the eye that looks at us") is a prime example of the unproblematized acceptance of militarism and the violence of war, and their assuming a central place in contemporary Jordanian popular culture. Pictures abound of the king dressed in military fatigues and participating in drills in the desert—while the status of the military as protectors of the homeland in a turbulent region, and the prohibition of any critiques aimed toward it, have only become more important. This social acceptance of militarism is the backdrop against which the Jordanian response to Muadh al-Kasasbeh's murder must be understood.

Militarist Masculinities: The King and the King's Men

The image of King Abdullah II as a military man was promoted in Jordan even before his ascension to the throne. Since then, however, his military training and credentials have assumed growing importance in boosting his standing with the Jordanian Armed Forces and, by extension, with large segments of the population. The king's official profile prioritizes his military training, going into great detail about its trajectory from 1980 to the present. It lists the beginnings of his military career at the Royal Military Academy Sandhurst in the UK, after which he assumed numerous positions within the Jordanian Armed Forces. His multiple skills, the profile reveals, allowed him to move between different parts of the Armed Forces—from tank companies to the air force to the Special Forces (Royal Hashemite Court, "Profile."). Clearly then, the king's military background is one of his most distinctive attributes and a major asset for his legitimacy as supreme commander of the Armed Forces. This may also go some way toward explaining the obsession with militarism in Jordanian popular culture since his ascension to the throne.

The response to al-Kasasbeh's murder, as noted earlier, was heavily mediated and focused on reinforcing the king's embodiment of an ideal militarist masculinity and on promoting male members of the Jordanian Armed Forces as also being representative of this masculinity. The monarch's stern threats to the Islamic State were notable for their directness and for constantly referencing the capabilities of the Jordanian Armed Forces to retaliate. For instance, immediately after the murder of al-Kasasbeh, the king held a meeting with senior military and political figures at the headquarters of the Jordanian Armed Forces, at which, as supreme commander, he said that "the martyr's blood will not be in vain, and the response from Jordan and the Arab Army . . . would be harsh" (Al Ghad). He added that "we will be on the lookout for these criminals and we will strike them on their own turf" ("King: We Will Strike"). Similarly, the Jordanian Armed Forces' first statement, read live on national television, was direct and threatening: "[Muadh al-Kasasbeh's] spilled blood will be avenged and the punishment that will be inflicted on the tyrants of earth who assassinated Muadh will be proportionate to the magnitude of the tragedy of all Jordanians" ("Text of the Army's Statement"). The emphasis on revenge and retribution as shorthand for justice and honor is significant here, as it is at the heart of Jordan's response to the Islamic State and a key strategy to highlight the need for militarist masculinity at that time of crisis.

The king's military career was cited as evidence of the seriousness of his threats to the Islamic State and his promise of severe retaliation, both inside and outside Jordan itself. In Jordan, the Royal Hashemite Court posted an image on its official Facebook page showing the king clad in military fatigues, a harness, and gloves—and looking ready for battle (Royal Hashemite Court, Facebook page). Western media in particular picked up this image as visual proof of the monarch's seriousness. He was dubbed the "warrior king" by the *Daily Telegraph*, which profiled him as "a free-fall parachutist, a biker and a military man" and added that "Jordan's King Abdullah is a force to be reckoned with" (Burke). To complete this picture, the *Independent*, among many outlets, reported that he had quoted Clint Eastwood (another paragon of masculinity) in a meeting with members of the U.S. Foreign Relations Committee directly after al-Kasasbeh's murder, allegedly saying "the only problem we're going to have is running out of fuel and bullets" (Sabin). In right-wing American media such as Fox News, articles and memes admiring the king's militarist masculinity and "tough-guy" style were used to attack then-President Barack Obama's "soft" stance on terror, as well as his masculinity ("Till we run").

This obsession with King Abdullah's performance of militarist masculinity was so pervasive that rumors circulated online (and even went viral) that he was personally taking part in the fight against the Islamic State. According to fact-checking website Snopes, the rumors emerged after the Royal Hashemite Court published the aforementioned image of the king in combat gear and were circulated, in part, by right-wing U.S. website Breitbart (Mikkelson). Even in reports debunking the rumors, however, the monarch's image was polished further. In *The Independent*'s article dismantling the rumor, the paper still maintained that he was "ready for action" like a "Hollywood action star" (Davies Boren). The desire to still portray the king in such a dramatic, hypermasculinized light, was enduring.

The linkages between the king's military career, his image, and the seriousness of Jordan's response to the Islamic State point to more than a fascination with "tough men" in Jordanian and Western media. This is especially so since, traditionally, "the dominance of men as decision makers of war . . . is assumed to be the result of so-called natural gender differences" (Khalid, n.p.). Even if these supposedly natural gender differences were not directly referenced in the representation of the monarch, they were an ever-present subtext. Furthermore, these linkages exist due to the dynamics of patriarchy and militarism, which reinforce each other in very gendered ways (Khalid). The unproblematized reception of the king's hypermasculine, militarist image in this context goes to show how deeply ingrained (and accepted) these dynamics are even beyond Jordan—and demonstrates their utility in times of crisis to inspire unity in the face of the enemy (the Islamic State in this case), to incite the violence of war, and to silence opposition to state policies.

Yet if the king embodied militarist masculinity *par excellence*, the power of his image and rhetoric rested on a ubiquitous and historical belief in the importance of the Jordanian military and its glorification as a *masna' al-rijal*, or 'factory of men.' It is here that the intricate and inextricable relationship between militarism and masculinity is clearest (Higate; Higate and Hopton; Khalid). As mentioned earlier, the importance of the Jordanian military as an institution and a symbol of regime stability cannot be understood without recognizing the central role it has played in national political and social life and its function as major employer and a pillar propping up the regime. In one example that illustrates all of these roles, *al-Ghad* newspaper published a round-up of statements issued by prominent military experts and veterans under the title "Our Army Represents the Strong Military Spirit of Jordan, Giving Us Our Sustenance, Our Dignity, And Our Tranquility" (Rbeihat). The military not only assures Jordanians of their security but also gives them sustenance, protects their dignity, and stands as a symbol of the very spirit of Jordanian-ness. The parallels here between these functions of the military and the traditional roles performed by men as providers and protectors cannot be missed; the reciprocal relationship between militarism and masculinity, in this case, is so intense that they become one and the same thing, performing the same functions.

This seeming overlap between militarism and masculinity in Jordan becomes most acute in times of political or social crisis, and a look at the history and dynamics of conscription in the kingdom provides a further example of this overlap. In 1967, the country introduced military conscription for all men who were between eighteen and forty years of age. Conscripts served for two years and had no recourse to a civilian service option. Later, after Jordan signed the peace treaty with Israel in the early 1990s, conscription was suspended and continues to be so. This experiment continues to occupy an important space in state–citizen interactions and in the understanding of militarist masculinity in Jordan. This is partly due to the fact that the Jordanian state still requires men of service age to perform certain duties in reference to the now-suspended conscription. For instance, they are obliged to obtain and hold on to "flag service" (or military service) documents, which they must periodically "defer." They are also not allowed to leave the country without having their documents in order. In addition to this, the Jordanian state actively keeps conscription in the limelight through periodic announcements and statements indicating the possibility of its return. In all of these ways, it remains a tool by which the Jordanian state maintains control over its male citizens. On the other hand, Jordanians themselves often call for the return of conscription as a solution to the current crisis experienced by heterosexual, traditional Jordanian masculinity. It is seen as the only way to "eradicate" male homosexuality, supposedly through teaching "correct" (read heterosexual) masculinity and punishing non-conformity. In this sense, conscription (and, by extension, militarism) are seen as the only way to create, protect, and promote the "right and desirable" Jordanian masculinity.

With the king as the epitome of militarist Jordanian masculinity and the role of the military as a "factory of men" thus established, the two came to be seen as part and parcel of Jordan's defence against the external threat of the Islamic State. In media coverage of the response to al-Kasasbeh's killing, this was referenced repeatedly. For instance, statements issued by various political and social parties in the country and widely circulated in the media all pledged allegiance to the king, sang the praises of the military, and emphasized Jordanian unity. In one example of this connectedness between the two, *al-Ra'i* newspaper published a roundup of statements from diverse political parties that "stressed the importance of internal unity in the upcoming period, and allegiance to the Hashemite leadership and the army" (al-Majali). In another, a statement by the speaker of the House of Representatives maintained that "our revenge will be earth-shattering, thanks to the efforts of our Armed Forces and security apparatuses, led by our beloved King" ("Al-Tarawneh Reaffirms MP Support"). Thus the king, and the king's men, were poised to retaliate and avenge al-Kasasbeh's killing, giving the Jordanian state the green light to increase its involvement with the campaign against the Islamic State along distinctly gendered lines.

Militarist Femininities: the Nashmiya and the Martyr's Mother

This discussion has so far focused exclusively on militarist masculinity as embodied in the person of the king and represented in the institution of the Jordanian Armed Forces. Yet as Connell and Messerschmidt argue, "women are central in many of the processes constructing masculinities" (Connell and Messerschmidt, 848). And indeed, they are also central specifically to sustaining militarism itself through embodying certain concepts of motherhood and femininity (Enloe, *Maneuvers: The International Politics of Militarizing Women's Lives*). In Enloe's words, "militarization may privilege masculinity, but it does so by manipulating the meanings of both femininity and masculinity" (Enloe, *Maneuvers*, 289). In Jordan's response to the Islamic State's actions, women played a key role in constructing and promoting militarist masculinity and in performing a militarist femininity that supported it. On the one hand, female soldiers propped up the militarist masculinity on display in Jordanian media. But on the other, Muadh al-Kasasbeh's mother (or the martyr's mother, as she came to be known) performed a key symbolic role bringing to the fore ideas about femininity, motherhood, and nationhood.

Following the initial statements by the king and the Armed Forces, Jordanian strikes against Islamic State targets started on February 4, 2015. Jordanian TV coverage of the beginning of this campaign featured several scenes showing fighter jets taking off to strike Islamic State targets. In a dramatic montage released by the Armed Forces on the same day and widely circulated in Jordanian media, a shorter version of this video included scenes of male and female soldiers writing messages of Qur'anic verses threatening the Islamic State on rockets attached to fighter jets about to take off (Armed ForcesJO). Male pilots were shown giving military salutes and thumbs-up before taking off. Female aircraft engineers, clad in fatigues and hi-vis vests, were shown marching toward a hangar of jets and then seemingly checking the aircraft before they took off. In two distinctive scenes, an image was shown of a rocket attached to a jet, with this message written on it in white chalk: "'[Their] assembly will be defeated, and they will turn their backs [in retreat]'.[1] To al-Baghdadi[2] from a Jordanian *nashmiya*,[3] February 4th 2015." The Jordanian female soldier, a true *nashmiya*, is thus also engaged in the fight against the Islamic State. Even though she is not directly involved in the attacks as a fighter pilot, she performs supportive roles such as aircraft engineering and morale boosting. Her visibility as she sends the Islamic State a direct threat is telling: she does this using a Qur'anic verse, couching it in explicitly gendered language that draws on Jordanian values and identity. This performance of militarist femininity props up the pervasive militarist masculinity and reinforces it while carving out a supportive role for women in the Jordanian military.

The other significant militarist feminine role that was noticeable in media coverage of the campaign against the Islamic State was that of the martyr's mother. Active and visible since his capture, Muadh al-Kasasbeh's mother came to be the focus of media attention after his killing. His young widow was also the subject of great attention yet did not appear in the media nearly as much as his mother, and therefore will be left out of this analysis. Drawing on already-established discourses about martyrdom as a high honor and motherhood as a gendered national duty, media coverage turned Muadh's mother into a symbol of militarist motherhood. If, as Enloe argues, "it takes a convergence of personal, societal, and state expectations to achieve the militarization of motherhood" (Enloe, *Maneuvers: The International Politics of Militarizing Women's Lives*, 256), then we must look beyond the fact that al-Kasasbeh's mother was simply a bereaved mother of a military man who lost his life in the line of duty. In a letter addressed to her, published by *al-Ra'i* newspaper, the writer maintains that "great motherhood means the making of men" and emphasizes the role she played in producing Muadh the hero: "you gave birth to Muadh, you breastfed him the milk of heroism, and you presented him on a platter of loyalty to the homeland" (Saleh). The "making of men" as a function of motherhood is one way in which militarist masculinity is dependent on certain ideas about, and performances of, femininity—and it echoes the "making of men" attributed to militarism itself.

But the function of militarist motherhood transcends the production and upbringing of male sons willing to serve and be martyred for the homeland. It extends to providing ideological support for war and military violence. An interview with al-Kasasbeh's mother aired on Jordan television shows her urging Jordanians to come together and to unite against terrorism. In the same interview, she also calls on the pilots of the Jordanian Air Force to avenge her son's death: "take care and avenge Muadh." She directly references air strikes against the Islamic State—"may god bless their hands, the hands that steer their fighter jets, carrying rockets, striking the dogs"—and she positions herself as their "mother and sister" ("Yis'id sabahak"). Thus, "the martyr's mother" became an advocate for war and military violence—and an influential political symbol, supporting the official message of the Jordanian state. And how could she not? As Sarah Ruddick asks, "if her son is killed while killing, should his mother deny herself the consolation of giving his 'sacrifice' a point?" (Ruddick, 87).

In another sense, "the martyr's mother" also became a representative of "the nation's mothers" as a whole (Enloe, *Maneuvers: The International Politics of Militarizing Women's Lives*, 297) and her mediated experience of grief triggered wide identification, solidarity, and calls to arms. A roundup of reactions from Jordanian mothers to al-Kasasbeh's killing underscored all of these elements. The article concerned begins by stating that "all Jordanian mothers felt the same way and they became one," then follows that with multiple accounts of shock, sadness, and solidarity from Jordanian mothers. In one account, a woman is quoted as saying "your son is the son of every Jordanian woman, O mother of the martyr, pride of all mothers," and another says, "our sons are your sons, they stand with you and will not allow [Muadh's] blood to be in vain" (Jaber). The mother of the martyr became the mother of nation, the mother of all Jordanians.

The roles that these militarist femininities performed in Jordan after al-Kasasbeh's death underline some of the functions of women in a militarist society. While the female soldier (the *nashmiya*) explicitly supported the military by being part of it and participating in launching the campaign against the Islamic State, the martyr's mother symbolized Jordanian nationhood as it intersected with ideal motherhood. She, too, participated in launching the military campaign by performing this militarist motherhood. She, too, participated in constructing and reinforcing militarist masculinity in Jordan. And, if on the surface the experiences of the soldier and the mother seem different, nonetheless they perform similar functions within a militarist society that uphold the ideology of militarism itself (Enloe, *Maneuvers*).

Conclusions

Jordan's response to Muadh al-Kasasbeh's burning at the hands of the Islamic State drew on a pre-existing discourse of militarist masculinity that venerated the king and the Armed Forces, and celebrated war and aggression. Social acceptance of militarism in Jordan is not new, and the ideology has long manifested itself in cultural productions and public discourse. But it is in times of crisis that militarist masculinity truly comes to the fore. In February 2015, Jordan's response to al-Kasasbeh's death was constructed along gendered lines and militarist masculinity was deployed to justify increased involvement in the war against the Islamic State. The king embodied this masculinity, given his military career, his image, his rhetoric, and local and international media obsession with his "warrior" credentials. The Jordanian military, on the other hand, was presented as a "factory of men," capable of avenging al-Kasasbeh's death through violent retaliation. However, the military was not just seen as capable of producing paragons of masculinity but also of performing the same functions that men tradition-ally do in Jordanian society (financial provision, protection, and so on). The blurred lines between militarism and masculinity, in this case, were com-pletely erased. Concurrently, militarist femininities performed by female soldiers and the mother of the martyr played an equally important role that upheld, and fed back into, militarism in Jordan.

This deployment of militarist masculinity and femininity in Jordan after al-Kasasbeh's killing was done in service of what the state defined as national security at the time: the avenging of Muadh's death and the eradi-cation of the Islamic State through increased involvement in the campaign against it. In Jordan's gendered response, masculinities and femininities were made to reproduce the violence inflicted on al-Kasasbeh, to call for and exact revenge, and to wage war in a multiplicity of ways. Crucially, these militarist masculinities and femininities drew on already-established gender discourses and roles, and were only effective due to the social and cultural acceptance of militarism in Jordan. These dynamics, in turn, mobi-lized ideas about national security, Jordanian identity, and nationhood—and reproduced the patriarchal order while simultaneously intensifying Jor-dan's war against the Islamic State.

Notes

1   This is a verse from the Qur'an: 54:45.
2   This refers to Abu Bakr al-Baghdadi, the leader of the Islamic State.
3   *Nashmiya* is the feminine of *nashmi*, an adjective used in the Jordanian dialect to describe someone who demonstrates positive traits such as chivalry, courage, honor, and bravery. The concept is used for both men and women, and is distinctly Jordanian.

Works Cited

Al-Ali, Nadje, and Nicola Pratt. *Women and War in the Middle East: Transnational Perspectives*. London: Zed Books, 2009. Amar, Paul. "Middle East Masculin-ity Studies: Discourses of 'Men in Crisis,' Industries of Gender in Revolu-tion." *Journal of Middle East Women's Studies* 7, no. 3 (2011): 36–70.

Armbrust, Walter. "Farid Shauqi: Tough Guy, Family Man, Cinema Star." In *Imagined Masculinities: Male Identity and Culture in the Modern Middle East*, edited by Mai Ghoussoub and Emma Sinclair-Webb, 199–226. London: Saqi Books, 2000.

Armed ForcesJO. "Royal Jordanian Air Force: Operation Martyr Muadh," February 5, 2015. www.youtube.com/watch?v=kpv9EzqaXCY.

Burke, M. "King Abdullah of Jordan in 60 seconds." *The Telegraph*, February 6, 2015. www.telegraph.co.uk/news/worldnews/middleeast/jordan/11395565/King-Abdullah-of-Jordan-in-60-seconds.html.

Cockburn, Cynthia. "Gender Relations as Causal in Militarization and War." *International Feminist Journal of Politics* 12, no. 2 (2010): 139–57.

Connell, R.W., and James W. Messerschmidt. "Hegemonic Masculinity: Rethinking the Concept." *Gender and Society* 19, no. 6 (2005): 829–59.

Davies Boren, Z. "King Abdullah of Jordan ready for action against Isis—but he won't actually be fighting." *The Independent*, February 6, 2015.

al-Dustur. "al-Tarawneh yu'akkid wuquf al-nuwwab khalf qiyadat al-malik wa yan'a al-shahid al-Kasasbeh, February 8, 2015.

Enloe, Cynthia. *Globalization and Militarism: Feminists Make the Link*. Lanham, MD: Rowman & Littlefield, 2016.

———. *Maneuvers: The International Politics of Militarizing Women's Lives*. Berkeley and Los Angeles, CA: University of California Press, 2000.

———. *Does Khaki Become You?: The Militarisation of Women's Lives*. London: Pluto Press.

al-Ghad. "al-Malik: sanadrib al-mujrimin fi 'aqr darihim," April 23, 2015.

Ghoussoub, Mai and Emma Sinclair-Webb, eds. *Imagined Masculinities: Male Identity and Culture in the Modern Middle East*. London: Saqi Books, 2000.

Higate, Paul. *Military Masculinities: Identity and the State*. Westport, CT: Praeger, 2003.

Higate, Paul, and J. Hopton. "War, Militarism, and Masculinities." *Handbook of Studies on Men & Masculinities*. Thousand Oaks, CA: Sage Publications, 2005.

Inhorn, Marcia. *The New Arab Man: Emergent Masculinities, Technologies, and Islam in the Middle East*. Princeton, NJ: Princeton University Press, 2012.

Jaber, M. "Ummahat al-urdun: la tahzani ya umm al-shahid," *al-Ghad*, February 5, 2015.

Khalid, Maryam. "Feminist Perspectives on Militarism and War: Critiques, Contradictions, and Collusions." In *The Oxford Handbook of Transnational Feminist Movements*, edited by Rawwida Baksh and Wendy Harcourt, 632–50, 2014.

Al Mahadin, Salam. "Gendered soundscapes on Jordanian radio stations." *Feminist Media Studies* 17, no. 1 (2015): 108–11.

al-Majali, K. "Hizbiyyun: istish-had al-Kasasbeh bidayat al-nihaya li-'Da'ish,'" *al-Ra'i*, February 4, 2015.

Mikkelson, David. "The King of Jordan Is Personally Leading Combat Missions Against ISIS?" *Snopes*, February 5, 2015.

Rbeihat, Ahmed. "Jayshuna ruhuna al-'askariya al-urduniya al-qawiya, tamna-huna khubzana wa karamatana wa tuma'ninatana," *al-Ghad*, February 5, 2015.

Royal Hashemite Court, The. "Facebook Profile." 2017.

Ruddick, Sarah. "Mothers and Men's Wars." In *Rocking the Ship of State: Toward a Feminist Peace Politics*, edited by A. Harris and Y. King, 75–92. Boulder, CO and London: Westview Press, 1989.

Saadawi, Nawal. *al-Rajul wa-l-jins* [Man and Sex]. Cairo: Maktabat Madbuli, 1973.

Sabin, Lamiat. "King Abdullah of Jordan 'quotes Clint Eastwood' in meeting over Isis killing pilot al-Kasaesbeh." *The Independent*, February 4, 2015.

Saghieh, Hazim. "'That's How I Am, World!': Saddam, Manhood, and the Monolithic Image." In *Imagined Masculinities: Male Identity and Culture in the Modern Middle East*, edited by Mai Ghoussoub and Emma Sinclair-Webb, 236–50. London, Saqi Books, 2000.

Saleh, H. "Ila umm al-shahid Mu'adh al-Kasasbeh", *al-Ra'i*, February 8, 2015.

Shalhoub-Kevorkian, Nadera. *Militarization and Violence against Women in Conflict Zones: A Palestinian Case Study*. Cambridge: Cambridge University Press, 2009.

Sinclair-Webb, Emma. "'Our Bülent Is Now a Commando': Military Service and Manhood in Turkey." In *Imagined Masculinities: Male Identity and Culture in the Modern Middle East*, edited by Mai Ghoussoub and Emma Sinclair-Webb, 65–92. London: Saqi Books, 2000.

———. "Preface." In *Imagined Masculinities: Male Identity and Culture in the Modern Middle East*, edited by Mai Ghoussoub and Emma Sinclair-Webb, 7–18. London: Saqi Books, 2000.

Tarabishi, Georges. *Sharq wa gharb, rujula wa unutha: dirasa fi azmat al-jins wa-l-hadara fi-l-riwaya al-'arabiya* [East and West, Masculinity and Femininity: A Study of the Crisis of Sex and Civilization in the Arabic Novel]. Beirut: Dar al-Tali'a, 1997.

"Text of the Army's Statement on Pilot." *Jordan Times*, February 4, 2015.

"Till we run 'out of fuel and bullets': Jordan's king vows to crush ISIS." *Fox News*, February 5, 2015.

"Yis'id sabahak: An Interview with the Mother of the Martyred Pilot Muadh al-Kasasbeh." JRTV Channel, February 13, 2015. www.youtube.com/watch?v=9ORo5y5VEuY.

CPSIA information can be obtained
at www.ICGtesting.com
Printed in the USA
LVHW081206140721
692666LV00014B/603/J

9 789774 169755